Economic Management and French Business

From de Gaulle to Chirac

Mairi Maclean
Professor of European Studies
University of the West of England
Bristol

palgrave
macmillan

First published 2002 by
PALGRAVE MACMILLAN
Houndmills, Basingstoke, Hampshire RG21 6XS and
175 Fifth Avenue, New York, N.Y. 10010
Companies and representatives throughout the world

PALGRAVE MACMILLAN is the global academic imprint of the Palgrave
Macmillan division of St. Martin's Press, LLC and of Palgrave Macmillan Ltd.
Macmillan® is a registered trademark in the United States, United Kingdom
and other countries. Palgrave is a registered trademark in the European
Union and other countries.

ISBN 0–333–76148–0

This book is printed on paper suitable for recycling and made from fully
managed and sustained forest sources.

A catalogue record for this book is available from the British Library.

Library of Congress Cataloging-in-Publication Data
Maclean, Mairi, 1959–
    Economic management and French business : from de Gaulle to Chirac /
Mairi Maclean. 1 0 0 3 3 3 4 6 3 3
        p. cm.
    Includes bibliographical references and index.
    ISBN 0–333–76148–0 (cloth)
        1. France – Economic conditions – 20th century. 2. France – Economic
policy – 20th century. I. Title.

HC276 .M323 2002
330.944'083–dc21   2002072840

10   9   8   7   6   5   4   3   2   1
11   10   09   08   07   06   05   04   03   02

Printed and bound in Great Britain by
Antony Rowe Ltd, Chippenham and Eastbourne

DATE DUE FOR RETURN

UNIVERSITY LIBRARY

3 0 JUN 2005 A

ANN HAL 63

UNIVERSITY LIBRARY

2 5 JAN 2005

SEM HALL 12

UNIVERSITY LIBRARY

2 5 JAN 2005

SEM HALL 22

UNIVERSITY LIBRARY

- 1 JUN 2005

SEM HALL 32

UNIVERSITY LIBRARY

- 7 JUN 2006

SEM HALL 22

SST

This book may be recalled before the above date.

Economic Management and French Business

Also by Mairi Maclean

EUROPEANS ON EUROPE: Transnational Visions of a New Continent (*with J. Howorth*)

FRANCE, GERMANY AND BRITAIN: Partners in a Changing World (*with J.-M. Trouille*)

FRENCH ENTERPRISE AND THE CHALLENGE OF THE BRITISH WATER INDUSTRY

MICHEL TOURNIER: Exploring Human Relations

THE MITTERRAND YEARS: Legacy and Evaluation

For my family

Modernisation is not a condition of things; it is a condition of mind.

Jean Monnet

Contents

List of Tables and Figures

Tables

Figures

Acknowledgements

Many people have helped, directly and indirectly, with this book. From the beginning, my father, Derry Maclean, has been a great source of inspiration, kindling in me an interest in other cultures and nations. I would like to express my thanks to the late Lockhart Whiteford, headmaster of Stirling High School, who encouraged me to pursue an academic career. My tutors in the French Department at St Andrews University inspired in me a love of French Studies; in many ways they helped to lay the groundwork for this study. Thanks are due to Dennis Ager of the Department of Modern Languages at Aston University, who encouraged me to spend a summer at Lyon Business School, and to complete an MBA degree. Interviewees who gave so freely of their time are also deserving of thanks, especially those who agreed to be interviewed on more than one occasion. Others kindly sent me valuable documents. In particular I wish to thank Tristan d'Albis, Anna Barnett, Jean-Louis Beffa, Daniel Bernard, Armand Bizaguet, Michel Bon, David Boughey, Georges Cagnard, Pierre-André de Chalendar, Dominique David, Yvon Desportes, Michel Drain, Jean-Pierre Helbert, William King-Gillies, Caroline Jackson MEP, Remé Lallement, Jacques Lauze, Jacques Maisonrouge, Mary Minch, Lindsay Owen-Jones, Michel Pauwels, Louis-Marie Pons, Alain Raoux, Jean-Cyril Spinetta, Philippe-Jean Terrasse, Henrik Uterwedde, David Wallace, Serge Weinberg and Katrina Williams. The library staff at Royal Holloway, University of London, processed and obtained numerous inter-library loans. The research assistance of Margaret Taylor, Claude Sumata and Holly Coombes was much appreciated. I am grateful to Felix Bihlmeier and Susan Price of the Faculty of Languages and European Studies at the University of the West of England for giving me the time to complete the manuscript on my arrival in March 2001. I also wish to thank my research collaborators over the years, whose influence is discernible in these pages: in particular Anthony Hayward, Susan Milner, Jon Press, Jean-Marc Trouille and, most of all, Charles Harvey. Thanks are due to Alison Howson and John M. Smith of Palgrave Macmillan for their kind assistance in the production of this book, and to an anonymous reader who made many constructive suggestions. Finally I would like to thank my family for their love and support. This book is dedicated to them.

MAIRI MACLEAN

List of Abbreviations

AGF	Assurances Générales de France
BNP	Banque Nationale de Paris
CAC-40	Cotation assistée en continu (top 40 listed French companies)
CAP	Common Agricultural Policy
CDU	Christlich-Demokratische Union
CEA	Commissariat à l'énergie atomique
CFDT	Confédération Française Démocratique du Travail
CFTC	Confédération Française des Travailleurs Chrétiens
CGC	Confédération Générale des Cadres
CGE	Compagnie Générale d'Electricité
CGM	Compagnie Générale Maritime
CGT	Confédération Générale du Travail
CIC	Crédit Industriel et Commercial
CII	Compagnie Internationale pour l'Informatique
CNP	Caisse Nationale de Prévoyance
CNPF	Conseil national du Patronat français (now MEDEF)
CNRS	Centre Nationale de Recherche Scientifique
CO	Comité d'Organisation
CRS	Compagnie républicaine de sécurité
CUMA	Coopératives d'utilisation de matériel agricole
DATAR	Délégation à l'aménagement du territoire et à l'action régionale
EADS	European Aeronautics, Defence and Space
EAP	Ecole des Affaires de Paris
ECB	European Central Bank
EC	European Community
ECSC	European Coal and Steel Community
ECU	European Currency Unit
EdF	Electricité de France
EEC	European Economic Community
EMI	European Monetary Institute
EMS	European Monetary System
EMU	Economic and Monetary Union
ENA	Ecole Nationale d'Administration
ERM	Exchange Rate Mechanism
ESCB	European System of Central Banks
ESPRIT	European Strategic Programme for Research and Development in Information Technology
ESSEC	Ecole Supérieures des Sciences Economiques et Commerciales
ETHIC	Entreprises de taille humaine industrielles et commerciales

EU	European Union
EUREKA	European Research Coordinating Agency
FDI	Foreign Direct Investment
FEN	Fédération de l'Education Nationale
FNSEA	Fédération nationale des syndicats d'exploitants agricoles
FRG	Federal Republic of Germany
GAEC	Groupements agricole d'économie en commune
GAN	Groupe des Assurances Nationales
GATT	General Agreement on Tariffs and Trade
GdF	Gaz de France
GDP	Gross Domestic Product
GM	General Motors
HEC	Ecole des Hautes Etudes Commerciales
IGC	Intergovernmental conference
IIASA	Institut International pour l'Analyse des Systèmes Appliqués
INSEE	Institut national de la statistique et des études économiques
IVD	indemnité viagère de départ
LSE	London Stock Exchange
M&A	Mergers and acquisitions
MEDEF	Mouvement des Entreprises de France
MEP	Member of the European Parliament
NATO	North Atlantic Treaty Organisation
OECD	Organisation for Economic Cooperation and Development
OPEC	Organisation of Petroleum Exporting Countries
PCF	Parti Communiste Français
PDG	Président Directeur Général
PME	Petite et moyenne entreprise
PS	Parti Socialiste
QMV	Qualified Majority Voting
RACE	Research and Development in Advanced Communications Technologies in Europe
R&D	Research and development
RFF	Réseau Ferré de France
RPR	Rassemblement pour la République
SAFER	Sociétés d'Aménagement et d'Etablissement Rural
SBF	Sociétés des Bourses Françaises
SEA	Single European Act
SEITA	Société nationale d'exploitation industrielle des tabacs et allumettes
SEM	Single European Market
SME	Small and medium-sized enterprises
SMIC	Salaire minimum inter-professionnel de croissance
SMIG	Salaire minimum interprofessionnel garanti
SNCF	Société Nationale des Chemins de Fer

SNECMA	Société nationale d'étude et de construction de moteurs d'aviation
SPRINT	Strategic Programme for Innovation and Technology Transfer
TEU	Treaty on European Union ('Maastricht Treaty')
TGV	Train à grande vitesse
UAP	Union des Assurances de Paris
UDF	Union pour la démocratie française
UN	United Nations
WEU	Western European Union
WTO	World Trade Organisation

Introduction: Economic Growth and the Transformation of French Business

This book examines the transformation of French business and the reconstitution of French capitalism over a fifty-year period since the watershed of 1945–50. How is it that the relatively modest pace of change which typified the French economy in the nineteenth and early twentieth centuries – compared to a bound Prometheus or a Gulliver in chains, the hallmark of which was restraint in competition[1] – gave way after the Second World War to a new, revived capitalism, a superior economic performance, characterised by a new, reborn cohesiveness and a greater confidence on the part of the French business elite? The French economic system is stereotypically defined as unchanging and stable.[2] Yet the changes apparent in French business at the dawn of the third millennium – including the large-scale presence of foreign actors, especially American institutional investors, in the equity capital of leading French firms, now averaging 40 per cent across the top 40 – are structurally profound and far-reaching.

It is argued here that the new French capitalism of the twenty-first century is the product of an ideological struggle, in which ultimately the forces of modernisation and change won out over the old guard of French nationalism. A strident call for a new beginning followed the humiliation of 1940–44.[3] The national crisis of the immediate postwar years was a potent catalyst for change, providing the opportunity for a modernising elite of technocrats led by Jean Monnet and supported by de Gaulle to win control of key agencies of the state. Modernisation was enshrined as the primary goal of economic policy and planning designated as the primary tool of economic management. The modernisers set out with their American allies to transform French business. Industries characterised by small firms and fragmented markets were to give way to large enterprises and mass production. The intention was revolutionary: the remodelling of the French national business system along the lines of American corporate capitalism, operating within the context of a more integrated European economy. There were many early victories, among which the remodelling of the French iron and steel industry and the formation of the European Coal and

1

Steel Community in 1951 stand out. The crowning achievement of the pioneering era came a few years later in 1958 with the formation of the European Economic Community (EEC).

Yet what began to emerge during the course of the Fourth Republic was not an economic order that resembled very closely that of the US, but a national business system that was distinctively French. Certainly there were profound and far-reaching changes. Industry became more concentrated and markets were progressively liberalised. There were, however, very powerful barriers to wholesale change, and along the way the demands of various stakeholders, often with mindsets inherited from the past, had to be accommodated. Compromise, it must be remembered, is a powerful shaping force. In France this meant that whole swathes of industry remained under state ownership while technocrats preserved their rights to intervene in the affairs of business, private and public, using the law and the public purse to ensure compliance. Likewise, the unions were unwilling simply to cede the rights of members and render them mere factors of production, undeserving of consideration. Industrialists themselves were reluctant to accept without question the logic of free competition, preferring instead, in time-honoured fashion, to work with the state and other business leaders to manipulate the rules of the game. What emerged was a French version of managed stakeholder capitalism, unified and held together by a ruling elite of like-minded technocrats, politicians and businessmen, educated in the same prestigious establishments and sharing common ideological suppositions. Foremost among these was the notion that while France needed desperately to modernise and compete internationally, this was an endeavour that should be managed in the French national interest.

The very success of the French economy during what economist Jean Fourastié famously described as the 'thirty glorious years' of expansion following the war,[4] helped in consolidating the new order, which down to the early 1970s grew progressively in self-assurance. This was manifest, for instance, in de Gaulle's two-time rejection of British membership of the EEC. Not before the trauma induced by the oil crises of the 1970s was the capacity of the system to sustain economic growth seriously called into question. The two oil shocks of 1973–74 and 1979 were a body blow to a country such as France with no oil and few natural energy sources of its own, giving rise to a decade of painfully slow economic growth. Yet in many ways it was France's reaction to that crisis that helped to create the conditions for the transformation of the French business system now so evident. Price liberalisation and orthodox financial management, as practised in the US and the UK, were introduced in 1976 in the form of the Barre Plan, best remembered for its domestic austerity programme.

The social and political tensions consequent upon economic slowdown and austerity in the 1970s found expression in 1981 with the election first of a socialist president, Mitterrand, and shortly afterwards a coalition government of socialists and communists. Economic policy was for a while thrown abruptly into reverse as the new regime sought to resist the logic of prudence in favour of state-led expansion. The financial markets meted out formidable punishment, which led to one of the most remarkable turn-arounds of modern times. With the U-turn of 1982–83, Mitterrand and his fellow socialists acknowledged that France was an integral part of Europe, interdependent with the economies of its Community partners. A new consensus emerged, lasting to the present day, on the primacy of business enterprise as the key determinant of wealth, welfare and economic progress. Privatisation from 1986 onwards served as a vector of change – though at the time it appeared largely as more of the same, with controversial hard cores of shareholders reproducing pre-existing patterns of cross sharehold-ings. In fact, privatisation has served as a catalyst in bringing France's for-mer state-owned firms to assume risk, and to expand at home and abroad. In creating 1.5 million employee shareholders, it has helped this risk-taking mentality spread beyond the boards of the CAC-40 (Cotation assistée en continu).

Many of the changes that we are witnessing today, however, do not make sense unless a longer-term perspective is adopted, unless we go back to the watershed of 1945–50 and the drive to modernise the economy that followed the Second World War.[5] Some features of the comparative long-run performance of the French economy are recorded in Table 1, which in general reflects the progressively rising prosperity enjoyed in developed countries in the nineteenth and twentieth centuries consequent upon industrialisa-tion and economic diversification. In France, rates of economic growth were unexceptional down to 1950. Between 1870 and 1913, GDP per capita grew at an annual average compound rate of 1.3 per cent compared to an unweighted average rate of 1.4 per cent for the six countries in Table 1. The French economy did comparatively well in the interwar period with GDP per capita growing at an average annual rate of 1.4 per cent between 1913 and 1950 compared to an unweighted average of just 1 per cent for the

Table 1 Comparative GDP per capita, 1870–1998 (1990 international $)

Year/country	1870	1913	1950	1973	1998
France	**1,870**	**3,485**	**5,270**	**13,123**	**19,558**
Germany	1,821	3,648	3,881	11,966	17,799
Italy	1,499	2,564	3,502	10,643	17,759
UK	3,191	4,921	6,907	12,022	18,714
US	2,445	5,301	9,561	16,689	27,331
Japan	737	1,387	1,926	11,439	20,413

Source: Adapted from Angus Maddison, *The World Economy: a Millennial Perspective*, Paris, OECD, 2001, p. 264.

sample group in Table 1. It was in the period 1950–73, however, that the French economy really took off, with GDP per capita growing at an annual average compound rate of 5.1 per cent. Living standards rose by two and a half times in the space of little more than two decades, with a consequent rise in public expectations and personal ambitions. Some developed economies, including those of Japan and Germany, performed even better than that of France, but in comparison to the majority of competitor nations, notably Britain and the USA, the French economy surged forward during this period at an enviable rate. Economic expansion was accompanied by profound social changes as the population grew at an unprecedented average annual rate of 1 per cent per annum compared to 0.2 per cent for 1870–1913 and the demographic stagnation witnessed between 1913 and 1950. By 1973 the French population was in excess of 52 million compared to 42 million in 1950. The French economy, in real and absolute terms, was more than three times larger in 1973 than it had been in 1950.

This period of rapid growth and development has become a reference-point in France and beyond for what went before and what came afterwards. The oil crises of the 1970s brought economic dislocation and an end to strong and sustained economic growth. This made for difficulties but not disaster. Between 1973 and 1998 GDP grew at an annual average compound rate of 1.6 per cent (0.5 per cent between 1973 and 1980, rising to 2.4 per cent in the 1980s, before falling away in the last decade of the millennium to 1.5 per cent). Other super-growth economies of the 1950–73 period, including Japan, Germany and Italy, experienced a similar slowdown, whereas Britain and the United States, especially the latter, experienced marked improvements in performance in the 1980s and 1990s. By the end of the 1990s, GDP per capita in France, as can be seen from Table 1, was 28 per cent below the United States level. By European and international standards, however, as the twentieth century drew to a close, the French economy was strong and well situated, standing proud near the top of the league table of national economies.

Economists like Angus Maddison have carefully charted the *proximate* causes of long-run economic growth in France in the years since 1950. Proximate causality, in this sense, is concerned with measurable factors in the growth process (on an input–output basis) that are themselves manifestations of less tractable social phenomena, referred to by Maddison as *ultimate* sources of economic growth. At the proximate level, the French economy has been powered forward in the later modern period by high rates of investment in fixed capital (plant, equipment, infrastructure, and so on) and human capital formation (education, skills development etc.). Together, these factors have encouraged and enabled unprecedented technological change and have resulted in a national productivity record that is among the best in the developed world. Yet French workers, unlike their counterparts in the United States, show no signs of paying a high price in consequence. Working hours in France are low by international standards while benefits in addition to salary are exceptionally high. As must be the case, relatively high employment costs (wages plus benefits), have lent impetus to the process of displacing labour with capital in manufacturing, so increasing the rate of technological change and levels of output per head. In turn, rising productivity within the national economic system has enabled the French to combine rising living standards with advantageous conditions of employment.

In drawing the distinction between proximate and ultimate sources of economic growth, Maddison warns against rushing headlong in offering general explanations of the economic performance of nations. Beneath readily observable structural features and regularities lie a myriad of micro-phenomena and interconnections. History, as the path to the present, invariably is conditioned by the cumulative impact of countless decisions, large and small, made within social institutions in a variety of realms – political, governmental, cultural and economic. The impact is gradual and progressive. Things that at first sight appear as revolutionary or discontinuous often turn out to have deep roots and compelling antecedents. This book, concerned as it is with ultimate rather than proximate causation, seeks to explain contemporary events and movements with reference to related and path-dependent phenomena. It is important that current developments be set against the background of incremental economic change that has taken place since 1945. Hence we aim here to present an appropriately broad and balanced picture, including in our analysis a brief consideration of French business and the French economy in the aftermath of Vichy and during the Fourth Republic, both in their own way harbingers of the Fifth.

The analysis which follows seeks to delve into the cultural substrata that underlie French society, often acting as powerful impediments to, or facilitators of change. As such it is concerned with cultural continuities, as well as with reform and renewal which is profound and far-reaching. However, the current tendency, as the twenty-first century begins, is to examine the business world in terms of sustained and rapid change. In such accounts, heightened competition and globalisation, the new 'bogeyman', loom large. The implication is that national systems must change correspondingly to keep pace with environmental change. Taking this argument to a logical conclusion, the eventual outcome must be the homogenisation of different forms of capitalism and the weakening of national and regional traditions. This argument, however, is far from proven. The French economy has undergone extensive and often very rapid change in the course of the past half-century, as the following chapters demonstrate, and it would be futile to deny this. But it is often more tempting and more exciting to emphasise change than underlying continuities. The fact that systems must adapt and accommodate in order to survive in itself does not sustain the thesis. Indeed, it will be argued here that in France there is a distinctive form of capitalism (based *inter alia* upon a particular concordat between state and business), with inherent flexibility, which is a source of stability amid change. According to this view, there are underlying systemic continuities and enduring traditions, which remain a distinctive source of national competitive advantage, and which France would not wish to discard lightly.

French economic growth has been one of the success stories of the second half of the twentieth century. The ruling elite remains concerned with growth, with national economic strength and with the extension of the national business system. This does not mean maintaining the status quo. Rather, it will be suggested that the French have done in the past whatever has been necessary in order to remain economically strong. In this respect, privatisation, mergers and acquisitions, network and alliance building, the projection of the national interest through European institutions, and a close and self-interested economic and industrial partnership with Germany are all part of a single process of structural refinement in pursuit of national competitive advantage. All the while, the French have sought to avoid what are often perceived to be 'Anglo-Saxon' excesses, such as the readiness to liquidate once-great companies in financial trouble before restructuring, with or without government support, in defence of established productive capabilities. Far from abandoning its national business system, with its emphases on stability, strategy and the longer term, France has sought through the European project to adapt and strengthen it. Far-reaching transformations are in train with respect to the internationalisation of production and ownership, paralleled by a change in corporate governance towards a more shareholder-value oriented or financialised economic system.[6] In providing the capital to fund expansion, foreign investors may also act as generators of change, or monitors of development, or serve as a model to be followed.[7] However, while these transformations are common in Western society, part and parcel of a general isomorphic tendency,[8] they are nevertheless taking place in France within the context of a distinctive national business system.

The French national business system, like that of other advanced economies, might be thought of as existing at three levels, each interrelated as depicted in Figure 1. Conceived as a pyramid, the most visible and easily apprehended features of a national business system are its formal practices, rules and regulations and these are shown in Figure 1 as close to the pinnacle. In terms of corporate governance, for example, we might think of the ways in which companies are set up and dissolved under the law, the composition of boards of directors and the ground rules for financial reporting. Equally, we might think of industrial relations with respect to the conventions and rules for worker representation and collective bargaining. Each of these is relatively simple to observe and document.

VISIBILITY   **LEVEL**

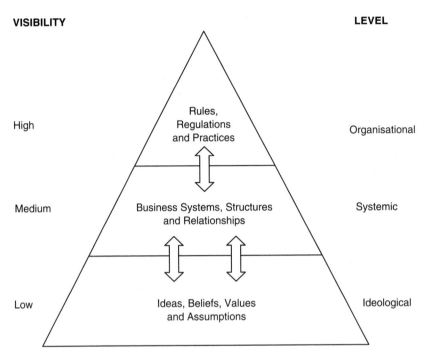

High

Rules,
Regulations
and Practices

Organisational

Medium

Business Systems, Structures
and Relationships

Systemic

Low

Ideas, Beliefs, Values
and Assumptions

Ideological

Figure 1 Dimensions of the French national business system
Compiled by the author.

Conversely, underlying ideologies, ideas, assumptions and deeply held values, on which rules and practices draw, are positioned closer to the base of the pyramid, being much more difficult to circumscribe and pin down. As with an iceberg, what is unseen is often the most important part, and the most treacherous to ignore. Business systems, structures and relationships mark the middle ground, linking unseen ideologies to the more easily apprehensible rules and regulations.

Each of the layers in Figure 1 – organisational, systemic and ideological – is of course an abstraction. However, the distinction between features of national business systems that are clearly seen, partially seen and largely unseen is a valuable one. The annual reports of quoted companies, for example, nominally open and transparent, are the means by which corporations report on their activities within the strictures of the law and prevailing conventions (the top layer). Yet a deeper ideological understanding is clearly required to decode their messages fully, in order to dig beneath the chosen rhetoric to reveal the hidden beliefs and values that lie behind (the bottom layer), the 'cultural baggage' in Hofstede's terms,[9] of which the authors themselves may not even be aware.[10] Similarly, changes at the organisational level, such as were introduced to corporate governance practices in France in the late 1990s following the recommendations of the Viénot and Marini reports, are likely to imply that changes have occurred at the base.[11] Changes at the organisational level are only ever likely to prove stable if matched by changes in assumptions, values and beliefs at the ideological level.[12] The question of how changes occur and impact elsewhere within the national business system is one of the enduring themes of this book. Particular attention is given to the ways in which defining ideas have surfaced and how these ideas have impacted on the business system in France both with respect to its *modus operandi* and its performance. Monumental ideas and choices, of necessity, are almost invariably articulated and contested in the political arena, and the voices of political leaders and their opponents are used frequently throughout the book in order to establish the complex rationales for decisions taken and courses mapped out.

Yet this book is most emphatically not about French politics and French political history. There is little reference to party politics and struggles for political power. Rather, the focus is on the shaping and reshaping of the French politico-economic system and its governance over more than half a century since the end of the Second World War. Two main themes are explored. The first is that of economic management and the drive to modernise French business. In exploring this theme, the purview of economic management is defined broadly to include the objectives, policies, measures and processes used to direct the economy, particularly with respect to the ownership, control, strategy and structure of business enterprises. The picture was far from static. In the course of the past half-century, for example, notions of national self-determination, of economic sovereignty as perceived by de Gaulle, have been increasingly at odds with the realities of economic management. Once the openness of the French economy had been accepted as a *sine qua non* of expansion in 1958, there was always the possibility that national goals and policies would run counter to the logic of international markets and the policies of international institutions. The assertion of national autonomy has been compromised time and again by the need to adjust to external constraints. Over the past fifty years, French politicians, like their counterparts elsewhere in Europe, have had to learn, sometimes the hard way, that national economies do not exist in a vacuum, but function within a complex and interrelated international economic system. Room for manoeuvre in economic affairs has been constrained, with the consequence that the grandeur of France has had to be preserved by other means, in particular as co-leader of the European Union (EU) with Germany for the past two decades.

Djelic has argued convincingly that the French founding fathers of the EEC – in particular Jean Monnet and Robert Schuman – understood the long-term consequences when they sowed the seeds of economic liberalisation and European integration.[13] There is no doubting the altruism and good intentions of Jean Monnet. Fundamentally apolitical, his genius lay in his ability to persuade his compatriots to rise above 'petty' politics, and to pursue supranational enlightened self-interest within concerted European action. But as the social theorist Pierre Bourdieu observes, drawing on Weber's sociology of religion, while all human actions may indeed be *interested*, the most successful are those that appear *disinterested* and consequently enjoy greatest legitimacy. This perhaps is one of the keys to French success in Europe. In Bourdieu's terms: 'The most profitable strategies are usually those produced, on the hither side of all calculation and in the illusion of the most "authentic" sincerity [...]'.[14]

As well as tracing the ups and downs of economic management in the postwar period, the book looks ahead to the challenges that confront France in the new millennium. The years ahead are likely to be dominated by continued internationalisation, as well as by the further development of the EU through Eastern enlargement, a project of which France is understandably wary, given the dilution of French influence in Europe it will inevitably bring. European integration may shortly encroach on the once-sovereign preserve of national fiscal law,[15] although tax harmonisation is viewed favourably by the French. The advent of the euro in 1999 has already wrested control of financial management from French bankers in favour of the European Central Bank, the former regularly frustrated by their inability to modify interest rates to suit national economic circumstances.[16]

The second main topic of this book is the ongoing reconstitution of the French business system. It is argued that French capitalism forms a distinctive set of social relations, founded on relationships between constituent agencies and in particular between the state and business, by which it is structured and conditioned. There have been important structural and ideological changes over the period covered by this book, but equally there have been notable elements of continuity and stability amid change. But in terms of fundamentals a paradox obtains, in that characteristics often viewed as rigid and bureaucratic, giving rise in Crozier's terms to a 'a stalled society',[17] have in the new era of Euro-capitalism turned out to be important sources of strength. The features of the system which stand out in this regard include organisational stability (emanating from a shared belief in the necessity for important companies to weather crises and survive), which in turn has created the capacity to harness resources and plan for the future. Secondly, organisational stability has promoted a long-term, strategic perspective in the French approach to Euro-capitalism. This has been manifest in shaping international institutions such as the General Agreement on Tariffs and Trade (GATT), the World Trade Organisation (WTO), and of course the EU where French influence has been pervasive, especially with respect to Economic and Monetary Union (EMU) and the Common Agricultural Policy (CAP). The cohesive nature of the national business system has thus enabled the French to be proactive in forging the rules of engagement for private enterprise within the European and global economic systems. Thirdly, continued close cooperation between leading politicians, civil servants and businessmen has made it possible for the French to manage the competitive landscape in several sectors, manipulating the rules of the game to the national advantage (a good example of this being energy). In several sectors of the economy, such as insurance and the utilities, this has given the French enterprises the capacity to generate the financial surpluses needed for business expansion at home and abroad. Fourthly, the availability of funds needed for sustained investment in research and development (R&D), information systems and the development of other organisational capabilities has been at the heart of the regeneration of numerous large French enterprises. The success of these companies has been fundamental to sustaining growth in GDP, international trade and foreign direct investment (FDI), inward and outward, since the 1980s.

This business model remains distinctively French and European because values such as stability, long-term planning, and a measured approach to business have not been abandoned in the flurry of euphoria which has accompanied the rise of the so-called 'new economy'. On the contrary, these values remain intact. At the same time, France has actively sought to manipulate and play global capitalism to its advantage, in a clever but determined fashion, encapsulating the French interest in the European whenever advantageous; yet always ready to flout European pressure to conform where it is not. As a former British Cabinet minister put it, 'The French have a block exemption on any directive they don't like.'[18] Postponing EU legislation, denying it or according it minimal interpretation are stratagems regularly employed by the French when the legislation in hand does not overtly serve French interests. Conditional support may be forthcoming if the legislation in question enables French companies to exploit market liberalisation by other member states. Meanwhile, delaying tactics are employed at home when it comes to implementation in order to afford French firms the opportunity to win market share and press ahead of rivals.

The opening chapter of this book explores the logic and general features of the French national business system and the pressures for change emanating from globalisation. The chapter examines a range of topics bearing upon these matters. An understanding of the main features of long-run economic change in France, for instance, or the quintessential and long-standing importance of the role of the state in the economy, dating back to Colbert, as well as the culturally specific referent of 'public service', are essential prerequisites to an understanding of French business in the twenty-first century. French Cartesianism is considered, together with the reasons why, following Kindleberger's analysis, it gave way in the period 1945–50 to greater empiricism. The nature of national 'sovereignty' – conceived in another era, yet the instinctive reflex of which still prevails in today's internationalised economy – is likewise discussed, together with Rousseau's concept of the 'general will', both useful tools in decoding and deconstructing ways of doing business in France. In short, we are concerned in this chapter with some of the underlying ideas and ideologies that inhabit the 'submerged' area at the base of our conceptual framework, and which are explored substantively in later chapters.

Chapter 2 focuses on the economic legacy of war and Occupation. Surveying the economic destruction that confronted de Gaulle on his return to France in 1944, this chapter considers the performance of French business and the economy in the aftermath of Vichy (1944–46), and during the immediate postwar years of the Fourth Republic (1946–57). The Fourth Republic has few friends among historians, traditionally presented as flawed by political weakness and financial laxity, fuelling inflation and leading to enormous public debt. It is true that budgetary deficits accumulated in the drive for reconstruction and modernisation immediately after the Second World War, causing the national debt to spiral, constraining the government's room for manoeuvre. However, while it is often assumed that the Fifth Republic was primarily responsible for the economic success that ensued, the reality is surely more complex, and the balance sheet less negative. As Berstein points out, the major structural reforms carried out at the time of the Liberation – in energy, transport, the supply of credit, welfare provision, and planning – provided the State with the necessary levers to play a leading role in economic management under the Fifth Republic.[19] Above all, perhaps, the Fourth Republic legated to its successor a new perspective on the international economy, characterised by the conviction that France could only 'catch up' if it abandoned traditional protectionist policies in favour of opening up the economy to international competition.

Chapter 3 provides an overview of the French economy under de Gaulle (1958–69) and Pompidou (1969–74), a period marked by the abandonment of protectionism and the opening up of cosy national markets to global competition, in the context of European integration and the progress of successive GATT negotiations. The internationalisation of the economy proceeded unequally: small and medium-sized enterprises enjoyed less export success than their larger counterparts; domestic demand continued to outstrip supply; and inflation was not brought under control. That said, the years of de Gaulle's presidency were nevertheless decisive in France's pursuit of rapid economic growth and structural change. The tools of France's economic performance during this time are accorded particular attention, informed as these are by the values and assumptions that underpin the French business model. These include devaluation, planning, industrial policy, and concentration in all areas of economic activity. Planning in particular was as vital to de Gaulle's pursuit of grandeur as technological independence or the nuclear imperative, in an effort to play 'catch-up' with the US. Conceived by Monnet as a participative endeavour, its participative dimension did not, however, go far enough. This chapter explores the view that through the *économie concertée*, the coherence and solidarity of establishment elites were strengthened; yet they remained strictly segregated from other social strata, thereby inadvertently fuelling the discontent that culminated in the social upheavals of May 1968. The chapter also examines the origins of the Franco-German relationship, one dominated by political and technocratic elites, in which de Gaulle was quick to recognise France's route to international standing and primacy in Europe. De Gaulle's successor to the presidency, Georges Pompidou, altered little of his predecessor's policies, despite the widespread desire for change that swept the general from office in 1969. In many ways, Pompidou's brief tenure at the Elysée was marked by more of the same; there was at one level little impetus for change, in that economically France was doing so well. Pompidou brought a new transparency and openness of style – subsequently belied, however, by the secrecy that surrounded his terminal illness, euphemistically described as a cold, reminiscent of the obfuscation of the deaths of Soviet presidents.

Valéry Giscard d'Estaing was elected to the presidency in 1974 in a radically changed economic climate, one for which Western governments and economies proved to be singularly unprepared. The French government had claimed credit for the 'thirty glorious years' that followed the war; this proved to be a problem when vigorous expansion gave way to an era of slow and faltering progress. Two oil crises in six years raised the price of oil tenfold – a major setback for a country with few natural energy sources, whose manufacturing industry depended heavily on imported oil. Chapter 4 surveys the extent and effects of the crisis, and the means adopted to deal with it. A key consequence was that from 1974 onwards, political room to manoeuvre came to be limited largely to the microeconomic level, constraining France's instinctive aspiration to economic sovereignty. The government's 'solution' to the crisis was to place the burden of adjustment squarely on the shoulders of employers in the form of higher employers' social security costs. In this way the working population was shielded from the costs of the economic difficulties (which, in the event, lasted almost a decade), borne instead by firms, together with the unemployed.[20]

That said, during the Giscard years France took a small – but significant – step towards reconceptualising her position in a world characterised by the interdependence of national economies. By the end of his mandate in 1981, Europe (Giscard's fundamental priority) had become more of a reality to the French. France's claims to a role on the world stage now relied more on the competitive performance of national champions, increasingly geared to export markets, and less on its maintenance of a nuclear deterrent. At the same time, the management of large firms improved significantly, taking advantage of a cadre of talented managers trained for public service by leading *grandes écoles*, as the Ecole National d'Administration (ENA) came of age. What increasingly concerned these managers was the maintenance and enhancement of France's competitive position in world markets.

In 1981, the French elected to the Elysée the first and, to date, the only socialist president of the Fifth Republic – an historic achievement rounded off by the landslide victory of a left-wing majority, comprising socialists and communists, in the parliamentary elections held in June. The new socialist administration pursued a Keynesian reflation policy immediately on taking office, aiming to achieve both a return to sustained economic growth and the restoration of full employment. The central plank of the government's economic policy was a vast nationalisation programme the like of which had never been seen in the West. Chapter 5 examines the economic priorities of the incoming administration and suggests that its objectives were compromised from the outset by the fact that it was running against the international trend towards austerity. The about-turn in economic policy, from reflation to *rigueur*, which took place from June 1982, reveals the extent to which the markets can punish governments and firms for disregarding the logic of their operation. The critical decision not to leave the European Monetary System (EMS) in March 1983 marked the point of realisation on the part of Mitterrand and the socialist administration that, ultimately, French macroeconomic policy is conditioned and constrained by the country's international economic environment, and by EC membership in particular. This decision set the tone for the remainder of the Mitterrand presidency and beyond. Paradoxically under a socialist administration (1981–86), this new consensus on Europe went hand in hand with another on the primary importance of business enterprise. During this time, many French firms came to view strategic management as concerned with more than planning and product positioning, seeking actively to develop the core capabilities and resources that might sustain their growth in the longer term.[21] A mark of success came when France overtook Britain to become the world's fourth largest exporting nation.

Chapter 6 examines the period 1986–95, the remainder of the Mitterrand era, and a momentous time for European construction. During the years of the first 'cohabitation' of the Fifth Republic (1986–88), the winds of change began to blow more fiercely in France. All price controls were abolished. Social legislation for hiring and firing was relaxed. State subsidy for industry was reduced. The French financial market was deregulated. The single market was conceived and became a reality. If the newly elected right-wing government (1986–88) had a mission, it was to encourage a more outward-looking and competitive 'liberal' economy, designed to prepare France for all that '1993' would bring, the hazards and the opportunities. In particular, a vast privatisation programme was launched, which sought to bring far-reaching change to the French economic landscape: as Finance Minister Balladur put it, this was to be 'the most important shift in the boundary between public and private sectors witnessed so far in the West'.[22] Indeed, the programme aimed to do no less than to produce a shift in mindsets by popularising capitalism. This chapter explores the 'liberal' years of the late

1980s and early 1990s, characterised by privatisation and by a wave of mergers and acquisitions as leading French firms strove to acquire the critical mass necessary to survive and compete in the harsher economic environment of the single market.

The undoubted strides taken by French business during this time, though, came at a considerable social cost. By the mid-1990s, the French had grown accustomed to, and had even come to tolerate, an unemployment rate that remained obstinately stuck at 12 per cent, despite healthy economic growth. It was the jobless and excluded who paid the price of budgetary stringency in the cause of European integration. As the year 1995 ended in a wave of strikes, triggered by welfare cuts and higher taxes, it was questionable whether internal pressures could continue to remain subordinate to European development.

Chapter 7 focuses on the Chirac presidency, dominated since its inception by the sweet air of scandal. *Les affaires* have reached a critical mass in France; nothing now can arrest the succession of prosecutions currently unravelling, which go all the way to the top. Whether or not the French have forgiven their president, as opinion polls in the run-up to the 2002 presidential election seemed to imply, is unclear. His re-election in May 2002 means a continuing immunity from prosecution. The concluding years of the twentieth century were also dominated by the appointment in 1997 of a socialist prime minister, Lionel Jospin (1997–2002), his arrival coinciding with the election of Tony Blair, as well as that of a left-leaning German chancellor, Gerhard Schröder, in 1998.[23]

The chapter begins by examining the experience of prudent fiscal management that characterised the late 1990s in the run-up to the launch of the single currency – an experience that seemingly revealed just how narrow are the straits that define the limits of government action in the new international economy. The margins of manoeuvre are likely to have been further reduced by the advent of the euro. To exchange the franc, symbol of national sovereignty *par excellence*, for the euro, simultaneously renouncing the right to control domestic monetary policy, including the setting of interest rates, has been a huge step. And yet, paradoxically, the chapter finds much evidence to support the view that in certain sectors at least (such as energy, utilities, transport, insurance, banking) French business and political leaders, who form a cohesive elite, continue to manage the competitive landscape effectively to their own advantage. This involves at times denying or deferring reciprocity in the liberalisation of domestic markets, while ruthlessly exploiting market liberalisation elsewhere in the EU.[24] In its purchase of West European grids, for example, the state-owned electricity company Electricité de France (EdF) has bought the rights to control the flows of electricity throughout continental Europe. Now in pole position, it has effectively acquired the right to dispense privileges. By way of a series of sectoral case studies, the argument is made that despite the ostensible loss of economic sovereignty through European integration, the French have continued successfully to defend and promote national business interests through skilful management of the new institutional landscape.

While seeking to present a balanced account of French business and the French economy as it has progressed along the route from economic nationalism to becoming a key European and global player, it is not however feasible to give one which is fully comprehensive in all respects. An all-embracing account would require additional volumes to the present study. Readers who look here for an extensive analysis of the French trade union movement or industrial relations system in particular will be disappointed. French trade unions, now embracing less than 7 per cent of the workforce, have been in decline since the 1970s, although the use of politically sensitive strikes, notably in transport and public service, makes them a force still to be reckoned with.[25]

Constraints of space have similarly restricted discussion in other areas. It has not proved practicable, for example, to provide a detailed analysis of the French pension system, the urgent reform of which is constantly postponed by a political class ever heedful of the next election. Socially divisive, with the potential to undermine intergenerational solidarity, this particular nettle has yet to be grasped effectively. While in 1950, there were as many as eight people in employment for each person in retirement, by 2050 there will be only two. The welfare states of France and Britain were set up in the postwar period; but, as Kindleberger observes, patterns of redistribution in war or which follow war are unavoidably different to those in times of peace. Failure to recognise this truth in France and elsewhere in the EU – where, with the exception of Britain and Denmark, pension funds remain significantly underdeveloped – arguably distorts behaviour with regard to both employment and retirement provision: 'fair shares carried into peacetime restricts inputs of labor and personal savings'.[26] EU governments are increasingly unable, and EU taxpayers ever more reluctant to pay. Though somewhat tangential to the present discussion, pension reform will have important implications for burden-sharing by French business, the state, employees, taxpayers and pensioners themselves in the future.

The French economy, at the start of the twenty-first century, notwithstanding the difficulties alluded to above, is well placed to exploit the opportunities and emerging potential of the new era of global capitalism. There is an essential robustness that stems from having a broad base in agriculture, manufacturing and a plethora of service activities from the prosaic to the culturally sophisticated. By and large, French companies are strategically well placed and have the organisational resources needed to compete successfully on the European and world stages. They have the advantage of being rooted in a supportive national business system characterised by long-standing interpersonal and intercorporate relationships and networks, and by a particular concordat between the state and business, all pulling in the same direction, especially since 1983. Because of the particular characteristics of French capitalism, the French business elite has been able to extend its influence very rapidly over recent years on the European stage, reproducing in the process elements of its ideology and institutional processes. This is a business community in transition, adapting to the logic of global capitalism. Network- and alliance-building is increasingly European and international; yet frequently the old rules still apply, albeit transferred to new spheres of action as appropriate. The accumulation and application of political capital at EU-level allows an asymmetric technocratic manipulation of rules, regulations and practices, in the pursuit of the national interest, the ultimate objective of which is to maintain or acquire hegemonic control of leading European and international enterprises.

1
Enduring Influences: French Business and the State

> Sovereignty, being but the exercise of the general will, cannot be alienated.
>
> Jean-Jacques Rousseau[1]

This book is concerned primarily with the changing economic realities of the French Fifth Republic, which, like the European Community whose development it has accompanied, was proclaimed in 1958, ushering in a new era of openness with France's European partners and, indeed, with the world at large. It traces the development of French economic and business life in long-term perspective, and in the context of the European and international economy, as these have evolved in the course of the Fifth Republic. It examines the main economic trends and events that have marked the last forty-five years, from nationalisation to privatisation, from war with Germany to reconciliation and *rapprochement* with the hereditary enemy, from the weak franc to the new franc to the strong franc and the euro, from national champions to mega mergers with foreign companies. But it also reaches back to the end of the Second World War. In many ways the immediate postwar period from 1945 to 1958, often seen as tarnished by economic and financial failures, was a truly revolutionary time for the French economy. There was an unprecedented surge forward in economic growth, with Gross Domestic Product (GDP) expanding by as much as 10 per cent in 1947, 13 per cent in 1948 and 7.5 per cent in 1949. The advance was spearheaded by a remarkable recovery in industrial production.[2]

This chapter differs in form and content from those that follow, which seek to explain specific developments within specific periods of time. Here we are more concerned with ideas and events that have cast a long shadow, that are in some way fundamental to the contemporary history of French business and economic management. In considering these enduring influences, the aim is to illuminate and contextualise the substance of later chapters. Following a brief overview of economic change in France in the years since 1945, we discuss the concept of a national business system and its relevance to France as a point of reference, as an ideal type. In this way we establish a basis for comparison between France and other national economies, identifying in the process what is said to make the national business system of France unique. This analysis is static, lacking the vitality of historically informed narrative, but it sets the scene for later sections. These range widely over formative ideas, events and issues, generally highlighting long-standing beliefs and practices that have informed the choices made by businessmen, technocrats and politicians, members of the ruling elite, at crucial stages in the economic and political history of France since 1945.

Economic change in France in the postwar era

The first three postwar decades of reconstruction and newfound prosperity, famously dubbed the 'thirty glorious years' by Fourastié and the 'golden age' by Maddison (1950–73),[3] witnessed the emergence of France as a modern economic power with far-reaching implications for lifestyles, consumption, behaviour and values. GDP grew in real terms at an annual average compound rate of 5.1 per cent during the *trente glorieuses*, rising as high as 5.8 per cent for the period 1959 to 1970 and culminating at a peak of 6.3 per cent in 1973. The era of sustained high growth was summarily ended by the first oil shock of 1973, the effects of which had begun to bite as early as 1974 (see Table 1.1). However, by this time, the national income of France was more than three times larger than it had been in 1950, such was the transformational power of historically high compound rates of economic growth in excess of 5 per cent per annum. In essence, France, like Japan and like other

Table 1.1 Real GDP growth 1870–1992 (annual average compound growth rates in percentages)

Year/country	1870–1913	1913–50	1950–92	1950–73	1973–92
Belgium	2.0	1.0	3.2	4.1	2.1
France	**1.5**	**1.1**	**3.8**	**5.0**	**2.3**
Germany	2.8	1.1	4.3	6.0	2.3
Ireland	0.5	0.6	3.3	3.2	3.5
Italy	1.9	1.5	4.3	5.6	2.7
Holland	2.2	2.4	3.6	4.7	2.1
Portugal	1.3	2.2	4.4	5.7	2.2
Spain	1.7	1.0	4.9	6.8	2.5
Sweden	2.2	2.7	2.7	3.7	1.5
UK	1.9	1.3	2.4	3.0	1.6
Europe av.	1.8	1.5	3.7	4.8	2.3
Japan	2.3	2.2	6.7	9.2	3.7
USA	3.9	2.8	3.3	3.9	2.5

Source: A. Maddison, 'Macroeconomic Accounts for European Countries', in B. Van Ark and N. Crafts, *Quantitative Aspects of Post-war European Economic Growth*, Cambridge, Cambridge University Press, 1996, p. 32.

countries in Western Europe, had been playing catch-up with the United States, taking advantage of the free flow of technology, investment and trade across the North Atlantic that was a feature of the new international order. As a natural consequence of expanded trade and investment flows, the French economy had become relatively open to international economic movements, fluctuations and influences, although still less so than the British or German economies. But with virtually no oil of its own and heavily dependent on energy imports, France paid dearly for the fourfold price rise imposed by the Organisation of Petroleum Exporting Countries (OPEC) in 1973. A further hike of 250 per cent in 1979 exacerbated the situation and made for a tenfold increase in six years. The effects of rising oil prices were compounded by sharply rising raw material prices in 1976–77 and the progressive increase in the value of the dollar. The consequential rise in import prices and the resulting pressure on the balance of payments came as further shocks to business confidence. Thereafter business life could no longer be planned with the same facility or certainty as before.

At the end of this golden age of growth, France's economy continued to expand, albeit no longer free from serious fluctuations, and at a slower rate than before. As the twentieth century drew to a close, France's trade surplus reached FF236 billion for the year 1998, about equal to the British trade deficit for the same year. GDP attained $1,150 billion in 1998. This was behind the mighty USA ($7,394 billion), Japan ($2,581 billion) and Germany ($1,460 billion), but ahead of the UK, $1,108 billion and Italy, $1,022 billion.[4] Yet achieving sustained economic growth had become more of a struggle, with the dual scourges of chronic unemployment and its close relation, social exclusion, looming large in the 1990s. Unemployment had remained low throughout the years of economic reconstruction, averaging 1.8 per cent of the workforce in the 1950s and 1.5 per cent in the 1960s, but by the end of the twentieth century it affected 11.2 per cent of the workforce. This fact stood out awkwardly, almost as a monument to modern society, capable of unprecedented wealth creation but not always jobs and the self-respect which accompanies them (see Table 1.2). While business ended the twentieth century on a buoyant note, with most economic indicators

Table 1.2 Comparative unemployment rates, 1950–95 (as percentage of workforce)

Period	France	USA	Italy	Japan	Germany	UK
1950–59	1.8	4.3	7.5	2.2	5	1.2
1960–67	1.5	5	4.9	1.3	0.8	1.5
1968–73	2.5	4.6	5.7	1.2	0.8	2.4
1974–79	4.5	6.7	6.6	1.9	3.4	4.2
1980–90	9	7	10	2.5	6.7	9.2
1990–95	11.2	6.6	11.3	2.5	8.7	9.4

Source: OECD.

reading positive and living standards at an all-time high, up to 5 million French citizens were deemed to be socially marginalised, living outside the social system. Once parodied as *le capitalisme sans capital*, capitalism without capital, French capitalism was now denigrated by writers such as Elie Cohen of the CNRS (Centre National de Recherche Scientifique) as 'capitalism without salaried workers'.[5]

The French national business system

The notion that the raw forces of capitalism are bounded, contained and directed according to different rules in different countries owes much to the work of Michel Albert. In his seminal study *Capitalisme contre capitalisme*, Albert explores the notion of two vying capitalist systems: one neo-American model founded on individual achievement and short-term financial gain; and one Rhenish model, of German extraction but with strong Japanese connections, which prizes collective success and consensus.[6] While the former is market-oriented and dominated by 'the tyranny of the quarterly report',[7] the latter is network-oriented, and characterised by a close partnership between banking and industry. Assuming a longer-term perspective, the Rhenish system is thus able to invest in industry, training and human capital.

Building on this analysis, Richard Whitley and his colleagues go so far as to speak in terms of 'divergent capitalisms', different models of capitalism that may be identified by comparing the main features of national business systems, thus challenging the view that national business systems are in the process of converging on the Anglo-American model. The Japanese business system, for example, is conventionally defined by the prevailing characteristics of ownership, inter-firm relationships, corporate finance and managerial authority. Japanese firms are bound together in vertical or horizontal groups united by cross-shareholdings, long-term supplier–customer partnerships and trade associations. They have a relatively high dependence on corporate debt relative to equity, and the company's lead bank occupies a key monitoring position, intervening directly whenever cause arises. There is a high level of managerial authority due to the lack of an active market for corporate control. In the Japanese system, the concept of 'shareholder capitalism' is subordinated to that of 'stakeholder capitalism'. Employees in particular are favoured by the advocacy of lifetime employment for all permanent employees. The Japanese state is perceived as the guardian of the national interest and an ally of business with a legitimate but not overriding strategic interest in business affairs. Under this system, the goal of business is not the maximisation of financial returns, but rather corporate growth and survival for the benefit of all stakeholders and in the general interest of society.[8]

Comparisons are often made in which the Japanese model, as described above, is placed at one end of a spectrum, as one ideal type, the so-called relational model of capitalism. The US model of competitive capitalism is placed at the other extreme, representing a second ideal type. Under this model, corporations are autonomous rather than bound together in business groups, equity finance predominates, and top managers, though powerful, influential and lavishly rewarded, are disciplined by vigilant groups of shareholders. There is a very active market for corporate control, with management teams regularly displaced for failing to maximise financial returns. The US national business system is thus depicted as the epitome of shareholder capitalism, with neither employees nor the state having legitimate rights with respect to the strategic direction of business corporations.

The national business system of France is generally perceived to be positioned towards the middle of the spectrum between the US and Japanese systems, and is often typified as a variant of the continental European model of managed capitalism. Its main features may be outlined with reference to the conceptual framework described in Figure 1 in the Introduction to this book. This identifies three levels or dimensions for the classification of system attributes: organisational, systemic and ideological. Organisational attributes are those features of the system that are the most readily observed aspects of a governance regime and relate to the ways in which the system is managed under national law. Systemic attributes are the structural properties that bind the system together and determine the ways in which it is managed in practice. Ideological attributes are the defining beliefs, values and assumptions of decision-makers within the system, including the businessmen at the front line, technocrats and politicians. Change at any level within the system, as it evolves, necessarily impacts upon other levels, effecting a state of dynamic equilibrium, although it is possible that one dimension might be out of kilter with another in the short term.

Some of the main attributes or defining features of the French national business system currently undergoing the assault of globalisation and its ideological counterpart – the doctrine of shareholder value – are presented in Table 1.3. At the heart of the system is the compact made between French business and the state, which in turn is held together by the shared ideology of a relatively homogeneous national elite. One of the products of the highly stratified French education system, by turns elitist and meritocratic, is that business, administrative and political leaders have mindsets forged in a common milieu and thus share numerous assumptions, prejudices and beliefs. That they have earned the right to run the system is not in question. Equally, there is a good measure of agreement over the fact that the business system exists primarily to serve the interests of the French nation, of which they, by virtue of their membership of the ruling elite, are the guardians. Thus while the system is managed by a confident elite, little interested in power sharing and supported by the state, the interests of other stakeholders are recognised, understood, respected and legitimised.

Table 1.3   Attributes of the French national business system

Organisational	Commentary
Board structure	Most boards are unitary as in the UK, though a few companies opt for the German two-tier model of management and supervisory boards. In unitary boards, the roles of Chairman and CEO are combined in the role of PDG (Président Directeur Général).
Board composition	Executive members are often home grown, especially in family firms, but in some large enterprises the PDG is appointed from outside. Many board members hold multiple directorships, often with reciprocal mandates within affiliated companies, with a consequent lack of 'independent' non-executive directors (NEDs).
Reporting and disclosure	Limited requirements for reporting to shareholders and for disclosure of detailed financial information. No compulsion to report on the remuneration of PDG or other directors.
Auditing and accountability	Limited use of audit committees to control executives and ensure conformance with rules and regulations. Few remuneration committees in existence. No tradition of shareholder activism. Generally passive annual general meetings.

Systemic	Commentary
Ownership	A system of closely held and reciprocal shareholdings linking banks, financial companies and industrial companies. Persistence of family ownership by founding families in many large firms.
Networks	Individual companies often form part of strategic groups united by cross-shareholdings. The group, often under the umbrella of a leading firm, is seen as a source of stability and security, defending against unwelcome takeovers.
Sources of funds	Traditionally a relatively high dependence on corporate debt in preference to equity. Equity financing and trading becoming more important following privatisation wave and stock-market reform.
Managerial authority	High level of managerial authority due to lack of an active market for corporate control. However, mergers and takeovers favoured as a means of industry rationalisation and international expansion.

Ideological	Commentary
Business goals	Survival and stability are paramount. Market share is more relevant than returns on investment or equity, producing a situation in which long-term strategy is more important than short-term dividends.

Table 1.3 (Continued)

Ideological	Commentary
The state	The French state is the guardian of the national interest, pursuing French business objectives in international forums, while imposing an onerous social settlement on business at home mitigated by the preservation of privilege.
Business elites	Business leaders are part of a fluid national elite. As such, some move with relative ease between the spheres of administration, politics and business. Members take for granted the right to govern, legitimised by educational attainment.
Stakeholders	The concept of the shareholder is subordinated to that of the stakeholder. Stakeholders include managers, employees, owners, communities, customers and the state.

Compiled by the author.

The compact forged between business and the state is characterised by recognition of the need for both parties to work together in pursuit of economic growth. In the context of global economic realities, this increasingly means that the state is charged with ensuring that the rules of the competitive game are forged to suit French business, working in the interests of firms rather than pursuing purely defensive goals such as the preservation of jobs. Strong French firms networked across Europe and beyond are seen to be the basis of long-term domestic economic prosperity. Firms such as these have the capacity to provide high-quality jobs and generate the wealth that might be redistributed for education, the national infrastructure and a plethora of social needs. High rates of taxation and social charges are the bitter pill that business has had to swallow in identifying so closely with the state in pursuit of its own interests.

Growth and corporate survival are the priorities shared by both French business and the French state. In order to reduce risk, achieve a higher degree of coordination and guard against hostile takeovers, firms have formed into affiliated groups bound together by cross shareholdings and directors with reciprocal mandates. Senior managers, members of the elite, have a large degree of authority with respect to strategic decision-making, traditionally unchecked by shareholders who have received information on a selective rather than mandatory basis. At the head of the corporate hierarchy is the Président Directeur Général (PDG), frequently combining the roles of Chairman and CEO, and serving as the embodiment of the corporation itself. Under French rules of corporate governance, typically little is known of the remuneration and personal affairs of PDGs, who have tremendous power at their disposal, moving smoothly within the upper echelons of French society.

Economic sovereignty as a national aspiration

The French national business system, as stylised in the preceding section, reflects in its practices the aspiration of France to retain control of its own economic destiny. This goal, however, is increasingly at odds with the reality of lost sovereignty stemming from inseparability from the global economic system. Globalisation refers to the 'quantum leap' in the interconnection of national economies that occurred in the late 1980s and 1990s, marked at the beginning of the twenty-first century by the growth of e-commerce and e-business. It goes beyond the internationalisation of business in terms of the extension of markets across national boundaries through exports and foreign direct investment (FDI).[9] What defines the globalisation phenomenon is the growth over the past two decades in the size and power of international financial markets, increasingly interlinked, often volatile and sensitive to information and the emergence of companies that appear to transcend national boundaries. Such transnational companies, it is alleged, no longer see the need for a national home base but have the power to source, produce and market products and services worldwide.

Globalisation is infused by risks, which must be understood and contained, such as financial and entrepreneurial risks, whose active embrace, Giddens writes, 'is the very driving force of the globalising economy'.[10] It is also marked by risks of global warming, which mankind must contain, or face disaster: a scenario which looms larger in view of the unwillingness of President Bush to confront the heavy costs imposed by the US on the natural environment. The most apparent consequence of globalisation is a reduction in the autonomy of national governments, limiting their ability to make decisions independently, without taking account of external economic actors and forces. One illustration of this truth was the Exchange Rate Mechanism (ERM) débâcle of September 1992, and again in summer 1993, throwing into relief the impotence of European governments (in this case the British, French, Italian and Portuguese), in the teeth of worldwide market speculation (see Chapter 7). According to Schmidt and Krugman, governments allow markets to boss them around since to do otherwise is to invite economic stagnation and hence to court disaster.[11] They also have little choice. The combined reserves of national banks such as the Banque de France, the Bank of England or the Bundesbank, considerable though these are, are nevertheless as a drop in the ocean when compared to the amassed power of determined global speculators scenting blood.

In France, fears over the adverse consequences of globalisation surfaced towards the end of the twentieth century in a series of public debates and protests, each lamenting loss of control and loss of national sovereignty. Unions and socialist politicians, in a flurry of rhetorical concern over *délocalisations* or 'social dumping', pointed to the loss of 'French' jobs as firms, driven by the need to compete on cost as well as quality, relocated manufacturing plants to low-wage economies. A public outcry against cross-border industrial concentration was triggered in January 1999 by the wave of giant mergers aimed at streamlining production in preparation for the launch of the euro. This was matched by a wave of public anger against US trade supremacy, as small farmers, union leaders and green activists joined forces to denounce an alleged American drive to rob nations of their livelihood and cultural identity under the banner of free trade. Under attack were the domination of American fast food, epitomised by the tentacular embrace of international markets enjoyed by chains such as McDonalds, and American entertainment. The perceived tyranny of the latter was especially unpalatable to a nation whose traditional eminence in literature and the arts was now limited by the fact of its own language (once the international language of European monarchs, courtiers and diplomats), in an era of English-speaking hegemony. In cinema, American films outperformed French films at box offices in France by a ratio of almost three to one in 1998. French films benefited from state subsidies worth £260 million for the year, but could only capture 27 per cent of the domestic audience.[12]

To what extent 'sovereignty' remains at the beginning of the new century is, of course, a moot point. National sovereignty is curtailed not only by internationalisation and globalisation but also, for member states of the European Union (EU), by the process of European integration. This proceeded apace in the 1990s, from one market in 1993 to one currency in 1999. The European Central Bank (ECB) now determines such vital matters as interest rates, once the preserve of national governments. Tax harmonisation, too, is on the cards, with the Commission contemplating a range of taxes relating to corporate taxation (including tax on cross-border interest, energy products, e-commerce, withholding taxes on interest and royalties, etc.). Viewed by many as a last bastion of sovereignty, taxation is no longer, it seems, taboo.

Rousseau and the concept of the general interest

French concern with sovereignty goes back a long way, to the economist Jean Bodin, author of *La République* (1576), but more especially to Jean-Jacques Rousseau, writing in the eighteenth century of a political sovereignty which he regarded as inalienable and indivisible, if under threat. Rousseau's *Social Contract*, published in 1762, has proved to be seminal and of lasting relevance. In this, Rousseau considers how individual citizens, with individual needs, can live harmoniously within a community, within society. He argues that in place of individuality and independence, individuals should cast aside their natural, harmful inclinations (termed *le moi humain*) and submit instead to the 'general will' (*la volonté générale*) of the integrated community (*le moi commun*), which permits no diversity of viewpoints. This single will of the whole – not equivalent to the will of all, potentially subjective and liable to be influenced by passion, but general and reasonable when its goal is for the common good – is presented as indestructible. Nevertheless, the sovereign authority of the collective state, which replaces nature, is likely to come under constant attack from the particular, sectional interests of private individuals, groups or factions. In passages that seem to presage the fall of the Fourth Republic, Rousseau warns of the dangers of subordinating the public weal to special interests. He writes that 'when the social knot begins to unravel and the state begins to weaken, when particular interests begin to make themselves felt and small communities begin to influence the greater community [...] the general will is no longer the will of all'. This, he admonishes, leads ultimately to the collapse of the state and the silencing of the general will, 'as the vilest of interests adorns itself with the sacred name of the public good'.[13]

There are many problems with Rousseau's concepts. How is the general will to be determined? How is it to be distinguished from the will of all? Does the universality of the law necessarily guarantee its justice? There is the danger that decision-makers may confuse their own interests with those of the state. When an individual is deemed to be unreasonable, according to Rousseau he is to be 'forced to be free', prefiguring Stalinist Russia. However, whatever the shortcomings of Rousseau's philosophy, his ideas remain fundamental and important to any understanding of contemporary French political culture and thought. His belief in a sovereign people endowed with a general will prey to special interests that seek to hijack and dominate it continues to permeate French political culture and remains deeply relevant. As the French economist, Jacques Plassard, once wrote: 'It is ideas that are essential. Ideas and not the economy – as Marxists and imbeciles believe – rule the world', a view supported by David Landes, writing in 1949 that 'ideas once formed are as powerful as the strongest material forces'.[14] They may also be as enduring. In a country which has long discarded its monarchy, which purports to be a meritocracy, yet where the particular interests of political, business and technocratic elites prevail and are jealously guarded, bolstered by establishment solidarity, these observations remain pertinent to this day.

The term 'economic sovereignty', a key concern of this book, denotes the power of the state to direct the economy as it sees fit without interference by other parties. It is thus concerned first and foremost with the autonomy of the domestic economy, but through trade and economic relations with other nations this necessarily spills over to notions of external sovereignty: the power to act in the domestic arena as on the world stage independently of foreign control. External sovereignty has, in the past, been taken largely for granted, perceived, as Stanley Hoffmann observes, as 'the normal and central characteristic of statehood', whether or not the state in question is a monarchy or a republic.[15] This is no longer the case. With the exception of the United States, which has acted in the past as 'international policeman' in matters of international security and trade, despite the existence of NATO (North Atlantic Treaty Organisation) and the WTO (World Trade Organisation), no other state can take its external sovereignty for granted. Even the US is now regularly challenged abroad, and increasingly at home. This has been one of the hard lessons of the twentieth century. France in particular has had great difficulty in coming to terms with the decline in its status from its former pre-eminence as a leading military and colonial power, to being a nation of the second rank. On the eve of the First World War, the French Empire spanned 11,755,000 square kilometres, embracing a population of 41.1 million outside the mother country. France had a plethora of colonies in several continents: Asia (in India, Indo-China, Kwangchou-Wan); Africa (Northern and Southern Algeria, Tunisia, Congo, West Africa and the Sahara, Réunion, Madagascar, Mayotte Comoro Isles, and the Somalia Coast); Latin America (Guiana, Guadeloupe, Martinique, St Pierre et Miquelon) and the Pacific (Tahiti and islands, New Caledonia). A quarter of a century later, in June 1940, this great imperial power was defeated in a matter of a few weeks by the might of the German army, the Maginot Line, its alleged state-of-the-art fortifications, easily breached. Added to this, it could be argued that in the twentieth century France's eminence in literature and the arts had begun to lose something of its former radiance. It is in the light of this decline in international standing that de Gaulle's obsession with grandeur and national prestige must be viewed.

Economic management, another main concern of this book, may be defined as the direction and guidance of the economy by the state. In this task, the state may have recourse to an array of incentives and controls, including fiscal, monetary, regional and industrial policies.[16] However, the state's capacity for economic management has been potentially greater in France than in other EU member states in the postwar period by virtue of the size of its public sector, ostensibly allowing the state considerable scope to intervene in the economy.

Colbertism, the state and business

There is a long tradition in France of state involvement in the economy, dating back to Jean-Baptiste Colbert (1619–83), variously superintendent of buildings (1664), financial controller (1665) and secretary of state for the royal household under Louis XIV. Colbert was an indefatigable public administrator, and in the tradition of France's great centralisers (including Philip the Fair, Richelieu, Mazarin and Louis XIV), he was above all an enlightened supporter of fledgling industries and commerce. He introduced protectionist measures, invited foreign craftsmen to France, and expanded the role of the state in manufacturing industry, albeit initially for the purposes of replenishing the monarch's depleted war chests. Some of the companies he nurtured in the seventeenth century remain in existence today, including glassmaker Saint-Gobain (created in 1665 as part of Colbert's economic reflation plan), which remains one of France's leading companies. However, of greater important is Colbert's intellectual legacy. He lends his name to the long-standing tradition of state intervention in the economy through discriminatory fiscal and public procurement policies, designed to favour and protect public and private national champions, as well as nascent industries, in order that they might withstand foreign competition. In the postwar period, economic management and economic sovereignty joined hands in an industrial policy whose principal objective, as Elie Cohen points out, was commercial success in the international marketplace through high-tech Colbertism. The State bolstered its 'national champions' (*champions nationaux*) in future industries with grants and public procurement measures designed to provide secure markets, and cushioned through subsidy its 'lame ducks' (*canards boiteux*) in sunset industries such as steel and shipbuilding. The general interest – national defence, national sovereignty and technological autonomy – has been customarily proffered as justification for what might be defined as 'offensive protectionism'.[17]

France's 'mixed economy', in which responsibility is shared by private and public actors, has not remained static during the postwar period. Following the Liberation in 1944–46, the public sector was significantly enlarged through the nationalisation of strategic financial and industrial sectors. The then Constituent Assembly adopted acts of nationalisation first for the banks (December 1945), next for electricity and gas (March 1946), followed by insurance (April 1946) and finally coal (April 1946). Linked to the Resistance movement, and to the vengeful atmosphere of the Liberation, nationalisation was perceived as 'democratic and patriotic retaliation against the alleged defeatist and collaborationist activities of the capitalist oligarchies'.[18] De Gaulle, however, as he confessed to his erstwhile Minister of Culture, novelist André Malraux, shortly before the general's death in 1970, perceived nationalisation above all as a means of resurrecting France.[19]

In February 1982, following the accession of the left to office for the first time in a generation, the state strengthened its hold on the economy (ostensibly at least) by taking control of another huge tranche of the financial and industrial sectors: 36 banks, two finance companies, and 12 leading industrial conglomerates. This gave rise to proportionately the largest public sector outside the Eastern bloc, accounting for some 24 per cent of jobs, 32 per cent of sales, 30 per cent of exports and 60 per cent of investment in the industrial and energy sectors (see Chapter 5).[20] Subsequently, from the mid-1980s, the tendency has been, in France as elsewhere, to reduce the role of the state in the economy in the interests of achieving greater efficiency and effectiveness, through the implementation of deregulation and far-reaching privatisation programmes. Thus France went from sweeping nationalisation to sweeping privatisation in the short space of four years. The disengagement or withdrawal of the state was now seen as a necessary precondition for a more efficient economy.[21]

Yet public service in France remains endowed with special meaning. Perhaps this goes some way towards explaining why France has faced such searching self-doubt in recent years regarding its particular model of state–society relations. Despite extensive privatisation since 1986, the French public sector remains one of the largest in Western Europe. At the birth of the Fifth Republic it represented just over 20 per cent of the French economy (excluding agriculture), in terms of its impact on levels of investment, value added, and the labour force. From a peak of 24 per cent in 1985, by 1998 it still accounted for a sizeable 13.5 per cent of investment, 11.5 per cent of value added, and employed 10.3 per cent of the workforce, representing an overall impact on the French economy of 11.8 per cent (excluding agriculture), against an EU average of 9 per cent (see Table 1.4).[22]

If the quest for national economic sovereignty is presented as a noble pursuit, the realities of economic management are concerned much more with compromise, relativities, and with the necessity of 'dirtying one's hands'. Clearly, the needs of economic management are not necessarily compatible with the aspiration for economic sovereignty. Tension and even conflict may arise between the quest for autonomy and prestige on the one hand and the necessity of managerial efficiency on the other, between 'national distinctiveness' and 'insufficient national means of action'.[23] In the course of the past forty-five years, the reality of economic management has come to diverge increasingly from the goal of economic sovereignty. Once the openness of the French economy was accepted as a *sine qua non* of expansion in 1958 – imports and exports rose from 13 per cent of GDP in 1953 to 23 per cent of GDP in 1983[24] – French economic management was likely

Table 1.4 Evolution of impact of public-sector firms[a] in EU economy, 1973–1998 (as a percentage) (excluding agriculture)

	1973	1979	1982	1985	1988	1992[b]	1995[c]	1998
Employees	8.3	11.9	12.8	11.5	10.6	8.9	7.6	7.1
Added value	11.0	13.2	14.1	13.4	12.0	10.9	9.7	8.5
Investment	22.0	22.5	22.9	21.0	17.3	15.6	13.6	11.0
Av. impact	13.8	15.8	16.6	15.3	13.3	11.8	10.6	9.0

[a] Public-sector firms are defined as those in which the state or local authorities or other organ of government own 50 per cent or more of the capital or are responsible for 50 per cent or more of administration.
[b] Europe of 12.
[c] Europe of 15.

Sources: Armand Bizaguet, French section, Centre Européen des Entreprises à Participation Publique; *CEEP Statistical Review 2000*, Brussels, CEEP, 2000.

to conflict with the aspiration for national autonomy. The latter has been compromised time and again by the need to adjust to external constraints, particularly in the wake of the first oil shock of 1973–74. Over the past half-century, French politicians have learned from experience that the French economy does not exist in a vacuum, but that it functions as part of a complex global economy. This became all the more obvious at the beginning of the Mitterrand era. Since the early 1980s, the quest for an increasingly unachievable national independence has been superseded by the goal of constructing an economically and politically coherent Europe that might better serve French interests.

Centralism and localism

Perceptions of French interests, however, are not always characterised by the unity to which Rousseau and later de Gaulle aspired. The paradox of a unifying state constantly beset by divisions wrought by sectional interests, is echoed elsewhere in French society, nowhere more so than in the apparent contradiction of bureaucratic centralising tendencies coupled with profound regional diversity. Centralisation was a long-standing ambition for the Bourbons; it was subsequently reinforced by the very revolution that ousted the monarchy. The difficulties of maintaining order drove the Republic proclaimed in 1792 to adopt even stronger centralising measures. The old provinces were legally abolished, replaced by *départements*. Yet for all his steps to unite France – through the Napoleonic codes of law, the Concordat, the creation of prefects and the introduction of measures to control departmental governments in legal, religious and educational matters – Napoleon could not make France entirely uniform. The loyalty that French people feel to Normandy or Picardy or to a certain *pays* is enduring, anchored in local history and culture. This diversity is accompanied by a lasting obsession with unity, exacerbated by growing social fragmentation. François Mitterrand, for example, aspired to be President of 'all the French', presiding over 'la France unie'. Yet the society that he left behind in 1995 was not the one – more equal and more tolerant of difference – he had set out to build in 1981, being characterised by *la fracture sociale* between the materially well off and an estimated 5 million 'have-nots'.

The French geographer Vidal de la Blache said that France has the history of its geography. As Dunham has written, it was geography that made Paris the natural capital of France, with its commanding position at the junction of the Seine and Marne, near that of the Seine and Oise, and its mastery of the routes in northern France. The counts of Paris became the Capetian kings of France.[25] The economic development of France has been greatly influenced by the domination of the capital, determining for example its road and rail transport systems. At the same time, the number and diversity of local *pays* help to explain the fragmentation of many markets until late in the twentieth century. In France, correspondingly, industrialisation was a gradual, protracted process marked by the persistence of small-scale operations in both agriculture and manufacturing industry. The relative smallness of French enterprises in many sectors of the economy for long worked as a counterbalance to the centralising tendencies of an ambitious state, helping preserve localism and regionalism as important social forces. This is in marked contrast to Britain, where the more pronounced trend towards industrial concentration from the late nineteenth century onwards brought most large companies to set up their headquarters in London. Economic and political power became geographically concentrated at an early stage, whereas in France a similar unification did not take place until after 1945.

War and the national consciousness

The end of the Second World War, which drew to a close in Europe in May 1945 but dragged on until September in Japan, marks an unrivalled watershed in twentieth-century international relations. With so many killed from so many nations (as many as 35 million in all), slaughter and destruction on an unprecedented and global scale, some of which, in its ill-treatment of human beings, plumbed the depths of human nature, there is a very real sense in which a nadir had been reached. The end of the war forms a *table rasé* or *degré zéro* which is a natural starting-point for our discussion and analysis. Paradoxically, that destruction also contained the seeds of new growth: inventiveness born of necessity and want; order and planning out of chaos; and, in the new Europe that began to assume shape and form after the war, understanding of enmity in a new environment more conducive to multilateral trade and international financial cooperation.

The First World War – in whose trenches 8.5 million had perished – legated to its participants an economic order born of acrimony and resentment, a product of the attempt to obtain reparations from Germany for the victors. These were due, as agreed by the 1924 Dawes Plan, primarily to France (52 per cent), the British Empire (22 per cent), Italy (10 per cent), Belgium (8 per cent) and the remainder to the other minor Allies. Negotiators at Versailles in 1919, notably John Maynard Keynes, were acutely aware of the potentially disastrous consequences to the continent of heaping too large a burden on the German economy. However, they faced huge budgetary problems of their own as a result of war debts and faced enormous pressure from public opinion to make Germany pay. As Feinstein *et al.* observe, 'le Boche payera' ('the Hun will pay') was a popular slogan in post-First World War France.[26]

In marked contrast, the end of the Second World War was not denoted by the imposition of an exacting peace treaty or a chorus of demands for reparations. Indeed, from 1947 defeated Germany received considerable sums to rebuild its devastated economy through the Marshall Plan for European reconstruction. So too did Europe's victorious powers, preventing the descent into difficult international relations, bitterness and ultimately revenge that scarred the years between 1918 and 1939. Altogether, from 1948 to 1951, over $13 billion was made available by the US to Europe through grants and loans as part of the European Recovery Progamme better known as Marshall Aid. The farsightedness of the US in this matter was recognised when the author of the plan, General George Marshall, was awarded the Nobel Peace Prize in 1953. In acting magnanimously towards both friend and foe, the US helped to secure its twin objectives of creating a viable and growth-inducing international economy (by helping financially beleaguered countries bridge the so-called dollar gap and procure the equipment and materials needed to rebuild) and fending off the menace of communism.

Imaginative thinking on the shape and direction of the postwar international economy was not, of course, exclusive to the US. In France, as elsewhere in Western Europe, businessmen, technocrats and politicians alike made the case for closer cooperation in economic affairs. France took a leading role in the process of European construction with Jean Monnet and Robert Schuman articulating the view that peace and wealth were likely products of market integration and economic cooperation. There followed the creation of a series of new institutions designed to reconcile the self-interest of businessmen with the structural necessities of industrial efficiency: the European Coal and Steel Community (created by the Treaty of Paris in 1951), Euratom (1957) and the European Common Market (created by the Treaty of Rome in 1957). In this way, France became firmly established at centre stage in Europe, hand-in-glove with its old enemy Germany. The Elysée Treaty of friendship with Germany, signed in 1963 by de Gaulle and Adenauer, formally ended centuries of hostilities stretching back over 23 wars to the time of Charles V and François I. According to Kuisel, the liberation of France in the summer of 1944 and the early postwar years were characterised by a new consensus in favour of reform and renewal and an overriding desire for a new departure. Ehrmann argues that these were joined by a strident call for the liberation of the economy.[27] Kindleberger meanwhile maintains that the new, potent ingredient was a new empiricism: 'In France [...] the Cartesian tradition remained vigorous, occasionally smothered by conservatism and business distrust. When it gained ascendancy after World War II, it added to itself the effective ingredient of empiricism.'[28] Together these ideas conspired to produce a major turning-point for the economic order of twentieth-century France.

French business in historical perspective

In general, the business history of France has been studied relatively little by those seeking to trace and explain the main features of capitalist enterprises as these have evolved since the eighteenth century, despite its current status as the fourth industrial nation and former status as the second. Porter omitted France from consideration in the *Competitive Advantage of Nations*. As Fridensen points out, 'among French or American business historians of France, nobody ever dared to write a general business history of France': the detailed studies needed for such an overview are lacking.[29]

The same is not true of French economic history, which is more concerned with the general features and mainsprings of economic growth. Richard Vinen even suggests that economic rather than political historians of France offer the most thought-provoking overview of French politics between 1945 and 1958. He observes that 'economic historians tend to describe a success story that begins in 1945 and lasts until the present day, where political historians describe a failure that started in the Third Republic and ended in 1958. This means that the economic history of the Fourth Republic is continuously rethought in the light of more recent events.'[30] Vinen points out that historians writing on the recent economic history of France tend to stress the close ties binding social, political and economic events.[31] It could be argued that the most successful accounts of the French economy and economic policy embrace the study of society and politics, and are therefore necessarily wide-ranging in perspective, offering a social and cultural analysis. It is important to stress that the political and economic spheres are enmeshed in France in a way in which they are not in the UK. The British government has tended historically to take the view that business is best left to business, interfering as little as possible in the micro-economy: the proper role of government according to this view is to manage the macro-economy through monetary and fiscal policy. Over the last fifty years French governments have assumed a rather different view. Thus the economist Maurice Parodi seeks to focus simultaneously on the economy and society of France in his examination of the second half of the twentieth century.[32] Likewise, American authors writing on French economic history, most notably David Landes and Charles Kindleberger, have portrayed social attitudes as illuminating and reflective of business life.

Landes' famous thesis, most eloquently expressed in his seminal article on French entrepreneurship published in 1949, ascribes the disappointing performance of the French economy in the nineteenth and early twentieth centuries to its atomistic structure and the predominance of inherently conservative family capitalism. In Landes' view, the family firm retarded economic growth in France, which in turn inhibited population growth (so-called Malthusianism). It is ironic that Landes should have written of French economic retardation just as economic growth was poised to take off. He was looking back on a nineteenth-century France that had forfeited its former political hegemony under Napoleon and which held a relatively minor place in the economic world. Supposed economic weakness and retardation thus stimulated his fascination with France: 'we must consider not only the more "modern" nations but those less industrialized as well. It will not suffice to study the progress of American or German business and deduce therefrom impressive theories on the importance of the business-man. The converse must also be examined.'[33]

Landes believed that most French businesses were structured in such a way as to bind them inextricably economically with the family, to the extent that business treasury and household purse typically were one.[34] Firms were family-structured, indeed, to the point of resembling pre-capitalist, even medieval economies. As for the entrepreneurs who ran them, Landes found them to be shaped by what he saw as the development of a single, conscious nation, albeit within great diversity – geological, climatic, ethno-graphic and cultural. Three typical characteristics of the average French businessman were identified. First, he was usually a small entrepreneur, acting alone or in concert with a small number of partners: the corpora-tion, certainly in its British or American sense, could not be said to exist. Second, he was deeply conservative, cautious and thrifty: company plant was intended to last, perhaps a hangover from the peasant mentality. And third, he was staunchly independent, as reflected in the self-sufficiency of the average firm. Growth was funded from family savings or by relatives or friends (the earliest investment banks did not appear in France until the 1850s and 1860s). The primary objective of the typical firm was the highest possible rate of profit, rather than expansion *per se*. Keeping prices high obviated the need to eliminate competition through competitive pricing, meaning that all but the most inefficient firms could survive. This desire for high profit margins was accompanied by a more general reliance on the state and on state aid, which coexisted paradoxically with a strong concern for secrecy, privacy and, as mentioned, independence, in what Landes terms an 'undeclared war between business and the state'. He explains the entrepreneur's childlike dependence on the state as follows:

Under the old regime the French manufacturer had been more a func-tionary than an independent entrepreneur; industry had been in large measure a sort of hothouse growth, nurtured by and derived from the central administration. The Napoleonic period, if anything, strengthened these characteristics. It is not surprising, therefore, that the businessman came to look on the government as a sort of father in whose arms he could always find shelter and consolation. This fundamentally infantile attitude, which must be distinguished from the predatory outlook not uncommon in the United States, was carried in this period to remarkable lengths and characterized businessmen from one end of the scale to the other. There is essentially no difference between the request of a wheel-chair maker of Belleville that the state purchase twelve of his devices for donation to various hospitals and the petition in 1848 of three of France's biggest iron firms, Schneider, Boigues and Bougueret-Martenot, that the government take over the defaulting Paris–Lyons Railroad and make good on four million dollars owed for delivery of rails.[35]

As Landes notes, the combination of these features was ill-suited to a harsh competitive environment: 'cautious management, obsolescent plants and high profits are not a combination designed to flourish in a world of cut-throat competition'.[36] Above all else, the typical entrepreneur prized security, reflected in his concern for a secure market protected from foreign competition – the remnants of which concern endure to this day.

The importance of stability over growth, expansion and even profit is confirmed by Eugène Schneider, writing in the 1920s from the perspective of one of France's leading elite industrial dynasties: 'What is essential and comes before all other things is stability. If we had to choose between exceptionally favourable but unstable general conditions and other less brilliant but assured of great stability, we would not hesitate to choose the latter.'[37] Reflecting on this, Ehrmann observes that the typical French businessman found it impossible to visualise a brilliant future for his company, so deeply ingrained was his sense of restraint in competition.

Writing on the Landes thesis in the early 1960s, Charles Kindleberger highlights its evident difficulties. First, he claims, Landes' conclusions on the nature of entrepreneurial behaviour were based on comparisons between France and Britain; yet differences in average growth rates between two countries cannot necessarily be ascribed to entrepreneurial behaviour without taking other factors into account, such as economic cycles and trends. Second, it is problematic to speak of an 'average businessman' in a country that is highly varied in terms of the size of its businesses, the nature of its industries, its regions and cities. Third, it is equally problematic to compare the behaviour of businessmen between countries when all other conditions are not equal, which is impossible. Lastly, entrepreneurial activity is multi-faceted and is not merely concerned with innovation, but embraces other functions, such as recruitment, training, marketing, capital accumulation, cost reduction and so on. Nevertheless, despite these qualifications, Kindleberger concedes that French economic growth may indeed have been as influenced by national character traits and social process as by more conventional determinants of growth, such as technology, savings and investment.[38] The organisation of the family is again highlighted as particularly relevant. Kindleberger further observes that in France, the family firm is preserved intact, while in the UK it is milked for profit. The French family firm achieves a plateau to which it hopes to adhere, while in Britain it changes from one generation to the next: the old cliché of 'clogs to clogs in three generations'. And while there may be many French family firms that function as efficient large-scale enterprises, the majority follow a different pattern. However, the main question, for Kindleberger, does not concern entrepreneurial behaviour *per se*, but rather, the relative lack of newcomers willing and able to challenge established firms;[39] no doubt some way explained by the chronic shortage of business capital, exacerbated by reams of red tape, legal difficulties, a deep-seated French distaste for speculation and risk-taking, and the limited role of the corporation in France (which in the US, as Landes points out, allowed thousands of anonymous small fortunes to be consolidated, and talented but penniless individuals to run them, the *société anonyme* tending on the contrary to consolidate existing fortunes).

In essence, the argument made by Landes and supported on a qualified basis by Kindleberger is that the influence of French entrepreneurial psychology on France's economic structure, and therefore performance, is significant and far-reaching. Of particular note, for Landes, is French Cartesianism, following the teaching of the French philosopher René Descartes (1596–1650), which values logic, deduction and mathematics according to clearly defined methodological principles, prizing intellectual rigour over pragmatic empiricism, theory over practice, thought over action. The whole of the French education system is informed by Cartesian logic, mathematics and methodology, including the *grandes écoles*, the hothouses in which France's business leaders are formed. Landes cites Lucien Febvre:

> We shall buy machines, fine machines, when we have acquired from top to bottom a mechanical mentality. We shall organize production effectively when we have freed ourselves of a certain Louis-Philippic petty-bourgeois psychology. Think first. Act afterwards. Then, yes, France, regenerated, will be able to resume a role of leadership in the world. Then, yes, the mortgage will be lifted, the heavy mortgage placed on our country by its cult of old ideas, its serene but stubborn museum-piece traditionalism.[40]

It was this which, for Kindleberger, changed dramatically after the French defeat by Germany in 1940: 'while on other issues the French might operate intellectually, verbally and theoretically, in economic reconstruction and growth there was a turn to empiricism'.[41] Nevertheless, French Cartesianism continues to exert a significant influence on French business life and decision-making. As an adviser to the Socialist minister of finance (1984–86) confirmed, contrasting France's undeniable prowess in the design and engineering of complex Ariane rockets with its relative inability to mass-produce altogether more mundane goods, such as washing-machines, which nevertheless meet the everyday needs of consumers: 'We know how to make the Ariane (rocket), but we don't know how to make washing machines.'[42]

French business culture

The preservation of all but the most inefficient firms through a tacit agreement between efficient and inefficient producers, centring on a regime of high prices, healthy profits, limited production and horizons, was a central feature of the Third Republic. In 1951, Fourastié noted that the productivity of labour was the 'variable driving power of social development'. Yet increased productivity, the consequence of rising technological sophistication and organisational effectiveness, most often goes hand in hand with a significant drop in prices. Growth-oriented firms embrace the challenge of falling prices and respond by increasing productivity still further, whereas conservative firms prefer to self-limit production as a means of preserving high prices.[43] In the France of the Third Republic and beyond, so the argument goes, conservative businessmen haunted by a fear of over-production and falling prices, conspired to limit output and maintain margins through output controls and price-fixing. Production was to be organised rather than expanded. With some exceptions (such as cars, steel, electricity and chemicals), the emphasis was on serving local markets rather than national or international ones. As Kindleberger points out, fragmented markets allowed small firms to behave monopolistically in a restricted area.[44] The emphasis was also on quality rather than on quantity, on bespoke items rather than mass-produced ones. The high-quality, made-to-order nature of much of French industrial production meant in turn that demand outstripped supply, even during the 'thirty glorious years', when the US and later the UK were in the grip of a marketing revolution. At the same time, keeping the economy on an even keel ensured greater stability of producers, fewer new entrants to markets as well as fewer casualties. Inevitably, though, in periods of more rapid growth such as the 1850s and 1860s, and again in the 1900s and 1920s, larger enterprises did gain ground and consolidate the position of producers in the national marketplace.

The nature of the 'concordat' between large and small producers, what Hoffmann terms the 'republican synthesis' uniting industrialists with peasants and small shopkeepers, lay in the fact that these small traders and producers were politically useful as a bulwark to the working classes. The constant need to appease them, however, as both Vinen and Hoffmann argue, was a key obstacle to rapid change in the Third Republic.[45] Nevertheless, it is important to emphasise that the quest for security that characterised French business throughout much of the nineteenth and twentieth centuries transcends business circles to embrace public authorities and other corporate bodies. Indeed, it is this search for security which some commentators pinpoint as the intimate link between public attitudes and corporate behaviour in France,[46] so often marked by the collision of economic and technical progress with a deep-seated desire for social stability.

As Alain Berger lamented in the early 1950s, businessmen in France valued regularity of income over profit. Profit ceased to be profit but became instead *rente*, income or annuity, not obtained through competition in the marketplace but protected from competition, something to be maintained rather than increased.[47] This had important consequences for taxation.

Businessmen had a vested interest in indirect taxation, which falls more evenly on employers and employees, large and small producers according to their consumption, in preference to direct taxation, more threatening to their income. Thus, progressive taxation was eschewed in favour of tariffs, price supports and subsidies as the preferred means of income redistribution.

The enduring search for organisational security in France is linked by various authorities to a deep-rooted need to avoid uncertainty and eliminate ambiguity. This is apparent in the traditional French predilection for land, gold, property or deposit savings accounts over other forms of investment, such as shares, perceived as altogether more risky. As André Maurois said of the rural population of France, 'the peasant has money, but the countryside doesn't spend; it saves up for the morrow'. Alfred Fouillée, writing early in the twentieth century in *Esquisse psychologique des peuples européens*, observed that the French love of saving was in marked contrast to the British predilection for spending.[48] The Dutch psychologist Geert Hofstede conducted in the 1970s a highly acclaimed study of work-related values across 40 countries in the subsidiaries of a sample of American multinationals (thus seeking to neutralise the impact of corporate culture on the results). Hofstede found that France scored particularly highly on risk aversion or 'uncertainty avoidance': the extent to which members of a society or company tolerate uncertainty in daily life. In this France achieved an index score of 86 (out of 100), far in advance of the UK with 35, and significantly higher than the average score of 64.[49]

Hofstede's basic premise is that the cultural values prevailing in a given society have important consequences for companies, and that these in turn impact on national economic activity and hence performance and competitiveness. Clearly, one of the fundamental problems of Hofstede's analysis is that the four socio-cultural variables used to elicit comparison were selected arbitrarily *a priori* and used as a preordained framework for the study. National cultures, however, are complex contextual structures, deriving from their own particular set of circumstances. A national culture is a self-referential system with its own integrity, as Lewis, Fitzgerald and Harvey point out: 'distinct values and attitudes do not exist in isolation, but rather in a well-defined relationship with other values and attitudes'.[50] Systemic rather than comparative analysis is therefore perhaps more appropriate to examining its unique composition. But to say that a culture can only be understood fully in its own terms is not to preclude attempts to decode or decipher it with reference to another, nor to deny the worthwhile nature of the exercise. The non-native 'foreign' observer inevitably carries his or her own cultural baggage, viewing French culture through the potentially distorting prism of another culture; at the same time, being at one remove affords a critical distance which may, in turn, yield privileged insights. This was certainly the view of the poet Robert Burns, for whom 'to see ourselves as others see us' was to enjoy a potentially enhanced understanding, not an impoverished one. Whether or not elements of French business culture have changed over time is a question that will be addressed in subsequent chapters.

The changing role of the state

The changing role of the state has been one of the defining features of the period under scrutiny, in particular the changing physiology of government intervention in the economy. Numerous writers have explored various aspects of the role of the state in France, and how and why this may have changed over time. Especially worthy of mention are Richard Kuisel, Peter Hall, Jack Hayward and John Zysman. All throw into sharp relief the political influences that permeate French economic policy. Economic policy is determined by governments, and governments are first and foremost political creatures. Hall argues that the political dimensions of economic management are paramount if we are to understand why nations pursue certain economic policies, and why these may undergo change.[51] Hall's *Governing the Economy* is informed by the notion of 'political culture', defined by Verba as 'the system of empirical beliefs, expressive symbols, and values which defines the situation in which political action takes place'.[52] This is highlighted as the determinative variable which explains why nations select different policy paths to confront similar economic problems, and why these may lead to different political outcomes. Critically, Hall argues, political culture is not set in tablets of stone and therefore the political dimensions of economic management may be amenable to change.[53] Hayward writes that the French may be more open to such change because they 'had acquired a style of authority that includes a capacity for crisis utilization for the purpose of imposing overdue changes'.[54] Zysman underlines the vital role played by the financial system (especially the Trésor) in determining the policy outcomes of the political conflicts which accompanied the implementation of industrial adjustment.[55] For Kuisel, France had moved from a traditional liberal political economy prior to 1914 to a managed dynamic order by 1950 because the prospect of relative economic decline was an unacceptable one for the French at the end of the Second World War. The nature of French liberalism, combining as it did competitive reserve with a long tradition of protectionism and authoritative centralisation by the state, meant that the transition to a more directive form of economic management was more straightforward for the French than for others.[56]

When the opulent era of the 'thirty glorious years' of sustained economic growth drew to a close, triggered by the oil-price hikes of the 1970s, the economic outlook for France suddenly looked much bleaker than before. In *The State and the Market Economy*, Hayward assesses how France, formerly acclaimed for its achievement of transcending under state guidance a long period of modest economic growth, and having embarked successfully on a process of modernisation and exposure to foreign competition, now functioned in an environment less responsive to 'the mobilization of industrial patriotism'.[57] By the mid-1980s public opinion had come to mistrust state intervention, whose wasteful failures and expensive successes were now firmly under attack, clearing the way for a rediscovery of liberalism as a panacea for economic inefficiency and stagnation.[58] The Mitterrand era was one of fundamental change in state–society relations, above all in the policies pursued by the French government towards business. In *From State to Market?*, Schmidt traces their development, from nationalisation in 1982, to privatisation from 1986, sweeping deregulation, and ever-increasing European integration, as the state-directed, *dirigiste* economy sought to become more market-oriented.[59] Modernisation required that the State exercise its role with greater efficiency than hitherto. As Hayward says, the guardians of the state required 'moins d'état' in order to achieve 'mieux d'état' – and, more importantly, 'mieux d'Europe': '[Despite] attempts to conceal the retreat and give it a semblance of order, the two periods of cohabitation in the Mitterrand presidency sealed the surrender of the attempt to use the state as the spearhead of French socio-economic policy that had already been conceded when the Socialists held power'.[60] By the end of the Mitterrand years, the state had lost much – but by no means all – of its legitimacy as the organiser of change.[61] It is hypothesised here that a transfer of some of the legitimacy that had formerly accrued to the state in favour of enterprise occurred in the early 1980s. The failed reflation of the economy and nationalisation of large swathes of French industry led to an economic U-turn and ultimately to the creation of a 'new right' by the French left, effecting the greatest shift in the political balance in France since 1958. This was marked in particular by a change in attitudes towards business enterprise and the pursuit of profit, now invested with a newfound legitimacy.

The French business model in transition

It may be argued, however, that it was the 1990s rather than the 1980s that marked the real watershed for French business. The decade witnessed numerous far-reaching changes in the business environment that could not be ignored by business leaders. The advent of the Single Market, the European Union and the euro each threatened heightened competition at home and in export markets. Likewise, the conclusion of the 1986–94 GATT round led to the erosion or removal of barriers to competition in new fields, especially within agriculture and the service sector, and the creation in 1995 of the WTO as supranational enforcer of the rules governing international trade. The general thrust of these developments has been towards creating a level competitive playing field, with national governments relegated to the sidelines, discouraged from granting subsidies or other forms of financial assistance to domestic firms. From a strategic standpoint, the message to firms has been that they must develop their internal organisational capabilities in order to remain competitive. To this end, large enterprises have sought to become stronger, more competitive, partly through internal investment in systems, technologies and research and development and partly through external investment in other companies, often resulting in mergers, often across national boundaries.

Pressures such as these are not unique to France. But they have come as a major shock to the system, given the long-standing ties binding the state and business. French firms, many until quite recently state-owned, have responded to the challenge to become world-class in terms of quality and productivity, by opening themselves up to foreign investors. In recent times, there has been a spectacular change in the ownership of French companies, distinguished by state withdrawal and the arrival of foreign institutional investors on an unprecedented scale, now collectively owning more than 40 per cent of the share capital of the top 40 French firms. These companies are tied up in a global process recently dubbed by Williams as 'financialisation' because the firm itself is no longer seen as historically rooted and context-dependent but rather as an entity driven purely by measures of financial performance.[62] According to this view, the owners of firms are motivated in the main by the pursuit of shareholder value (maximum financial returns) and directors and senior managers are rewarded, hired and fired on this basis. Effective corporate governance regimes are seen to be those that enable the owners of firms to control managers and measure their performance. The rise of the corporate governance movement in France in the 1990s should be seen against this background, constituting in effect an ideological assault on the model of French capitalism forged in the aftermath of the Second World War.

How deeply grounded are these changes? How much of this is likely to be enduring, to represent a genuine sea-change, and how much is merely superficial and cosmetic? History reminds us, as Charkham points out, that France is 'always on the verge of change', and 'only the provisional is permanent'.[63] That said, events on the European corporate scene are unfolding fast. The growing internationalisation of European business, particularly of French business, exemplified by the much-expanded role for foreign investors, and the new wave of merger and acquisition activity fuelled by the arrival of the euro, may well lead to some cross-fertilisation from one business model to another. Are the changes that are taking place in the French business model really in the direction of Americanisation and globalisation, as foreign institutional investors bring with them the logic of the financial market economy, accompanied by new techniques and demands on management?[64] Or are they on the contrary towards hybridisation?

Cassis finds that convergence is the overriding feature of the evolution of big business in Europe in the course of the twentieth century. Convergence has occurred in many areas of business – 'in the number and sectoral distribution of large companies; in the educational levels of business leaders and the professionalization of business careers; in the social integration of business elites and the form and content of their political intervention'.[65] This has led some experts to broach the idea that big business in Europe is moving towards a European model,[66] a networked-based stakeholder model, whose 'social interest' is key, where financial holding companies (as in France) or banks (as in Germany) play a prominent role in company decision-making and restructuring, which take a longer-term view than that which is commonly assumed in market-oriented systems, and which are innately resistant to hostile takeovers as the means to replace inefficient management by better management teams. The European Commission has long favoured the introduction of a European Company Statute, proposing in particular that the boards of quoted European companies adhere to a two-tier business model such as that currently in use in Germany. The draft fifth directive for a European Company Statute first appeared in 1970 and has been on the table since 1991. It has foundered thus far on the requirement for worker participation, fiercely resisted by the UK and a number of other member states.[67] Arguably, the increasingly multinational emphasis of French business may well take some large companies further down the road towards a European model, whatever is agreed in Brussels, thus continuing a natural process of convergence in European business.

Cassis also finds, however, that convergence has not led to uniformity. Even cross-border mergers, which might be seen as driving towards convergence by giving birth to European as opposed to British or French large companies, 'might also be organized on the basis of national specializations and reinforce them in the process'.[68] Britain and France retain distinctive characteristics legated by their individual historical experiences, ranging from distinct legal and institutional frameworks to the dominance of specific business elites; it would be unwise to underestimate their enduring influence. Despite general isomorphic tendencies common in Western societies,[69] the national 'embeddedness' of transnational companies[70] works against the 'transplantability' of organisational forms developed in one country to another with the same degree of effectiveness,[71] perhaps because national business systems are path-determined, not goal-determined.[72] This leaves open the possibility of culturally specific variations, as the French business model is adapted to suit international structures. This seems a likely outcome. As Djelic writes, 'Cross-national processes of transfer or diffusion cannot be uncoupled from a parallel process of diffraction, partial reinterpretation, or "translation" of the original model to be transferred.'[73]

Conclusion

The years since the end of the Second World War in 1945 have in general been good ones for the French economy and the French people. For much of the period, the economy and consequently living standards grew more rapidly than ever before. Economic performance was well above the world average and exceeded that for other leading industrial nations. This success, particularly marked during the thirty glorious years immediately following the war, has been identified as a triumph for the French national business system. Under this system, the state played an important role directly and indirectly in business affairs. It formed a compact with French business based upon mutually supportive relationships aimed at generating wealth and developing industrial capabilities. The existence of a coherent national elite, legitimised through educational attainment, was vitally important to economic development because of the beneficial consequences for coordination, mutual understanding and strategic thinking.

This is not to say that the relationship between the state and business has been an easy one, untroubled by disagreement. The high employment-related costs imposed on industry have been a source of conflict, and so too periodic waves of nationalisation have met with understandable resistance. Yet, overall, a consensus has prevailed with respect to a number of fundamentals. Most importantly, agreement has existed over the goals of business enterprise, the need to invest for the long term and the sharing of risks between the private and public sectors. The state has therefore sanctioned and at times promoted institutional arrangements to maintain stability, reduce uncertainty and protect French firms from takeover while at the same time encouraging expansion abroad. This form of defensive–offensive behaviour is likewise characteristic of the French approach to rule-setting and enforcement within the EU and other supranational economic organisations.

The roots of state involvement in French business are long, and over time the *modus operandi* of the state has changed dramatically, and so too have many of the attitudes, beliefs and practices of French business. It is one of the ironies of intellectual history that David Landes should have published his critique of French business enterprise at the very time when the French economy had just been launched on the path to super-growth. The 'dependency' of business on the state that Landes condemned turned out in the postwar era, with different internal and external drivers of change, to be part of a unifying, strategic and growth-oriented partnership for economic modernisation. This is not to say that Landes was wrong in all aspects of his interpretation, but it does illustrate the frailty of any mono-causal interpretation of the causes of national economic growth. In the postwar era, the advantage lay with the centralising state and with modernising members of the ruling elites in business, administration and politics that were able to harness national resources in pursuit of business expansion and economic growth. The goal of national economic sovereignty, of self-determination in pursuit of the general interest, so prized by de Gaulle, may ultimately have proved chimerical, but for a while it was a valuable source of cohesion, inspiration and vision.

One of the great enemies of national self-determination in economic affairs is, of course, globalisation. In France, the dramatic reversal induced by the oil price shocks of the 1970s might have served as an early warning sign that it was time to rethink the fundamentals of the national business system. But this did not happen, and when the socialists came to power in 1981 their faith lay initially in retreating into what had worked in the past rather than facing up squarely to the insistence of global forces. Only when the markets punished false logic did nationalisation give way to privatisation and the progressive renegotiation of the concordat between French business and the state. Under the prevailing consensus, what matters most is to develop the capabilities of French and Franco-European firms – knowledge, technologies and systems – in order that they might compete successfully on the world stage. There are very serious implications. A significant part of the equity of many nominally French firms is owned outside France, in the United States, in Japan and elsewhere in the EU. Such internationally mobile shareholders have little truck with traditional French values and aspirations. They worship at the Universal Church of Shareholder Value where the God of Money is supreme. An ideological battle is taking place under the banner of corporate governance reform and the outcome as yet is uncertain.

2
Liberation, Modernisation and the Fourth Republic

I regarded the state [...] as [...] an institution of decision, action and ambition, expressing and serving the national interest alone.

Charles de Gaulle[1]

The French economy at Liberation

At the end of September 1944, six weeks after the Allied landings in the North, at Avranches, and in the South, where Toulon and Marseilles proved the hardest nuts to crack,[2] France was almost entirely freed of the German invader. The German Army was expelled with extraordinary rapidity, in less time than it had taken to occupy the country four years previously. Although the war dragged on until May 1945, for many French people the Liberation signified the end of the war.

After four years of Occupation, war, devastation and pillage, the state of the French economy was dire indeed. This chapter explores the economic legacy of war and Occupation, surveying the *degré zéro* of the economy in post-Liberation days and during the Fourth Republic, an essential prerequisite to an appreciation both of the war as a watershed and of the measure of subsequent economic success. It is argued that, despite the almost exclusively negative political commentary that has been written on the Fourth Republic, economically there were important strengths. In particular the groundwork was laid – through the nationalisation of energy, transport and the main banks, the introduction of planning and the reorganisation of welfare provision – to furnish the state with the necessary tools to assume a key strategic role in economic management under the Fifth Republic. The impact of these programmes continues to be felt in the twenty-first century. Interlaced with the analysis is an exploration of the major intellectual currents of the day, ideas such as *dirigisme*, the notion that the state should assume a key role in the organisation of economic activity in the interests of the greatness of France, championed by de Gaulle. Despite the fundamental

long-standing conservative liberalism of French society, this rose to prominence in the post-Liberation era. Though not a new idea, it coalesced in
1945 with calls for *rattrapage* and the modernisation of the economy,
together with the obvious need for state-directed reconstruction, becoming
in time part of the dominant ideology.

Amid the chaos that followed the Liberation, it is inevitable that precise
statistics, facilitating prewar and international comparisons, are lacking. This
dearth of statistics is exacerbated by a tendency to secrecy that traditionally
has characterised French business (and which continues to this day), the
withholding of information having been commonplace among French businessmen, with owners concealing business details even from family members. During the war this intensified. A modern industrialised economy, such
as the Germans needed to achieve their military objectives, required the systematic gathering of statistical data. Under Vichy, the patriotism of many
businessmen found expression in the lies they told the occupier. Since the
enemy could use the information provided, it made sense to distort the picture given to their agents, the French businessmen who became presidents of
the Comités d'Organisation (CO), created in August 1940 to ensure that
industrial production would continue. In the summer of 1940, following the
armistice of June, the economy was in confusion, unemployment was high
and rising, factories were shut and machines lay idle.

The German authorities swiftly launched a campaign to encourage
employers to return to their posts and resume production, leading to the
passage of a law in August 1940 on the organisation of industrial production. The CO were entrusted with functions essential to the German war
machine, including inventories of plant, raw materials and manpower; the
establishment of manufacturing programmes; systems for the purchase and
distribution of raw materials; the development of standards of production,
quality and competition; price fixing, and so on.[3] The CO presidents effectively became civil servants, since the law accorded all those employed in
the administration of vital raw materials, so crucial to the German war
effort, the status of public officials. As Ehrmann notes, the presidents of the
committees – almost always leading businessmen who had been prominent
in the trade associations with which the CO became fused – enjoyed extensive powers with respect to all aspects of industrial production. Through
industrial self-government they asserted themselves as the country's elite,
in the process perhaps becoming identified unavoidably with the government which had entrusted them with running the economy – albeit under
the jackboots of the occupier. It is a severe indictment of the employers'
movement during the war that no part of it ever took up a position that
might be seen as hostile to Vichy.[4] As Vinen observes, having a record of
service in the Resistance became a valuable currency after the war in business and the civil service, precisely because such records were so rare.[5]
Henri Weber deems only a few individuals as worthy of mention: the

bankers Blocq-Mascart, Aimé Lepercq, and industrialists Pierre Lefaucheux, Joseph Laniel and René Mayer.[6] The lack of reliable data and estimates relating to the devastation suffered during the Occupation and Liberation means that first-hand testimony regarding the state of the French economy in 1945 is especially valuable. The work of Dorothy Pickles, for example, published in 1946 and written at the time of the events described, provides an evocative account based upon first-hand interviews with protagonists.[7] The testimony of de Gaulle himself, as head of the provisional French government in the months immediately following the Liberation until September 1944 and subsequently as head of the 'government of national unity' until January 1946, benefits from access to such economic data as were available. Later, from 1946 to 1958, during his years of self-imposed 'exile' from political life at his home in the village of Colombey-les-deux-Eglises in Champagne, he had the time to reflect and write about the situation.[8] These poignant testimonies offer a privileged insight into the state of the French economy in the early days after the Liberation, thereby enhancing our appreciation of the extent of French economic development in the ensuing 'thirty glorious years' and beyond.

In *Le Salut*, the third volume of de Gaulle's trilogy of war memoirs, he describes his tour of the country in autumn 1944. France was now struggling to play a full part in the war, with de Gaulle intent on restoring France's former standing and prestige in the world. Yet he was battling against the stigma of the country's former conquered-nation status, as well as understandable Allied perceptions of its inherent weakness following the disappointing capitulation in June 1940 without taking arms, to the country's enduring shame. Communications and transport were clearly paramount, but the provinces were almost entirely cut off from the poverty-stricken capital. Telephone and telegraph lines were broken at innumerable points, radio stations destroyed, and liaison planes unable to land on shell-covered fields. An average of 100 civilians were killed or maimed each month by exploding mines which littered farmland, with an estimated 1,000,000 hectares (2,500,000 acres) of land unusable; it was reckoned that a thousand million man-hours would be required to rid French soil of mines.[9] The railways were paralysed: of 12,000 locomotives at the start of hostilities, only 2,800 remained. Nor could any train reach the key provincial cities of Marseilles, Toulouse, Bordeaux, Lyon, Nancy or Lille. As many as 3,000 rail bridges had been blown up, and over 3,000 kilometres of rail-track destroyed. Of three million prewar vehicles, only 300,000 remained roadworthy. Petrol was in very short supply, making car journeys hazardous. De Gaulle lamented the frequent stoppages of the French army due to lack of fuel as it advanced eastwards into Germany, exacerbated by the fact that the first claim on petrol supplies went to American and British forces. Much-needed supplies of food, raw materials and manufactured goods could not be imported, despite support from

Washington, because France's main ports were unusable. Many had been badly damaged during the Allied landings (including Calais, Boulogne, Dieppe, Rouen, Le Havre, Cherbourg, Nantes, Marseilles and Toulon), whether by Allied bombs or German retribution, 'offer[ing] nothing but ruined docks, flooded harbours, jammed floodgates and waterways choked with wrecks'.[10] Others were still under German garrison: Dunkirk, Brest, Lorient, St-Nazaire and La Rochelle. Of these, Dunkirk, St-Nazaire and La Rochelle had to wait until the German capitulation of May 1945 to be liberated. Pickles cites a description of French ports, laid to waste, by a war correspondent of the day:

> Everywhere, conditions are lamentable and heartrending. The same desolation everywhere, the same mutilation, the same systematic destruction: lock-gates blown to bits, sea-walls disembowelled, jetties demolished, sunken craft blocking the fairways, dismantled cranes raising their twisted arms above mine-wrecked wharves, sheds in ruins, railway tracks torn up, the rails themselves like serpents writhing in agony, warehouses lying open to the wind and rain, vessels lying on their sides tugging at useless moorings and groaning like mortally wounded beasts ....[11]

In 1938, French imports amounted to 35 million tons.[12] Five years later French ports could not have coped with one-third of that amount. Of goods imported during the first year after the Liberation, less than one million tons was destined for ordinary citizens. Vast stocks of raw materials had been removed during the Occupation. Stocks in many cases were virtually non-existent, although not always; what was so tragic, in Pickles' view, was that 'there was always *something* lacking':

> Most of the iron and steel, chemical, rubber and textile factories could have resumed production *if* – if they had had the necessary stocks, or coal, or if they had had the necessary transport to bring raw materials and coal to the factories, if the ships had been available to import rubber, textiles, paper pulp and leather, and if they had had enough skilled labour. As it was, the early months of the liberation saw mounting unemployment, more and more men and women standing idle with work crying out to be done.[13]

Recovery depended also on the health of workers. Observing the pale, sunken-cheeked, emaciated faces of workers in Lille at the end of September 1944, de Gaulle noted that under the Occupation they had been compelled to accept wages fixed at subsistence level. In 1944, official food rations amounted to just 1,200 calories per person per day, stimulating a buoyant black market. Livestock had been reduced to half its prewar numbers, and tools, fertilisers, seeds and plants were lacking, partly due to systematic theft and pillage by the occupiers. The lack of wool, cotton and leather meant that many civilians wore threadbare clothes and wooden clogs. The small amount of coal being mined was reserved for hospitals, basic industries, power plants, railways and the army; none was available to heat homes, schools or offices in the first winter of the Liberation, one of the harshest on record. Electricity supplies were intermittent (in turn affecting the resumption of work in the factories) and gas pressure low. De Gaulle estimated that up to one-quarter of the population had been uprooted. Homelessness was rife, with displaced people living in ruins or shanties – an estimated half a million in Normandy alone, amounting to one-fifth of the population of the region's five *départements*. Traditionally one of the richest parts of France, blessed with apple orchards, its dairy herds fed on lush green pastures yielding copious supplies of butter, cream and cheese, Normandy in 1944 was badly damaged. In some places the Germans had carried out the systematic, planned destruction of homes and buildings. Pickles reported that of 532 *communes* in the Vosges department, one-fifth had been laid to waste and 25 obliterated.[14] An official report published in July 1945 estimated that 1,750,000 buildings had been damaged or destroyed nationwide.[15] De Gaulle put the figure higher at two million, with 500,000 completely destroyed and 1,500,000 seriously damaged.[16] An estimated 91,000[17] factories were inoperative, while an estimated 40,000 farms required rebuilding.[18] Reconstruction, moreover, was hampered by a shortage of manpower. In 1944 as many as two-and-a-half million Frenchmen remained in Germany as prisoners of war, deportees or forced labourers. A further 700,000 had been drafted into the armed forces. At the same time, there are reports of harvests rotting in the fields while men sat idly by in cafés: 'English and American troops commented on the lack of local initiative and solidarity and compared France unfavourably with their own countries and even with Germany.'[19] Altogether, France suffered approximately 635,000 human casualties in the war: a quarter of a million in combat, 160,000 the victims of bombings or executions by the occupiers, 150,000 in concentration camps, and 75,000 as forced labourers or prisoners of war, while a further 585,000 became invalids.[20] French losses exceeded the casualties endured by Britain and the Commonwealth, just over half a million killed in total, and the United States, which lost 300,000. They are dwarfed however by the terrible casualties endured by countries such as the USSR, a staggering 21.3 million dead, Poland, 5.5 million, or Germany itself, 7.1 million, not to mention China (13.5 million), in fighting little reported in the West, or Japan (2.1 million).

It was clearly incumbent upon the provisional government to restore the country to work and to raise living standards as quickly as possible. Wages were increased by 40 per cent in September 1944. A 50 per cent rise in family allowances was enacted a month later. These measures did not go as far as to restore incomes to 1938 levels in real terms, however, given price increases during the war.[21] In the course of 1945–46 the social security system was revamped and extended,[22] inspired by the wartime Resistance movement and Britain's ambitious Beveridge Plan (1942), which was to form the basis of the British social security system. An ordinance of 4 October 1945 sought to cover all citizens for all risks, regardless of employment status, and secondly, to provide uniform benefits, irrespective of income – although its actual achievements fell short of these goals. In particular, it failed to create a universal system, as in Britain, and gave rise instead to a number of disparate agencies responsible for distinct aspects of social security, further accentuated in 1967.

To finance these measures, sustain the war effort and restore communications and essential energy supplies, without which recovery was impossible, a major public loan was urgently required. State coffers were empty after years of German levies on public funds, estimated by de Gaulle at FF520 billion. The so-called 'Liberation Loan' of November 1944, devised by Finance Minister Lepercq, was one of numerous government borrowings during the years of reconstruction. It yielded FF165 billion (FF127 billion in cash and the remainder in treasury bonds), more than had ever been raised by any previous public issue. The funds it provided were all the more necessary given the inadequacy of tax receipts: in September 1944 economic activity stood at approximately 40 per cent of its 1938 level. The loan also helped to control inflation, which proved to be an enduring postwar problem, as banknote circulation (FF630 billion) rose to three times its prewar level.

The business community and symbolic retribution

The legacy of war was social as well as economic. It was loudly demanded that businessmen who had collaborated with the occupier, or who had earned illicit profits during the Occupation, or who through their actions had caused the deaths or endangered the lives of their compatriots be brought to justice. The same people simply could not be allowed to remain, and be seen to remain in positions of power or in charge of business life. Bringing them to justice was also perceived as a means of restoring order and much-needed stability by stopping the anarchy of spontaneous lynching as old scores were settled.

The wartime collaboration of the French business elite in general, and certain members of the business elite in particular, is well known, and has entered the realm of popular mythology. It is fair to say that businessmen in France have suffered traditionally from a poor image, despite the fact that by the end of the nineteenth century top industrialists such as Scheider and de Wendel were integrated into the uppermost rank of Parisian society.[23] Often more concerned with pride and status than balance sheets, the old industrial dynasties tended to treat their firms as an aristocrat might his lands.[24] In 1936, at the time of the Popular Front and the nationalisation of the Bank of France, the elite oligarchy of '200 families' was reviled and charged with exploiting the working classes. Further, as some commentators observe, in a country renowned for its literature, the portrayals of businessmen and financiers in novels such as Balzac's *Le Père Goriot*, or Zola's *L'Argent*, are entirely unsympathetic. They are depicted as swindlers and bloodsuckers or, at best, as in Zola's *Germinal*, as ignorant, misguided rentiers that know not what they do.[25] Perhaps because of this unflattering image, businessmen have tended to define themselves not as *hommes d'affaires* but rather as administrators, as the title of François Bloch-Lainé's book makes explicit: *Profession: fonctionnaire.*[26]

The conduct of French businessmen during the years of Occupation reinforced this negative image. Public perception of their wartime activities is encapsulated in de Gaulle's chiding remark on 4 October 1944 to business leaders, who had come to protest against the flood of accusations being directed at them: 'Where were you, sirs?', to which he allegedly added that he had seen none of them in London.[27] The remark may be apocryphal, as claimed by Jean-Noël Jeanneney, as there is no record of it in the minutes of the meeting. Authentic or not, it nevertheless conveys the virulence of national feeling against employers, who had been seen to profit from the country's misfortunes, in the wake of the Liberation.

The *leitmotif* of employers' conduct during the Occupation seems to have been an attitude of 'business as usual', of keeping the factory wheels turning, of accommodating the particular circumstances in which they found themselves. Weber claims that cohorts of employers became fully integrated into the Vichy administrative machine, many of whom collaborated to the fullest extent. Ehrmann writes that in 1940 French business, whether modern or traditional, unanimously supported the armistice regime of June 1940 that had charged them with running the French economy. It is by no means clear, however, whether or not French employers were more Pétainist than the general population. Ehrmann and Weber agree that they seem to have followed closely the general trend of public opinion: 'a shrewd observer remarked afterwards that a Gallup poll in wartime France would have shown 95 percent of the population "Pétainist" after the armistice, 50 percent until the Allied landings in North France and still 30 percent on D-Day'.[28] The ambivalent relationship of the French to Vichy and the Occupation, and their difficulties in coming to terms with the often large overlap between collaboration and resistance inhabited by many French people at the time – 'between the heroes and the traitors there were [...] the mass of people [...] thrown off their balance by the policy pursued by the traitors'[29] – is captured in the classic film *Le Chagrin et la pitié*. Tellingly, however, the steel magnate François de Wendel records his amazement at the speed with which following the armistice in June 1940 it became fashionable among top industrialists to be Anglophobic, and to avoid Jews with whom they had once socialised.[30] In Kolboom's opinion, the French business elite viewed the birth of Vichy as a stroke of luck: 'it cannot be denied [...] that the events of 1939/1940 brought about a situation in social affairs and politics that matched the wishes of the majority of the political and social elites at the time, especially the employers'.[31] This would seem to have been the case in 1940. But thereafter the balance began to shift, slowly but perceptibly, especially after the entry of the US into the war on the Allied side, triggered by the Japanese bombing of Pearl Harbor on 7 December 1941, as the French population began to question the permanence of the German victory.

Spectacular expropriations of firms were carried out against those employers who had been seen to profit from the nation's darkest moments. The alleged collaborationist activities of Louis Renault led to the takeover of his automobile company by the state. What is less well known is that Renault's 'showcase trial' never took place: he died in prison awaiting trial, and was therefore not convicted. The car manufacturer Marius Berliet suffered the same fate of expropriation. At his trial in September 1945, Berliet claimed in his defence that his company had produced fewer cars for the German occupiers than any other French car producer: 2,239 cars for Germans as against 6,548 for French clients. This he compared to Renault, which had delivered 32,887 vehicles to Germans and only 1,697 to French customers, a pattern also followed by Citroën (32,248 vehicles produced for Germans and 2,052 for French clients).[32] Meanwhile, managers at Renault insisted, for their part, that they had deliberately slowed down production, producing 7,677 fewer vehicles than the target of 41,909 set by the Germans. This argument, however, cut no ice with the Communist-backed workers union, the Confédération Générale du Travail (CGT), which alleged the go-slow had been masterminded by workers, not by managers.

Louis Renault may have been punished more for his attitude than for his actions, which resembled those of other employers, the majority of whom were treated less severely. Aron reports that, when visited by a Gaullist seeking his support for the Free French, Renault is alleged to have replied: 'De Gaulle, don't know him!'[33] Ultimately, Renault's punishment was undeniably symbolic, serving as a warning to other members of the business elite of the fate that might befall them should they fall from grace. As such it fulfilled an important function: a symbolic reaffirmation of the collective sentiments and ideas which make up the unity and personality of French society, such as are periodically enacted throughout French history since the 1789 Revolution. French society is extraordinarily tolerant of power distance and, indeed, of abuses of power, as its remarkable equanimity in the face of the widespread corruption and financial misdemeanours of its ruling political elite amply demonstrates. But from time to time, in a symbolic catharsis and confirmation of national identity and values (as exemplified by the 1848 Revolution, the seizure of power by Louis Bonaparte in 1851, and the 1871 Commune), heads must roll.[34] This exemplary punishment of a member of the elite, it could be argued, works to support the stability and cohesion of the group as a whole, 'cleansed' and thereby absolved by the act of retribution, however collaborationist or similar the experiences of individual members. How ruling elites treat those who fall from grace arguably provides a useful key to the ways in which they achieve self-preservation in a changing world.

In 1944–45, several thousand employers were temporarily removed from the management of their firms, the running of which was assumed for the duration by workers or vigilantes. Most were never brought to trial, and most recovered their businesses within a few short weeks; but the experience of near-expropriation was bitterly resented by the business class as a whole.[35] It might be argued that businessmen served as convenient scapegoats in a country where a large proportion of the population had engaged in collaboration of one form or another, however passively or actively. Yet the prosperity of a small group contrasted with the nation's general penury and made them easy targets. In 1944 the property-owning classes certainly seemed to be at risk from the growing power of the Communist Party,[36] whose legitimacy derived from its contribution to the Resistance. Research conducted by Ehrmann into the activities of employers' associations in France was sufficiently close to events to benefit from numerous first-hand accounts by managers directly involved in wartime business activity. At the same time, the passage of time enabled him to ascertain the extraordinary stability of the French business elite, even following their universal condemnation for alleged unpatriotic conduct. Notably, Ehrmann confirms at first hand that the post-war boards of directors of large French corporations consisted invariably of *the same men* – the vast majority were *still there* – and almost always of the same social groups, as before the war. This was despite the publicly proclaimed goal of unseating the upper bourgeoisie and permanently eliminating it from positions of economic and administrative power, promoted by a Resistance bent on targeting what it termed an 'oligarchy of big business leaders'.[37] As argued above, the spectacular punishment of an unfortunate few made it possible for the vast majority to stay in post, while bolstering establishment solidarity. Such threats against the business community had dissipated largely by the early 1950s, following the ousting of the Communist Party from government in 1947. The extraordinary stability of the French business elite over time, and often in the face of adversity and scandal, emerges as a fundamental characteristic of the French business model to which we shall return in subsequent chapters.

In his memoirs, de Gaulle documents the punishments meted out to alleged collaborators, of all classes. A total of 2,071 death sentences were pronounced by the courts, some being passed *in absentia*, of which 1,303 were pardoned, including all women and almost all minors, and 768 executed – a modest number in de Gaulle's view. A total of 39,900 prison sentences were pronounced, as compared to 55,000 sentences in Belgium and 50,000 in the Netherlands.[38] The confiscation of business profits deemed illegal by decree in October 1944 was systematically pursued. Thereafter, top businessmen remained conspicuously absent from the entourage of de Gaulle – although not, however, from positions of power: Antoine Pinay, a businessman and former supporter of Pétain, went on to become prime minister in 1952.

Nationalisation and economic renewal

De Gaulle's primary goal was to renew the economy 'so that it served the collectivity before furnishing profits to private interests'. At the same time he sought to improve the living and working conditions of what he rather condescendingly referred to as the 'labouring classes'.[39] The Resistance was inextricably bound up with deeply felt aspirations for social reform. In the event, however, de Gaulle restrained post-Liberation plans for immediate and far-reaching nationalisation, arguing that only a properly elected government could take such steps. To this end a Consultative Assembly was swiftly established. The National Council of Resistance in its 'Charter of Resistance' of March 1944 had called for 'the return to the nation of the major, monopolized means of production'. All the main political parties – the Communists, Radicals, and the Socialists – shared this objective with de Gaulle,[40] who at Algiers on 18 March 1944 had presented nationalisation as fundamental 'to the improvement of national resources'.[41] In 1945 and 1946 the Assembly voted overwhelmingly in favour of the nationalisation of the banks, electricity and gas, insurance and coal industries. As Kuisel notes, however, the motivation for nationalisation was not primarily ideological. Reasons of economic recovery, renewal and management certainly dominated; but nationalisation was also informed by a vengeful spirit of democratic, patriotic retribution against the monied oligarchy who, according to public perceptions, had 'thwarted the people's will at critical moments and corrupted the Third Republic'.[42]

The nationalisation wave of 1945–46 was the second in French history. The first was at the time of the Popular Front in 1936 when the state had begun the quest to control directly the commanding heights of the economy. At this stage the Bank of France was reorganised and the arms and aeronautical industries were nationalised along with the rail transport network, giving rise to the Société Nationale des Chemins de Fer (SNCF). The nationalisations of 1945 may be classified under three headings. First, companies nationalised for strategic investment reasons, including the coal, electricity and gas industries.[43] The creation in December 1944 of Houillères nationales du Nord et du Pas-de-Calais facilitated postwar coal production, while Electricité de France (EdF) and Gaz de France (GdF) came into being in April 1946 with the amalgamation and nationalisation of utility companies. The costly modernisation of such basic industries greatly exceeded both the means and the will of those private-sector firms holding concessions. Guaranteed nationwide energy supplies were quintessential to economic recovery and prosperity, clearly going beyond the natural responsibilities of individual, often local companies. In de Gaulle's words:

> The country's activity depended on coal, electricity, gas and petroleum, and would eventually depend on atomic fission and in order to bring France's economy to the level that progress demanded these resources must be developed on the largest possible scale. Expenditure and efforts were necessary, therefore, which only the state was in a position to realize and nationalization was a necessity.[44]

The second set of companies brought into public ownership was seen as pivotal to the effective functioning of a modern economy. Included under this heading were the Bank of France and the country's four main deposit banks, the Crédit Lyonnais, Société Générale, Comptoir national d'escompte de Paris and the Banque nationale pour le commerce et l'industrie, transferred to state ownership in December 1945.[45] Also in this category were 34 insurance companies and the Bank of Algiers, nationalised in April 1946. Finally, there was the nationalisation of the Régie Nationale des Usines Renault in retribution for alleged collaboration. The remainder of manufacturing industry remained virtually untouched.

At the same time, the public sector was extended by other means, such as the creation in 1945 of the Commissariat à l'Energie Atomique, the Bureau de Recherche du Pétrole, and the Paris Airport at Orly. However, plans to nationalise airlines that had benefited from state subsidies before the war were abandoned in 1948. Instead, Air France was created on the basis of a public–private partnership in which the state held a majority share. This served as a model for other partnerships in shipping and maritime transport. Additional impetus for change was provided with the setting up in 1945 of the High Commission on Plans for Equipment and Modernisation (see Chapter 3), its primary task to encourage the new economy to invest for the future.[46]

Nationalisation was just part of the solution to the postwar economic crisis proposed by de Gaulle and his advisers. It was apparent in France, as in the UK, that industry in the United States was far more technologically advanced and better managed than that in Europe. The productivity gap that had existed in 1939 had widened considerably during the years of conflict. Economic modernisation now demanded professional management. This perception led in December 1945 to the inauguration of the Ecole Nationale de l'Administration (ENA), the brainchild of Michel Debré, adviser to de Gaulle. The new school was conceived as providing future members of the administrative elite, rigorously selected and highly educated, that would direct and manage the apparatus of an expansive, modernising and transformatory state. Together with Polytechnique, ENA has educated large numbers of top executives of leading French companies over the past fifty years. Its continuing relevance is amply demonstrated by the fact that in 1998 two-thirds of the chairmen of the top 40 firms came from ENA and Polytechnique, despite the recent popularity of other, less elitist business schools.[47] This shared educational background has reinforced the cohesion of the French business elite. It has increased elite solidarity across the ruling class and has fostered common ideological positions and mindsets, a 'pensée unique', which in turn encourages business leaders to pull together in the same direction. This has been beneficial both to French business and the economy in general.

Despite standing unquestionably on the right of the political spectrum, it is important to stress that de Gaulle did not adhere to conventional *laissez-faire* economics. Indeed, some of the policies he supported are more generally associated with the left than with the right: that, above all, of nationalisation, in which he perceived 'a means of resurrecting France'.[48] De Gaulle's support for nationalisation was entirely in tune with his adherence to *dirigisme*, the intervention of the state in the economy, directed and conducted[49] in the interests of the greatness of France to the collective benefit of the French people as a whole. As de Gaulle acknowledged, this would depend in the future far more on economic and technological achievement than on military prowess:

> Today [in 1945], as ever, it was incumbent upon the state to create the national power, which henceforth would depend on the economy. The latter must therefore be directed, particularly since it was deficient, since it must be renovated, and since it would not be renovated unless the state determined to do so. This was, in my eyes, the chief motive of the nationalisation, control and modernisation measures adopted by my Government. But this conception of a Government armed to act powerfully in the economic domain was directly linked to my conception of the state itself. I regarded the state not as it was yesterday and as the parties wished it to become once more, a juxtaposition of private interests which could never produce anything but weak compromise, but instead an institution of decision, action and ambition, expressing and serving the national interest alone.[50]

De Gaulle remained true to this vision of a state-directed economy, and of the state as 'an institution of decision, action and ambition', pursuing the national interest. Towards the end of his life he wrote that: 'Although freedom remains an essential lever of economic activity, the latter is nonetheless collective, directly determines the fate of the nation and at all times affects social relations. That implies an impulsion, harmonization, rules that can only come from the state; in other words, *dirigisme*.'[51] Simply to 'orient' the economy was not, in de Gaulle's view, sufficient: it had to be directed and conducted by the state.

De Gaulle was a dogmatic and sourly critical visionary who throughout his career was tormented by the idea of France on the brink of greatness, 'dedicated to an exalted and exceptional destiny'. Yet, in his view, the nation was held back by conflicting private interests, intent on serving their own ends, vying with one another for supremacy, all too often dragging the state back into chaos, mediocrity or exemplary misfortune,[52] 'condemned by governmental weakness and political cleavages to stagnation'.[53] Rousseauesque in inspiration, de Gaulle's views were informed by the works of Charles Maurras that he had read as a young man, together with the political doctrines of the neo-royalist Action Française. This advocated a return to the strong executive authority of a monarch or military leader, and decried the parliamentary republic. As de Gaulle explained in *L'Appel*, the first volume of his war memoirs: 'France is not really herself unless she is in the front rank; [but] only vast enterprises are capable of counter-balancing the ferments of disintegration inherent in her people.'[54] It was these forces of disintegration – governmental weakness and political fractures – that de Gaulle blamed for the humiliating capitulation of the armistice in June 1940. Later, in October 1944, following Liberation, Giraud reportedly exclaimed to de Gaulle, 'How things have changed!', alluding to the transformation of a nation which only weeks previously had been under the yoke of a hated invader. De Gaulle's response is illuminating:

> 'True enough – for things', I thought. But as I looked at the noisy and excited crowd, I doubted if this was the case for the French.[55]

The continuing paradox perceived by de Gaulle – that France needed greatness but was constantly thwarted in its pursuit by inherent forces of disintegration – ultimately led to his withdrawal from politics on 20 January 1946. He proclaimed himself weary of having to negotiate with political parties and splinter groups in order to get things done and was contemptuous of their incessant intrigues and quarrels. Doubtless he expected to be swiftly recalled; but for this he had to wait twelve years. He left behind him an economy that had embarked on the road to recovery. According to Kuisel, France was now ready to listen to the advocates of growth and progressive change, liberal modernisers like Jean Monnet and François Bloch-Lainé. They played effectively upon the postwar collective sense of national economic decline during the first half of the twentieth century to promote economic management and growth in the second.[56] But acceptance of the need for change and renewal was far from universal. On his return from incarceration at Buchenwald, where he had survived for two years, the socialist leader Léon Blum did not find an overwhelming desire for renovation, as asserted by Kuisel and Kindleberger. Instead he found only 'a tired, nonchalant and lazy convalescence', prompting him to exhort his fellow countrymen not to let the sacrifices of war serve as an excuse for laziness and exhaustion. The alternative confronting the country, as Monnet succinctly expressed it, was one of 'modernization or decadence'.[57]

The political and economic tribulations of the Fourth Republic

The Fourth Republic is traditionally presented as marred by political weakness – the 'ferments of disintegration', as prophesied by de Gaulle, skewering the quest for international prestige and power. With de Gaulle no longer at the helm, France's parliamentary parties fought for control and repeatedly brought down governments, the average duration of which was just six months. The most enduring government, that of left-of-centre socialist Guy Mollet, lasted sixteen months; the most transitory, led by Christian democrat Pierre Pflimlin in May 1958, a mere fourteen days. On 13 October 1946 a new constitution was accepted by popular referendum, following the rejection of that of the previous May. This dramatically reduced the role of the president and the Senate of rural notables, both rendered effete, leaving the way clear for the parliamentary parties of the Constituent Assembly to battle it out among themselves. On 14 January 1947 Vincent Auriol was elected president of the nascent Republic – the first of two presidents of the Fourth Republic, being succeeded by René Coty in 1953.

It is often said that France alternates between periods of strong leadership – by Philip the Fair, Richelieu, Mazarin, Louis XIV, Napoleon, Doumerge, Clemenceau, Poincaré and de Gaulle – and periods when the social cement, the 'glue' which binds the nation together in a common cause, seems to dissolve. Warring factions and parliamentary stalemate typify these latter periods, when strong men at the top are no longer tolerated or able to achieve consensus.[58] The Fourth Republic has come to represent the second model in its purest form. Described by historian Pierre Goubert as an unloved regime, it was also one of France's most ephemeral, lasting less than twelve years.[59] It suffered an ignominious end, cut short by a lethal combination of bankruptcy, worsening civil strife in Algeria, and political deadlock at home.

Although the Fourth Republic is usually disparaged for its political failings, which lie beyond the scope of this study, it is also denounced for its economic failures, being depicted as a friend of inflation and purveyor of enormous public debt, characterised by financial laxity. This judgement is unfair and the reality more complex. It is easy to forget that the 'thirty glorious years' also embraced those of the Fourth Republic. The undeniable economic progress achieved during the golden age of growth following the war is attributed to, and claimed by the Fifth Republic, but it was nevertheless begun under the Fourth. Berstein argues convincingly that the success of the Fifth Republic was rooted in the major structural reforms carried out in the wake of the Liberation and under the Fourth Republic. These embraced the nationalisation of energy, public transport, the principal clearing banks and insurance companies, as well as the Bank of France (enabling the government to control the credit supply), the introduction of welfare provision and above all of planning. The cumulative effect of these reforms was to allow the government to assume a leading role in economic and financial management. The planning process in particular, introduced in 1947, allowed the state to become the principal architect of economic modernisation.[60] Viewed in this light, the main economic policies pursued by the two Republics are characterised by continuity rather than rupture. As Berstein asserts, 'In all these areas the Fifth Republic simply realised the considerable profits derived by its predecessor.'[61]

At the same time, crucially, through a fortuitous coming together of the collapse of empire[62] and the logic of Europe, the Fourth Republic bequeathed to its successor a new perspective on the international economy. This was marked by the conviction that the process of 'catching up' (*rattrapage*) could only be achieved through the abandonment of protectionism in favour of opening up the economy to international competition.[63] It was under the Fourth Republic that France entered the Organisation for Economic Cooperation and Development (OECD), and joined the European Coal and Steel Community (ECSC), when it came into effect on 18 April 1951. The Western European Union (WEU) came into being in May 1955. (The proposed European Defence Community, established by the Treaty of Paris in May 1951, which aimed to establish a third military defence community independent of the US and USSR, was effectively scuppered by Mendès-France in 1954.) The climax of this process was the historical signing on 25 March 1957 of the Treaty of Rome, together with Germany, Italy and the Benelux countries, thus creating the Common Market.

It is nonetheless true that high inflation became a defining feature of the Fourth Republic. The German occupiers, who had regularly ordered the issuing of large amounts of paper money, had drained the economy. The machines and material urgently needed for modernisation were costly. Budgetary deficits accumulated in the drive for reconstruction, which called for the building of roads, railways, bridges, factories, houses and ports, causing the national debt to spiral, the interest payments on which significantly restricted the government's room for manoeuvre.[64] Inflation was stimulated further by the outbreak of the Korean war in June 1950, causing the price of raw materials to rise, fuelling wage demands, and adversely affecting the trade and foreign exchange balances. The minimum wage, the *salaire minimum interprofessionnel garanti* or SMIG,[65] created in 1947, was regularly reviewed and increased thereafter, becoming indexed to the cost of living from 1952. The situation was partially stabilised in 1952–55, following the intervention of Antoine Pinay, a provincial businessman turned politician who served as an independent deputy for the duration of the Fourth Republic, at the time President of the Council, when 'expansion amid stability', as Edgar Faure put it, was achieved.[66] But inflation took off again with the start of the Algerian war, with whose outcome the fortunes of the Fourth Republic became intimately bound up, propelled by the renewed wage demands of a reduced labour force rather than the costs of financing the war effort *per se*.

The accession to power in January 1956 of a socialist government under Guy Mollet, a member of the Section française de l'internationale ouvrière (SFIO), the forerunner of Mitterrand's Parti Socialiste (PS), intent on implementing a raft of social policies, exacerbated the budget deficit and increased the salary burden on companies. In particular, Mollet introduced improved old-age pensions (the elderly were now living longer), higher salaries for civil servants, and a third week of annual paid holiday. Mollet resigned when he failed to convince parliament that taxes should be raised in order to fund military operations in Algeria, where civil strife had intensified. Following a number of pernicious price and taxation policies introduced by Paul Ramadier, Minister of Finance, this unfortunate state of affairs culminated in demeaning requests for financial aid from the International Monetary Fund and the US (Eximbank). Financial support was granted contingent upon the return to health of the public finances. In external affairs, it seemed, 'the Fourth Republic knew only how to seek shelter under the American umbrella', returning to a point of near-submission to the Western bloc dominated by the US.[67] Bankruptcy discredited the Fourth Republic in the eyes of the French public. Together with its reputation for political weakness and financial corruption, this effectively sealed its fate. With the fall of Mollet's government in May 1957, France entered a state of semi-paralysis until the mutiny of the French Army in Algeria in May 1958, which led to the return of de Gaulle to office.

Endemic inflation, however, was not a purely negative phenomenon since high levels of indebtedness on the part of both firms and state were eroded all the more quickly in consequence. Inflation also functioned as a useful political tool. In the course of the Fourth Republic it helped to finance public expenditure, eating into the debt which was unavoidably required to fund vast reconstruction projects, while satisfying the expectations of wage earners that incomes would continue to rise. At the same time, reconstruction, which fuelled inflation, created thousands of jobs and led to full employment. Additional manpower was needed, triggering an influx of immigrant workers from North African and Mediterranean countries. State, employers and trade unions colluded in their collective refusal to control rises in prices and wages. This, as Elie Cohen has defined it, was to prove a lasting feature of the postwar period, promoting relatively painless hidden transfers of resources. The key issue, in Cohen's view, was how to facilitate social change, how to transform a largely rural country dominated by small businesses without destroying the very fabric of society. Strong growth created the economic resources to ease this transformation, alleviating the pain of population shifts and providing the wherewithal to fund infrastructural improvements. The sanction of the 'inflationist social compromise', as Cohen puts it, was regular currency devaluation.[68] Eight devaluations occurred between 1944 and 1958, as the franc tumbled on foreign exchange markets, losing more than 90 per cent of its value between the outbreak of war in 1939 and the birth of the Fifth Republic in 1958.

Reconstruction and Marshall Aid

It is almost a convention to ascribe the speedy recovery of the West European economy after the Second World War to American financial munificence in the form of what quickly came to be known as Marshall Aid. This commonly shared judgement of history is plausible but a gross over-simplification. By the time George C. Marshall, the US Secretary of State, made his famous speech at Harvard University in June 1947, in effect offer-ing large-scale financial assistance to all the war-torn economies of Europe, economic recovery was already well underway. By the end of 1946 indus-trial production in France, Belgium and the Netherlands had recovered to between 85 and 95 per cent of prewar levels (from between 30 and 40 per cent when hostilities ceased).[69] Meanwhile, in the UK, the economic transi-tion from war to peace was accomplished so smoothly that the prewar level of national output had been fully restored. These achievements, however, were not made without considerable costs and sacrifices. Spending, by states and citizens, ran ahead of the capacity of economies to deliver. Budget deficits and inflation were the natural concomitants of large-scale invest-ment in reconstruction projects. And, notwithstanding American loans and other forms of financial aid, foreign exchange reserves quickly dwindled, threatening the continuation of postwar recovery efforts. This contrasted with the situation on the other side of the Atlantic where the US balance of payments surplus was running at the rate of $10,000 million per annum.[70]

The economic disequilibrium that had emerged between the US and Western Europe, and its potentially destabilising consequences, became apparent during the early part of 1947 when continued shortages of food, coal and other essential commodities caused industrial production to falter across Europe. Earlier hopes of a rapid and sustained recovery from the effects of war began to fade, and it is against this background that Marshall made his offer of aid to Europe on behalf of the US. A flurry of diplomatic activity followed, which led swiftly to the Soviet Union, fearful of capitalist domination, declining to participate in the European Recovery Programme. Sixteen nations pressed ahead under the auspices of the Committee of European Economic Cooperation that grew out of a specially convened conference held in Paris in July 1947. The sense of desperation felt by many of the participants was confirmed in the following month when the UK was forced temporarily to suspend the convertibility of sterling into US dollars, and the government of France announced the suspension of all dollar imports except for cereals, coal and other vital supplies.

The Committee of European Economic Cooperation, which in time was to grow into the OECD, came forward with a diagnosis and a proposed solution to the problem of European economic recovery.[71] The diagnosis was that a huge disparity had grown up during wartime between the productive potential and competitiveness of the United States, on the one hand, and Europe, on the other. In order for the international economy to function effectively once more, the European economies must rapidly increase levels of production and productivity. And in order to do this they needed to import American technology and raw materials, which in turn required the foreign exchange, specifically dollars, they so conspicuously lacked. The solution to this dilemma, the only way to bridge the so-called 'dollar gap', was for the US to grant vast sums of money to replenish the coffers of European governments and central banks over a four-year period beginning in 1948. In return for this assistance, the sixteen members of the Committee of Economic Cooperation pledged to make a mighty production effort (especially in food, fuel and power), to modernise their factories and transport systems, to create internal financial stability, to increase exports, and to cooperate with others in reducing barriers to trade and developing common resources.

The distribution of Marshall Aid was by formula based on need. Some indication of the plight of the French economy can be gauged from the escalation of the wholesale price index (1938 = 100) from 469 in 1945 to 846 in 1946 to 1,217 in 1947 and 1,974 in 1948 – a more than fourfold increase in the space of just three years.[72] Meanwhile, the country recorded a balance of payments deficit in 1946 of $2,049 million (with exports of just $453 million), severely eroding gold and dollar reserves before the imposition of controls in 1947 limited the deficit for that year to $1,676 million.[73] Plainly, the French government, in pushing ahead so rapidly with reconstruction, had reached the limit of current policy. Marshall Aid was thus both timely and necessary if forward momentum were to be maintained. In the event, France came second only to the UK as a beneficiary of the recovery programme, receiving $1,776 million between 1948 and 1950 in direct aid (21 per cent of the total budget) compared to $2,237 million for the UK (26 per cent of the total budget).[74] Moreover, in addition to Marshall Aid, France was the beneficiary of financial aid through several other schemes and agreements. Over the period 1945–53, the country received aid from the US amounting to a formidable $10,901 million.

The significance of financial aid from the US to the postwar reconstruction of the French economy is not so easy to evaluate as the figures cited above might indicate. Certainly there were huge and highly beneficial transfers of resources in absolute terms. But the scale of the problem was even more massive. The official French estimate of the scale of the damage inflicted on the nation in consequence of the Second World War was $98,000 million, and if this is accepted as true then US aid was equivalent to just 11.1 per cent of French losses.[75] It is hard to resist the conclusion that domestic resources in the main were applied in the economic reconstruction of France. However, this should not detract from the fact that Marshall Aid played a key role in economic expansion over the course of the Fourth Republic. In this regard, it is important to recognise that American aid, in whatever guise, directly targeted the main constraint on economic expansion: the general lack of foreign exchange in Europe. In releasing this constraint, participating countries were able to import both vital foodstuffs and capital equipment on a large scale. Food imports prevented shortages, cutbacks and renewed austerity after years of sacrifice, fending off any tendency to disharmony and social dislocation. Capital equipment imports were likewise beneficial in preventing bottlenecks, so raising productivity levels much faster than would otherwise have been the case. The French steel industry in particular made spectacular progress through the wholesale importation of two state-of-the-art wide strip rolling mills. More generally, the importation of large numbers of American machine tools encouraged the modernisation of production across a wide range of industries.

At a less direct and more qualitative level, acceptance of Marshall Aid in France and elsewhere did much to create the right climate for economic recovery and industrial regeneration. The architects of the European Recovery Programme recognised the need, nowadays so familiar, for financial stability as a condition for sustained economic growth. Participating nations pledged themselves to that objective and it is no coincidence that after 1948, when the French introduced the Mayer Plan for economic stabilisation, retail price inflation declined sharply to be contained at an average annual rate of 10 per cent between 1948 and 1953.[76] This was still uncomfortably high but the threat of complete loss of control had been dissipated. The Marshall Aid planners displayed similar foresight in bringing the countries of Western Europe to think of national economic efficiency as dependent on collaboration across borders. Trade liberalisation was placed high on the agenda of participating countries, and cross-border planning was urged in order to make the most of massive capital investments in basic industries.[77] The most important outcome for France was the systematic modernisation of its iron and steel industry, which in turn paved the way for the formation in 1951 of the European Coal and Steel Community, the precursor to the European Economic Community.

Economic planning and the quest for modernisation

France stands out as the only country in Western Europe to have embraced planning as a tool of economic management in pursuit of reconstruction, modernisation, growth and social justice. The impetus towards economic planning lay in the devastation caused by Allied bombardments and four years of Occupation. Yet as Jean Monnet, author of the first plan, articulated, the underlying weakness of the French economy predated the war, the extent and degree of the rot being thrown into sharp relief in the lightning speed with which the country fell. In Monnet's view, France's dearth of investment, its tendency to import more than was exported, its antiquated agricultural and industrial machinery and lack of business acumen constituted as immediate a cause of the collapse of 1940 as moral lassitude and the absence of military preparations. (The average age of French industrial equipment was 25 years prior to the war, as opposed to six years in the US and nine years in the UK.)[78]

Nowhere is the spirit or motivation behind the adoption of planning in France more clearly articulated than in the introductory section to the 1946 Monnet Plan for the reconstruction and modernisation of the French economy.[79] This opens with the charge that before the war France had spent more than it had earned, making up the shortfall with profits from overseas investments. These assets had been liquidated during the war and thus 'in the years to come France [would] have nothing to live on but the product of its labour'. The situation had been worsened by ravages of war and the fact that 'other countries continued to progress at a tempo accelerated by the very requirements of war'. France had been left far behind. Hence it was 'necessary to increase productivity and, in order to do that, to modernise and mechanise the economy'. Modernisation meant not only technological improvement but also better production methods and improved corporate structures. Monnet concluded that 'efficiency must be a primary concern throughout the economy', famously asserting that 'modernization is not a condition of things; it is a condition of mind'. France must develop its economy 'according to a coherent plan; must make the best use possible of the means available; must increase key resources to the maximum; must utilize its disposable national resources in an order of priorities that reflects the exigencies of the situation'.

The compelling and highly influential analysis of the plight of the postwar French economy put forward by Monnet was singular, yet cast within the same mould as the European Recovery Programme. There was general agreement that the fundamental problems of Western Europe stemmed from international economic dislocation, from the gulf in productivity and productive capacity that had opened up between the US and Europe, and from the chronic shortage of foreign exchange that plagued recovery efforts across the continent. There was general agreement also that the solution to these problems ultimately lay in Europe grasping the nettle of economic modernisation and industrial regeneration within an open economic system free from barriers to trade and capital mobility. Modernisation and sustained growth in production and exports were universal rather than uniquely French goals. But France, consequent upon protracted depression in the 1930s and defeat in 1940, differed from other countries in the depth of its conviction that present problems were due to institutional failings in the past. Thus economic modernisation demanded, as a condition of success, a completely new approach supported by new techniques and new institutions. This in essence is the logic that led the French, alone in Western Europe, to embrace planning as a central plank of economic management.

However, Monnet, at heart a moderate rather than a revolutionary, was at pains to allay private-sector distrust of a strong state. His sensibilities in this regard had been heightened by the spectacular expropriations for alleged wartime collaboration, the confiscation of profits judged illicit and the temporary incarceration of some businessmen. A businessman himself, the son of a cognac salesman, Monnet sought to promote the view that the state was not the enemy of business, and to foster enlightened self-interest among business circles in the collective pursuit and management of wealth. In his memoirs, Monnet explains the genesis of French planning in a conversation with de Gaulle, which he reports as follows:

> 'It will take some time', I told [de Gaulle], 'to repair the towns, ports, railways, but it will be done because we cannot do otherwise. On the contrary, it will take a firmness of purpose and many explanations to convince people that the fundamental evil lies in the archaism of our equipment and our methods of production. [...] I do not yet know exactly what should be done, but I am sure of one thing, that we cannot transform the French economy without the participation of the French people in this transformation. When I say people, I do not have in mind an abstract entity, I mean trade unions, industrialists, administrators, all those who will be associated in a plan for equipment and modernization'. 'This is what must be done, and therein lies its name', concluded General de Gaulle.[80]

In a note to the general, dated 4 December 1945, Monnet outlined the plan for modernisation and investment. The result was the creation of the Commissariat Général du Plan by the decree of 3 January 1946, with Monnet at its head, its mission 'to illuminate the future, facilitate economic debate, improve coherence'.[81] Monnet conceived of the plan as, fundamentally, an instrument of *concertation*, of dialogue, discussion and consultation, essentially a collective enterprise and participative endeavour.[82] Committees dubbed *Commissions de modernisation* were established, bringing together representatives from the worlds of business (top managers, white-collar workers, with some representation from blue-collar workers), government and administration (civil servants and planning staff) alongside experts in relevant fields. In 1946, a total of ten Commissions involved 494 individuals.

By the time of the fifth plan in 1963, there were 32 Commissions with 1,950 members.[83] At the same time, the plan's purpose was also one of heightening awareness: to alert decision-makers to the needs of the economy, to which manufacturing could then be aligned. Thus in 1946, when Tollet, head of the Commission of manual workers, and also a leading official in the Confédération Générale du Travail (CGT), was confronted with the statistical reality of the French economy, he unhesitatingly advocated a working week of 45 hours, beyond the legal norm of 40 hours. If the working week of 48 hours was not restored, wrote Monnet, this was due not to the unwillingness of workers, but rather to the shortage of supplies necessary for production.[84]

The earliest plans of the reconstruction era were direct in both their conception and execution. The Monnet Plan for equipment and modernisation (1947–50, extended to 1953 to utilise Marshall Aid) focused on the country's basic needs in the early stages of reconstruction. Five priorities were established. In first place was the modernisation of 'coal, electricity, metallurgy, cement, agricultural machinery and transportation, and to increase considerably their production ... on which the life of the entire nation' was seen to depend. Second came the modernisation of agriculture as a means of improving nutritional levels and relieving pressure on the balance of payments. Third was the reconstruction of the national infrastructure, which in turn required the modernisation of the construction industry. Fourth was the development of manufactured exports, 'at first by taking advantage of the exceptional shortage of goods in the world, later by the lowering of production costs through modernisation and increased output'. Fifth was the modernisation of the capital goods industries that provided 'the equipment for the above activities'.[85] All were undisputed motors in the reconstruction process. These sectors alone benefited from Marshall Aid and they received massive additional funding directly from the state. A total of 7,057.4 thousand million current francs were invested in the French economy between 1947 and 1952, of which 51 per cent came from public funds.[86] Central direction of production and resource allocation was further reinforced by the setting and achievement of specific targets for import licences, building permits and financial credits, lending credence to the view that French planning, particularly in its early stages, transcended the merely 'indicative' to embrace the 'dirigiste'.[87]

The second plan (1954–57) coincided with the waning of the Fourth Republic. It maintained the emphasis on heavy industry, but broadened its remit to incorporate new sectors, such as public investment in schools and hospitals. Detailed investment and production targets were specified, covering the whole of manufacturing industry, which was to be rationalised and modernised. International competition was no longer to be shunned, resulting in the removal of a raft of restrictive practices. Despite the regime's serious financial difficulties, aggravated by social turmoil in Algeria, the plan met, and even exceeded most of its targets. Notably, it aspired to a GDP increase of 25 per cent over the period, whereas in fact a commendable 30 per cent increase was achieved.[88] Consumer demand had been stoked up by years of hardship, and the ensuing expansion of the economy fuelled inflationary wage claims. At the same time a surge in imports exacerbated an already existing balance of payments deficit, compelling Monnet in January 1958 to go cap-in-hand to Washington to seek emergency financial aid totalling $600 million. This was seen by many as deeply demeaning.

Economic management and the American model

History has not treated the French Fourth Republic kindly. Political bungling and ignominious collapse have weighed far more heavily in the balance than a highly creditable record of economic growth and structural change. Recovery proceeded apace such that France had regained its 1938 level of national income by 1948. In the decade that followed, real GDP grew at a compound rate of 4.5 per cent, slower than West Germany at 7.4 per cent and Italy at 5.9 per cent, but well ahead of the UK at 2.4 per cent. By historical standards this was exemplary. Growth was a product of modernisation, capital investment and rising productivity. At first investment was concentrated in a limited number of industries, reflecting the priorities of the first and second plans; but it was sufficient to secure an overall annual average increase in labour productivity of 4.3 per cent between 1949 and 1959, a record only bettered in Europe by West Germany (5.7 per cent) and the Netherlands (4.8 per cent).[89] The active labour force grew by just 0.1 per cent per annum, and consequently the labour market became progressively tighter, unemployment falling to a low of just 160,000 in 1957.[90] The vast majority of the French population enjoyed year-on-year rises in living standards as per capita incomes grew (in 1990 dollars) from $5,270 in 1950 to $6,890 in 1957, an increase of 31 per cent.[91]

The pursuit of rapid economic growth, dubbed 'growthmanship' by economists of the day, was shared across Western Europe, motivated by a general desire to catch up for lost time and transcend the shortages and suffering of the recent past. The conditions were propitious. Under the stable international payments system installed after the war, and with the progressive relaxation of tariffs and quotas, international trade flourished, growing more rapidly than output and serving as an engine of economic growth. Between 1948 and 1962 the exports and imports of European countries grew at an annual average rate of about 7 per cent whereas GDP growth averaged about 4 per cent. In France, exports grew at an annual average rate of 7.6 per cent, a little above the European average, as French firms took advantage of periodic sharp devaluations of the value of the franc.[92] Meanwhile, in order to shield French industry from the full force of foreign competition, the government resisted the removal of physical limits on imports for entire classes of goods. France in the early 1950s, while having similar tariff levels to other countries, had the most protected economy in Western Europe. In resisting pressure from the US and UK for speedy liberalisation, the French government bought time for domestic firms to invest and become competitive by international standards.

Economic management under the Fourth Republic had two main facets. The first of these was planning with general objectives specified in terms of macroeconomic targets for variables such as production, investment and employment. Beneath the generalities lay the detailed specifications for inputs and outputs, industry by industry. Each of these specifications required elaborate negotiations between officials and industrialists, which in turn required commercial and technical understanding at the level of industries and enterprises. This explains why the various components of the plan varied so much in their effectiveness, working best when the industry concerned was a top priority and the targets laid down were prescriptive, working poorly when forecasts were little more than statistical guesses. Prescription and the leverage exerted by the state at the enterprise level were greatest within the nationalised industries wherein 'the plan was compulsory and had the force of law'.[93] In other industries, the plan was in theory indicative, guiding decisions through the provision of information, but in reality a barrage of tools and techniques were used by planners to control the investment process. The granting of modernisation funds for investment, for instance, was conditional upon accepting direction from the authorities. In exerting leverage through the granting or withholding of funds, the state was able to restructure core industries through a process of consolidation and rationalisation, as in the case of iron and steel. The extent of power held by planners is evident from the fact that 57 per cent of the funds invested in modernisation projects between 1948 and 1951 came directly from the state.[94]

The second main facet of economic management during the Fourth Republic was the subordination, though not abandonment, of orthodox principles of budgeting in favour of large-scale deficit financing. This was a matter of active choice, not passivity. If reconstruction and modernisation were to proceed apace, fulfilling national aspirations, then the state had to channel resources actively in support of the plan. There was a big gap between government income and expenditure. Income as a proportion of expenditure averaged 73 per cent between 1946 and 1951, although the recorded funding gap falls from an average of 27 per cent to 21 per cent if allowance is made for American loans and grants.[95] Remedial measures were taken. Tax reforms were introduced, income tax increased and a new tax on value added was introduced in 1954. Public loans were issued and there was a sharp increase in the national debt. But these measures were not enough to bridge the gap between income and expenditure. Inflation raged in consequence, a natural counterpart to the deliberate policy of rapid recovery, growth and modernisation, without any attempt to clamp down hard on consumption. However, by the mid-1950s, after several years of growth, rising tax receipts and a marked shift from government to the private financing of investment, there was the prospect of an early return to budgetary orthodoxy. The rate of inflation plummeted between 1953 and 1956 before escalation of the conflict in Algeria brought this interlude of relative stability to an end. Only in 1958, with the introduction of the Pinay–de Gaulle stabilisation plan, were definitive steps taken to curb excess demand and the onward march of inflation.

Notwithstanding the tensions caused by inflation, it is hard to resist the conclusion that the strategy for economic management pursued under the Fourth Republic was on the whole very successful. The particular style and methods of planning adopted by the French led to a focus on the concrete problems of investment, technology, management and industrial organisation, purposefully discriminating between individual sectors, industries and in some cases firms. In Caron's view, for example, the Monnet Plan constituted a true turning-point in the history of energy in France. It did not aim to restore what had existed before, but rather to put in place proper foundations for deep-seated industrialisation. In this way it sought to break with the so-called Malthusianism (low growth cycle) that had for long impeded growth in energy production.[96] In bringing together a large number of the country's key economic actors and decision-makers, the plan yielded detailed knowledge and a vital overview – and in this sense, perhaps, greater certainty – of the whole to which the individual contribution of each could to some degree be geared. That the state provided the leadership and wherewithal, through deficit financing and Marshall Aid, needed to deliver on the promises of the first two plans is a tribute to those who after the war seized responsibility for economic management and the modernisation of French business.

It is this select group, first and foremost among whom was Jean Monnet, that Marie-Laure Djelic, in *Exporting the American Model*, refers to as France's modernising elite. In the minds of the modernisers, the American business model of corporate capitalism, characterised by large firms, advanced technology and mass production, was inherently more productive than the French system, blighted by technological backwardness and small-scale operations. It followed that France must learn from the US experience and reform itself from within. Modernisation was thus an ideologically loaded concept vehemently opposed to traditional French institutions and ways of doing business. It stood, on the one hand, as shorthand for massive investment in large, rationalised firms, industries and sectors and, on the other hand, for economic liberalisation, for the abandonment of protectionism and barriers to the free movement of capital and labour. It succeeded in gaining credence because of the depth of the institutional crisis faced by

France after the war. According to Djelic, a small group of modernisers took advantage of the prevailing power vacuum to create a fresh dialectic associated with Jean Monnet and the planning commission, top civil servants linked to the Ecole National d'Administration (ENA), and opinion-forming politicians and journalists led by Pierre Mendès-France and Jean-Jacques Servan-Schreiber.[97] In essence, the new mission of the state was to lead France into the corporate age within an economically unified and newly liberal European order.

The modernising elite found its greatest allies not inside France but in the US. Here the supporters of Marshall Aid were convinced that American interests, political and economic, were best served by tying a regenerated and competitive Western Europe into a robust international economic system that embraced and promoted by degree the free movement of goods, services and capital. The best way to do this, it was reasoned, was to export to Europe the core features and practices of the US corporate economy, and to encourage the integration of national economies so as to create markets large enough to support competition between large and cost-efficient enterprises. Money and know-how were to be injected into Europe to promote these ends. Cash came in the form of Marshall Aid and was tied to promises of liberalisation. Know-how came in the form of the US technical assistance programme, which supported the transfer of technical knowledge and management practices from America to Europe. By the end of 1953 France had organised 291 productivity missions to the US, involving thousands of managers in spreading the credo and values of corporate capitalism throughout French business.[98]

This marked the beginnings of a long process that has slowly gained momentum with the formation and enlargement across France of business schools wedded at core to the technologies and practices of US management. However, neither ideological nor systemic changes have been sufficient to eradicate the distinctive features of the French national business system. Indeed, while it is fair to say that the modernising elite has progressively gained in strength and numbers, it is equally the case that it has met with resistance and reaction that have forced compromise, which in turn has led to uniquely French ways of thinking and acting. Most conspicuously, the compact forged between the state and business has preserved a mentality that puts the French national interest well ahead of any abstract consideration based on the ideals of economic liberalism.

Conclusion

In examining the calamitous state of the French economy in the immediate aftermath of war and Occupation, this chapter has sought to highlight the fundamental importance of the war as a watershed. The ensuing overwhelming desire for economic modernisation was underscored, of course, by the technological defeat of 1940, in which the country had failed to take to arms. At the same time, it is suggested that the postwar treatment of alleged collaborationist business leaders sheds important light on the ways in which French ruling elites preserve and regenerate themselves in the face of *forces majeures*. Expropriation serves as a symbolic act of retribution and catharsis that reaffirms the identity and values of the group as a whole, while reinforcing its stability. In this it serves a useful social function. However collaborationist the wartime activities of business leaders may (or may not) have been, to destabilise business excessively, beyond the level of punishment deemed necessary to anchor society by staving off anarchy, was clearly not in the country's interest as a whole. Hence, as Ehrmann observes, the postwar boards of French companies consisted almost invariably of the same men as before the war.

This chapter has also elicited the importance of the preliminary but nevertheless fundamental steps taken to reconstruct the economy immediately after the war, many of which contained the seeds of future success. De Gaulle's insight that French economic progress depended on the development of energy resources 'on the largest possible scale' emerges as almost visionary in view of the spectacular success currently enjoyed by energy giants EdF and GdF (see Chapter 7).[99] The establishment of ENA was likewise significant. Whatever criticisms may have been levied against it subsequently, ENA, together with other leading *grandes écoles*, has gone on to produce a significant proportion of top business leaders, politicians and civil servants over more than five decades *from a common mould*, educating them in a common world-view. The usefulness of this institutional framework to business and the economy as a whole, encouraging it to proceed along agreed ideological lines according to agreed formulae, while ensuring the preservation of the business elite in particular, is arguably considerable.

This argument is supported by the evidence of this chapter regarding economic management, planning and economic performance. The drive to modernise the French economy under the Fourth and Fifth Republics originated in the immediate postwar years in the public sphere, with leading technocrats and opinion-formers who were highly critical of French institutions and intellectual traditions. From key positions within the establishment, the modernising elite, on its own initiative, took the lead in transforming French business with unbridled support from the planning commission and progressive forces in the US. They enjoyed considerable success within the economic realm despite the political turmoil and factionalism that have tarnished the memory of the Fourth Republic. As the values of corporate capitalism spread, the ranks of the modernising elite swelled and extended to younger business leaders better able to accommodate themselves to the challenges of the postwar international economic order. They owed this ability not only to the thoroughness of their training and expansive outlook, but also to the myriad of personal and cultural links, stemming from a common education, which bound them to France's technocratic, political and intellectual elites. More than anything else it was elite cohesiveness, lending stability amid change, that enabled France to manage the economic transition from Fourth to Fifth Republic largely unscathed.

3
The 'Golden Age' of the Gaullist Era

> In economy as in politics or strategy, I do not believe that there can be absolute truth, but only circumstances.
>
> Charles de Gaulle[1]

The 'thirty glorious years' of economic expansion following the Second World War, during which GDP per capita grew at an annual average rate in excess of 5 per cent, are closely identified in the public mind with the return of de Gaulle to power, the restoration of order, and the establishment in 1958 of the Fifth Republic. This golden age of economic growth witnessed the modernisation of the French economy, the transformation of living standards and the birth of consumer society. In the 1960s France emerged as one of the world's leading industrial economies: 'France has married her century', as de Gaulle theatrically put it.

This chapter provides a *tour d'horizon* of the French economy during the Gaullist years, under de Gaulle (1958–69) and his successor, Pompidou (1969–74), a period marked by the relinquishment of protectionism and the opening up of complacent domestic markets to international competition. It accords particular attention to the Gaullist tools of economic management, including devaluation and the creation of the new franc, the planning process, industrial policy, and concentration, the maxim 'big is beautiful' coming to predominate in all areas of economic activity. It explores the view that de Gaulle's *économie concertée* enhanced the dominance of politico-administrative and business elites, leaving little room for social outsiders. Cohesive at the top, the establishment remained segregated from other social classes. In this sense, it may have contributed inadvertently to the downfall of a presidency that bore the hallmark of obduracy and arrogance. De Gaulle's response to the crisis of May 1968, to promote the 'participation' of the man in the street in the economy, arguably came too late.

The origins of the Franco-German relationship, one dominated by technocratic and politico-administrative elites, are also explored in this chapter. Recognised by de Gaulle as early as May 1945 as the key to French ascendancy in Europe, and hence to prestige and status on the world stage, it resulted in a fortuitous co-leadership of the European Community (EC) to mutual advantage. With Eastern enlargement imminent, perhaps as early as 2004, this co-leadership, and with it the considerable benefits that accrue to France as a result, are nevertheless now under threat. Foremost among these benefits are the huge financial advantages enjoyed by France over four decades due to membership of the Common Agricultural Policy (CAP), also reviewed in this chapter. Despite several attempts at reform, this survives largely intact, as introduced by de Gaulle in the 1960s.

Economic historians nevertheless vary in their judgement on the period. The predominant view that the achievements of the period were exceptional has been challenged on the grounds that economic modernisation had in fact begun earlier in the twentieth century. According to this interpretation, the chronic depression of the 1930s and the disaster of the Occupation should be seen as interrupting a process of vigorous expansion begun by French firms in the 1920s.[2] From 1918 to 1929, the French economy was arguably more buoyant than ever before, with the birth of new, prosperous industries in chemicals and engineering.[3] In this light, postwar economic growth may be seen not as a turning-point, but rather as a return to the healthy economic growth that had existed previously.[4] Table 3.1 presents economic growth in the each of the main European countries from 1896 to 1963 in three broad periods. In each case a considerable postwar boost is noticeable, which would seem to contradict this view. Other commentators are of the opinion that during this period of sustained economic growth, business in Western Europe grew in size and scope regardless of national origin, with individual national characteristics persisting, but becoming less clearly defined over time and tending to converge. Certainly postwar growth was by no means a uniquely French experience, as Fourastié acknowledged, but one that France shared with other European and industrialised nations.[5] France's average annual growth rate of 5 per cent for the period 1950–73 is only slightly above the European average of 4.8 per cent, and below that of Germany (6 per cent) and Spain (6.8 per cent) (see Table 1.1). Cassis suggests that the trend towards convergence has been the dominant feature of big

Table 3.1   Annual average growth rates, 1896–1963

Period	France	Germany	Italy	UK
1896–1929	1.7	*	2.1	1.0
1929–63	2.2	*	2.7	2.1
1949–63	4.6	7.8	5.8	2.6

Source: Parodi, M., *L'Economie et la société française de 1945 à nos jours*, Paris, Armand Colin, 1971, p. 63.
* Cannot be compiled due to frontier changes.

business in Europe in the twentieth century.[6] Critically, though, Cassis insists that convergence does not imply uniformity. Nor did the so-called 'thirty glorious years' always appear to be so wonderful at the time. This was demonstrated most spectacularly by the crisis of May 1968, itself 'the child of economic growth',[7] when profound social upheavals motivated by qualitative aspirations (e.g. status in the firm) rather than quantitative demands (e.g. shorter hours, higher wages) unseated de Gaulle. The *trente glorieuses*, wrote Fourastié, were glorious purely because of their dramatic impact on the standard of living and quality of life in France. They were not glorious in any other domain, whether philosophy, art, literature, spirituality, demographics or virtue.[8] That said, French authors won the Nobel Prize for Literature three times during this period: in 1947 (André Gide), 1957 (Albert Camus), and 1975 (Saint-Jean Perse). The Nobel Prize for Science was awarded to a French scientist in 1964, while in philosophy the period saw the emergence of such influential thinkers as Jean-Paul Sartre, Michel Foucault, Jacques Derrida and Pierre Bourdieu, as existentialism, structuralism then post-structuralism and post-modernism came to the fore. Nevertheless, in Fourastié's eyes, the thirty glorious years failed above all to restore France's national character and social consensus, enfeebled by the years of Occupation. In the foreign policy domain, he laments, 'despite the brilliant feats of Jean Monnet, we were unable to take (or keep), in Europe and elsewhere in the world, the place which, up to 1954, our partners were *keen to accord us*, and which our economic renewal allowed us to take'.[9]

The 1950s were dogged by problems of persistent inflation and labour shortage. France's low birth-rate over the preceding century was a longstanding cause for concern. Now it compounded the problem of the scarcity of labour, in turn exacerbated by an ageing population, life expectancy being prolonged by better health and hygiene. The postwar baby boom nevertheless saw births rise from 600,000 annually before the war to 800,000 in the years of reconstruction, while an influx of immigrants from North Africa and the Mediterranean countries helped to make up the shortfall in workers. The 1960s saw new anxieties emerge. In 1966, French industrial management was severely taken to task by Michel Crozier in his critique of the 'stalled society'.[10] One year later Jean-Jacques Servan-Schreiber warned against the impending invasion of France by US conglomerates.[11] It was perhaps not until the early 1970s, as Vinen observes, that French people became conscious that in many respects, they had never had it so good. The budget remained continuously in deficit for the first decade of the Fifth Republic, followed by a few brief years in surplus – 1970, 1972, 1973 and 1974 – before plunging into the red once again in 1975 as recession began to bite. Ironically, it was on the eve of recession, dubbed 'la crise', in 1973, that growth peaked at 6.3 per cent.[12]

It is often said that de Gaulle's economic problems remained ill-defined and open to interpretation due to his lack of interest in the subject (a feature

Table 3.2   Five-year annual averages of imports and exports (as percentage of GDP)

Period	1956–60	1961–65	1966–70	1971–75	1976–80
Imports	12.0	11.8	13.1	17.3	20.8
Exports	11.6	11.7	12.2	17.4	20.2

Sources: Smith, W.R., ' "We Can Make the Ariane, but We Can't Make Washing Machines": the State and Industrial Performance in Post-war France', in Howorth, J. and Ross, G., eds, *Contemporary France: a Review of Interdisciplinary Studies*, Vol. 3, London, Pinter, 1989, p. 197.

shared with François Mitterrand, who understood little about economics when he became president in 1981). De Gaulle's interests resided first and foremost in issues of foreign affairs, defence and the constitution.[13] Nevertheless, the Gaullist economic record stands on its own merits. During the Gaullist era France renounced its long-cherished protectionism and opened itself up to international competition. Thus, at the start of the Fifth Republic, imports and exports accounted for 12 per cent and 11.6 per cent respectively of annual GDP. By 1980 these figures had risen to 20.8 and 20.2 per cent (see Table 3.2), percentages which have varied only slightly since. Small businesses and the countryside, both of which had acted as brakes on economic growth, lost their former predominance. The need for industrial concentration was accepted and the nation embraced modernisation as the precondition of economic success. The state served as 'director, catalyst, initiator and regulator' of growth,[14] perhaps at the expense of economic liberalism for which governments of the right are more commonly renowned.[15] This reflects, as Kuisel points out, a deep-seated French preference for *faire faire* over *laisser faire*, favouring an economy that is directed by the state over one which allows greater scope for the free play of market forces.[16]

Devaluation and deflation

De Gaulle set out radically to reform economic policy and state finances in preparation for entry into the European Economic Community (EEC). Central to this objective was the Pinay–Rueff plan of December 1958, drawn up by de Gaulle in conjunction with his first finance minister, Antoine Pinay, together with Jacques Rueff, former adviser to Poincaré.[17] A provincial conservative politician associated in de Gaulle's mind with the mediocrity of the Fourth Republic, Pinay was nevertheless known for his integrity and was popular with small savers and the business community. Liberal in inspiration, and marked by budgetary austerity, the Pinay–Rueff plan set the tone for French economic policy under de Gaulle, characterised by obstinacy and endurance, heedless of any unpopularity this might provoke. In 1958, France's economy was fundamentally inward-looking, cushioned from external competition by high tariffs and import quota restrictions. The plan aimed to open markets to international competition, which it was hoped would foster dynamism and innovation. Taking a gamble on the balance of payments, 90 per cent of trade restrictions with Europe and 50 per cent of those with the US were removed. The gamble paid off: between 1959 and 1973 France's annual balance of trade was 11 times in surplus.[18] The plan's main target on the domestic front was inflation, perceived as the greatest threat to France's international position. Deflationary measures were adopted. State sector subsidies and social welfare payments were cut, public-sector salary increases were held at 4 per cent, and dispensable social expenditure was withdrawn. At the same time, taxes were levied on personal incomes, company profits and mass-consumption items such as alcohol and tobacco.

Deflation was accompanied by devaluation, designed to stabilise the currency and correct the imbalance of payments by stimulating exports and reducing imports. The franc was devalued by 17.5 per cent in December 1958, hailed as a once-and-for-all devaluation to end the humiliating periodic devaluations consequent upon the 'inflationist social compromise'.[19] Linked to this, on 1 January 1960 the existing franc was replaced by a 'heavy franc' or 'new franc', equal to 100 old francs. This was a symbolic step, emblematic of French economic revival, which sought to give the franc parity with the German mark and the Swiss franc, and to endow it with the credibility of a major international currency. While monetary policy did not rise to the top of the French political agenda until 1983, in fact de Gaulle attached particular importance to the value of the *nouveau franc*. Its international standing was bound up in his eyes with a desire for grandeur, a break with the hegemony of the US dollar, and a return to the stability once associated with the gold standard. De Gaulle was exasperated by the fact that the US could run an international trade deficit financed through the perpetual creation of new dollars. In his view, US financial pre-eminence amounted to a form of subjugation; to submit to it was tantamount to slavery.[20] In February 1965 de Gaulle delivered a scathing attack on the international monetary system, accusing the US of deliberately acquiring trade deficits abroad in order to pay its debts with dollars which it alone could issue, instead of paying them fully in gold.[21] The worker–student insurrection of May 1968 effectively put an end to de Gaulle's monetary defiance against the dollar. When widespread strike action halted production, paralysing the country, fuelling inflation, the trade deficit, the balance of payments, and prompting flights of capital, de Gaulle doggedly refused to devalue despite the seeming inevitability of so doing. In the name of the 'once-and-for-all' devaluation of 1958, he rejected the adjustment of a currency regarded by many as overvalued. Devaluation took place in the relative calm of August 1969 under de Gaulle's successor to the presidency, Georges Pompidou, who was perhaps better able to comprehend the impossibility of monetary autarchy, and hence more willing to countenance the 'loss of face' which devaluation might bring.

Economic planning

Economic planning, adopted in the Fourth Republic as a means of organising and directing the process of reconstruction and economic modernisation, normally over a four- to five-year period, was one of the principal economic tools of the Gaullist era.[22] It is also, in the minds of many commentators, one of the most interesting aspects of the French economy in the postwar period, being without precedent in the West, especially during the 'thirty glorious years', when its relevance to economic and business life was at its peak.[23] Planning formed a central plank of the Gaullist strategy of state-led growth. Intended as a means of reducing economic uncertainty (confirming the strong uncertainty avoidance index accorded to France by Hofstede), French planning was essentially indicative in character, particularly from the fourth plan onwards. In this respect it differed from the central planning typical of the command economies of the former Eastern bloc (notably favoured by Stalin, whom de Gaulle admired and with whom he got on well). Indicative planning is nevertheless something of an oxymoron. As Hough points out, the plan's claim to have been indicative is to some extent belied by the battery of support mechanisms at its behest, particularly in the form of investment funding and financial incentives.

The advent of the Fifth Republic coincided with the launch of the third national plan (1958–61). This marked a new departure as reconstruction ceded to growth as the main economic objective. The third plan was more ambitious, elaborate, scientific and technical than its predecessors were. Inspired by the apparent success of the planning process, it examined 'the effects of changes in the size and structure of the national population, of scientific and technical progress, of the creation of the European Communities, and of links with France's former colonies'.[24] Detailed growth projections were prepared for almost every area of the economy, integrated with a parallel programme of resource allocation, with an overarching target of a GDP increase of 20 per cent, which was easily met. Both the national and international contexts were now radically different to the early postwar years. The period was marked by the launch of the Common Market, the intensification of social crisis in Algeria, and the impending arrival on the job market of the young people of the postwar baby boom (see Tables 3.4 and 3.5).[25] In particular, the plan focused on reducing imports and stimulating exports, in an attempt to solve the growing balance of payments problem.[26] To this end the economy was deflated and the franc devalued under the Pinay–Rueff stabilisation plan, triggering recession. An 'interim plan' (1960–61) was prepared, and in the event recovery occurred more swiftly than anticipated, but at the cost of slowing down economic growth, the plan's primary goal. As Hall puts it, the planners' elaborate projections were rendered meaningless by the disruption caused by 'short-term macroeconomic management',[27] which to some extent defeated the original purpose of the exercise.

The fourth plan (1962–65), approved in August 1962, was aimed at 'economic and social development' and assumed a social and redistributive character previously eschewed. It embraced social security, pensions, schools, hospitals and the regions, as the scale and scope of the planning exercise became ever wider. By 1960, it was apparent that the French economy had embarked on a path of sustained growth. Boosted by the postwar population increase,[28] the urban explosion, and the 'embourgeoisement' of the working classes,[29] the domestic market continued to expand as the 'consumer society', marked by mass consumption, came into being. The main purpose of the plan was no longer the allocation of scarce resources. Rather, it was more concerned with the problems of sharing out the fruits of expansion – 'the apportionment of surplus' as Pierre Massé, then Commissaire Général du Plan, put it.[30] Redistribution targeted the poorer, underdeveloped west of France, the disadvantaged, the elderly (now increasing as a percentage of the population, see Table 3.3), and public services (whose share of GDP was growing at twice the growth rate). Under Massé's leadership, the fourth plan was one of the best executed. The target of 24 per cent growth in GDP was achieved exactly (24.1 per cent). The plan also benefited from de Gaulle's

Table 3.3 Changing age distribution (as percentage of population)

Age	1954	1962	1968	1973
>20	30.7	33.1	33.8	32.5
20–64	57.8	55.1	53.6	54.4
65+	11.5	11.8	12.6	13.3

Source: Berstein, S., *The Republic of de Gaulle 1958–1969*, Cambridge, CUP/Editions de la Maison des sciences de l'homme, 1993, p. 126.

Table 3.4 Evolution in sales outlets, 1962–94 (as percentage)

Sales outlets	1962	1970	1980	1990	1994
Grand Commerce	14.0	21.1	30.2	41.1	46.7
Petit/Moyen Commerce	63.0	55.9	46.1	39.5	36.1
Other*	23.0	23.1	23.8	19.1	17.2
Total (FF billions)	142	282.3	955.5	1,985.7	2,143.1

* Includes bakeries and cake shops, sales of tyres, car accessories, petrol, wholesale purchases, etc.

Sources: INSEE; Parodi, M. *et al.*, *L'Economie et la société françaises au second XXe siècle*, Vol. 2, *Les Mutations sectorielles*, Paris, Armand Colin, 1998, p. 229.

Table 3.5   Number of small retail stores, 1961–71

Type of store	1961	1967	1969	1971
Grocery, dairy stores (<400 m²)	149,100	111,900	96,480	85,090
Chain stores, cooperatives	35,000	31,980	29,295	26,050
Drug stores	19,500	14,280	14,280	13,710
Total	203,600	158,160	140,055	124,850

Source: de Monnet, J. and Harvard Business School, 'Carrefour, S.A.', Harvard Business School case study no. 273-099, 1974, p. 2; *Points de Vente*, March 1972, p. 125.

unstinting support. He famously hailed the plan in 1961 as 'an ardent oblig-ation',[31] 'compensating for the disadvantages of liberty without forgoing its advantages',[32] which he considered to be as critical to the success of his quest for grandeur as the nuclear imperative or technological independence.

From 1966 onwards, however, boosted by its apparent early successes, planning became increasingly extensive and elaborate in nature, setting ever more quantitative goals. As it grew in ambition, so forecasting errors became more frequent. The fifth plan (1966–70) coincided with the waning of de Gaulle's power (despite his victory in the presidential elections of December 1965, the first of the new Republic, over Mitterrand, who took the general to an unexpected second round)[33] and the end of his two terms in office. It aspired to interweave the needs and products of all French industrial sectors, in a grandiose, excessively complex input–output model.[34] Its execution was thrown off course by the events of May 1968; perhaps one of the reasons why Pompidou distrusted economic planning. While economic growth con-tinued to rise steadily under the fifth plan, inflation spiralled. To some extent planning became the victim of its own success: the plan's growing ambition was one of the root causes, albeit not the only cause, of its decline from the mid-1970s. With the heightened competition brought by the open-ing of frontiers, and the gradual displacement of the domestic market by European and international markets, the ability of planners to direct the economy in the manner of the first three plans was increasingly curtailed.

Few topics in French economic history have aroused so much contro-versy as that of planning. The crux of the debate rests on whether planning made a major contribution to economic growth, or whether high and sus-tained growth would have occurred anyway. In short, was planning responsible for the French 'economic miracle'? Or was it rather a case of 'a cockerel who fancies his crowing makes the sun rise', to quote Jacques Rueff?[35] Commentators are divided as to whether it did or did not enhance French economic success. Carré *et al.* suggest that the plan fostered a cli-mate of optimism and business confidence, which had a positive impact on investment, boosting economic growth which was its primary objective, even if its precise effects cannot be measured or pinned down. The government accepted the expanding outlook of successive national plans, but this acceptance in turn may have had a positive effect. Productive public investment accounted for over one-third of all productive investment throughout the 'thirty glorious years', spilling over into the private sector, playing 'a strategic role as prime mover, stimulating growth in every sector of the economy'.[36] Carré *et al.* highlight the role of the first plan in particular, which gave absolute priority to the development of productive capacity in basic industries, for which it was criticised, ignoring as it did housing and social investment. But the first plan coincided with the first of three intense growth phases that occurred during the *trente glorieuses*: 1946–50, 1956–59 and 1962–66. Hough concurs with this view, while accepting the plan's obvious difficulties, particularly during the years of slow and faltering growth in the 1970s.[37] Hall argues that the planning process was fundamentally flawed in that what emerged as its dual purpose – on the one hand, the modernisation of the nation's productive apparatus in the search for efficiency and, on the other, the prevention and alleviation of social conflict – was essentially contradictory. The reorganisation of production inevitably kindled the social unrest that the plan sought to assuage.[38]

One of the most positive aspects of planning, however, was its participatory nature. The plan brought together a wide range of social actors – businessmen, government officials, union leaders – and fostered communication and the exchange of information and ideas between them, thereby helping economic actors to make informed choices. This dialogue took place, moreover, in a culture where secrecy had been commonplace. The fact that in 1967 80 per cent of top industrialists claimed to be familiar with the plan's general objectives, and 60 per cent to conform to them, speaks for itself.[39] It was also a useful stocktaking exercise for those involved, even when the plan in question was aborted and had to be redrawn. As Massé put it, 'the planning process [was] more meaningful than the plan itself'.[40] Notably, writing at the end of the 1970s, Fourastié accorded pride of place to the plan as the single most important institutional factor contributing to the economic progress of the 'thirty glorious years':

> Among the institutional factors of progress, it is necessary to cite in the first place the 'commissariat au Plan', founded and directed by Jean Monnet [...] Although a plan drawn up by leading civil servants, however enlightened and knowledgeable they may be, has always struck me as impotent to promote properly a complex, progressive economy, on the contrary, a national *plan*, a national economic *policy* for the medium term has always appeared and still appears to me to be necessary, on the one hand to direct the immense economic power of the State, too often determined by short-term considerations, and on the other hand to correct the

errors and lacunae of the market, irreplaceable though this is, but also all too often falsified by the frenzy of profit, the lure of immediate gain, psychological temptation and insufficient information.[41]

Industrial policy and technological independence

Key to de Gaulle's idea of economic sovereignty was his fear of financial and technological domination by the US. The foremost expression of the former was the hegemony of the dollar. As regards the latter, US mastery of nuclear technology, in both the military and civil spheres, smacked to de Gaulle of technological imperialism. This de Gaulle was determined to resist at all costs. The dual goals of national independence and the need to restore France's standing in the world necessitated in turn the 'nuclear imperative', whereby a strategic priority was accorded to the development of an independent nuclear arsenal.

The development of nuclear weaponry had a threefold purpose. First, it sought to 'sanctuarise' French national territory, serving as a deterrent to potential invaders. Second, it aimed to underline the absolute independence of French military choices, while agreeing to provide unspecified conventional support for Allies, especially in Europe. Finally, it aimed to enable France to play an international role, ensuring that its Allies would never again disregard it as had been the case during the Second World War.[42] On 13 February 1960 French atomic tests began in the Sahara. In 1967, a fleet of 62 Mirage IV fighter planes, built by Dassault and capable of carrying 60-kilotonne atom bombs, became France's nuclear strike force. In March of the same year, France's first nuclear submarine, appropriately named 'Le Redoutable', was launched. It came into service four years later, armed with 16 sea-to-land ballistic missiles with a firing range of 2,500–3,000 kilometres, each with a nuclear warhead of 500 kilotonnes.[43] In August 1968 at Mururoa in the Pacific, France successfully exploded the hydrogen bomb. Mururoa continued to serve as the chosen site of French nuclear tests subsequently, even as recently as September 1995 when President Chirac ordered the resumption of nuclear testing in a defiant gesture of national independence and would-be sovereignty, flouting widespread international condemnation. Chancellor Kohl of Germany was shocked not to have been consulted beforehand, prompting a cooling of relations between the two Community partners.

Technological independence was also deemed necessary for reasons of prestige. As Berstein notes, de Gaulle saw it as primordial to persuade the French people of the excellence of French technology, especially in the face of American disdain. The image of France in the US was essentially one of wine, women and song, trivialised by its association with Maurice Chevalier and Brigitte Bardot, *haute couture*, good food, perfume and champagne.

It did not enjoy a credible reputation for high-quality industrial goods. Enormous support and publicity were thus granted to technological projects of international significance.[44]

The growth of American Foreign Direct Investment (FDI) in France in the postwar period, initially welcomed and even encouraged by the French government, actually accentuated the feeling of technological dependency. While such investment brought jobs and factories, the headquarters of such firms remained at home where the bulk of profits was repatriated. When the company fell on hard times, foreign subsidiaries were often early casualties in terms of redundancies. The takeover of Simca by Chrysler and the attempted takeover of Bull by General Electric were viewed with suspicion by the Pompidou government. In 1963, the official view of foreign multinational companies operating in France was pronounced. Henceforth US multinationals would continue to be welcome, provided that they were in sectors deemed essential to economic development, and provided that they did not lead to a given sector or region becoming excessively dependent on foreign-owned enterprises.[45] Public distrust of the presence in France of US multinationals was encapsulated in 1967 by Servan-Schreiber's seminal work, *Le Défi américain.*

It was also fear of the growth of US influence in Europe that led de Gaulle to turn down, twice, in 1963 and again in 1967, British membership of the EEC. De Gaulle was concerned that the UK, through its privileged links with the US, might serve as an 'aircraft-carrier' or Trojan horse for US multinationals intent on conquering European markets. Angered by the Anglo-American Polaris agreement ('We intend to have our own national defences', he insisted), de Gaulle argued that a US-led Atlantic Community might well seek to swallow up the EEC. Mischievously, he justified his decision by asserting the need for Britain to get its house in order, economically and politically, prior to membership, rather inappropriately given Britain's then superior economic standing to France.[46] At a press conference on 14 January 1963, de Gaulle insisted that Britain neither thought nor acted like a European nation; to qualify for membership Britain must first sever its links with the Commonwealth. To add insult to injury, he broached the possibility of some kind of junior associate status for Britain. Clearly, de Gaulle was at pains to prevent Britain from potentially queering France's pitch as one of the undisputed leaders of the fledgling Community before it had been firmly established. The general's decision prevailed (Community decisions depending on unanimity, not a majority view), despite the fact that France's partners in the Community were all in favour of British membership. Following the decision of January 1963, the British Foreign Office claimed that de Gaulle had got something off his chest, implying that a future application might be treated more sympathetically. But in May 1967, de Gaulle expressed identical sentiments, giving Labour leader Harold Wilson the same brush-off as he had given his Tory predecessor, Harold Macmillan.

He now set as conditions for membership an end to the US–UK special relationship, the dismantling of the sterling area, and proof that the British had begun to think as good Europeans. On 27 November 1967, de Gaulle formally vetoed British entry into the Common Market. Britain had to await his departure and the arrival of Pompidou for the veto to be lifted.

It is perhaps true to say that the consequences of European integration, which underwent considerable, if rather haphazard progress during the 1960s, were ill thought-through in 1958, when European construction had been embraced with such alacrity by member states, reeling from the ravages of war. The liberalisation process occurring first and foremost within the EEC (in July 1968 internal tariffs were abolished and common external tariffs introduced), but also internationally through the various GATT rounds (General Agreement of Tariffs and Trade) boosted competition. However, as Community member states were increasingly exposed to foreign competition, so national governments found themselves obliged to fall back on attempts to regulate the market domestically, practising in the manner of 'Keynes at home and Smith abroad'.[47] In stark contrast to the liberal ideology which came to hold sway in the 1980s, the 1960s were imbued with an optimistic belief in the ability of political institutions to influence and guide the 'invisible hand' of the market, as France's planning process exemplifies.[48]

Industrial concentration and national champions

The French response to growing competition was largely through sectoral, industrial policy. The state promoted 'national champions', and encouraged greater industrial concentration in both the public and private sectors, on the assumption that France could not be great without great companies. Recognising that France's large firms often fell far short of the optimal size for competitiveness, profitability and efficiency,[49] the route to international competitiveness was believed to lie in the acquisition of critical mass. As Lionel Stoléru asserted in *L'Impératif industriel* (1969), only large companies could exploit and develop new technologies. The takeover of medium-sized firms by larger companies was openly encouraged by government policy, especially during the period of the fourth and fifth plans, which sought to restructure French manufacturing industry through concentration.[50] Tax incentives for investment, public procurement (the tendency of public bodies to purchase mainly from their own national companies, thus limiting competition), and half-disguised measures of external protection were employed in the drive to build up companies that could take on 'the American challenge'. Between 1962 to 1970 there was a proportionate increase in the number of firms with 1,000 or more employees, while the proportion of firms with 10 or less employees fell by about 20 per cent. Plant size similarly increased from 1962 to 1968, with the average employee base of plants employing 50 workers or more rising from 215 to 250.

Concentration occurred in most industries, but especially in machinery, transport equipment and intermediate products.[51] The majority of the French ruling elite accepted the logic of industrial concentration whether in business, politics or administration. The model in mind was that of the US, which paradoxically in seeking to resist France sought to emulate. Only very large firms had the resources needed to compete internationally. Economies of scale attached not only to production but also to research and development, marketing and other business functions. Economies of scope, from operating in related areas of business, likewise were largely the preserve of rich and powerful enterprises. Competitive markets demanded competitive prices allied to high quality in design, functionality and manufacture. If French firms were to equal American or German firms in their chosen markets, then they must be major producers with low unit costs and capable of winning significant market share. These were the firms that had the resources to invest on a large scale, to recreate themselves, to become ever more sophisticated in their products and technologies. The precise situation was bound to differ from industry to industry, but in France in the mid-1960s and early 1970s there was a remarkable consensus about the way forward for business. The state lent direction through building a united strategic front and by providing resources and support when it had direct control of the situation.

In 1966 state aid for the struggling steel industry became conditional upon the industry's restructuring around three large concerns, namely Creusot-Loire, Denain-Nord-Est-Longwy and Wendel-Sidélor. Similarly, state funding for research in nascent hi-tech industries was conditional on firms agreeing to state-inspired mergers. In this way, CII (Compagnie Internationale pour l'Informatique) came into being in 1967, and SNIAS was created from amalgamated state-owned aviation companies. The total number of mergers increased from 32 per year in the period 1950–58 to 74 per year in the years 1969–75. Between 1966 and 1972 the number of large mergers peaked at an annual mean of 136, embracing most sectors of the economy. The total annual value of mergers in each of the years 1966–69 was more than double the total value of merger operations during the period 1950–58.[52]

The petrochemicals giant Elf-ERAP (Entreprise de Recherches et d'Activités Pétrolières) was created by merger in December 1965. It united in one state-owned company the Bureau de Recherches de Pétrole (BRP), established in 1945 by de Gaulle to encourage oil and gas exploration in France and its colonies 'in the exclusive interest of the nation',[53] and the Régie Autonome de Pétroles (Rap), created in 1940, retaining as its most dynamic subsidiary the SNEA (Société Nationale Elf Aquitaine). In chemicals, a government commission recommended industry restructuring on account of perceived institutional instability. The outcome was the creation of Péchiney-Ugine-Kuhlmann and Rhône-Poulenc in heavy, agricultural chemicals, petrochemicals and basic health products. The history of

Rhône-Poulenc has been described as a 'history of mergers', stretching back to its origins in the merger of Poulenc Frères and the Usines du Rhône in 1928.[54] Through a series of acquisitions (notably that of a majority stake in two research facilities, the Laboratoire Roger Bellon and the Institut Merieux, and the takeover of two small chemical companies, Progil and Péchiney Saint-Gobain), by 1969 Rhône-Poulenc had become France's largest company. The spread of merger fever reflected a myriad of convergent conversations in French boardrooms. In 1970, Saint-Gobain merged with Pont-à-Mousson, a world leader in cast-iron pipes, justified on the basis of technological, product and market synergies. In the event, at Saint-Gobain and elsewhere, much-lauded prospective synergies proved impossible to realise in practice. In the 1970s Saint-Gobain shed its chemical and petroleum investments, as well as its iron and steel interests legated by Pont-à-Mousson. The fact of negative outcomes, however, was not enough to stop the merger roller-coaster. In car manufacture the positions of Peugeot and Citroën were strengthened, as were those of Thomson-Brandt and Compagnie Générale d'Electricité (CGE) in electrical equipment. In banking, the state-owned BNP was created, the result of the merger between the Banque Nationale pour le commerce et l'industrie (BNCI) and the Comptoir d'escompte de Paris.[55] The Crédit Agricole grew to be one of France's – and indeed of the world's – most powerful banks, cash-rich from the accumulated deposits of farmers and *petits paysans*, in whom the habit of 'saving up for the morrow' was deeply ingrained.

In investment banking Suez and Paribas, both private banks, established rival financial empires, held together by extended families of interlocking directorates and elaborate networks of 'crossed shareholdings'.[56] The development of financial relationships among firms was another form of concentration favoured by the French since it did not require a dynamic stock market, which to some extent it replaced, immobilising large proportions of shares. Financial relationships between firms also compensated to a degree for lack of firm-size and the absence of company reserves, the muscle of corporate allies replacing the backing of companies' own reserves. Financial links proliferated in the 1960s, although Denuc observed the trend as early as 1939, documenting that the accounts of companies quoted on the Paris Bourse in 1911 and 1936 displayed remarkable growth under 'portfolio investment and stockholding' items. Stockholding by leading French companies declined during and immediately after the Second World War, but increased from 1957 and 1966, in the course of which stockholding in 400 quoted French companies rose from 17 to 27 per cent of total capital employed.[57] Suez and Paribas, the two 'godfathers' of French capitalism, went on to dominate the French corporate landscape throughout the 1970s. Cross-shareholdings and cross-directorships came to form the bedrock of French capitalism for more than three decades, giving rise to a brand of capitalism caricatured as 'capitalism without capital', where blocks of shares were exchanged without any money actually changing hands. It was not until the mid-1990s that these began to unravel in response to the growing pressures of globalisation, coupled with a call for changes in corporate governance practices on the part of employers' federations, international shareholders and the state (see Chapter 7).

Linked to the promotion of national champions were the 'grands projets', examples of hi-tech Colbertism founded in offensive protectionism and the quest for national prestige, in transport, information technology (IT) and infrastructure. They included Concorde, a joint Franco-British project for a supersonic airliner, built at Toulouse, completed in December 1967; the new airport at Roissy outside Paris to complement Orly, now overstretched, appropriately named 'Charles de Gaulle'; the shipliner Le France; the Rhine-Rhône Canal; and the French colour television system SECAM. Added to these were plans for high-speed railways, a fleet of nuclear submarines and the manufacture of enriched uranium. The 'plan Calcul' in IT aimed to provide France with its own computer industry following the refusal by the US in 1963 to sell France the control systems needed for its nuclear strike force. Some of these were costly multibillion-franc projects, yielding low returns and quickly branded 'white elephants'. Concorde, for example, recovered but a fraction of the development costs invested by the French and British governments and took many years to prove its commercial viability even when these had been written off as irrecoverable.

The 'grands projets', irrespective of financial viability, formed an integral part of a comprehensive system of state support for French industry. At one end of the spectrum was support for high-technology industries of the future for which state support was justified on an infant-industry basis. In such cases, the argument made was that France would be forever excluded from these industries unless the state spent large sums of money up front to develop the required organisational capabilities. Investment was largely an act of faith, made on a strategic rather than purely commercial basis, part and parcel of the state's heroic industrial patriotism.[58] In economic terms, it might be argued that the state was intervening in order to correct market failure; certainly an argument favoured by the administrative elite.[59] At the other end of the spectrum, state support for sunset industries such as steel, textiles and shipbuilding, the so-called 'lame ducks', was short-term and defensive and justified mainly on social grounds. Many of these *canards boîteux* came to depend for survival on constant government subsidy in dwindling markets subject to fierce international competition. They came to be viewed by many as bottomless pits engulfing billions of francs of public subsidy.[60]

In conjunction with these industrial policy measures were spatial policies, conceived in the mid-1950s to promote industrial investment in 'problem regions' such as Nord-Pas-de-Calais, Lorraine and St Etienne. These were expanded in 1964 following the creation in 1963 of DATAR (Délégation à l'aménagement du territoire et à l'action régionale) to embrace a much wider range of areas, including much of the west and south west, the Massif Central and northeastern France. Eight provincial cities were designated as counterweights to Paris (*métropoles d'équilibres*) in an effort to address questions of regional inequality, attract industrial investment to the provinces and thus end Parisian hegemony.

Concentration in services

The doctrine of 'big is beautiful' embraced services too. The term 'services' includes an ever-expanding range of non-materially-based activities, as France moved headlong in the postwar period from being a primarily industrially and agriculturally based economy to one increasingly dominated by the service sector. The Gaullist years witnessed a clear and accelerated decline in the proportion of small establishments, although medium-sized and larger establishments remained fairly stable as a proportion.[61]

Concentration was especially pronounced in distribution. The caricature of France as a nation of small shopkeepers is woefully obsolete, yet lingers occasionally in international perceptions. In 1960 retail distribution was a highly fragmented activity, with small shopkeepers accounting for almost all sales in food and non-food products, while product lines in individual stores were relatively narrow. Shopping for food was on a daily basis, with visits to four different shops required to buy bread, meat, vegetables and dairy produce.[62]

The beginning of the Fifth Republic, however, coincided with the decline of small corner shops as supermarkets and hypermarkets, based on the postwar American model,[63] came into being. In 1960 Carrefour opened its first supermarket in Annécy in the south of France. At 650 m^2 in size, it served to test shoppers' reaction to a one-stop, self-service shop selling goods at discounted prices. The first hypermarket, opened on 15 June 1963 by Carrefour at Sainte-Geneviève-des-Bois south of Paris, five years after the appearance of the first supermarket in France, occupied 2,500 m^2. These relatively modest dimensions rapidly gave way to gigantism: the hypermarket established by Carrefour at Porter-sur-Garonne covering a massive 24,000 m^2.[64]

The success of 'les grandes surfaces', which mushroomed in the 1960s on the perimeter of large towns and cities where parking was available, derived from convenience and price. They benefited from the development of 'Fordist' mass production techniques, rising car ownership, urban growth and the tendency for more women to go out to work, boosting household income, and favouring a weekly shop under one roof. The philosophy of these large stores was to achieve a rapid turnaround in stock by selling all kinds of goods on one site at prices that small shopkeepers could not match. In the 1970s they expanded their non-food goods, in which they often achieved higher profit margins. The success of the *grandes surfaces* spawned other hypermarket giants, both in the same sector (e.g. Euromarché, Hautchamp) and in other specialised sectors, such as DIY (Castorama), furniture (Conforama), electrical goods (Darty), sports clothing (Sparty), books, records and photography (FNAC, Fédération nationale d'achats de cadres). By 1970, approximately 250,000 m^2 of new hypermarket space was being added each year. Business analysts predicted that a total domestic hypermarket selling area of 2.2 million m^2 was required to reach market saturation, almost half of which had been achieved by June 1972.[65]

The *grandes surfaces* proliferated in the richer half of France – in the Paris basin, the North, Lorraine, the Rhône-Alpes, and in the Midi along the Mediterranean coast – where their impact on the livelihood of small shopkeepers, especially the smallest shops termed 'Petits Libres Services' (PLS), was dramatic. While in 1962 small and medium-sized shops (*le petit et moyen commerce*) accounted for some 63 per cent of retail sales, by 1970 this had fallen to 55.9 per cent. Meanwhile the share of sales attracted by larger shops (*le grand commerce*) grew from 14 per cent to 21.1 per cent over the same period (see Table 3.4). Almost 80,000 or 40 per cent of the 203,600 small retail stores operating in 1961 had closed their doors by 1971 (see Table 3.5).[66] As shoppers left the town centre for the periphery, eroding the incomes of small storeowners and distributors, shopkeeper unrest grew. Small shopkeepers constituted a significant political force in France. Demonstrations were organised at the opening of new hypermarkets. These were similar to the current unrest prompted by globalisation, as individuals target the trappings and symbols – McDonalds restaurants, genetically modified crops, G8 summits – of global trends beyond their control. May 1970 saw the destruction of Carrefour's largest store by fire: arson was suspected. Shopkeeper protest prompted the 1973 Royer law (la loi d'orientation du commerce et de l'artisanat), designed to ensure that 'the disorderly growth of new forces in distribution did not crush small enterprise'.[67] Under the new law, departmental committees of urban commerce, Commissions départementales d'urbanisme commercial (CDUC), were set up. These were invested with the authority to grant or refuse any proposal for a *grande surface* that exceeded a threshold of 1,000 m^2 in communes of less than 40,000 inhabitants, and one of 1,500 m^2 in larger townships. Legislation was passed to tax retail outlets in order to furnish pensions for shopkeepers forced to close their businesses, to be paid by all retail merchants, and especially by operators of *grandes surfaces* established after 1962. This resulted in an estimated bill of FF3 million for Carrefour alone.[68] While the Royer law at first slowed the growth of new hypermarkets, in the late 1980s their seemingly relentless development proceeded apace. By 1997 there were 1,114 hypermarkets nationally, of which 501 exceeded 5,000 m^2, and 7,300 supermarkets. Today France has more hypermarkets than her main European partners: 1.5 hypermarkets per 100,000 inhabitants, as against 1.3 in Germany and 0.2 in Italy.

Modernisation in agriculture

State-backed concentration and a concomitant drive towards modernisation and efficiency took place also in agriculture, complemented by the actions of farmers themselves. The agricultural revolution that took place in some Western countries as they industrialised occurred relatively late in France. Structural change and improved productivity took place very gradually during the nineteenth and first half of the twentieth century. There were numerous pockets of technical excellence and commercial specialisation, but it is only during the past fifty or so years that the full productive potential of French agriculture has been unlocked. Agricultural machinery was one of the six high-priority sectors specified in the 1946 Monnet Plan, anticipating the investment of FF10 billion.[69] Yields rose dramatically following the Second World War, albeit unevenly, as farming became ever more intensive through the use of fertilisers and pesticides. During this time the number of farms and holdings declined steadily, as did the number of people working the land (see Tables 3.6 and 3.7) – a trend that still continues early in the twenty-first century.

One of the paradoxes of French agricultural modernisation is that its very success undermines its demographic base, resulting in rural exodus (see Chapter 6). A poignant account at grassroots level of the social

Table 3.6   Evolution of working population in three sectors, 1946–68 (as percentage)

Year	1946	1954	1962	1968
Agriculture	36.46	27.69	20.60	15.62
Industry	29.26	36.37	39.07	40.21
Tertiary sector	34.28	35.94	40.33	44.17

Adapted from Parodi, M., *L'Economie et la société française de 1945 à 1970*, p. 95.

Table 3.7   Evolution of working population in agriculture, 1954–90

Year	1954	1962	1968	1975	1982	1990
Working population (Agricult.) (in 000)	5,135	3,841	3,048	2,024	1,752	1,264
As % of total working population	26.8	20.0	14.9	9.3	7.5	5.0

Adapted from Parodi, M. *et al.*, *L'Economie et la société françaises au second XXe siècle*, vol. 2, *Les Mutations sectorielles*, p. 62.

transformation accompanying postwar modernisation in the South West is provided by Amann in his book *The Corncribs of Buzet*. The celebrated films *Jean de Florette* and *Manon des Sources* likewise provide insights into changing village life as the peasant economy collided with the galloping progress of the postwar world with which it was incompatible. Peasants who refused to change their ways were doomed literally to disappear, since young farmers who rejected modernisation could find no marriage partners. The initial phase of modernisation was often a 'bribe' by the older to the younger generation to persuade it to stay on the farm by making a gesture in the direction of its demands.[70]

It is not proposed at this juncture to explore the manifold complexities of French agriculture. Nor is it proposed to document its relative postwar decline in terms of its contribution to GDP and diminishing population in the face of spectacular productivity increases and, from 1979, considerable export success.[71] What does concern us here is the longstanding fragmentation of French agriculture, symptomatic of inefficiency, low productivity, dependence on state subsidy, and conspiring in the nineteenth and early twentieth centuries to prevent France from achieving the same degree of progress in agriculture as in Britain and elsewhere in Northern Europe. As Tables 3.8 and 3.9 illustrate, holdings of between one and 5 hectares in size were preponderant from 1892 to 1955 inclusive, when they represented a tiny 5 per cent of the total agricultural arable area. They were located especially in the poorer south and west, whose inefficient smallholdings, often operating at subsistence or near-subsistence level, contrasted starkly with the large wheat and cattle farms of the Northeast plains and the Paris basin. This gave rise to the term, 'les deux agricultures', implying the existence of

Table 3.8 Size distribution of agricultural holdings above one hectare, 1892–1967 (in 000s)

Area* (ha.)	1892**	1929	1955	1963	1967
1–5	1,829	1,146	649	454	375
5–10	788	718	477	364	308
10–20	430	593	536	485	413
20–50	335	380	377	394	372
50–100	52	82	75	85	85
100+	33	32	20	23	24
Total	3,467	2,951	2,134	1,805	1,577

* Includes woods in 1892 and 1929, and 'arable agricultural area', excluding woodland, thereafter.
** Excludes Alsace-Lorraine, then part of Germany.

Source: Carré, J.-J., Dubois, P. and Malinvaud, *French Economic Growth*, translated by J.P. Hatfield, Stanford and London, Stanford University Press and Oxford University Press, 1976, p. 171.

Table 3.9   Holdings as proportion of agricultural area, 1955–67 (as percentage)

Area (ha.)	1955	1963	1967
1–5	5	4	3
5–10	11	8	7
10–20	23	22	20
20–50	35	37	38
50–100	16	17	19
100+	10	12	13
Total	100	100	100

Source: Carré et al., *French Economic Growth*, p. 171.

two distinct agricultural systems. Fragmentation has been exacerbated by French inheritance law, whereby farms were not legated intact to the eldest son or daughter, following the practice of primogeniture, but rather, according to the Napoleonic Code, were divided up equally among surviving offspring. While this mandatory equal division among siblings has been amended to favour the son or daughter who stayed on the farm, division nevertheless remained the norm. This made for smallholdings that were non-viable due to their size and often to their shape, such that a hencoop belonging to one family member might stand in the middle of a field belonging to another.

The Pisani Law of 1960 did much to correct this fragmentation, consolidating land and encouraging the processes of modernisation and mechanisation. The measures introduced by Edgar Pisani as Minister of Agriculture were multifaceted, but their overall goal was to promote land consolidation or *remembrement*.[72] A new pension fund was established to encourage the retirement of older farmers at 65 through the IVD or *indemnité viagère de départ*, in order that he might hand over his farm to his heir and thus reduce the average age of those working the land. Often, though, he had no successor, because his children, if he had any, were not willing to eke out a living on the farm working all hours when they could earn far more working shorter hours in the town. In addition, subsidised, low-interest, start-up loans, accompanied by a modest gift of capital from the state, were to be provided by the Crédit Agricole to enable young farmers to purchase land. Absentee landlords, who brought no investment to the countryside, were henceforth to be dealt with more severely. Most importantly, the Pisani Law set up an agency to buy up land, leading to the establishment of regional Sociétés d'Aménagement et d'Etablissement Rural (SAFER). Their mission was to buy land, improve it, and sell it on in larger, consolidated parcels to a single owner, often to younger farmers with more agronomic training.

Concentration was marked between 1955 and 1967 when the number of farms of fewer than 20 hectares declined while holdings of 50 hectares or more increased (see Tables 3.8 and 3.9). By 1967 farms of 20 hectares or more accounted for 70 per cent of the total, compared to 61 per cent in 1955, while those of 20 hectares or less represented 30 per cent in 1967, as against 39 per cent in 1955. The total number of holdings of one hectare or less decreased from 3,467,000 to 1,577,000 over the period 1892–1967 as land was consolidated, but the rate of change underwent a clear acceleration from 1955. The figures testify to an annual rate of change of 0.5 per cent during the period 1892–1929, of 1.0 per cent during the period 1929–55, followed by 1.9 per cent during the twelve years 1955–67.[73]

As in manufacturing industry, the general aim of the state was to expand the scale and scope of productive operations. Young farmers were encouraged by tax and interest rates to form cooperative partnerships, Groupements agricole d'économie en commune (GAEC), with siblings or parents. The cooperative purchase and use of farm equipment through Coopératives d'utilisation de matériel agricole (CUMA) was likewise encouraged by the granting of tax concessions. If a farmer combined forces with at least two of his neighbours to build, say, a joint irrigation pond, the government and departmental administration would pay almost half.[74] Gradually the full potential of the cooperative movement came to be recognised as farmers combined their resources for marketing and purchasing. Some went further by integrating their activities vertically into processing and distribution. To this end a number of industrial companies and cooperatives were formed to organise large-scale processing or product distribution, requiring that farmers sign production contracts for an agreed amount of poultry, fruit etc., and then requiring that they adopt the most up-to-date techniques.[75]

Concentration accompanied by increased mechanisation and intensive farming methods led to a huge rise in agricultural productivity. From 1952 to 1972, agricultural production increased by an average of 2.5 per cent annually, amounting to a 64 per cent increase over twenty years. The rate of increase rose to 2.7 per cent per year between 1959 and 1969. Cereal production grew by 7 per cent per annum from 1950 to 1970, vegetable and fruit production by 2 per cent, while wine production remained static. Much of this was due to the use of fertilisers to boost yields, up 7.3 per cent per year. In the 1950s extensive maize cultivation resulted from the adoption of hybrid maize while in the 1960s the artificial insemination of livestock became the norm. The number of tractors, meanwhile, increased exponentially from 30,000 in 1938 to 150,000 in 1950 and 1,300,000 in 1970, while productive fixed capital per head grew at an astonishing annual rate of 8.3 per cent.[76]

Land consolidation certainly made life easier for farmers – through the convenience of working less dispersed fields, perhaps freed from encroaching hedges or grouped around the farmstead. Amann nevertheless disputes the view that *remembrement* was the core experience of modernisation. For him it was largely a symbolic gesture whereby one generation acceded in some way to the demands of the next in the hope that it would entice them to stay on the land. However, such was the success of the SAFER movement that by 1978 as many as 106,000 farms had increased in size, equal to approximately 15 million acres of land, 10 per cent of the land which had been sold during the intervening years. By 1978 the SAFER were involved in more than a quarter (26 per cent) of all land sales. Their influence became less predominant, however, with the introduction of guaranteed product prices under the CAP, boosting farm incomes and providing farmers with greater security.[77]

Carré *et al.* present two alternative hypotheses to explain the acceleration of change in French agriculture. According to the first hypothesis, mechanisation and technical progress liberated a growing proportion of farm workers for non-agricultural employment. The second hypothesis postulates that the growth of production in other sectors of the economy increased the demand for labour, making it easier for younger farmers to find employment elsewhere, while at the same time reducing hidden underemployment in farming. Where these two views meet is in the certainty that the rise in farming incomes over the 'thirty glorious years', such that they broadly kept pace with wages elsewhere in the economy, would not have been possible without large-scale migration to the towns. Gross financial returns in agriculture grew from FF14.8 billion in 1954 to FF45.6 billion in 1972. This rise, though, was less than the growth in production that occurred in other sectors and insufficient to sustain the agricultural population of the early postwar years at income levels comparable to the remainder of the population.[78]

In the above examples of concentration in the primary, secondary and tertiary sectors, as in the case of planning, it is clearly problematic to pin down the precise degree to which the state actually contributed to the process. To what extent was concentration the result of an autonomous *prise de conscience* on the part of economic actors and decision-makers, aware of technological and market opportunities and determined to take advantage of these? Certainly individual companies played a vital role in the processes of reconstruction and modernisation. In many cases, the state exerted little direct influence on merger decisions, except where struggling companies required an injection of public funds to keep them afloat. State aid to ailing industrial sectors, often occurring as part of an international shakeout, as in the cases of steel or shipbuilding, may have actually postponed or impeded rationalisation. One top manager of the merged Saint-Gobain-Pont-à-Mousson reported that the state had played no part in the merger, Pompidou having been informed after the deal was struck, merely out of politeness.[79]

Industrial concentration was an international phenomenon after 1945 and was by no means unique to France. This said, down to the 1960s France had not progressed as far down the road of industrial reorganisation and rationalisation as other West European countries. In 1962, large companies in France (employing more than 1,000 employees) accounted for only 21 per cent of all employees in industry, as against 33 per cent in

Germany, 32 per cent in the US, 31 per cent in the Netherlands and 27 per cent in Belgium.[80] Large French companies remained significantly smaller than British large companies or German large companies. This was true as late as the year 2000 when relative small size was cited as a major reason for numerous high-profile international mergers involving French companies.[81] Moreover, while the state sought to produce large national champions endowed with the 'critical mass' deemed to be conducive to international success, Carré *et al.* find the tendency to concentration to be more pronounced in medium-sized firms, less susceptible to state influence.[82] They deduce that the theory that the rapid development of modern capitalism toward highly monopolistic forms played a major part in French economic growth is non-proven – with the exception of agriculture, where expansion did make a big difference, accompanied by a concomitant attitudinal and technical transformation.[83] Where the state did influence the situation, however, was in promoting an investment climate for growth, inspiring a confidence that it would continue to pursue and finance its objectives, as specified in successive plans, thereby creating opportunities to which businesses, or small farmers for that matter, could respond. As Vinen observes:

> The civil servant who laid down objectives for government plans, the industrialist who decided to build a new factory, the peasant who decided to buy a new tractor and the housewife who decided to buy a new washing machine may have had little in common, but they did all share a belief that the French economy was growing and that growth would make their ambitious projects feasible. If the *trente glorieuses* were a myth then it was one that came to influence reality.[84]

In this way the state came to propagate something of a self-fulfilling prophecy, fostering a climate in which business confidence – intangible but potent – could flourish, in turn stimulating economic growth and structural change.

The Franco-German relationship and primacy in Europe

De Gaulle cites in his memoirs a handwritten memorandum sent to him in 1945 by Himmler, clutching at straws in the final days before German capitulation:

> Agreed! You have won. Considering where you started from, one bows low indeed to you, General de Gaulle .... But now what will you do? Rely on the Americans and the British? They will treat you as a satellite, and you will lose all the honour you have won. Ally yourself with the Soviets? They will restore France to their own pattern and liquidate

you ... . Actually the only road that can lead your people to greatness and to independence is that of an entente with defeated Germany. Proclaim it at once!

No reply was sent to the author, but as de Gaulle wryly observes, beneath its flattery, anguish and treachery the note concealed more than a grain of truth.[85] After the war, de Gaulle was quick to grasp that Germany's annihilation, Europe's laceration and Anglo-American friction offered France a unique opportunity. The route to French leadership in Europe lay in binding vanquished Germany into a political, economic and strategic Western European bloc that might function collectively as a world power, if not comparable to the US or the USSR then at least able to act as arbiter between them.[86] In short, a relationship with Germany might serve as a means of asserting French primacy in Europe, a source of international standing, prestige and mutual prosperity.

The precondition for such an alliance was reconciliation with Germany. In May 1945, at a troop inspection in Stuttgart and Konstanz following Germany's surrender, instead of glorying in vengeance de Gaulle observed the possibilities of a new understanding between the two enemies. As he clarifies in his memoirs, 'amid the ruins, mourning and humiliation that had submerged Germany in her turn, I felt my sense of distrust and severity fade within me. I even glimpsed possibilities of an understanding that the past had never offered; moreover, it seemed to me that the same feeling was spreading amongst our soldiers.'[87] De Gaulle displayed considerable vision in recognising at such an early stage that geopolitical factors favoured a Franco-German entente. These factors included possession of a common border and the location of the Rhine as central artery. But of greater importance was the postwar settlement that had created two superpower blocs, leaving Europe divided with Germany as a bulwark to the West. The division of Germany itself and its capital Berlin, with Soviet troops ever present on the eastern borders of the new Federal Republic (FRG), meant that Germany desperately needed dialogue with its neighbour in the West, albeit its former adversary now turned ally.

The process of reconciliation began immediately, assisted from 1950 by Robert Schuman and Jean Monnet, both of whom favoured *rapprochement*. While the Paris–Bonn axis in its early years has been criticised as 'stillborn'[88] and as disappointing the hopes of grandeur invested in it by de Gaulle, nevertheless from its earliest stages reconciliation transcended mere rhetoric. It was expressed in deeds and acts, not only in town-twinning but also in integrated education – in the Franco-German University of Mainz, in the schools, *lycées* and study centres opened in the aftermath of war. While the goods with which these projects are concerned are the intangible ones of 'human infrastructure', nevertheless they have the power to reach the hearts and minds of participants in a direct and immediate way rarely achieved by political argument.[89] Youth exchanges were set up, leading to the official opening of the Franco-German Youth Office in July 1963.

Rapprochement was cemented by a genuine personal friendship between Chancellor Adenauer and President de Gaulle, laying the basis for future political entente. On 23 January 1963 they signed the Elysée Treaty of Cooperation in Paris, formally concluding centuries of conflict. There had been no fewer than 23 wars between the two countries since the days of the Hapsburg ruler Charles V (1500–58), emperor of the Holy Roman Empire, and François I of France (1494–1547). On 8 May 1963 the Bundestag ratified the Elysée friendship treaty. It did not do so, however, in the spirit that its two signatories would have wished, appending a statement to the effect that the document existed within the framework of West Germany's major commitments. These included NATO, the Alliance, European unification following the creation of the European Communities, and the inclusion of the UK within these. Given the global balance of power, and the dependency of the FRG on the US within that power structure, *Realpolitik* determined that the 'special' nature of the Franco-German relationship be put in context. When compared to John F. Kennedy's declaration five months later, in June 1963, 'Ich bin ein Berliner', effectively guaranteeing American defence of West Berlin in the event of a Soviet threat, the Elysée Treaty appeared little more than window-dressing. As Berstein observes, 'when asked to choose between the United States and an autonomous Europe dominated by France, Germany had no hesitation in opting for the former'.[90]

Nevertheless, over the decades the relationship between France and Germany has deepened and widened, especially during the Kohl–Mitterrand era. The last forty years have been characterised by reconciliation, growing *rapprochement*, genuine friendship and an ever-closer cooperation. Despite its complexities, ups and downs, occasional misunderstandings and periods of cooling off, over the years Franco-German cooperation has expanded to include a multitude of activities.[91] Beyond politics, the partnership has come to embrace the economy, finance, monetary policy, industry, R&D, science, aeronautics, space, foreign affairs, security and defence, social policy, immigration policy, the recycling of nuclear waste, agriculture, media, culture, youth exchange, education, and even espionage.[92]

Cemented by regular biannual summits between heads of state and governments,[93] the Franco-German relationship came to be perceived in the 1980s as Europe's 'engine' and driving force. Co-leadership of the Community by France and Germany brought to fruition de Gaulle's dream of primacy in Europe through reconciliation with the hereditary enemy. It has guaranteed the safety of France from German aggression, henceforth kept at bay, while simultaneously promoting French grandeur, both in terms of prosperity and an enhanced European and international role. When, on the other hand, the European integration process has ceased to move forward, the Franco-German relationship has functioned alternatively as an 'ersatz' to that process, taking a step forward *à deux* which for whatever reason could not be taken by six, nine, ten, twelve or fifteen. It remains to be seen, of course, to what extent the relationship can continue to function as a loco-motive of European integration in an enlarged EU of 27 member states.

Jean-Louis Bourlanges, a member of the European Parliament, has notably likened the Franco-German relationship to a Vespa motorbike, inadequately powered to pull the European train.[94] Yet too much engine power might prove counterproductive in that it would underline Franco-German hegemony in a way that might jeopardise co-leadership, imply-ing the existence of a Franco-German 'directorate'. This was something Mitterrand and Kohl, both great defenders of the Franco-German relation-ship, were at pains to deny – or to disguise, as Jacques Attali, Mitterrand's erstwhile special adviser, reports:

Mitterrand: We must avoid saying that we are jointly running Europe.
Kohl: You're right. If we are suspected of that, then that's the finish.
Mitterrand: We have a dominant role, but we must never impose anything, we must be modest.[95]

Kohl and Mitterrand clearly intuited that the acceptance of their often far-reaching joint proposals for European integration by other member states depended critically on the *appearance*, as opposed to the reality, of disinter-estedness, as posited by Bourdieu (see Introduction). The full extent to which French ideas with German backing have come to dominate EU policy is epitomised by the realisation of EMU (Economic and Monetary Union). Achieved through the combined efforts of Jacques Delors, Mitterrand and Kohl, together with Pierre Bérégovoy, Jean-Claude Tricot and Elisabeth Guigou, this project culminated in the launch of the euro in 1999.[96] At the heart of the Franco-German relationship are the myriad relationships between the technocratic and political elites that comprise numerous joint commissions of civil servants and leading experts, respective ministries and national representations to the Community. The opaque, abstruse nature of the EMU negotiations combined with the mastery of technical detail required implied an in-built technocratic advantage in this critical area, arguably enhancing the power of the technocratic elites involved.[97] The subsequent creation in 1998 of the European Central Bank has further extended the role and power of technocrats in the EU, sparking a fierce battle for control of the ECB by the French, who sought to impose Jean-Claude Trichet, former head of the Banque of France, as its head. France's inability to control ECB bankers, in particular to influence their decisions on interest rates, has prompted French calls for 'gouvernement économique' of the EU to complement the ECB.

Such has been the chemistry of Franco-German relations that when fac-ing difficult issues, 'bilateral empathy' often frames the expectations of other participants at EU negotiations, including those of the Commission, prompting third parties to fall into line. At the same time, the democratic deficit at the heart of the Community has given French and German negotiators greater room for manoeuvre, leaving the way clear for deals and side-deals to dominate. In this way it has tended to encourage 'French and German negotiators to prepare bilaterally the side-deals which would permit a broader compromise to emerge'.[98] At times, though, it has left third parties with the distinct impression of a *fait accompli*, a Franco-German 'stitch-up', which after the event they are powerless to undo (see Chapter 7).

Grandeur through Europe

Before the launch of the Common Market in 1958, France's economy was focused on the domestic market and shielded from external competition by a battery of quota restrictions and high tariffs. Foreign trade was geared towards French colonies and former protectorates. As the restrictions on the free movement of goods and services between Community member states were gradually removed, however, there was a real sense in which 'what concerned France also concerned Europe, and vice versa'.[99] It has been said that the French of the Fifth Republic live not only under the constitution devised by de Gaulle; they also live under the economic system created by Jean Monnet. Architect of the first plan, Monnet is also hailed as the 'father' of the Common Market and the ECSC that preceded it. His enduring economic legacy through the EU is every bit as significant and far-reaching as the political legacy of Charles de Gaulle through the Fifth Republic.

What concerned de Gaulle, however, was not primarily economics but rather the creation of a political Europe. The Europe he wished to construct was essentially a 'Europe of nations' ('l'Europe des patries'), not one which would eventually come to challenge, supersede or absorb the nation-state. For de Gaulle, the nation-state was sovereign, and its relations with other nations should be dictated solely by self-interest. (Somewhat ironically, it might be argued, it has fallen to the British not the French to promote the vision of Europe as a looser, wider union in which the nation-state retains its essential integrity and sovereignty.) Yet despite his aspirations to French grandeur, in a world dominated increasingly by two superpowers, de Gaulle could not ignore the fact that France was now a second-rank, medium-sized power. Thus the Community was intended primarily as a vehicle to amplify the voice of France in world politics, and to serve French interests.

In the event, however, it was the so-called 'low politics' of economic affairs that quickly came to dominate the newly created EEC. As French markets became more open to international competition, external rather than internal conditions increasingly set the parameters of French economic policy. The French government became progressively less interventionist and more liberal in orientation. This was matched at the corporate level, as companies became more astute at marketing, at stimulating demand and creating fresh markets. At an earlier stage in the development process, when domestic demand exceeded supply, marketing had been a much less pivotal capability. The execution of the Pinay–Rueff plan, critical to France's preparations for entry into the Community, proved so successful that France was able to participate in the first lowering of tariffs on 1 January 1959, and even requested that the process be accelerated. In fact, the customs union came into being ten months earlier than anticipated in the Rome Treaty, on 1 July 1968.

It was in exchange for this goodwill in lowering tariffs that France demanded the creation of a Common Agricultural Policy, which came into being in the 1960s.[100] Over the years the CAP has dominated the relationship between France and the Community in many respects (see Chapter 6). It was conceived under de Gaulle as a means of protecting the small farmers of France's south and west. Its overriding aim was to shift the burden of agricultural subsidies for farmers – who remained a powerful political force despite their dwindling population – from French to European taxpayers.[101] In this end it succeeded very well: from the outset France received as much as 36 per cent of agricultural subsidies while contributing only 26 per cent of the costs.[102] While understandably the Community does not wish to be perceived in terms of winners and losers, nevertheless the distribution of agricultural subsidies has determined which member states gain financially from membership and which lose out. In the 1970s the CAP devoured as much as three-quarters of the Community budget. By 1980, this had fallen slightly to two-thirds of the budget. By 1999 the CAP's share of the EU budget was 42 per cent, costing approximately E40 billion annually. This is a massive budgetary share allocated to a single sector of the European economy, which accounts for less than 5 per cent of the current EU population.[103] Nor is agriculture a sector of the future, but is essentially one of the past in which self-sufficiency, while a legitimate concern of the postwar period when food rationing applied, was achieved in full by the mid-1970s. It should be noted, moreover, that at no point did the decline in budgetary share represent a decline in real terms for agricultural support. On the contrary, the overall size of the 'cake' continued to increase following the accession of new, generally wealthy member states (with the exception of Greece in 1981 and the Iberian nations in 1986).

The Treaty of Rome outlined five general targets for agricultural policy, namely: to increase agricultural productivity; to guarantee a good living standard for farmers; to stabilise markets; to ensure security for suppliers; and to ensure reasonable prices for consumers. The CAP's three guiding principles – unity of markets, financial solidarity and Community preference – have meant that it has flown in the face of growing international competition and the opening of markets through successive GATT rounds. Community organisation of the agricultural market was based on the abolition of quantitative obstacles towards inter-Community trade, a uniform pricing system, equal guarantees to all EC producers, the adoption of a common position to Third World countries, and common management of markets and budget.[104] As such it was bound to benefit those member states with large farming populations, irrespective of their overall economic status. France became an immediate primary beneficiary of the CAP due to the sheer size of its farming sector. It was not until 1982 that France became an overall net contributor, due partly to the entry of poorer countries into the EC. Its net contribution of E0.8 billion in 1999, though, remains small, particularly when compared to the sizeable net contribution made by Germany (E10.9 billion), amounting to 60 per cent of the Community budget.[105]

Other problems have resulted from the CAP, beyond its domination of the budget and the inequity of redistribution. Agricultural productivity, for example, was enshrined as an end in itself, without any inbuilt mechanism of declining subsidy on a sliding scale beyond a certain level, which might have helped smaller farmers without privileging productivity for its own sake. Once self-sufficiency was achieved, the CAP's drive to productivity resulted in perpetual accumulation, through which the CAP lost much of its meaning. It generated enormous surpluses, butter and grain mountains, milk surpluses and wine lakes, which were expensive to store, and often ended up being 'dumped' (disposed of at bargain prices) on world markets, often in Eastern Europe, to the annoyance of other agricultural producers, especially the US and Cairns group. In seeking to protect small farmers, it benefited large, wealthy farmers, such as the wheat farmers of France's northern plains, who grew fat on EC support they did not actually need. Uniform prices implied that target prices were set at their highest existing level in the Community. In the case of soft wheat, the common target price was that which had applied in the region with the least adequate supply, namely Duisburg in the Ruhr, on which prices in the remainder of the EC had to conform.[106] Despite purporting to fairness across the board, so-called reasonable prices for consumers were bound to conflict with reasonable prices for farmers. The CAP has generally resulted in higher prices for consumers than would have been the case had world market prices applied, effectively subsidising farming incomes out of consumers' pockets. This was the case throughout the 1960s; although in the mid-1970s the Community benefited from prices considerably lower than those applying on world markets, when many basic foodstuffs, such as sugar, were in short supply. By the 1990s, however, the CAP was putting an estimated £16 per week on the food and tax bills of a family of four living in the EC.[107] Meanwhile producers have enjoyed what have amounted to guaranteed incomes, cushioned from market fluctuations.[108]

The European Community, of course, is concerned with much more than just agriculture. It impacts on industrial policy; competition policy; transport; regional policy; monetary policy; equality in the workplace, industrial relations, social policy; foreign policy and security issues; consumer policy; relations with the Third World, and so on. Nevertheless, it is noteworthy that until EMU and the successful launch of the euro in 1999, no other economic sector had seen the elaboration of a common policy comparable to the CAP. Its continuation serves as a powerful lure to membership for the countries of East Europe. For current EU members, however, the potential budgetary pressures of extending the CAP to new East European member-states are enormous (see Conclusion).

The special relationship between France and the Community did not always proceed as de Gaulle would have wished, and in this Mitterrand was perhaps more successful through his partnership with Kohl. As Tsoukalis observes, de Gaulle overshadowed the Community throughout the 1960s.[109] He failed notably to construct a political Europe that would speak with one voice – that is to say, amplifying France's voice on the world stage. Nevertheless, over the years France has enjoyed remarkable success in 'punching above its weight' in the European policy arena. De Gaulle was especially concerned to quash the supranational aspirations entertained by the Commission that might threaten French national interests. The low point of France's relations with the Community was the 'empty chair crisis' of June 1965 to January 1966, during which de Gaulle paralysed Community business by boycotting meetings, jeopardising the EEC's existence. His grievances included the financing of the CAP, about which France's partners were understandably uneasy; the role of the Commission, which sought more extensive, executive powers; and the application of articles 145 and 148 of the Rome Treaty on majority voting in the Council of Ministers, a collective expression of national interests where power was concentrated. The resolution of the crisis was through the 'Luxembourg compromise', which reintroduced the national veto, undermined the supranational element of integration, strengthened the intergovernmental aspect (compelling the Council constantly to seek agreement with member states, even on relatively trivial issues), and settled the financing of the CAP. In short, French demands on all counts were satisfied.

The downfall of de Gaulle's Republic

The end of de Gaulle's reign is inextricably bound up with the social upheaval of May 1968. The new, postwar 'baby boom' generation was beginning to come of age, approaching twenty years, at odds with authority of all descriptions. This new generation contested the authority of the Church, the paterfamilias, refused the principle of hierarchy according to which much of French society was structured (and in many respects still is), and vehemently rejected the concept of an authority according to which one commands and others obey. Large French companies were characterised by bureaucracy, often viewed by industrial sociologists as a social tool that legitimises control of the many by the few. They laid much emphasis on the *organigramme*, the pyramid according to which they were structured. They were marked by a traditional rigidity accentuated by the hierarchical social stratification within them. This was bolstered in turn by the *grandes écoles* training of engineers and managers, inculcated in the view that they were an elite, omniscient, a superior caste set apart from the rest, to whose demands they seemed unable to listen. Partitioning (*le cloisonnement*) was rife. It was not, however, the preserve of the elite alone, but was all-encompassing, as Michel Crozier argues: 'At all levels of society the French, once they gain entry into an influential group, instinctively try to keep others out.'[110] Some firms, such as dairy producer BSN (Boussois Souchon Neuvesel) Gervais-Danone, did attempt to adapt, to improve communication by changing the nature of middle management (*l'encadrement*) to render it more heedful of others. But most did not, and this notion of a ruling hierarchy remains something of an enduring feature of French business. Nor was far-reaching cultural change and social transformation reflected in the make-up of the government, many of them old men who had served in the war, with de Gaulle himself now in his late seventies, arrogant, out of touch and unrepentant.

At the same time, it seems that many French people simply did not realise that things were getting better. Opinion polls suggest that the French remained discontented with their lot, with between 80 and 90 per cent of respondents regularly claiming that their standard of living was the same as, or worse than previously, even though the facts belied such perceptions. Fewer than 10 per cent of interviewees perceived any improvement.[111] May 1968 was not simply the expression of frustration on the part of workers and students, the former no longer amenable to being directed as before, the latter dissatisfied by inadequate university provision. Nor was it a phenomenon unique to France, being part of a wider, international movement, which took root in the US, the UK, West Germany and even in Japan, but whose manifestation was especially acute in France. As a movement it caught the imagination of a generation of young French people who rejected the outdated hierarchies and rigid autocratic structures which permeated French society.

There are numerous detailed studies of the process of escalation from student protest to general strike. Student unrest focused upon the inadequacy of facilities and teaching within the French university system, which had expanded dramatically as a consequence of admission being granted to all awarded the *baccalauréat*. High rates of failure were accepted as the norm by the authorities with seeming indifference. It is against this background that in early May 1968 a local protest at the University of Nanterre spread first to the Sorbonne and then the streets of Paris. The extent and potency of the brewing crisis was misjudged by the government, which responded with indifference, illustrated by Prime Minister Pompidou's departure for

Afghanistan the same day, on a ten-day visit. The crisis swiftly spread to other establishments. As many as 2,000 student demonstrators took to the streets, erecting barricades in the Latin Quarter, assailed by CRS (Compagnie républicaine de sécurité) troops who tried to disperse them, culminating in the 'night of the barricades' of 10–11 May. By mid-May the crisis had spread to workers and factories, although on the face of it there was little to unite workers and students. The workers contested the high cost of living and lack of input in workplace decision-making; the students demanded improved academic facilities. Their social backgrounds and aspirations were quite different. A general strike was called by trade unions on 13 May, when an estimated 200,000 demonstrators marched from the Place de la République to the Place Denfert-Rochereau. As Berstein notes, this critical date marks the turning-point at which the crisis shifted from the student population to society itself.[112] The strikes spilled over on to every area of working life, impacting on the private as well as state-owned sectors, managers as well as employees, manufacturing and service industries, and administration. There was not a sector of the economy that remained unaffected. It is estimated that more than one-third of the French workforce went on strike, while students occupied university buildings the length and breadth of the country.

What concerns us here is the collision of values that contributed to the social turmoil of May 1968. Traditional nineteenth-century values that permeated French society and social organisations clashed with the new values that emerged with the arrival in the 1960s of a consumer society, fashioned by two decades of uninterrupted economic growth. A yawning gap was opening up between the country's preoccupations with social justice and the quality of life on the one hand, and the president's dogged pursuit of grandeur on the other. Seemingly from a bygone era, the latter seemed increasingly divorced from the reality of everyday life for most French people, yet was prosecuted ever more obsessively.[113] At an organisational level, employees increasingly expressed their need for new forms of social organisation on a human scale, more flexible and worker-friendly, less formal and bureaucratic, which might include an element of co-management.

De Gaulle's response to the crisis and to the qualitative demands of workers was to pursue the idea of worker participation in management, on which he intended to hold a referendum. Quintessentially authoritarian, de Gaulle nevertheless supported a rather vague policy in labour relations that he called 'the association of capital and labour', the idea that capital and labour might be able to work together for the good of France, which he came to call 'participation'. As he explained to Malraux, 'I saw in participation a means of waking up the country [...], of shaking it!'[114] Its intended purpose was to surmount class conflict by associating all citizens in the task of national development, in the hope that they might freely accept its goals. Business and technocratic elites dominated France's *économie concertée.* Through *participation* others, such as small shopkeepers, peasant farmers and trade unions might be included in the process.[115] Participation was doubtless too reformist-minded for the centrists who, in joining the ranks of the discontented, effectively scuppered de Gaulle's chances of winning the referendum. Its *raison d'être*, however, did not lie in industrial democracy *per se*, but was similar to the way de Gaulle conceived of nationalisation as a means of resurrecting France. The triumph of the 'no' vote on 27 April 1969 was interpreted by de Gaulle as a fundamental rejection of what participation stood for:

> Participation was a symbol, if you see what I mean.... The standard of living became the source of vexation of the whole country. It determines half of world politics. However, there is so much more than that. Our ancient rural society has been transformed by access to property; our industrial society will be transformed likewise. Participation was, rather tentatively, the route to this transformation. And you know that France, in voting against me, has not discarded its regions, the Senate, and so on: it has rejected what participation symbolized.[116]

De Gaulle's ideas thus expressed were farsighted and far-reaching. In a limited sense, the transformatory potential of property ownership was recognised eighteen years later in 1986 under the socialist President Mitterrand in launching mass privatisation. By 2001 there were more than 1.5 million salaried shareholders in France: still a small minority of the population but a big change from what had gone before.[117] French workers, however, had to wait until 1982 and the passing of the Auroux employment laws for the introduction of a measure of democracy in the workplace, which for the first time granted the right of free expression at work. Viewing this as symptomatic of the sheer rigidity and compartmentalisation of French organisational structures, one businessman retorted, 'Did we really need a law for that?!'[118]

De Gaulle never really recovered from the worker–student insurrection of May 1968, despite his seemingly masterful restoration of order the following month; nor indeed from the growing unpopularity of the fiscal austerity programme devised by finance minister (1962–65) Giscard d'Estaing. In April 1969 he failed to win a referendum on his proposals for restructuring the Senate and granting more power to regions, drawing the conclusion that he had lost the popular mandate that was the basis of his authority. He withdrew once more to his home at Colombey-les-deux-Eglises and died in November 1970.

De Gaulle's successor as President, former prime minister Georges Pompidou, a graduate of the Ecole Normale Supérieure and one-time chairman of the Rothschild bank, fought the 1969 presidential election on a Gaullist ticket, promising 'continuity in change'. Once elected, in fact, the emphasis was firmly upon continuity rather than change. Pompidou changed none of de Gaulle's policies and practices. Barring the strident demands for social change voiced in May 1968, prior to 1973 there was, it must be said, little reason to change: economically France was doing very well indeed. Change under Pompidou was thus limited to the immediate devaluation of the franc for which business leaders had long campaigned; the lifting of the veto on British entry into the EC, leading to admission in 1973 along with Denmark and Ireland; and a new openness and accessibility of style. Greater transparency and informality, however, did not extend to admitting his own illness; Pompidou's terminal cancer was made public on the brink of his death on 2 April 1974, catching France off-guard. Following on from where de Gaulle had left off, his primary aim was to achieve the full modernisation and industrialisation of France. Central to this was the construction of a new up-market, contemporary business complex at La Défense, outside Paris, which became the chosen headquarters of leading firms such as Saint-Gobain and Elf-Aquitaine, dramatically altering the Paris skyline but arousing much hostility. The Centre Pompidou (Beaubourg) was also built in central Paris; controversially a British architect won the commission. As the historian Pierre Goubert summed up Pompidou's short presidency: 'In 1969 Pompidou was elected easily [...] but he died in 1974 without having had time to finish his chosen task of disfiguring Paris.'[119]

Conclusion

This chapter has sought to provide an overview of the French economy under de Gaulle. In this it has accorded particular emphasis to the main Gaullist tools of economic management, including devaluation, planning, industrial policy, and concentration in all areas of the economy, in the belief that without critical mass France would remain a second-rank economic power. Faced with US supremacy on all fronts, planning in particular was as crucial to de Gaulle's quest for grandeur as the nuclear imperative or technological independence, in the drive to play 'catch-up'. In bringing together key decision-makers from the worlds of business and administration, planning arguably lent a positive impetus to economic life, contributing to a national *prise de conscience* on the part of economic actors. It promoted an investment climate for growth, instilled a confidence that the state would persist in its objectives, creating opportunities that business leaders could identify and to which they could respond. At the same time, however, it might be argued that participation in the planning process did not go far enough, despite numerous wide-ranging committees. The *économie concertée* reinforced the cohesion of business and politico-administrative elites at the pinnacle of the social hierarchy, thereby arguably strengthening the culture of authoritarianism and partitioning, emphatically rejected in the 1968 worker–student insurrection. The establishment was indeed coherent and robust at the top; but it was separated from other social classes, thus contributing to disengagement, the feeling of 'them and us' that fuelled the social upheavals of May 1968. Technocratic and political elites were strengthened too by *rapprochement* with the hereditary enemy. Actively pursued by de Gaulle as soon as hostilities had ceased, reconciliation with Germany was recognised by de Gaulle as the key to French primacy in Europe, a vision that came to fruition in the 1980s and 1990s. In many respects the fledgling Community, dominated by de Gaulle, emerged as a cipher for French interests in Europe, especially French farming interests. This amplification of French power depended in part, de Gaulle believed, on keeping Britain out of the Community, thus preventing American influence from infiltrating EC affairs; this he succeeded in doing throughout his lifetime with unswerving resolve.

In the Gaullist era, the instinctive French preference for *faire faire* over *laisser faire*, for an economy directed and orchestrated by the state rather than one that fully embraces the free play of market forces, came to the fore. From the mid-1980s, however, following the 'aberration' of the early Socialist years when state intervention in the economy reached a paroxysm, the balance began to tip once more in favour of greater liberalism. During this time, deregulation and privatisation gathered momentum first in the US, then the UK, followed by Western Europe and elsewhere in the world. In the twenty-first century, the free play of market forces is on a global scale. Yet much of de Gaulle's vision for economic management arguably applies today. It is apparent in the systematic pursuit by French business leaders of European and international mergers and acquisitions. Empire-building abroad is accompanied in certain sectors, in particular energy, by a fierce resolve to keep domestic markets closed for as long as possible. The interpretation of EU directives to suit the national agenda, while exploiting market liberalisation elsewhere, remains true to de Gaulle's vision of a Community in France's image. In key respects, *dirigisme* survives, and the Gaullist vision of economic sovereignty and economic management lives on in the face of changing global economic circumstances.

4

The Giscard Years: from Prosperity to Deepening Crisis

> Just as houses retain in their thick walls, at the beginning of autumn, heat soaked up during the summer, so our entire economic and social system remained impregnated for several years with the illusions and easy terms of the preceding period.
>
> Valéry Giscard d'Estaing, 1981[1]

Valéry Giscard d'Estaing was elected to the presidency on 19 May 1974 in a radically changed economic climate, one for which Western governments and economies in general – and France in particular – proved to be singularly unprepared. Narrowly defeating his socialist rival, François Mitterrand, by 50.7 per cent to 49.3 per cent in the second round of voting, Giscard had campaigned as an independent Republican candidate on a left-leaning platform of reform, promising in particular a rise in basic wages. His campaign was based on 'four ideas, three securities and nine changes' and was encapsulated in the slogan 'change without risk'.[2] Europe was highlighted as the essential priority, with Giscard predicting union by 1980.

In the event, two oil crises in six years – in 1973 and 1979 – obliged him to reject much of his reformist agenda in favour of an austerity programme that steadily eroded his popularity. The French government had claimed credit for the 'thirty glorious years' of prosperity following the war. This proved to be a problem when expansion gave way to recession. The French, alongside other Western nations, had become accustomed to a state of affairs in which they had never had it so good, and in which things kept on getting better – even if it did not always appear to be so. By 1973 there were 14 million cars in circulation, as against 4.5 million in 1959, 12 million televisions, as against only one million in 1959, and 500,000 new houses completed annually as against 290,000 twelve years previously.[3] But the oil crises raised the price of oil tenfold: first by 400 per cent and then five years later by a further 250 per cent. For a country with few natural energy sources, whose manufacturing industry was heavily dependent on cheap imported oil, this was a major blow.

This chapter examines the extent and effects of the economic crisis, as well as the steps taken to deal with it. These included a short-lived reflation programme in 1975 followed by a deeply unpopular austerity package (1976–81). The realisation of the extent to which the country had become dependent on cheap imported oil brought a new awareness of vulnerability, driving a search for new energy sources and the rapid construction of nuclear plants. It also raised awareness of France's economic interdependence with her Community partners; although this did not emerge fully until the failure of the Mitterrand–Mauroy experiment in 1982–83 highlighted the extent of this interdependence and the consequent need for European construction.

When the first oil crisis began to bite in 1975, it initiated a recession that arguably was more severe and enduring in France than those of her major European partners. Britain's North Sea oil came onstream in June of that year, partially compensating for the cut in oil imports; that said, in 1975 inflation rose to 25 per cent in the UK.[4] 'La crise', as it became known in France, lasted almost a decade, blighting the Giscard presidency, as well as the first socialist government of the Mitterrand presidency that succeeded it (see Chapter 5).

The two oil crises had rather different origins. The first arose when, following the Arab–Israeli Yom Kippur war, oil-producing Arab states determined to deny supplies to some countries, in particular the US, punished for its support for Israel, while at the same time limiting supplies to most other client countries. On 17 October 1973 the oil states instilled panic in Western Europe, dependent on Arab producers for 80 per cent of its oil, by raising the price by 70 per cent. Hitherto oil price rises had been agreed in negotiation with Western oil companies. The oil price hike of October 1973 sent a powerful signal to the Western world that henceforth prices would be determined unilaterally by the Arab oil-producing states. The second oil crisis was linked to the driving into exile of the Shah of Iran. Between December 1978 and December 1979 the price of crude oil more than doubled from $12 to $26 a barrel. Following the failure of OPEC (Organisation of Petroleum Exporting Countries) ministers to agree a single price for a barrel, prices reached a staggering $40 a barrel. OPEC's point was that some of the wealth enjoyed by Western nations in the postwar era, often achieved through the exploitation of other regions and continents, should be secured for the oil-producing countries of the Middle East, in possession of a lucrative, but ultimately finite, natural resource. OPEC's decision to cut output in 1980 exacerbated and prolonged the effects of the second crisis.

The effect on business life in the West could hardly have been more devastating. Prior to 1973, business life in France, as elsewhere in the West, could more easily be predicted, helped by healthy growth rates which enabled realistic targets to be attained; from 1973, this was no longer the case. The decline of French national planning illustrates the impact of this turning-point. Such was the faith in the planning exercise, indeed, that even in 1978 the Parti Socialiste (PS) wrote 'the Plan will fix a growth rate',[5] as if all were ultimately controllable by technocrats.[6] That the demise of planning was a long and protracted affair, and ultimately incomplete, testifies perhaps to the reluctance of a nation to abandon a powerful symbol of postwar growth and a tool of economic management that had made it feel secure.

French dependence on imported energy

In *Le Mal français*, one of the most politically influential books of the 1970s, Alain Peyrefitte highlighted the quintessential importance to France of achieving international competitiveness.[7] Peyrefitte made the case that a lack of natural energy explained the protracted nature of the industrialisation process in France:

> Why did England enjoy an early industrialisation? 'Because she possessed coal', the history and geography textbooks reply. Why was industrialisation much less spectacular in France? 'Because her coal mines were poorer.'[8]

The quadrupling of the price of oil in 1973 exposed to French public opinion the country's inordinate dependence on imported energy. There is little doubt that prior to the Yom Kippur war France had been lulled into a false sense of security, living in an artificial environment characterised by a super-abundance of energy that was relatively cheap. Since the early 1960s France had negotiated directly with oil states with regard to supplies and prices. By the early 1970s France's energy dependence clearly placed it in a more precarious economic position than many of its competitors. To some extent this had been a calculated gamble on the part of the French government – the Jeanneney Plan had deemed that the overall competitiveness of the national economy mattered more than the particular provenance of energy supplies – which had served France well initially[9] but that had now come unstuck. Caron notes that the amount of primary energy imported into France was 76.3 per cent of total consumption in 1973 – as against 47 per cent in Britain and 50 per cent in Germany – having risen dramatically from 49.6 per cent a decade earlier.[10] In 1973 as much as 67 per cent of France's primary energy needs were supplied by oil, up from 18 per cent in 1950 and 30 per cent in 1960 (see Table 4.1). Paradoxically, the decline of coal in the 1950s and 1960s had been hastened by the low price and availability of fuel oil.

The initial response of the French government to the oil crisis was twofold. First, it sought to improve its relations with the oil-producing states, in particular Iran, Iraq and Saudi Arabia, to which it sold high technology in the form of armaments or nuclear power stations. Second, it attempted to locate new national sources of energy. In this there was little

Table 4.1   French energy consumption by source (as percentage)

Source/year	1950	1960	1968	1972	1975
Solid fuels	74	54	32	19.1	16.6
Oil	18	30	51	65	62.1
Gas	0.5	3.5	6	8.3	10.6
Hydro.	7.5	12.5	10.5	6.6}	10.7}
Nuclear			0.5	1.9}	}

Source: Caron, F., *An Economic History of Modern France*, translated by B. Bray, Columbia, Columbia University Press, 1979, p. 228.

room for manoeuvre. As far as coal was concerned, it was possible only to slow down its dramatic decline; following the first oil crisis, the projected target of 13 million tons of coal for the year 1980 was increased to 20 million tons. Domestic supplies of natural gas were similarly limited. Production commenced in 1942 at St Marcet, near Pau in southwest France, and in neighbouring Lacq fifteen years later. Yet, as Caron observes, by 1972 domestic production of natural gas covered only 54 per cent of domestic needs. Additional supplies were imported from Algeria and the Netherlands to slow the consumption of precious domestic resources as much as to supplement national supplies.[11] Hydroelectricity was earmarked for further development, but lacked the considerable potential required to meet national energy needs. Electricity obtained through nuclear power seemed the obvious choice.

The decision to develop nuclear power had already been taken in 1955, with the construction of four nuclear plants promised in the fourth plan. But little was done, with the subsequent fall in the price of oil in the 1960s casting doubt on the wisdom of a nuclear programme – until the Yom Kippur war sharpened government resolve. In March 1974, it was decided to begin construction of six nuclear energy plants that year and seven in 1975. These were built with enormous speed. In Britain the development of nuclear energy attracted widespread public protest, epitomised by the high-profile demonstration at Windscale, its name changed to Sellafield in an effort to erase public memory. In Germany the success of the anti-nuclear movement is encapsulated in the popular slogan, 'Atomkraft, nein Danke!' In France, however, the nuclear programme met with limited resistance, being greeted on the contrary by general public acceptance of the need for a secure, national energy supply. Indeed, it elicited national pride when, in the early 1980s, France became self-sufficient in electricity thanks to the nuclear programme, and began exporting electricity to other countries, including by the mid-1980s oil-rich Britain. Resistance in France has been limited largely to technicalities: whether the so-called 'French system' as opposed to American technology of fast-breeder reactors should be adopted.[12] In the event, the

American system won the day when French companies Framatome and the Compagnie Générale d'Electricité (CGE) acquired the rights to use the pressurised water reactor patented by General Electric and Westinghouse. Interestingly, when following the nuclear disaster at Chernobyl in 1986, other countries took the decision to scale down or halt their nuclear-plant construction programmes outright, the French took the opposite course of action, and actually speeded up construction. Nuclear energy was promoted by Electricité de France (EdF) at the time in an advertisement featuring a sole pair of ballroom dancers surrounded by fighting pairs of boxers in a large ring, confirming French ease at doing things differently.

The search to locate new national sources of energy was not without its lighter moments, however, particularly the scandal of the so-called 'sniffer planes', *les avions renifleurs*, in 1976. In a financial tragi-comedy reminiscent of the adventures of Tintin, the management of Elf-Aquitaine were hoodwinked by the Count Alain de Villegas de Saint-Pierre-Jette and Aldo Bonossoli, who persuaded them that they had invented an aeroplane capable of detecting oil fields and other deposits located underground. The company pumped FF750 million of public funds into the development of the so-called 'invention of the century', baptised Mirza. One top company official, Paul Alba, noted with satisfaction in August 1977 the apparent results the device had so far yielded:

> Today, the plane has flown over 60,000 square kilometres in Aquitaine and Atlantique [...]. Already the device revealed at Berenx the existence of 5 million cubic metres of gas, 5 million tonnes of oil at Grau-du-Roi and a large oil field in the Loire-Atlantique, 450 million tonnes of which should be recovered.[13]

So convincing were Villegas and Bonossoli that, incredibly, a demonstration was arranged before President Giscard on 5 April 1979. To his credit, Giscard seems to have smelt a rat. But the whole extravagant affair did not become public until late 1983, in the irreverent pages of *Le Canard enchaîné* – having been hushed up by Elf in 1980, then picked up by a tax inspector in early 1982. When it finally came to light, the former president was able to produce a note, from the 5450 boxes deposited in the national archives, in which he clearly expressed his fears of a fraud.[14] For investigative journalists Derogy and Pontaut, however, the real significance of the affair lay in the fact that 'in our era of high profitability and great realism, two enlightened poets were able to share their madness with one of the greatest oil companies in the world, and that this company should agree to give its gold to these alchemists for them to transform into a dream'.[15] Unfortunately for Elf, the company was at the centre of a much more important scandal in the late 1990s, one in which leading members of the political and business elite were directly implicated.

The economic effects of crisis

The economic crisis engendered by the oil shortage, of course, affected far more than supplies of energy. The oil shocks fuelled inflation – which reached 13.7 per cent in France in 1974, and 25 per cent in Britain in 1975 (see Table 4.2) – raising the price of imports generally, and triggering a world-wide recession as demand slumped. Supply was reduced as company profitability declined. Between 1973 and 1980 the mean gross profit margin of private-sector firms in France fell from 27.6 per cent to 23 per cent of total value added,[16] with manufacturing industry bearing the brunt of the decline. Factory prices rose sharply, while soaring inflation drove many firms out of business. In 1975 bankruptcies increased by 23–24 per cent over the preceding year in France, West Germany and the USA, and by an unprecedented 40 per cent in the UK, causing unemployment and public deficits to rise dramatically.[17] Particularly badly affected were small and medium-sized firms (SME), which did not have access to state aid from which firms like Boussac in France or British Leyland in the UK continued to benefit.

Unemployment across the OECD (Organisation for Economic Cooperation and Development) reached 15 million by May 1975, equal to 5.5 per cent of the total workforce. Unemployment rose sharply throughout the European Community (EC), with Denmark (+103.5 per cent), Britain (+81.4 per cent), Belgium (+79.5 per cent) and France (+71 per cent) registering the sharpest increases (see Table 4.3).[18] As many as 1.3 million Britons were out of work by January 1976. Under the government of Jacques Chirac, France's jobless swelled from 425,000 at the time of his appointment in May 1974 to 925,000 by the time of his resignation in August 1976. The south and west of France were particularly badly affected. As the baby-boomers reached maturity, an estimated 880,000 additional workers entered the labour market between 1976 and 1983.[19] In the last six months of the Giscard presidency, unemployment was growing at an average rate of 37,000 per month (seasonally adjusted).[20] During the crisis as a whole

Table 4.2 Inflation in industrialised nations, 1971–75 (as percentage)

Country	1971–72	1972–73	1973–74	Oct. 74–Oct. 75
USA	3.2	6.2	11	7.5
UK	6.8	8.3	16	25.6
FRG	5.5	6.9	7	5.8
France	5.9	7.3	13.7	10.2
Italy	5.6	10.4	19.4	11.8
Japan	4.9	11.6	23.2	8

Source: Adapted from 'Modération générale sauf en Grande-Bretagne', *L'Année économique et sociale: 1975, 'la crise'*, *Le Monde Dossiers et Documents Supplément*, January 1976, p. 17.

Table 4.3   Unemployment in industrialised nations, October/November 1973–October/November 1975 (as percentage of workforce)

Country/ year	Italy	USA*	Belgium	*France*	FRG	UK	Japan*
Oct./Nov. 1973	7.5	4.7	3.4	**2.7**	1.5	2.2	1.3
Oct./Nov. 1975	8.3	8.2	8.2	**6.2**	5.3	4.9	1.9

* OECD method of calculation, which differed from the EEC method of calculation, by which all other percentages were derived.

Source: 'Partout l'aggravation', *L'Année économique et sociale: 1975, 'la crise'*, p. 14.

unemployment in France quadrupled (rising from 2.6 per cent of the workforce to 10.5 per cent in 1986). It affected white-collar as well as blue-collar workers, dubbed the 'new poor'.[21] By September 1975, it was nonetheless clear that the main victims of unemployment were young people, women and manual workers. Young people under 25 years of age now accounted for 46 per cent of the unemployed (430,000, up from less than 200,000 in December 1973); women accounted for 50 per cent (475,000); and manual workers accounted for 48 per cent of those out of work (450,000).[22] From 1978, unemployment hit the male workforce hard, as industries such as steel, shipbuilding and textiles, reeling from foreign competition, were obliged to lay off workers massively and rapidly – workers who had come to expect lifetime security in their job – despite large-scale public subsidy.[23] This combination throughout the Giscard presidency of endemic inflation, low growth and high unemployment, which proved to be structural rather than cyclical, was branded 'stagflation'.

Some idea of the scale of the first oil crisis can be gleaned from the estimated cost of the additional oil bill in 1974 as a percentage of national GDP in 1973: for France this was reckoned to be as high as 3–4 per cent.[24] Developing countries fared worse, with Uruguay, Thailand and South Korea facing additional oil bills estimated at 4.9 per cent, 5.4 per cent and 9 per cent of GDP respectively. Between 1974 and 1975, industrial production across the OECD nations receded by an average of 15 per cent. Meanwhile, GDP fell sharply by 3 per cent in the USA, 2 per cent in France, 3.7 per cent in West Germany, 4.5 per cent in Italy, and 2.2 per cent in the UK, averaging 2 per cent across the OECD.[25]

Some sectors were especially badly affected, such as chemicals. In 1975 German heavyweights Bayer, Hoechst and BASF saw their profits fall by as much as 70.9 per cent, 57.6 per cent and 55.8 per cent respectively from the preceding year.[26] Steel production declined by 20 per cent in the Community of nine, by 19 per cent in the US, 11 per cent in Japan and by 14 per cent in the rest of the world (excluding Eastern Europe). Initially, car manufacturers were also badly affected by the recession, with the American giants Ford, Chrysler and General Motors faring worst, and the French constructors managing rather surprisingly to hold their own against the odds – Renault even emerged as European leader in the first semester of 1974, a rare achievement.[27] Unsurprisingly, the most profitable companies in 1974, accounting for ten of the top twenty global companies by turnover, were oil companies. The only French firm to feature among the top twenty, which contained three British and no German firms, was the Compagnie Française des pétroles in nineteenth position (see Table 4.4).

The reasons advanced by the OECD and other commentators for the continuing severity of the recession, beyond what had been anticipated, included the speculative restocking which took place at the start of the crisis in many countries, including France, West Germany, Italy, Canada and the USA (but not in Britain). This may have actually boosted annual growth by 1 per cent in 1973. But as stocks were depleted by firms in the ensuing year, this in turn acted as a brake on growth equivalent to 4–5 per cent, tantamount to an overall reduction in GDP of about 3 per cent in 1974.[28] Meanwhile the savings rate increased, as individuals, fearful for their jobs and attracted by higher interest rates, put more aside, thereby depressing demand and prolonging the recession. Even the British,

Table 4.4 Top 20 global companies by turnover, 1974

Company	Turnover ($ million)	Business	Workforce
Exxon (USA)	42,061	Oil	133,000
Shell (Neth/UK)	33,037	Oil	164,000
GM (USA)	31,549	Cars	734,000
Ford (USA)	23,620	Cars	464,731
Texaco (USA)	23,255	Oil	76,420
Mobil (USA)	18,929	Oil	73,100
BP (UK)	18,269	Oil	68,000
Stand Oil Cal (US)	17,191	Oil	39,540
Nat. Iran. Oil (Iran)	16,802	Oil	50,000
Gulf Oil (USA)	16,458	Oil	52,700
Unilever (Neth/UK)	13,666	Food/Household	357,000
GE (USA)	13,413	Electric goods	404,000
IBM (USA)	12,575	IT	292,350
ITT (USA)	11,154	Tel./Electric	409,000
Chrysler (USA)	10,971	Cars	255,929
Philips (Neth)	9,422	Electric goods	412,000
US Steel (USA)	9,186	Steel	187,503
Stand Oil Ind (USA)	9,085	Oil	47,217
Cie Fr. des Pét (Fr)	8,908	Oil	27,400
Nippon Steel (Jap)	8,843	Steel	97,814

Source: 'Les "grands" des affaires', *L'Année économique et sociale: 1975, 'la crise'*, p. 9.

renowned as consummate spenders and reluctant savers, increased their savings rate from 9.8 per cent of disposable household income in 1970–71 to 13.5 per cent in 1975.[29] The unwillingness of Western governments to reflate their economies for fear of fuelling inflation, while other governments tightened their belts, has been cited as a further reason for the continuation of the crisis. The fall in investment is also cited as a contributory factor. Corporate investment in France declined slightly from an average of 17 per cent of value added between 1963 and 1973 to 14 per cent during the period 1976–81. But as Smith observes, in intermediate goods, such as chemicals, steel and rubber, which formed the core of French industry, the fall in investment was considerably more marked. Corporate debt, which had been consistently high in France, increased, while self-financing, never prominent, declined further.[30]

In all, the cost of the two oil price hikes on the French economy amounted to an estimated 8 per cent of GDP. What the oil crises threw into salient relief above all was the growing interdependence of national economies; although, arguably, it was not until the crisis was nearing an end, in 1982–83, and for different reasons, that the French registered the full impact of this lesson (see Chapter 5). Under Giscard, French policy-makers became increasingly obsessed with the balance of payments, as a surplus of $773 million in 1973 was turned almost overnight into a $3.9 billion deficit in 1974, due largely to the quadrupling of the oil price.[31] The fact that oil prices were denominated in dollars ruled out any attempt to devalue the franc relative to the dollar. Exports might be cheaper and therefore more competitive, but devaluation would also have increased the price of oil imports; as Hall observes, 'One of the traditional weapons in the arsenal of French economic management was no longer of much use.'[32] Exports continued to grow at a rate of 5 per cent in value during the Giscard presidency, but declined in volume for the first time in 25 years. The developing countries, which absorbed a growing amount of exports (18 per cent in 1973, 25 per cent in 1977 and 30 per cent by the end of Giscard's tenure in 1981), were also increasingly unable to pay their debts.

From 1971, with the Bretton Woods system of fixed exchange rates, based on the dollar–gold convertibility, beginning to break down, the international monetary system had been in crisis, stoking up inflation. In 1973 the Bretton Woods system collapsed. The European monetary zone attempted to cope with floating exchange rates by seeking to maintain bilateral exchange rates within tight margins, constructing in 1972 a rudimentary exchange rate block dubbed the 'snake in the tunnel' after its shape. The dollar served as the anchor currency, providing the broad constraints within which currencies could float. Under this scheme, individual member currencies (including some from outside the EC) could float up and down against the dollar to a limit of 2.25 per cent; against other member currencies, individual currencies could float up and down to a maximum of 1.25 per cent.

The snake was essentially an attempt to preserve some of the benefits of the Bretton Woods system at a regional, European level. It failed, however, when a number of key currencies were forced to withdraw, such as the pound, which joined the snake in May 1972 only to leave it six weeks later, and the Italian lira, which left in February 1973. Its fate was sealed by the departure of the French franc, forced to withdraw in January 1974, rejoining temporarily in July 1975 only to leave again in March 1976.[33] There was therefore by the mid-1970s no viable alternative to the generalised floating of exchange rates. The European Monetary System (EMS), at the centre of which was the Exchange Rate Mechanism (ERM) which the snake had prefigured, was not launched until 1979, following the 1978 conference at Bremen. In the meantime, among European currencies the German mark became especially prominent, creating in this way a 'Deutschmark zone'.

French responses to the crisis

Ultimately, the Giscard presidency was caught between 'a rock and a hard place', between the Scylla of international constraints and the Charybdis of internal pressures. On the one hand, as a centre-right administration, which lacked the natural support of the trade unions, it feared the electoral fall-out of an austerity programme in a climate of rising unemployment. On the other hand, a balanced budget was crucial to keep the crisis within manageable limits, but was desperately hard to achieve, given escalating energy costs, growing unemployment, index-linked salaries and continuing financial subsidies to threatened groups. The crisis was the first such crisis faced by France as a fully-fledged welfare state. It followed three decades of growth during which every social group had become used to a continual improvement in the standard of living, and during which conflicts about income distribution had occurred 'within a positive and increasing sum game [where] [...] social progress and economic efficiency were no longer perceived as competitors'.[34]

Planning, which had served the French well during the thirty glorious years, failed to help the government out of crisis. The sixth plan (1971–75), which announced 'the industrial imperative' in the teeth of foreign competition,[35] had been drawn up in better days. It was thrown off course by a recession that was all the more painful for the fact that people had come to believe that things would carry on getting better. Its successor, the seventh plan (1976–80),[36] was founded on the misplaced expectation that recovery was imminent, necessitating the drawing up of a whole new plan incorporating more modest objectives. The primary concern of planning now switched to economic management in crisis, one that lasted for almost a decade (1975–84).[37]

The government's solution to the conundrum was to place the burden of adjustment to the crisis squarely on the shoulders of employers in the form of higher employers' social security costs (*les charges sociales*). It has become widely recognised since that the additional oil bill was largely borne at the time by business enterprise, despite falling profits.[38] Friction between business and government was one of the hallmarks of the Giscard presidency. The leading French employers' association, the Conseil National du Patronat Français (CNPF), had to a degree already burnt its boats with Giscard, having withdrawn its support during the 1974 presidential campaign, preferring to remain neutral. Its bargaining power thus diminished, an uneasy stalemate between 'patronat' and president ensued.[39] Employers' social security costs had already been high in France relative to other industrialised nations at the start of the crisis. They included aspects of social security, which, in other countries, would normally be borne directly by the state, paid for by general taxation, such as family allowances (*les allocations familiales*). This was compounded during the course of the decade: French employers' costs rose from 12 per cent of GDP in 1973 to 15.7 per cent seven years later, suffering the highest increase of any leading industrialised nation (see Table 4.5). Under Giscard, the overall tax and social security burden (compulsory deductions in their widest sense, *les prélèvements obligatoires*) increased as a percentage of GDP by an estimated one percentage point per year from 35 per cent of GDP in 1974 to 42.5 per cent by the end of his presidency.[40] The political advantage of concentrating the costs of the recession on business, as well as on the unemployed, was that it helped to prevent widespread electoral discontent by shielding the working population from the crisis. The downside was that the rising cost of salaries in real terms exacerbated its effects. The burden of social welfare on employment has remained a cause of friction between employers and government to the present day. With the 2002 presidential election imminent at the time of writing, more recently concessions have been made to employers

Table 4.5 Employers' social security costs as percentage of GDP, 1973–80

Country/year	1973	1980	% change 1973–80
France	**12.0**	**15.7**	**+3.7**
USA	4.4	5.1	+0.7
Japan	2.7	4.2	+1.5
West Germany	7.7	8.8	+1.1
UK	3.6	5.1	+1.5
Italy	10.6	11.2	+0.6

Source: Smith, W.R., ' "We can make the Ariane, but we can't make washing machines": the state and industrial performance in postwar France', in Howorth, J. and Ross, G., eds, *Contemporary France: a Review of Interdisciplinary Studies*, III, London, Pinter, p. 201.

by Finance Minister Fabius, following unexpectedly buoyant tax receipts in 2000–2001 (the so-called *cagnotte*).[41] But the issue is unlikely to be addressed fully until tax harmonisation is finally achieved in the EU. This is eagerly desired by the French, but vehemently opposed by the British, who, seeing it as a last bastion of sovereignty, refused at the Nice summit in December 2000 to relinquish the national veto on this important issue.

Abortive reflation

French responses to the two oil crises, which took place under two separate administrations, led by premiers Jacques Chirac (1974–76) and Raymond Barre (1976–81) respectively, were nevertheless significantly different. Prime Minister Chirac favoured a reflation policy. In the event this was followed only tentatively. Deepening deficits and rising inflation militated against a full-blown reflation of the economy: inflation reached almost 14 per cent in France in 1974, averaging 10.5 per cent for the period 1973–79, against an average of 6.2 per cent in 1970–73. Reflation, moreover, would have had to be pursued in isolation to France's economic partners. That said, during his premiership Chirac put in place two plans to bolster the economy. The first, a plan to sustain productive investment, which cost FF15.7 billion, was launched in April 1975. Its follow-up, launched five months later, costing FF30.5 billion, aimed to develop the French economy. The two plans included measures to sustain consumption, tax breaks for productive investment, together with additional public investment, loans at privileged rates for exporters, and the postponement of business taxes by six months from 15 September 1975 to 15 April 1976. It also included industrial 'grands projets'; in particular a major revamp of the French telephone system, long derided by foreigners as a stain on France's reputation. In all, they cost 2.3 per cent of GDP over 1975–76, 1.3 per cent in 1975, and 1 per cent the following year (excluding loans and the postponement of tax receipts), the full costs of which were borne by the budget.[42]

Aged only 42 on taking office, Jacques Chirac was a youthful, energetic and clearly able prime minister, attributes he shared with the president under whom he served – Giscard, at 48, was one of the youngest presidents in the history of the French Republic. Prime minister and head of state had a lot in common. Both men were technocrats, both 'énarques', products of the prestigious Ecole Nationale d'Administration (ENA), both had served under Pompidou (Chirac was a particular favourite of the former president), and both had risen rapidly in their political careers. Initially the Giscard–Chirac tandem had seemed the perfect combination to solve the country's difficulties. But the two men fell out, leading to Chirac's resignation in August 1976, on the grounds that Giscard had denied him sufficient freedom of action. He was replaced as prime minister by Raymond Barre, an economist and academic by profession, who had taught at the

Institut d'Etudes Politiques de Paris (Sciences Po). Barre was also asked to assume the portfolio of economic and finance minister.[43] A relative newcomer to government, having been appointed to his first ministerial post in January 1976 as minister for foreign trade and commerce, Barre worked more closely with Giscard than his predecessor had done. Meanwhile, as mayor of Paris from 1977, and fashioning himself as the genuine successor to de Gaulle, Chirac used his new office at the Hôtel de Ville as an RPR (Rassemblement pour la République) power base from which to challenge Giscard's policies, burdened by the worsening economic recession.[44] Formed by Chirac in 1976, the RPR was conceived essentially as a vehicle for his political and, indeed, presidential ambitions.[45] He served as its head until 1994.[46] (According to recent allegations, Chirac is also reputed to have used his time at the *mairie* to feather his own nest financially.)

The 'Plan Barre'

Overtly pro-European, having served at de Gaulle's behest as vice-president of the European Commission responsible for economic affairs from 1967 to 1973, Barre brought to the premiership a liberal approach to running the economy, coupled with a natural conservatism. Giscard described Barre at the time of his appointment as 'the leading French economist [...] best able to resolve the most important problem for France at the present moment, which is that of inflation'.[47] To his critics, though, he remained the professor of economics, too independent (he did not belong to any political party despite his loose affiliation to the Union pour la démocracie française, UDF), detached and inflexible.

Two years prior to his appointment as prime minister, Raymond Barre had denounced the laxity, wastefulness and sheer consumption of Western economies, which, in his view, ought to become 'economic' once again and privilege 'savings and investment'.[48] Once installed at Matignon, Barre's solution to the crisis was a deflationary package known as the 'Plan Barre'. It was designed to restore the country to economic health principally by combating inflation without stifling investment. It also sought to address the huge balance-of-payments deficit. At the core of Barre's strategy was a determination that business enterprise should bear the burden of adjustment to the new international economy, characterised by increasing foreign competition.[49]

The plan, however, was regarded by many as too extreme. It was certainly wide-ranging. Presented to the National Assembly on 22 September 1976, the austerity package included the following measures: a three-month price freeze; an immediate income tax rise of 4 per cent or 8 per cent for millions of taxpayers, depending on the level of contribution;[50] a 4 per cent increase in business taxes; increases in the price of road tax, petrol (up 15 per cent) and alcohol (up 10 per cent); a 1 per cent increase in social security contributions (from 12.95 to 13.95 per cent, up to a specified ceiling); a 0.4 per cent rise in pension contributions (from 10.75 to 11.15 per cent of earnings). In addition, the package included compensation for farmers affected by the drought of summer 1976, amounting to FF6.2 million. At the same time, the threshold for paying income tax in 1977 was to be maintained at its 1976 level of FF4,500, despite a substantial increase in the cost of living due to inflation, meaning that overall the tax burden would rise.[51] To counter public discontent and foster national solidarity, the salaries of the wealthy were frozen, luxury items like yachts or golf taxed, and expense accounts were to be closely monitored. To improve the trade balance, the basic rate of value added tax (VAT) was reduced from 20 per cent to 17.6 per cent for intermediate goods from January 1977.[52] Oil imports were to be restricted to an overall bill of FF55 billion in 1977, and an emergency fund of FF2.5 billion was to be made available to industry.

Unsurprisingly, the Giscard–Barre administration failed to win public acceptance of its austerity plan. Reflation policies, though potentially fuelling inflation and damaging public finances, are consistently more popular with electorates, who are not required to tighten their belts. The trade unions had asked Raymond Barre to reduce social inequalities; but salary increases were to be limited to 6.5 per cent, below the rate of inflation, on the government's recommendation.[53] In a concerted rebuttal of the austerity package, the leading trade unions, the CGT (Confédération Générale du Travail) and CFDT (Confédération Française et Démocratique du Travail) supported by the FEN (Fédération de l'Education Nationale), immediately sought and obtained the support of left-wing parties for a general strike on 7 October 1976.[54] This proved to be the first of numerous one-day stoppages to hit the public sector, disrupting electricity supplies, rail and underground services, postal services, waste collection and schools.[55] The PS and PC (Parti Communiste) naturally opposed the austerity plan, their joint agenda having been formulated in the Common Programme of 1972, conceived at a time of high growth prior to the oil crises.[56]

Meanwhile the business community, as represented by the CNPF, gave the plan its qualified support, uniting with the government in condemning the strikes, while making a number of requests designed to help firms recover from the crisis. In particular the CNPF asked Prime Minister Barre to promote investment; to adopt the American 'carry back' system that allowed businesses to set deficits against profits in the subsequent year, recently introduced in West Germany; and to reduce the tax payable on share dividends in order to stimulate equity finance. The managers' union, the Confédération Générale des Cadres (CGC), rejected the plan outright and launched a protest to be channelled through national deputies.[57] The CGC was supported by the Confédération Française des Travailleurs Chrétiens (CFTC), which registered a more measured response. While deploring the strikes, it nevertheless expressed its alarm in November 1976 that two months after the introduction of a new stability plan, key economic indicators, such as employment and the cost of living, continued to move in the wrong direction.[58] Small and medium-sized businesses, meanwhile, voiced their concerns about the financial burden borne by SMEs to fund unemployment.[59]

Ultimately the Plan Barre and its successor, designed to pave the way for the 1978 parliamentary elections, led to its author becoming one of the most unpopular prime ministers of the Fifth Republic. Barre showed himself to be inflexible and unyielding, turning a deaf ear to public demands and a blind eye to the strikes. He refused to change course, ostensibly at least, affirming that there would be no reflation of the economy.[60] As he put it in January 1977:

> The right to strike exists. The strike will take place. But government policy will not change.... I have already told you that I am not susceptible to demonstrations. Those who have not yet understood this will understand it. They will take their time and I shall wait until they have understood.[61]

Despite plumbing the depths of political unpopularity, Barre was nevertheless reappointed to a second term as prime minister following the legislative elections of April 1978. He immediately abolished price controls, in what Frears describes as potentially the most liberal gesture of the Giscard years.[62] Prices for the traditional *baguette* were liberated for the first time in a century.[63] Barre explained his logic as follows:

> As long as employers could not fix their prices, they lost interest. [...] In a protected society, people make no effort to adapt to competition. In France, I am sure there are reserves of imagination, creativity and courage, which are untapped because we are conditioned by the society about us, and are made to carry out tasks whose object we do not understand.[64]

Barre also began the process of bolstering the equity market, which Laurent Fabius and Edouard Balladur would take further in the 1980s under the Mitterrand presidency. A new form of preferred share was introduced, along with tax benefits for share buying, doubling the number of small shareholders in just three months.

Industrial policy

In industrial policy, President Giscard sought to break with a past characterised by state support for key growth sectors, such as aerospace, nuclear energy, computing and electronics. Rather, his primary objective, announced at the end of 1973, was the 'redeployment' and restructuring of industry. At stake was the dependency of French industry on the state for financial resources and direction, which in the eyes of Giscard and Barre was unlikely to foster national competitiveness. It was also a drain on the public purse that France could ill afford at a time of recession. At the heart of Giscard's thinking was a desire to make France a more liberal nation – as well as a more admired one.[65] During the Giscard years France did move to some degree in the direction of a predominantly free enterprise economy. Market mechanisms were privileged, such as lucrative 'development contracts' awarded to firms willing to match public with private funding for the development of new technologies, robotics, biotechnology, etc.[66] There was clearly a need for greater flexibility and responsiveness to the market. However, the problem was that for firms to acquire the efficiency and profitability that underpin competitiveness, substantial lay-offs were called for immediately beyond what the government could countenance politically.

Whatever his initial ambitions, the Giscard years on the whole were marked in the industrial sphere by continuity rather than change. Yet, as Berger points out, there was one significant difference. Whereas previously the negative objectives of government policy had been left largely to the market (such as allowing inefficient industries to disappear or the peasant population to decline), while growth industries were supported by the injection of resources, during the Giscard years the reverse applied. After 1974, resources were channelled at 'lame ducks' such as shipbuilding, steel, shoes and textiles, which had increasingly come under pressure from cheap Third World imports. The preservation of these 'sunset' industries was potentially more problematic than their demise. Arguably, public funds would have been more judiciously spent easing the transition to new market realities rather than perpetuating their existence. State intervention in steel, for instance, encouraged the sector to retain outdated capacity (steel production had fallen to two-thirds of capacity, from 27 million tonnes in 1974 to 22 million tonnes in 1977 to 23.4 million in 1979).[67] At the same time the industry was encouraged to create new capacity that world markets could not absorb. The result was increased corporate indebtedness, putting off but ultimately exacerbating the problem of large-scale industrial restructuring.[68] The combined debts of Usinor and Sacilor in 1979 amounted to FF38 billion, exceeding their total annual turnover.[69] Moreover, firms that incorporated government hopes for the future were increasingly left to their own devices. One adviser to the president summed up government policy as *'faire faire* not *laisser faire'*.[70] As Berger writes:

> While the state nationalizes steel to save it from bankruptcy, bails out the largest textile manufacturer, and salvages hundreds of tottering small- and medium-sized enterprises, its role in the construction of a new economic structure has been defined in progressively narrower and less activist terms. Asked how the state intended to encourage the *redéploiement* and *restructuration* that Giscard has defined as the principal objective of French economic policy in the seventies, the *Commissaire au*

Plan explained that it was up to individual industries: 'Redéploiez-vous!' [Redeploy yourselves!][71]

At the same time, there was growing disillusionment with the Gaullist policy of state-backed industrial concentration. Mergers and acquisitions promoted by the state had been a major plank in Gaullist industrial policy, such that by the beginning of the Giscard era France had the highest rate of corporate mergers in Western Europe for two decades. Size had come to be conceived as an end in itself, deemed necessary for survival and prosperity in an increasingly cut-throat competitive environment. As French national champions were consolidated through mergers, however, no attempt had been made to verify the link between size and efficiency. Yet research and development (R&D) expenditures often decline in relative terms as firm size increases, as firms seek to reap economies of scale or simply become absorbed in the internal processes of managing the merger. Many firms that had grown through mergers in the 1960s became automatic candidates for nationalisation by the left, as featured in its Common Programme. Some of these firms would have liked, had they been able, to have turned the clock back and avoided the mergers which led to their nationalisation in 1982.[72] Due to their size, even relatively small decisions on their part had potential political ramifications, curtailing their room for manoeuvre and slowing the decision-making process. By contrast, small and medium-sized firms began to appear more responsive to market changes, less unwieldy, less alienating to work in, and potentially more able to create jobs – although it was not until the early 1980s that the *petite et moyenne entreprise* (PME) really caught the public imagination.[73] In 1976, the government established a new body to help SMEs, the *délégué à la petite et moyenne entreprise*, designed to facilitate company start-ups, which were relatively low in France, encourage the expansion of existing firms, and provide management consulting, although there was little take-up of this service.

However, the real focus of public funding throughout the Giscard years was the rescue of firms from bankruptcy,[74] to such an extent indeed that Véronique Maurens, writing in *Le Monde* in March 1979, described France as 'the largest cemetery for bankrupt firms in the world'.[75] At the same time, the success of some expensive, high-prestige technological projects, including Concorde – which despite considerable public investment from Britain and France could not cover the cost of its operations – was increasingly called into question. The Plan Calcul, an attempt to forge a viable computer industry by creating in CII (Compagnie Internationale pour l'Informatique) a national champion through the merger of various small firms, likewise absorbed substantial public investment. But the wisdom of ploughing public money into an industry that could only compete in protected markets, in a symbolic but ultimately futile gesture of strategic independence, appeared increasingly suspect. Eventually, following the logic outlined by Stoléru in his influential book *L'Impératif industriel* (1969),[76] France was forced to increase international (read American and later Japanese) participation in her electronics industry.[77] Under Giscard a merger was arranged between CII, which suffered from low market share despite protected markets, and Honeywell, while Matra joined forces with the Harris Corporation to manufacture microchips.

The end of the Giscard era

By 1978–79, the economic outlook had begun to look brighter. Buoyant exports in 1978 suggested that firms that had restructured through public funds were increasingly geared to international markets. Agriculture, described by Giscard as 'our oil', was earning large surpluses: as much as FF17 billion with other EC nations in 1979.[78] The balance-of-payments deficit had been transformed into a surplus (see Table 4.6).[79] The franc was beginning to appreciate in real terms against the mark following its entry in 1979 into the EMS (admittedly with devastating consequences for sectors exposed to international competition, such as cars).[80] In short, the French economy was arguably just beginning to crawl its way out of recession when the second oil shock sent it reeling once again.

The impact of the second oil shock was most pronounced in 1980, when it reduced growth in OECD countries by an estimated 2.3 per cent (see Table 4.7). The restrictive policies put in place by several Western governments to combat the crisis, and prevent inflation from spiralling out of control, actually exacerbated its effects, suppressing growth by an estimated additional 1.0 per cent in 1979, and 1.2 per cent in 1981. During the winter of 1980–81, moreover, Prime Minister Barre actually implemented a slight reflation of the economy, both to stimulate internal demand as well as to soften up the electorate in preparation for the presidential election of May 1981. Key to this reflation was the suppression in

Table 4.6   French balance of payments and current account, 1978–80 (FF millions)

Year	1978	1979	1980
Exports	336,061	400,846	454,812
Imports	−332,967	−409,179	−505,263
Trade balance	+3,094	−8,333	−50,451
Curr. Acc. Balance	+16,850	+4,913	−31,113

Source: Adapted from Hough, J.R., *The French Economy*, London, Croom Helm, 1982, p. 191.

Table 4.7 Impact of second oil crisis and economic policies on growth, OECD, 1978–81

Year	1978	1979	1980	1981
Change in GDP	4.0	3.1	1.2	2.0
Oil crisis	0	−0.5	−2.3	−0.5
Budget policies	+0.5	−0.5	−0.5	−1.5
Monetary policies	0	−0.5	0	−0.7
Total impact	+0.5	−1.5	−2.8	−2.7

Source: Fonteneau, A. and Muet, P.-A., *La Gauche face à la crise*, Paris, Presses de la Fondation nationale des sciences politiques, 1985, p. 74.

February 1981 of the additional percentage point on national insurance contributions introduced in August 1979. An award of FF4.1 billion was made to farmers to maintain their 1980 level of income. The minimum level of retirement pension was increased, as were benefits for the disabled, while the price of petrol and road tax remained unchanged in the 1981 budget.[81] Few, however, seemed to notice, Fonteneau and Muet observing that the 'overlooked reflation' of spring 1981 was consistently underestimated by the incoming socialist administration.

Meanwhile Giscard grew increasingly remote, aloof and discouraged as his presidency neared its end, assailed moreover by a growing number of scandals. One such scandal was the Bokassa affair, which hit the headlines in autumn 1979.[82] It was alleged that the president, alongside other leading members of the government, had accepted valuable gifts of diamonds from the emperor of the then Central African Empire (renamed Republic in 1978), Jean-Bedel Bokassa, dictator of a brutal regime and a suspected perpetrator of atrocities. The Central African Empire was a client state of France and exceedingly poor, except for its diamond mines and an estimated 8,000 tons of uranium reserves, virtually untapped. Had the diamonds been given to Valéry Giscard d'Estaing, the man? Or were they instead intended as a gift to the French nation, of which Giscard was merely the representative? Giscard's refusal to explain went down very badly with the populace. Another charge levied against him was that he had made large stockmarket gains during his presidency. Yet another scandal was inspired by the president's predilection for tall, long-legged black women. There is a deep-rooted tolerance of adultery in France, which goes hand in hand with an acceptance of the demarcation of public and private life, reinforced by draconian privacy laws. François Mitterrand is rumoured to have had several mistresses, whom he provided with state apartments and, allegedly, *châteaux*, and even, in the case of Edith Cresson, the job of prime minister. The appearance of Mitterrand's illegitimate daughter, Mazarine, an attractive young student, at her father's funeral in January 1996, sparked a fascination on the part of public and paparazzi to which France, with its long-standing tolerance of adultery and protection of personal privacy, was unused. In the case of Giscard, his predilection for *minettes*, and even the scandal of the Bokassa diamonds, could have been forgiven him by the electorate. Frears insists, perhaps with an element of special pleading to which biographers may at times be susceptible, that any charge of corruption is misplaced: 'the idea that Giscard is corrupt, or corruptible is, in the eyes of almost everyone, simply not a credible accusation'.[83] But what the man in the street was perhaps less able to forgive was that such behaviour should be accompanied by an overbearing arrogance suggestive of an authoritarian president who not only considered himself to be far superior to those he served, but who was ultimately contemptuous of their criticism. 'Porphyrogenetic' or 'born to the purple' was the epithet used by Duhamel to characterise Giscard.[84] While encapsulating his demeanor, this characterisation obscures the fact that the title 'd'Estaing' had been purchased by Giscard's father and was not in fact a mark of nobility.

The triumph of François Mitterrand in the second round of the presidential elections on 10 May 1981, by 51 per cent to 49 per cent of votes cast, is commonly perceived as a victory for Mitterrand and the left. It is probably more accurate, however, to view the result as a defeat for Giscard.[85] Irrespective of inflation, the growing army of unemployed, or deepening public deficits, it is likely that the tarnishing of Giscard's personal reputation, coupled with the president's innate but ultimately inappropriate arrogance, lost him the 1981 presidential election. Writers, however, are much more interested in the socialist experiment of François Mitterrand that followed than in Valéry Giscard d'Estaing. In his final televised broadcast to the nation as president, on the evening of Sunday, 10 May 1981, following the announcement of Mitterrand's win, Giscard, at 55 years of age still a relatively youthful head of state, promised that he would be back. In a theatrical gesture worthy of Racine, Giscard left the scene, the camera lens focused on an empty chair. He did not return.

Giscard's years at the helm of the nation were dominated by the two oil crises, which effectively scuppered the reformist agenda outlined in his election campaign. It would be wrong, however, to see his presidency purely in the light of an economic agenda thrown off course by world events outside his control. For Giscard, Europe – in which he aspired to '[conserve] what exists, that is the CAP [Common Agricultural Policy]' while 'proposing what is lacking'[86] – was the fundamental priority. The launch of the EMS in 1979, a critical stepping-stone on the path to Economic and Monetary Union, represented the fulfilment of a key election promise. He formed a close personal friendship with West German Chancellor Helmut Schmidt, with whom he had much in common, which served to amplify French influence on the European stage. One of Giscard's main achievements in Europe was to introduce the European Council, a key decision-making body of the European Community, holding regular summit meetings. His ultimate ambition for France in Europe was that of 'a united France in a confederal Europe'.[87] This is arguably one which he has lived to see largely fulfilled, above all through the advent of the euro in 1999 to which he contributed through his promotion of the EMS, even if this was introduced eighteen years after his own presidency had elapsed. Subsequently, at the Laeken summit in December 2001, the importance of Giscard's role in the European project was recognised when he was appointed as the convenor of a convention to shape the future of the EU, examining in particular the possibility of a European Constitution.[88]

During the Giscard years, France took a small but significant step towards reconceptualising her position in a world characterised above all by the interdependence of national economies, thrown into sharp relief by the crisis in the Middle East and its impact on world oil supplies and prices. A full understanding of this position, however, did not emerge until the early 1980s. This developing awareness nevertheless conditioned Giscard's views on economic sovereignty, national independence and prestige cherished by de Gaulle. The idea that France could remain fully independent and detached from what occurred beyond its borders was at odds with its ambition to play a leading role in Europe.

For Giscard, French prestige lay first and foremost in serving as an example to other nations: France should be admired for its economic policy, its intellectual prowess, its emphasis on justice (the last execution had taken place under Pompidou, in November 1972).[89] French claims to a role on the world stage, moreover, relied increasingly on the competitive performance of her national champions and less on the maintenance of a nuclear deterrent. Following the recommendations of Stoléru, France strove to preserve at least one national champion in critical industrial sectors, such as Dassault in aviation, or Framatome and CEA (Commissariat à l'énergie atomique) in nuclear technology, in a monopolistic or oligopolistic form of capitalism that sought increasingly to manage the competitive landscape.

While, under Prime Minister Thatcher, British firms that got into financial difficulty were increasingly allowed to go under, French national champions derived considerable organisational stability from the state's determination that they should survive. If the rhetoric under Giscard was of economic liberalism, this was fundamentally an *organised* liberalism. Essentially, this gave firms the knowledge that they had a future even if in a slimmed-down form, that they would still be there tomorrow, and hence could look to the longer term. It was not until summer 1984, paradoxically under the socialist government of Laurent Fabius, that a household name, the private steel company Creusot-Loire, was allowed to go bust.

Conclusion

The year 1973–74 witnessed an end to the availability of the cheap imported oil that had fuelled thirty years of economic boom. This chapter has explored French responses to the crisis this provoked. In key respects, French reactions to the crisis continue to influence French decision-makers in the here and now. The oil shocks threw into sharp relief the full extent of French dependence on imported energy. The tenacious, aggressive stance adopted by French business leaders and politicians in European energy markets, marked by a state-funded strategy of international expansion while home markets are fiercely protected, often in contravention of EU directives, has its origins in the vulnerability revealed by the oil crises of the 1970s.

While the reflation plan of 1975 may have contributed inadvertently to the ensuing crisis, boosting inflation, the Barre Plan (1976–81) was arguably a step along the road to greater realism, despite its deep-rooted unpopularity. Deflationary and pro-European in essence, it set the tone for much of the following two decades. Vernholes notes that, having nationalised large swathes of the industrial and financial sectors in 1981–82, the socialist administration reverted essentially to the economic strategy outlined by Raymond Barre. In abolishing price controls from 1976, the Barre Plan was also a first step in the restoration of managerial responsibility, which emerged in the 1980s under the socialists and which went from strength to strength in the 1990s.[90] This emphasised the importance of management over *dirigisme*, readjusting the balance in a small but significant way in the direction of the former. Companies that embodied government hopes for the future relied increasingly on their own initiatives. Barre's measures to stimulate the equity market likewise paved the way for major reforms of the stock exchange in the 1980s and 1990s, initiated by left and right alike.

At the same time, the management of large French firms improved enormously during the Giscard years, able to draw on a talented body of managers trained for public service by the leading *grandes écoles*. The fact that members of the managerial and administrative elite had a common educational background led to a pronounced cohesiveness and continuity of thought. They were educated in particular at ENA, created in 1945, whose intake came largely from Sciences Po, and Polytechnique, many of whose graduates went on to join the Ecole des Mines or the Ecole des Ponts et Chaussés. Together ENA and Polytechnique educated approximately 50 per cent of top managers. France's key decision-makers thus shared a technocratic ideology, essentially pragmatic, yet characterised by continuity with respect to institutional structures, and a deep-rooted belief in the close cooperation between state and industry. This was fostered in turn by the networks of personal relationships linking the heads of leading firms with top civil servants and politicians. In the late 1980s this common vision – characterised now by an unswerving belief in German-style financial orthodoxy – came to be dubbed 'la pensée unique'.

As the Giscard years drew to a close, what concerned leading managers was above all the maintenance of France's competitive position in world markets. From 1978 large firms were increasingly geared to export markets. Meanwhile the process of European economic integration, moving on apace, served 'to prick the sides of [their] intent'.[91]

5
The Socialist Experiment: Coming to Terms with Economic Realities

> Marxism is dying; Catholicism reminds us that there is nothing more capitalist than that other elder daughter of the Church, Italy; analysts are silent – an elementary prudence in the face of the new idol, the firm!
>
> Alain Minc, 1985[1]

When, on 10 May 1981, the French elected to the Elysée, albeit by a narrow margin, the first and to date only socialist president of the Fifth Republic, it marked the end of 23 years of right-wing rule. This 'historic victory' of the left was complete when a coalition of socialists and communists won a landslide victory in the legislative elections held in June. This was Mitterrand's third attempt at the presidency. That it was successful owed much to his realisation that only a united left could come to power in France. Giscard's imperial bearing also played its part in the election result, as did the twin difficulties of mounting inflation and unemployment, after seven long years of *crise*, stoking up popular demand for economic and social reform.

This chapter examines the new economic priorities of the incoming left-wing administration, in particular the nationalisations of February 1982, the cornerstone of the government's ambitious economic programme. It suggests that the success of these priorities was jeopardised from the outset by the fact that they were against the international trend, which was towards deflation and austerity. The speed with which the subsequent U-turn on economic policy was effected throws into sharp relief the extent to which governments can be punished by the markets for denying the constraints bearing upon them. The chapter also explores the new business mentality that emerged in the early 1980s as the socialists converted the French to the virtues of the market economy: an ironic outcome for an administration that initially had aspired to effect a break with capitalism. The growth of provincial French business schools reinforced the new ideology, as did the rise of a new generation of businessman, more worldly, more attuned to the exigencies of the market.

A generation spent in opposition had given the left time to dream, to nurture great ambitions. Armed with an unambiguous mandate for social change (*le changement*), and persuaded that the voters had made a *choix de société*, the left immediately embarked on a far-reaching programme of reform, whose objectives were at once ideological and social as well as economic. On the ideological plane, the programme aspired to a rupture with capitalism, an end to establishment domination, and the elimination of private profit. As Mitterrand put it in his pre-election debate with Giscard, his aim was '*une nouvelle politique*'[2] founded on respect for mankind, and not determined by the profit of a small but powerful and dominant elite.[3] In a similar vein, Prime Minister Mauroy proposed, in his inaugural speech to the National Assembly, 'a new style of citizenship'.[4] The bold ambition articulated by the *Projet socialiste*, and aimed at the youth of the day, was 'to make [France] the melting pot for the liberation of man and the construction of socialism'.[5] These were aims and ambitions that delved deep into the cultural substrata, the deep-rooted values, beliefs and basic taken-for-granted assumptions that characterise French socio-economic and business culture. Likewise, on the social plane, the left aimed to instil democratic relations in the workplace, in particular the implementation of workers' control, and a strengthening of the unions.

On the economic plane, the programme aimed to get the country out of recession. Beyond this basic objective, it aspired to the rescue and modernisation of France's industrial base through a new mode of production and continued investment despite an unfavourable environment; a return to full employment through job creation; and a new type of growth. As the *Projet socialiste* expressed it, 'A strong and different type of growth is necessary to achieve our objectives [...] We want growth which is egalitarian, independent and creative.'[6] This was to be achieved through the Plan, through an active budget and a vibrant public sector. Meanwhile, with import penetration perceived as a direct cause of deindustrialisation and therefore of unemployment, the left sought to 'reconquer the domestic market'. An estimated 700,000 industrial jobs had been lost during the Giscard era.[7] At the same time, 98 per cent of tape-recorders, 86 per cent of hi-fi sets, 79 per cent of domestic freezers, 66 per cent of refrigerators, 58 per cent of machine tools and 50 per cent of textiles sold in France now came from overseas.[8] It was not difficult to perceive a correlation between these two sets of statistics.

With such radical ambitions, and with four Communist ministers appointed to government, it is perhaps not surprising that the left's agenda might be viewed by some as threatening. Following Mitterrand's election to the presidency, prices on the Paris stock exchange fell so sharply that trading had to be suspended after five minutes. Lack of confidence in the left's programme prompted substantial flights of capital to Geneva and New York. Mauroy tells how in the run-up to the presidential election

$8 billion left the country, followed by a further half a billion to one billion dollars daily in the early days of the socialist administration.[9] In the ten days between Mitterrand's election and his inauguration as president, the Banque de France lost one-third of its total reserves in a futile battle to defend the franc.[10] For many leading businessmen, 1981 represented another Popular Front,[11] their expectations for the future direction of the economy under socialist management encapsulated in the anti-left election slogan, 'Work less, spend more, and borrow the difference!'[12] Weber describes relations between government and *patronat* in the left's first year of office as 'trench warfare'.[13] As one leading businessman explained:

> Their desperation was sincere. The thunderbolt had shaken them terribly. They suspected the government of aspiring to put enterprises and entrepreneurs under its control, to replace them by the unions, to appropriate for itself the largest firms through the subterfuge of nationalisation, to break up the CNPF [Conseil National du Patronat Français] by promoting other organisations, to replace its leaders by political cronies. This is why 1981 was a year of total opposition.[14]

They had good reason to fear: in 1981, the incoming administration ousted as many as 29 of the chairmen of the top 36 public-sector companies. Admittedly it replaced them with individuals from the same privileged background, that is to say who had graduated from a leading *grande école*, who were members of a prominent *grand corps*, and who normally had followed a politico-administrative career path as opposed to one in business.

The world economic outlook had begun nevertheless to look more promising in the spring of 1981, such that it seemed that the recession might be drawing to a close – as it had, indeed, several times since 1974.[15] In July 1981, as the left took office, the Organisation for Economic Cooperation and Development (OECD), alongside other economic and business analysts, including the European Community (EC) predicted a 2 per cent increase in GDP in 1982. In the event this did not materialise. GDP fell by 0.4 per cent in the EC in 1981, rising again by 0.4 per cent in 1982.[16] But it was on the assumption that the economic climate would improve, and in the heady atmosphere accompanying its dual victory, that the left set about implementing its electoral programme, as set out in Mitterrand's '110 propositions'.

Educated in law and political science, Mitterrand lacked any formal training in economics. He was also determined to implement to the letter the manifesto on which he had been elected, despite warnings from some of his advisers, who advocated immediate devaluation of the franc, over-valued at the time by about 15 per cent, as well as greater protectionism.[17] To renege on his electoral promises would have been to betray the *peuple de gauche*. As Mitterrand later admitted, 'I was carried away by our victory; we were intoxicated. Everyone [...] predicted the return of growth by 1983. Honestly, I lacked the necessary knowledge to say they were wrong.'[18] Naïvety in economic affairs conspired with inexperience of office,[19] after a generation in opposition, to ensure the immediate implementation of the socialist programme of far-reaching reform. Politics took precedence over economics, as the socialist government embarked on a headlong rush for growth despite a difficult international context, which, in the initial euphoria of victory, was largely ignored.

L'état de grâce

Scarcely had the victory celebrations quieted when laws designed to bring about 'le changement' came thick and fast. These announced widespread nationalisation. The retirement age was to be lowered at a stroke from 65 to 60, while the working week was to be cut from 40 to 39 hours without loss of pay (the first reduction in working time since the 1936 Matignon Agreements had consecrated the 40-hour week).[20] Other concessions to working people included an additional fifth week of paid holiday and measures to bring democracy to the workplace.[21] Mitterrand announced the reduction in the working week publicly without prior consultation with key ministers, an indication of his extensive presidential powers. (Pierre Mauroy subsequently argued that the 39-hour week should be accompanied by a commensurate reduction in salary; Mitterrand disagreed.)[22] Nor were business leaders consulted on the granting of a fifth week of annual paid leave and the reduction in the working week. The CNPF estimated the yearly cost of this 'double whammy' to industry at FF75 billion.[23] Adding to this the cost of raising the minimum wage (Salaire minimum interprofessionnelle de croissance, SMIC), the increase in the business tax (*le taxe professionnelle*), and the implementation of the Auroux laws on workplace democracy, the whole bill was reckoned to amount to FF100 billion.[24] The result was a tax and social security burden that France's leading employers association claimed was twice that of the country's leading competitors.

Admittedly the CNPF had got off to a bad start with Mitterrand by openly campaigning against him during the 1981 presidential elections. For years past its leaders had been complaining of the substantial social charges burdening French business, which had mounted steadily during the Giscard years,[25] and in return for whose alleviation many businessmen were willing to sacrifice state aid (see Table 5.1). 'Less aid and fewer charges!' was the slogan adopted by Yvon Gattaz, a small businessman who rose to prominence as founder of ETHIC (Entreprises de taille humaine industrielles et commerciales), elected CNPF leader in December 1981. In the eyes of the CNPF, the incoming administration severely overestimated the ability of French business to withstand a further onslaught on costs and remain competitive. On 10 March 1982, in an interview published in *Le Monde*, Gattaz denounced

Table 5.1 Employers' social security and payroll taxes in France, 1970–91 (FF billions)

Levy	1970	1975	1980	1985	1990	1991
Soc. Sec. contributions	100,991	219,799	500,068	905,143	1,253,142	1,305,687
Paid by employees	19,248	46,591	130,216	246,399	376,695	387,420
Paid by employers	73,942	158,976	332,845	585,915	773,348	808,581
Paid by self-employed	7,801	14,232	37,007	72,829	103,081	109,686
Other payroll taxes *of which*	3,338	10,499	25,811	42,980	54,021	56,679
Salary	3,162	6,923	15,831	26,413	34,165	34,785
Apprenticeship	176	234	1,129	827	661	678
Professional training	–	250	1,550	668	195	178

Source: Revenue statistics of OECD Member Countries, 1965–92, cited in Blotnicki, L. and Heckly, C., 'France', in Messere, K., ed., *The Tax System in Industrialized Countries*, Oxford, Oxford University Press, 1998, p. 105.

the 'bleeding dry' of business by government: 'I know that our discourse on employers' payments is always greeted with a certain scepticism. [...] But it is as an economic expert that I raise the alarm [...]: our firms are being bled dry; we must put a stop to this haemorrhage imposed in the name of social progress.'[26] Mitterrand had promised in his election campaign not to increase the total tax and social security burden, which, in the event, was increased by two further percentage points under the socialist government, rising from 42.5 per cent to 44.5 per cent of GDP by 1985.[27]

The Keynesian reflation policy pursued by the Mauroy administration (1981–84) from its accession to government in June 1981 until the devaluation of the franc in June 1982 (the second in a series of three devaluations) aimed to achieve a return to economic growth and the restoration of full employment. Redistributive measures designed to stimulate internal demand included raising the minimum wage, which affected 1.7 million workers. The SMIC was revised upwards as many as nine times from June 1981 to March 1983. This represented an overall increase of 38 per cent, about 15 per cent in real terms, to be borne by France's increasingly beleaguered enterprises, boosting the black market for labour, *le travail au noir*. There was no compensatory reduction in national insurance contributions. Provision for pensions, health and the unemployed were increased in real terms by 5.1 per cent in 1981 and by 6.7 per cent in 1982. Of this, Muet attributes about 1 per cent of the 1981 increase and half of the 1982 increase to government economic policy, the rest being due to the lowering of the retirement age, the continued rise in health spending, and the greater numbers receiving unemployment benefit.[28] Government spending on public housing, centrally authorised capital projects and subsidies to industry also rose. Family allowances for those with two children rose by 50 per cent in 1981–82.

These redistributive measures were accompanied by a vigorous employment policy. Lowering the retirement age was designed to reduce the labour supply and encourage the hiring of younger workers who accounted for 50 per cent of the unemployed. Reducing the working week was intended to boost job creation. In addition, as many as 240,000 new administrative posts were created in the public sector in the period 1981–83.

Nationalisation and economic progress

The central plank of the incoming government's economic policy was an extensive nationalisation programme, dwarfing those carried out in the heady days of the Popular Front under Léon Blum or in the aftermath of the Liberation under de Gaulle.[29] The programme was implemented rapidly, only eight months after the left came to power, because the socialists and communists had been planning it for a decade, separately at first, then together in their 1972 *Projet commun de gouvernement*. Indeed, that its completion was delayed until February 1982 was due to the participation of foreign partners in some companies earmarked for nationalisation, requiring complex negotiations on the part of the government. These concerned the computer manufacturer CII-Honeywell-Bull, 47 per cent of which was owned by the American Honeywell; the pharmaceutical house Roussel-Uclaf, part of the German chemical group Hoechst; and CGCT (Compagnie Générale des constructions téléphoniques) controlled by the American giant ITT.

A law was passed on 11 February 1982 transferring ownership of twelve industrial groups and their subsidiaries from the private to the public sector. Seven featured among France's top twenty largest companies, including five international groups: Compagnie Générale d'Eléctricité (CGE) in electrical construction, electronics, telecommunications, heavy engineering and shipbuilding; Thomson-Brandt in domestic appliances, electronics and telecommunications; Saint-Gobain-Pont-à-Mousson in glass, paper and metals; Péchiney-Ugine-Kuhlmann in aluminium and chemicals, and Rhône-Poulenc in pharmaceuticals, fertilisers and chemicals. In addition, the state purchased a majority stake (51 per cent) in two privately owned arms and aeronautical manufacturers, Dassault-Greguet and Matra. Two major iron and steel firms, Usinor and Sacilor, in which the state had held a majority stake since 1978, were also nationalised. In the banking sector, two investment banks were nationalised: the two 'godfathers' of French capitalism, the Compagnie financière de Suez and the Compagnie financière de Paris et des Pays-Bas, better known as Paribas. These were joined by 36 smaller banks and the remaining private shares in the previously nationalised Crédit Lyonnais, Banque Nationale de Paris (BNP) and Société Générale.[30] Mitterrand decided in favour of complete nationalisation and against purchasing a controlling interest (51 per cent) in the majority of companies selected for nationalisation, as Michel Rocard and Laurent Fabius advised. Perhaps, had he done so, the Communist Party, which had contributed to the left's victory in the presidential and legislative elections, would have perceived this as immediate betrayal. But all-out nationalisation cost the Treasury dearly. Shares were purchased at the going market rate lest the socialists be accused of Soviet-style appropriation. Estimates of the cost of the nationalisations vary, but the initial cost was probably around FF47 billion of public money, while an estimated FF50 billion was to be paid annually in the form of bonds over the next 15 years in compensation to shareholders.[31] The combined turnover of the nationalised firms in 1981 was in the order of FF300 billion.[32] They employed approximately 800,000 workers, of whom 250,000 were engaged abroad. Together they brought the total number of French workers in public employment from 1,633,000 to 2,295,000, increasing the percentage of public-sector workers in industry from 6.1 to 18.6 per cent and in banking from 46.8 to 68.5 per cent.[33] The French public sector was now the largest outside the Eastern bloc, with an overall impact on the economy of 22.8 per cent of GDP, excluding agriculture, by the end of 1982, reaching a peak of 24 per cent by 1985 (see Table 5.2). After the 1981–82 nationalisation programme was complete, the public sector embraced 24 per cent of employees, 32 per cent of sales, 30 per cent of exports and 60 per cent of annual investment in the industrial and energy sectors.[34]

Ideas expressed in the presidential campaign speeches of François Mitterrand now found themselves woven into new laws on the statute books.

Table 5.2 The public sector in France, 1973–98, excluding agriculture

End of year	Employees (as % of total workforce)	Value added	Fixed capital employed	Mean of three criteria
1973	10.7	12.3	24.3	15.8
1979	11.8	13.9	29.3	18.4
1982	16.7	17.3	34.3	22.8
1985	17.6	19.5	34.9	24.0
1988	13.3	16.0	25.4	18.3
1991	13.4	15.1	24.2	17.6
1998	10.3	11.5	13.5	11.8

Sources: Centre Européen des Entreprises à Participation publique, *Les Entreprises à participation publique dans l'Union Européenne*, Brussels, CEEP, 1994, p. 132; *CEEP Statistical Review*, CEEP, Brussels, 2000, p. 12.

The hopes vested in nationalisation were considerable. Nationalisation was to be 'an efficient instrument of action in the strategy against the recession', contributing to 'an objective of social growth and the development of employment'. The nationalisation of credit completed the process begun in 1936 with the nationalisation of the Banque de France, and pursued in 1945 with the nationalisation of the four main deposit banks, subsequently reduced to three through merger. It was designed to furnish the state with 'an innovative and decentralised financial instrument'.[35] The nationalised companies were to be the vanguard or 'strike force' in the state's attempt to regenerate France's industrial base. That the term *'force de frappe'* was employed, normally reserved for France's nuclear deterrent, implied that the nation's hopes for independence and prestige now lay firmly in the nationalised industries.

State-owned enterprises were also to be the *'fer de lance'*, spearheading the government's policy to introduce democracy in the workplace, to be achieved through employment legislation known as the Auroux laws, named after Jean Auroux. After all, it was argued, there was little point in nationalising firms if workers were not to be given the right to express themselves, to have an input into issues affecting their company or their jobs, thereby influencing and contributing to corporate growth. The Auroux laws consequently stressed negotiation at the level of the firm.[36] Work councils (*les conseils d'atelier*) and the boards of nationalised firms as well as the planning commission were to participate together in a bottom-up as well as top-down democratic process.[37] The Auroux laws were in many ways the government's most ambitious project; they were also, in the eyes of some commentators, its greatest achievement.[38] They did not contribute, however, to a strengthening of the unions, as the socialists had hoped. On the contrary, union membership fell quite dramatically under the socialists. In 1979–80, the strongest union, the Confédération Générale du Travail (CGT), boasted 1.9 million members; by 1983 this had fallen to 1.1 million, while membership of the rival Confédération Française Démocratique du Travail (CFDT) dropped beneath 1 million. Meanwhile membership of the managers' union, the Confédération Générale des Cadres (CGC), shrank by more than 50 per cent: from 320,000 in 1979–80 to 140,000 by 1983.[39] In all, over the fourteen years when Mitterrand was at the helm, trade union membership declined from approximately 25 per cent of the workforce in 1981 to just 7 per cent in public-sector firms, and 5 per cent in the private sector, by 1995.[40]

Industrial policy

Having control of a significant part of French industry, it was argued, would facilitate the government's implementation of industrial policy. French industry, the government felt, was too specialised, having pursued a policy under Giscard centred on niche markets or *créneaux* and overly focused on the strengths of individual star firms. It was in the early 1980s that attention began to shift from building industrial capabilities to building corporate capabilities. This was the time when the discipline of corporate strategy came of age. Chief architect of the strategy revolution was Michael Porter, whose ideas, cogently presented in *Competitive Strategy* (1980) and *Competitive Advantage* (1985), quickly became a new orthodoxy, not only in the USA but also in Western Europe.[41] At the heart of Porter's worldview lay the idea that a firm should seek and maintain a distinctive position in the market. Customers, it was reasoned, would respond positively to a clearly delineated value proposition that would allow the firm to command good prices and earn above-average profits, creating in turn a platform for reinvestment and growth. By investing in those things that it did particularly well, so creating value for customers, the firm would secure a competitive advantage over its rivals that might sustain it into the future. Strategy was thus about finding a sound position in the market, putting forward a distinctive value proposition and developing the organisational capabilities needed to sustain that proposition. The lesson for French business leaders was that big alone did not mean beautiful. Industrial leadership could not be secured purely by the pursuit of economies of scale and scope, the logic of the past associated with the Giscard era and the thinking of Lionel Stoléru.

Beyond the recognition that corporate strategy mattered, it would be wrong to identify the thinking of the French socialists of the early 1980s with that of Porter and other American business ideologues. The underlying assumption in the US was that rivalry between domestic and foreign firms in open markets, free from state interference, was the natural context for the development of competitive strategies. In France, however, the messages were paradoxical: strategy was recognised as necessary to the pursuit of competitive advantage, but the context was that of technocratic planning as a substitute for the free play of the market. Under the socialists, firms were now required to concentrate on their core businesses, a policy known as *recentrage*. The restructuring of industry would comprise a new policy of *filières* or production chains, which sought to develop synergies between firms through vertical integration, to build capabilities that could be shared up and down the production chain with nationalised firms leading the way. Nationally organised vertically integrated manufacturing processes – such that the output of one activity became the input of another, like the interconnected links of a chain – were to embrace whole sectors, of which nationalised industries would comprise the main 'poles', the new term for 'national champion'. This new policy of *filières* was not to be determined primarily by world market forces. On the contrary, its objective was one of de-specialisation, in an effort to reconquer the domestic market and regain competitiveness lost to foreign firms in industrial processes that were not championed by a national star.[42]

In taking responsibility for the restructuring of industry, the government hoped to rise above trade union distrust as well as the petty rivalries of individual management teams. The policy, however, led to the bureaucratisation of industrial policy through a proliferation of public and para-public agencies. By 1984 more than thirty agencies were involved in the electronics production chain alone.[43] In a peculiar way, the present (competitive strategy) had collided with the past (industrial planning) to produce an extraordinary corporate hybrid: the nationalised firm of the early Mitterrand years.

Evaluation

The nationalisations of 1982 were not generally perceived as a success. The fact that the ideology that came to dominate in the latter half of the 1980s – not only in France but elsewhere – was opposed to *dirigisme*, centring instead on the disengagement of the state, privatisation, and on the assertion of the individual rather than the collectivity, reinforced this perception. The balance sheet, however, is not as bleak as it has been painted. Seven of the twelve industrial conglomerates purchased were already in the red at the time of their nationalisation. In 1982, the nationalised firms made a combined loss of FF19.6 billion. In steel, Usinor-Sacilor fared particularly badly in a world market characterised by over-capacity. Rhône-Poulenc lost FF787 million, Thomson lost FF2.2 billion, and Péchiney FF4.6 billion. In the following year the total losses of nationalised firms amounted to FF16 billion.[44] The newly nationalised firms had also lost time and money through the transition from private- to public-sector companies. Interference in their affairs on the part of various ministers of industry was merciless, reaching a paroxysm when Jean-Pierre Chevènement was in post, one of four ministers of industry to be appointed in just two years.

Impecunious, in the teeth of world recession, and with so many other demands being made on the Treasury, the 'shareholder-state' proved unable to provide the newly nationalised firms with sufficient funds for investment – all the more necessary in that these had been sorely lacking under Giscard. Large amounts of public money were indeed ploughed into them (see Table 5.3). But state funds promised in 1982 were received by nationalised firms only in 1983.[45] The French right is firmly of the view that the reflation and nationalisation programme of 1981–82 was almost entirely responsible for the escalation of the national debt throughout the remainder of the 1980s and into the 1990s.[46] From a total debt of FF500 billion in 1981, France's national debt had more than doubled to FF1,195 by the end of the socialist mandate in 1986, equal to 23.8 per cent of GDP.[47] Yet there was a positive side to the mounting national debt. At a time when many large British firms, especially in manufacturing industry, were simply allowed ignominiously to enter receivership, necessary sacrifices on the altar of Thatcherite market dogma, their French counterparts

Table 5.3 French industrial investment
1982–83 (FF billions)

Company	1982	1983
Renault	8.58	9.99
CGE	2.32	2.58
Saint-Gobain	3.49	2.89
Thomson	2.37	2.80
Rhône-Poulenc	2.16	2.50
Péchiney	2.03	2.70
Sacilor	1.69	2.05
Usinor	1.03	1.64
CdF-Chimie	0.63	0.78
EMC	0.37	0.45
Bull	0.55	1.05
CGCT	0.04	0.10
Elf Aquitaine	15.04	15

Source: Jublin, J., 'Les nationalisées ont perdu
16 milliards de F en 1983', *Le Monde*, 12
March 1984.

survived and were ultimately regenerated. Arguably, the survival of these
firms was due in no small measure to the persistence in France of the
Colbertist tradition and the cohesiveness of the French ruling elite.

However, the rising indebtedness of the state in the wake of budgetary
expansion and large-scale nationalisation, together with the slowdown of
the international economy, conspired further to undermine confidence
in the administration of the French economy. High inflation in France –
averaging 12.5 per cent in 1981 and 11 per cent in 1982 – contributed to a
loss of competitiveness on the part of exporters. This exacerbated the trade
deficit, which climbed to FF93.5 billion in 1982, 50 per cent higher than
had been forecast in the finance bill (FF61 billion) (see Table 5.4).[48] France's
external debt reached one-fifth of GDP, severely curtailing the government's
room for manoeuvre. While France pursued a reflation strategy designed to
kick-start the economy, her main economic partners, in particular West
Germany and the UK, were pursuing an austerity policy, thereby depressing
imports. At the same time, while business increased production, this failed
to achieve the desired aim of reconquering the domestic market, since
French consumers often preferred to buy German or Japanese imports than
French-made products, which did not always have the same reputation for
durability or quality. Ultimately French reflation collided with world deflation. The Mauroy–Mitterrand reflation policy, pursued at a time when
France's economic partners were tightening their belts, soon came to be perceived as an expensive mistake. Admittedly, the employment measures
introduced by the socialist administration did have a positive impact in the

Table 5.4   French trade balances in the Mitterrand years (1981–95) (FF billions)

Year	Trade balance	Year	Trade balance
1981	−59.4	1989	−43.9
1982	−93.4	1990	−50.1
1983	−43.2	1991	−29.5
1984	−21.0	1992	31.1
1985	−24.0	1993	87.7
1986	0.3	1994	88.1
1987	−31.6	1995	100.0
1988	−32.8		

Source: *Le Parisien*, 22 February 1996, p. 8, cited in Szarka, J., 'French Business in the Mitterrand Years: the Continuity of Change', in Maclean, M., ed., *The Mitterrand Years: Legacy and Evaluation*, Macmillan Press – now Palgrave Macmillan, Basingstoke, 1998, p. 155.

battle against unemployment in France, which in 1982 increased by 4 per cent as against 29 per cent in West Germany and 22 per cent in the US.[49] Less positively, though, one could argue that this simply postponed the much-needed modernisation of industrial structures, especially the downsizing of large French firms, which in 1983–84 were compelled to shed hundreds of thousands of jobs – particularly in the coal, steel, textiles and shipbuilding sectors – in the struggle for international competitiveness.

From *relance* to *rigueur*

The government's U-turn (*le virage*) from expansion to austerity measures ushered in a freeze on prices (with the exception of milk, fruit and vegetables) and wages (bar the SMIC) from June to October 1982. This proved deeply unpopular, triggering a wave of public demonstrations against government policy. The deindexation of salaries, combined with tax increases, contributed to a decline in household consumption and a loss of purchasing power, which fell in 1984 for the first time in 30 years (by 0.2–1.0 per cent).[50]

The U-turn is commonly cited as occurring in March 1983, when the fight against inflation, double the German rate (increasingly the main point of reference), became the top priority. However, Jacques Delors, then Finance Minister, traces the beginning of austerity to June 1982,[51] while some commentators situate the president's realisation that a change of direction was essential even earlier.[52] CNPF leader Yvon Gattaz, for example, insists that Mitterrand was already aware in April 1982 that things had gone too far just weeks after the nationalisation programme was complete. It was at this point that Mitterrand ruled out a further increase in employers' charges until July 1983, as well as a second reduction in the working week to 35 hours, both of which would have been severely detrimental to business enterprise.[53]

The new policy of *rigueur* marked a departure from the policy of a 'rupture with capitalism' introduced in 1981. It also, more significantly, marked a break with the centralised economic model put in place in the aftermath of the Second World War.[54] As Cohen points out, it saw a left-wing government breaking the indexation of salaries to the cost of living, arresting the increase in compulsory levies on employers, deregulating the economy, clawing back some of the gains made by workers in 1981–82, boosting unemployment, demanding that nationalised firms break even, and ultimately making entrepreneurs the key players in the economy. It was a groundbreaking change of direction that was implemented, moreover, without a genuine ideological debate commensurate to its importance, at least at grassroots level.[55] Within the governing socialist party a debate did take place between traditional socialists and modernists. Whereas the former advocated greater protectionism, championing the interests of declining sectors, small farmers and small businesses, under threat from foreign competition, the latter, in particular Jacques Delors, insisted that the franc should stay in the European Monetary System (EMS). Delors argued that it was not by eschewing competition that French firms would prosper. The fundamental problems of French industry sprang from an intrinsic lack of competitiveness, which could only be achieved through major restructuring and modernisation. As McCormick observes, of FF863 billion worth of imports in 1982, France could have produced at best just 45 per cent.[56]

In the teeth of a rising dollar, against which the franc lost more than half its value between 1980 and 1984, the pressure to reverse socialist reforms proved irresistible.[57] The decision not to devalue immediately on accession to office – as Mitterrand put it, 'one cannot go up the Champs Elysées and devalue the franc'[58] – led to three humiliating devaluations against the mark (on 4 October 1981, 12 June 1982 and 21 March 1983).[59] Thereafter, the promised socialist transformation of the economy was postponed indefinitely. It was replaced by a new emphasis on economic and industrial efficiency and a deflationary austerity programme that targeted consumption in the name of national financial health or 'assainissement national'.[60] In the eyes of Vernholes, this essentially amounted to the implementation by the socialists of the economic strategy of Raymond Barre.[61] Growth, the government's primary aim on acceding to office, was sacrificed for price stability, the balance of payments and a stronger currency. Overwhelmingly the new priority was to restore corporate profitability and investment, the urgency of which was brought home to the government by the unpalatable fact that in 1983 a majority of the top 100 French companies (52) made a loss.[62]

Foremost among the critical lessons learned by the socialists in 1982–83 was the tyranny of the *conjoncture* in a problematic economic environment compounded by the interdependence of national, especially EC economies.

A Keynesian reflation policy, which flew in the face of the austerity programmes being implemented by France's EC neighbours, served little purpose. The critical decision not to withdraw from the EMS in March 1983,
when the franc had again come under pressure, marked the point of realisation on the part of Mitterrand and the Socialist administration that
French economic policy is constrained and conditioned by France's economic environment. In particular it is conditioned by membership of the
Community and the financial and economic relations that obtain with
other member states (especially Germany), restricting government room
for manoeuvre. Decisions that affect French economic policy are taken not
only in Paris but also increasingly in Brussels.

In terms of economic management, the decision to remain in the EMS
was a defining moment, setting the tone for the remainder of the
Mitterrand presidency and beyond. It led above all to the unswerving
pursuit of the orthodox deflationary policy known as the 'strong franc' or
'stable franc', characterised by tight monetary policy and fiscal restraint.
This was closely associated in the 1980s with Pierre Bérégovoy, who, in the
role of Finance Minister (1984–86, 1988–92) and later Prime Minister
(1992–93), earned the respect and confidence of the business community.
'Competitive disinflation' gave France the financial credibility it had lacked
earlier in the Fifth Republic, but at the cost of low growth and rising unemployment throughout the 1980s and 1990s, peaking at 12.7 per cent of the
workforce in 1995.[63]

With hindsight, the U-turn of 1983 emerges as something of a watershed. It marked the turning-point between the quest for an unachievable
level of national economic independence, epitomised by the socialists'
failed go-it-alone reflation of 1981–82, and the pragmatic realisation of systemic interdependence with Europe and the wider international economy.
French economic policy since that time has been set entirely within the
parameters of European construction and the strong franc – a decision
born not of idealism, but rather of enlightened self-interest, realism and
diplomatic necessity.[64]

The rehabilitation of the firm

The year 1983 marked the abandonment of the socialist dream; but it also,
much more positively, witnessed the beginnings of the reconstitution of
French capitalism, and the rehabilitation of the firm. This was played out at
the level of an ideological struggle, in which the forces of modernisation
and change ultimately won out over the old guard of French socialism and
nationalism. The turning-point of 1983 was critical to the process of transformation, going some way towards healing the two-hundred-year-old
schism of a conflict-ridden society, and marking the birth of a new consensus. This new consensus revolved around two poles: the primacy of business

enterprise on the one hand and the importance of Europe on the other. French economic policy became more sensitive to market forces; from now on the economy took precedence over politics. That this cultural revolution took place under a socialist regime was not a remarkable coincidence but rather a precondition for its success. As one top director put it, 'It was necessary for the left to come to power for the importance of market forces to be admitted by all.'[65]

A major feature of the rising status of business enterprise, increasingly apparent after 1983, was the revamping of France's archaic, unsophisticated, 'chalk-and-blackboard' stock exchange. With the traditional French predilection for debt over equity finance, the Parisian and regional *bourses* had long remained underdeveloped relative to the size of the national economy. Compelled to tighten its purse strings following its spendthrift years of reflation, the state began to encourage other, non-governmental sources of capital for industry. On 3 January 1983 a law was passed on the development of investment, followed by a flurry of measures designed to bolster the Bourse.[66] February 1983 saw the birth of the 'second market'. To be listed here cost one-third of the price of a listing on the 'first market'. The fact that it was possible to be listed with only 10 per cent of the firm's shares available for sale (as against 25 per cent for the *premier marché*) prompted one hundred or so medium-sized firms to seek listings in as little as thirty months.[67] The introduction in 1984 of participatory shares (*titres participatifs*) allowed individuals to buy non-voting shares in nationalised companies (Saint-Gobain, Rhône-Poulenc, Thomson-Brandt, the CGE and Renault all took advantage), as did investment certificates (*certificats d'investissement*). Industry Minister Laurent Fabius introduced a new savings certificate, the CODEVI (Compte pour le développement industriel), which was a complex mix between a bond and a share bearing tax-free interest for three years. Several other products were launched, such as non-voting priority dividend shares (*actions à dividende prioritaire sans droit de vote*) and subscription bonds (*obligations à bons de souscription*). These investment products allowed the state to 'have its cake and eat it', by retaining control of nationalised firms while securing equity finance, and at the same time giving the Bourse a much-needed shot in the arm. During the five years of socialist government (1981–86), the total market capitalisation of the Paris Bourse increased by as much as it had in the previous twenty. That said, the relative dearth of significant listed stocks reflected the nationalisation programme of 1981–82.[68] The market capitalisation of the Paris Bourse in 1986 (FF600 billion) was unimpressive when compared to the capitalisation of stock exchanges around the world. It was scarcely above Amsterdam, below Zurich, half the size of Toronto and less than half of Frankfurt, less than a quarter of the City of London, a twelfth of Tokyo and just a twenty-fourth of Wall Street. As far as daily transactions were concerned, there were four, five, 17 and 50 times as many in London, Frankfurt, Tokyo and New York respectively.[69]

The first signs of resurgence in French capital markets were accompanied more generally by a change in public attitudes in favour of business values and against traditional collective values. The results of a 1983 *Le Figaro–SOFRES* opinion poll suggested that the terms 'competition', 'liberalism' and particularly 'profit' – which had never before been seen in a positive light – were all in the ascendant, while those of 'socialism', 'nationalisation', 'trade unionism' and 'planning'[70] had all declined in popularity. Similarly, a BVA–*L'Expansion* survey published in September that year discovered that a majority of interviewees (62 per cent) considered the well-being of industry ('la santé des entreprises') to be more important than the standard of living of individuals.[71]

In July 1984 a new and youthful prime minister, Laurent Fabius, only 37 years of age, replaced Pierre Mauroy at Matignon, his appointment symbolising the supersedence of old, outworn patterns and ideologies by a new pragmatism. His appointment also signified an end to the Union of the left that had brought the socialists to power, provoking the resignation of the four communist government ministers. As early as December 1982 Fabius had begun to suggest that 'the state should intervene better, and no longer incessantly more'.[72] This discourse contained the seeds of an idea born in the paroxysm of state intervention that constituted the nationalisations and which continued to gather momentum throughout Mitterrand's second term as president. In order for '*mieux d'Etat*', a better state, there had to be '*moins d'Etat*', less state.[73] In July 1984, Prime Minister Fabius publicly recognised the state as having 'reached its limits', which it ought never again to exceed.[74]

Fabius embodied a new style of socialism: dynamic, flexible, open and entrepreneurial, seemingly more concerned with image, perhaps, than with content. This change of direction, however, was not merely superficial and cosmetic. It also marked a deeper ideological shift, brought about by a new understanding of the limits of the government's room for manoeuvre. What the state could not do for individuals, they must now do for themselves. The word 'socialism', in fact, was dropped from Fabius' vocabulary, replaced by new buzzwords such as 'désétatisation', the withdrawal of the state, and 'modernisation', his preferred verbs being 'modernise', 'communicate' and, most important of all perhaps, 'win', *gagner*.

From 1984 the nationalised companies, which were now expected to be profitable, were increasingly treated like other companies and ceased to be sacrosanct in socialist eyes. The efficient management of public-sector companies became an important appraisal criterion for their chairmen. Mitterrand himself articulated the new pro-market mentality making headway among socialist ranks in a televised address to the nation in January 1984. He insisted that the government's focus was now securely on the firm: 'The French are beginning to understand: it is the firm that creates wealth, it is the firm that creates jobs, it is the firm that determines our standard of living and our place in the world hierarchy.'[75]

This did not necessarily signify warmer relations between government and *patronat*, who were warned by Mitterrand in 1984 that they faced prison sentences should they boycott the *taxe professionnelle*, as they had threatened.[76] That better relations did not ensue is suggested by the fact that Mitterrand, who had met Yvon Gattaz, head of the CNPF, a dozen times during the period 1981–84, refused to meet with him in 1985–86. This is odd, since it was precisely at this time that the government was seeking to present itself as more heedful of the needs of business enterprise.[77] One of Fabius' first acts as Prime Minister, moreover, was to refuse to bail out the crippled private steel firm Creusot-Loire, sending a powerful signal to business that government–industry relations had changed irrevocably. Partly, the decision was due to the government's reluctance to do anything that might be seen as nationalisation by the back door. But it also reflected the government's impatience with Creusot-Loire shareholders for refusing to recognise that they might have a responsibility to commit their own resources to help the stricken firm.[78]

To reconcile the French with industrial enterprise and the market economy, *le jeu du marché*, now became a key government objective. The emphasis was henceforth on individual effort and enterprise; it was the state's mission to provide the structural conditions in which individual initiative could thrive, not to supplant or suffocate this, and flourish in its stead. That individual initiative had been sorely lacking in France was suggested by the low birth rate of new businesses. It was also evident in the large numbers of young people who were out of work: 50 per cent of the unemployed were under 26 years of age – normally among the most dynamic and creative members of society, and the most open to new ideas. Crozier's notion of France as a stalled society, burdened by bureaucracy, is again relevant here.[79] The mindset of the *grandes écoles* graduates who ran top French companies was predominantly risk-averse, their undoubted talents employed in scaling the bureaucratic hierarchy rather than exploiting entrepreneurial opportunities. With mathematical competence a *sine qua non* of a successful passage through their rigorous selection procedures and competitive examinations, the *grandes écoles* fostered an approach to business which was theoretical and Cartesian rather than practical, creative or intuitive. They tended to breed desk men rather than managers concerned with change and opportunities. As one observer put it, 'They train people who have a greater chance than others of becoming the chairman of a large firm, but rarely entrepreneurs.'[80] Crozier believed that business in France was further undermined by the isolation of the individual, the lack of face-to-face contact, the compartmentalisation of the firm, the struggle for privileges, and the absence of constructive solidarity.[81]

It was not so much in large French firms (500 employees or above) that the government now sought salvation, but increasingly in the PME, the *petite et moyenne entreprise* (with between 10 and 499 employees). This was partly ideological. Large firms, characterised by sclerotic bureaucratic structures built up over the years through state-backed mergers, began to appear increasingly unwieldy and inflexible, burdened with social costs and legislation on hiring and firing, unable to adapt with the necessary speed to changing economic conditions. In contrast, small and medium-sized enterprises seemed more flexible and friendly, not distant and alienating but operating on a human scale, more in touch with, and able to adapt to changing market realities. The government's faith in small businesses was also, however, pragmatic: in 1984, only 50 firms were created with assets in excess of FF1 million.[82]

The regeneration of business at a regional level, particularly the small firms sector, depended on decentralisation. The headquarters of large French firms was (and is) almost invariably in Paris, or just outside the capital at La Défense, with the notable exception of tyre-manufacturer Michelin, based in the Auvergne at Clermont-Ferrand, sometimes called 'Michelinsville'. The policy of national champions pursued during de Gaulle's presidency contributed directly, whether intentionally or otherwise, to the centralisation of business enterprise in the Paris basin. The 1982 Defferre decentralisation reforms sought to correct this imbalance, striking at the heart of the long-established dichotomy of 'Paris et le désert français'. These remain one of the major departures of the first Mitterrand presidency, devolving resources and responsibilities away from the capital to local authorities. They strengthened all levels of local government, and provided *inter alia* for the direct election of regional councils (*conseils régionaux*), the first taking place in 1986, and a reduction in the powers of the *préfet* (functionaries of the central state). Thus, at a time when Britain was seeing the power of local authorities curtailed by the Thatcher government, France was pursuing the opposite path, introducing a much-needed element of legitimacy and democracy into local politics.

That said, the impact of the Defferre reforms was less than it might have been, since they did not seek to upset the domination of the politico-administrative system by traditional elites, inviting local elites instead to associate themselves consensually with the established administration.[83] Nevertheless they instilled hope of economic renewal at the local level, thus helping to create a climate of confidence in which businesses could flourish, encouraging company start-ups. Business confidence was fostered in turn by the upswing in the economy in 1985–86: in 1986, for the first time in a decade, France's trade balance was once again positive, albeit marginally (see Table 5.4). Since the first Mitterrand presidency, this small-firm revival has, as Szarka observes, been ongoing and real, if not always as capable of generating jobs as is sometimes claimed. It should also be noted that the jobs created by small firms in the late 1980s and early 1990s were often precisely those that had been lost by large firms as they downsized and contracted out activities. Company start-ups were often presented in terms of individuals standing on their own feet, not dependent on the state for protection and employment. It is nevertheless the case, ironically, that during the Mitterrand era as a whole no fewer than 1,500 different types of public aid became available for this purpose.[84] At the same time, a form of performance-related pay was introduced in many companies (*l'intéressement*). This recognised that employee motivation was higher where their involvement in the company was greater, seeking to link workers' contributions directly to company performance by dividing among employees a share of the profits.

The provincial business schools, the so-called 'Sup de Co', have also been instrumental at the regional level in changing attitudes in favour of business. Machinery for the production of top French managers – the elitist Parisian *grandes écoles* – has been in place since 1794 in the case of Polytechnique, and since 1945 in that of ENA (Ecole Nationale d'Administration). These two elitist establishments continue to educate the majority of the chairmen and chief executive officers (Président-Directeur Général) of France's top 40 listed companies, the CAC-40 (Cotation assistée en continu).[85] Attendance at a leading *grande école*, followed by membership of a *grand corps*, remains one of the most secure routes to the pinnacle of the French business hierarchy. But the managerial base these schools produce is woefully inadequate to the country's needs as a whole. A growing number of provincial graduate management schools, such as the Sup de Co at Lyon, Montpellier, Amiens and Nantes, have played a critical role in broadening this managerial base, particularly at middle management level and among medium-sized firms. They have also helped to spread the new managerial ideology throughout France. The prestige of a private business education over that acquired at a traditional state university reflects this new ideology, which seeks to promote French interests as encapsulated in European interests. The courses offered by the provincial business schools are more practical and international than the traditional *grandes écoles*, encouraging *stages*, preferably abroad. The Parisian *grandes écoles* have likewise sought to become less narrowly focused on mathematical theory, and more international in their perspective.[86] EAP (Ecole des Affaires de Paris, linked to the Paris Chamber of Commerce) set up a three-venue graduate management course, based in Paris, Berlin and Oxford or Madrid, with multiple points of recruitment. There were, however, relatively few takers for such a linguistically exacting trilingual course, which demanded study in two further countries in addition to the host nation, and in 1998 EAP, failing to recruit in sufficient numbers, was subsumed as part of ESCP, Ecole Supérieure de Commerce de Paris.

In recent years a small number of universities, in particular those of Aix-en-Provence, Paris II and Paris IX-Dauphine, have sought to emulate the role of the provincial business schools. They have introduced candidate selection, as opposed to admitting all those with the *baccalauréat*, and are now competing with the graduate management schools for students while charging much-reduced tuition fees (£200 per annum at the time of writing as opposed to £4,000 for the provincial business schools).

At the same time, the personal success of prominent businessmen, such as Trigano of Club Med, Edouard Leclerc and the non-establishment figure Bernard Tapie, did much in the 1980s to promote the cause of entrepreneurship. A poor boy from Le Bourget near Paris, Tapie made good by buying up bankrupt businesses for the nominal sum of one franc and turning them around. Kicker shoes, Wonder batteries, La Vie Claire (a leading French health-food chain) and the football club Olympique de Marseille all owed their rebirth to his apparent Midas touch. Tapie's rise to prominence coincided with the new socialist emphasis on business enterprise and prominent politicians like Pierre Bérégovoy and even President Mitterrand courted him. At one point Tapie even aspired to the Elysée. His political career – the high point of which was a televised gladiatorial debate with Jean-Marie Le Pen in December 1989, beating him soundly to Mitterrand's admiration[87] – culminated in his appointment in March 1992 as Minister for Urban Affairs. Financial scandal forced his resignation after seven short weeks in office. Tapie was eventually jailed for match-fixing and numerous instances of tax evasion and fraud. From being a 'golden boy' of the 1980s, providing – briefly – an example of what it was possible for the underprivileged to achieve, he became a figure of ridicule in the 1990s. Tapie became the exception that proved the rule. The black sheep that had forced his way into the elite's pen had demonstrated conveniently his unworthiness for admission in the eyes of the ruling business establishment, thus confirming and reinforcing the status quo. The business community was preserved intact, albeit with its feathers ruffled. On emerging from prison in 1998, Tapie, irrepressible, took to theatre, becoming a classical actor on stage, and expressing his desire for a film part. He provides a convenient symbolic example of the fate that might lie in store for unqualified individuals (i.e. neither a member of the establishment nor legitimated by educational achievement) who overstep the mark.

Despite this, the changes, subtle yet significant, taking place at this time in France's *grandes écoles* and business schools and among industrial leaders nevertheless promoted a radically new business climate that was much more conducive to enterprise than hitherto. Ideological change, on this reading, was the product of a broadly based movement from below rather than politically inspired from above.

Denationalisation in vogue

Counterfactual propositions in history may be thought of as reasoned speculations supported by evidence, and with this in mind it seems reasonable to suppose that had the socialists not lost the legislative elections of March 1986 they would have begun to unwind the nationalisation programme of

1981–82. By this stage the ideological march in favour of free enterprise was well advanced, with fellow travellers joining the ranks from across the political spectrum. Privatisation under the left would doubtless have been on a more modest scale than the far-reaching privatisation programme on which the incoming right-wing coalition government embarked in 1986. In all likelihood it would have been partial – the privatisation of subsidiaries of state-owned firms, for example, such as was later implemented by the socialist administration of 1988–93. Perhaps, too, it would have been carried out without daring to speak its name. The socialists never spoke overtly of privatisation in 1985–86, doubtless a bridge too far given their massive nationalisation programme only four years earlier. But they did speak, while preparing for the parliamentary elections, of denationalisation. As Industry Minister Edith Cresson pertinently remarked in May 1985, 'Denationalise public companies? Why not? I don't have any religious theory about it, neither one way nor the other.'[88] A bill was drawn up on denationalisation in 1985, with a view to a law on privatisation being promulgated by spring 1986.[89] This was despite the fact that most of the companies nationalised in 1981–82, with the exception of the two steel firms and the CGCT, had begun by 1985 to make a profit.[90] In the first semester of 1985, Rhône-Poulenc and Pechiney announced interim profits of FF1 billion and FF451 million respectively.[91] Privatisation under the left – had the leadership the confidence to tap into the wave of liberal sentiment then in vogue – would have had the advantage of pulling the rug from under the feet of the right, widely expected to win the forthcoming elections. The right, moreover, had made no secret of its plans to privatise.[92]

It is likely, too, that the left would have deregulated widely had it won the 1986 election.[93] The theoreticians of 'less state' had accused the socialist administration of putting in place '*toujours plus d'Etat*', always more state.[94] In their eyes it was necessary to liberate French firms from the 'iron corset' of social charges and bureaucratic structures in which they were tightly bound, to 'unchain Gulliver' as Paul Mentré put it.[95] Deregulation had originated in California, following a referendum in 1978 on lower taxes. It had gathered momentum throughout the US, in the UK, but also throughout Europe, under governments of both left and right, even ultimately in Eastern Europe, in Hungary, Japan and China, as governments throughout the world sought to reduce the total tax burden and increase mobility and flexibility. To liberate energies previously imprisoned in a yoke of rules and regulations seemed a fitting response to a decade of recession. Running out of time as the election approached, the Fabius government began to deregulate, reducing the tax burden, lowering income taxes, partly lifting price controls, freeing up exchange controls – proof, if any were needed, that the intellectual tide was running against the old socialist ideology. The government did not, however, relax legislation on hiring and firing, for which the business community clamoured as a spur to job-creation. In the event this was announced by the incoming Chirac administration on 1 July 1986.

That the left lost the ensuing parliamentary elections was partly due to the end of the Union of the left. It was also due, however, to the left's seeming inability to accept and assume its own metamorphoses after five years of government. A good manager, but a mediocre reformer, the left was ultimately caught in the trap of its own contradictions. It had succeeded in converting France to the market economy, but had failed in its cherished objective of introducing 'une autre politique' and thus effecting a rupture with capitalism. In bringing inflation under control, the left nevertheless achieved an 'assainissement national' which was necessary to a durable recovery. The increasing interdependence of national economies, particularly within the EC, limited government scope for managing the economy. From 1983 this was now fully understood, marking the beginning of a new commitment to international competition, founded on a remarkably broad recognition that protectionism coupled with industrial policy is not ultimately a viable option for a medium-sized economy.

Conclusion

This chapter has reviewed the economic priorities of the new socialist administration in 1981, proposing that these were fundamentally flawed by their incompatibility with those of partner countries in the EC. Having nationalised widely in one of the most radical government agendas enacted in the West in the postwar era, the socialist administration reverted essentially to the Plan Barre. It is argued here that what the complete about-turn in policy in the early 1980s, from reflation to austerity, reflects above all is the extent to which markets can punish governments for denying their logic and constraints. This punishment was apparent in the budget deficit and national debt that snowballed, in the trade balance that grew deeper, in unemployment that got worse, and in the currency, exacting three humiliating devaluations. The socialists learned a hard lesson from this punishment, and in the event, somewhat ironically, succeeded in converting the French to the values of liberal capitalism.

Under the socialist administration of 1981–86, French business culture and capability were transformed. French firms developed more sophisticated strategies that recognised the need to offer customers carefully thought-out value propositions supported by appropriate business structures, systems and processes. It was around this time that France overtook Britain to become the world's fourth largest exporter. From 1985, large French companies, once famous for their ostrich-like insularity, their unhealthy dual dependence on the state and on the protected home market, found new wings: by 1986, France's trade balance was positive. The state's apron strings were gradually being untied, helped by deregulation and the external expansion of France's nationalised companies, soon to be candidates for privatisation. Three years later France became the main cross-border acquirer in Europe, while French direct investment in the US rose to fourth position.

In the course of the early 1980s, attitudinal upheavals transformed French business culture. The year 1983 in particular was a turning-point from which France has never looked back. It stands out as a year of revolution and reconciliation, which went some way towards healing the two-hundred-year-old schism of a conflict-ridden society, and marking the birth of a new consensus. This new consensus revolved around two poles in particular. The first was the primacy of business enterprise. As Roger Fauroux, a future Minister of Industry, put it: 'In the first rank of all the consensuses on which the political class feeds, the agreement on the firm, above all the industrial firm, is probably the most complete.'[96] The second element of consensus was the importance of Europe. First came the realisation that France's economy was inextricably interwoven with those of her European partners. That had been the hard-learned lesson of the failed 1982 reflation of the economy, at a time when Britain and Germany were pursuing austerity programmes. Then there was a growing sentiment among France's political leaders that Europe might prove to be the means for achieving national goals such as prosperity and prestige, goals which national action alone could no longer guarantee.[97]

At the heart of the consensus on Europe and the firm lay pragmatism, an enlightened self-interest born of bitter experience, not ideology. Nevertheless it is argued here that it is at the level of an ideological struggle for the hearts and minds of the nation that the consensus over business enterprise in particular has been played out and won. The ideological change effected under the socialists was not the transformation, the so-called break with capitalism, they set out to achieve. The firm now became, as Alain Minc put it, the 'new idol', before which the socialists bowed low.[98] The important point here is that the changes that took place were not cosmetic or superficial. Rather, they were profound and far-reaching, beginning at the base of the pyramid depicted in Figure 1 in the Introduction, and paving the way for later changes in the national business system and its supporting rules and regulations.

What made France's new business orientation so remarkable was the fact that it was forged under a socialist administration – an unlikely mid-wife to this conversion, but perhaps in consequence all the more effective. The economic strategy of Raymond Barre in itself, irrespective of its deep unpopularity, was not enough; it required the victory of the left and the pursuit, and subsequent abandonment, of its radical agenda for greater realism to emerge. The discovery by the socialists of the firm, their conversion to the market economy as they shed their old, outworn skin of collective socialist values, emerging phoenix-like from the ashes, has had profound consequences for the reconstitution of French capitalism. It has contributed to a revival in small and medium-sized enterprise, engendering a new confidence and greater cohesiveness on the part of the French managerial elite, however improbable this may have seemed in 1981 on the eve of nationalisation. Firms began to engage in more marketing; there was a new focus on image and presentation. Suddenly it was acceptable, even desirable to be an entrepreneur, at the sharp end of business life, responsible for wealth creation: 'It is good to be a boss', wrote the editor of the business magazine *L'Expansion* with audible relief. 'At last!'[99]

6
Competitive Liberalism and European Ambitions

> It is Europe that constitutes one of our best chances to ensure the progress of our economy and the radiance of France. [...] Let us take the paths of competitiveness, of economic growth and job creation.
>
> Jacques Delors[1]

In the 1960s French firms had faced 'le défi américain'.[2] By the mid-1980s, reeling now from the Japanese challenge, they were calling more stridently for a European market that was whole and supportive, and for pan-European companies big enough to challenge the American and Japanese invaders. The Single European Act (SEA) came into effect on 1 July 1987. This established a deadline of 31 December 1992 for the completion of the Single European Market (SEM), defined as 'an area without internal frontiers in which the free movement of goods, persons, services and capital is ensured'.[3]

In many respects, the SEA set out to achieve what the Treaty of Rome had failed to bring about in thirty years. This had given rise not to a common market but rather to the fragmented 'uncommon' market of 'non-Europe', as Albert and Ball put it, hampered by costly red tape and customs delays.[4] Economic growth across Europe lacked the vitality of the three decades following the Second World War. It was hoped that the removal of barriers to the movement of goods, persons, services and capital in a single market would propel them into a new era of expansionism. Replacing the requirement for unanimity with qualified majority voting (QMV), except for issues of strategic national interest, the SEA ended the decade-long stalemate of Community indecision dubbed 'Eurosclerosis'.

Although an amendment to a treaty, and not a treaty in its own right, nevertheless the Single Act was dynamite. The 1985 White Paper *Completing the Internal Market*, produced by Lord Cockfield, was low-key and non-threatening to governments concerned with potential loss of sovereignty.[5] It united European integrationists, like François Mitterrand, who rightly saw in the single market an important step in the process of European construction, with free-marketeers such as Margaret Thatcher, hugely relieved that Europe was now at last about down-to-earth practical matters, about business. Some European Community (EC) member states embarked on a period of frenzied preparation, rich in hype. France ran a televised publicity campaign featuring an undersized but determined French boxer up against more muscular American rivals. Announcing, 'we are fighting for a Europe which is strong, free and independent', the advertisement ended with the slogan: 'Europe, it's future will be ours'. Mitterrand saw Europe as the top priority for business: 'can there be any other dimension for any man or woman in a position of responsibility – particularly if they run a company – than Europe, France and Europe, France in Europe, Europe in the world?'[6] This echoed his much-quoted address to the nation in December 1986: 'France is our country, Europe is our future.' In short, in the late 1980s, as one director put it, Europe emerged as 'an extension of France's cultural revolution begun in 1983'.[7]

The date 1993, as Project 1992 was referred to in France, became synonymous with the challenge of restructuring industry and rendering it more efficient in the face of international competition. The single-market campaign in France became bound up with the strong franc; a move towards the German model of capitalism; the concentration of firms; and with a wave of acquisitions abroad, especially in the US. It engaged all sectors of the economy. Enthusiasm for 1993 was especially pronounced in France because it tapped into the French need for involvement in grand designs and epic productions.[8] In the UK, on the other hand, the Department of Trade and Industry's (DTI) high-profile campaign, 'Europe open for business', masked widespread complacency. A 1988 survey revealed the proportion of British firms with a strategy for the internal market to be less than half that in France.[9]

This chapter examines the extensive privatisation and growing Europeanisation that characterised the late 1980s and early 1990s, a decade in which French business became increasingly competitive, both in Europe and globally. 'It is no longer the French market that counts, it is Europe', one company director pointed out, 'but it is also the world'.[10] The years 1986 to 1994 coincided with the Uruguay Round of GATT negotiations (General Agreement on Tariffs and Trade), culminating in the creation of the World Trade Organisation (WTO) in 1995, long desired by the French to counterbalance American influence. It is suggested here that despite the difficult nature of the talks, and the apparent jingoism that characterised French attitudes towards them, they nevertheless marked, particularly in the final stages of negotiations, a subtle but perceptible shift in understanding France's long-term interests. These were now more concerned with international realities and business competitiveness than with holding on to rights and privileges that might ultimately prove untenable in the global economy.

But the years in question were not ones of unalloyed French success. This chapter also explores the scandals that have tarnished the ruling elite since the late 1980s. Many of these have involved business and the financing of political parties. Scandal went right the way to the top, damaging the reputations of Mitterrand and Chirac. It has even been suggested somewhat fancifully that Mitterrand, a master of timing, may have chosen the moment of his death in January 1996 to avoid the humiliating fall from grace to which his friend Chancellor Kohl, less fortunate, was subjected.

Privatisation and popular capitalism

If, in March 1986, the newly elected right-wing government, headed by Jacques Chirac, had a mission, it was to foster a more outward-looking and competitive liberal economy designed to meet new challenges, preparing France for all that 1992 would bring. Preparations for the single market coincided with a new wave of liberalism nourished by the apparent successes of Reaganism in the US, now gathering credence throughout the industrialised world, and centring on the removal of rigidities in labour markets and the perceived need to roll back the state.[11] During the years of 'cohabitation' from 1986 to 1988 – the coexistence of a president and prime minister of different political persuasions, a new experience for the Fifth Republic, but one to which it has since become used – the winds of change began to blow more fiercely in France. Government led the way in making a series of bold moves. All price controls and most exchange controls were abolished. Social legislation for 'hiring and firing' was relaxed. State subsidies for industry were reduced. The French financial market was deregulated (the so-called 'little bang'). And France embarked on a vast privatisation programme that aimed within five years to return to private ownership the whole of the banking and insurance sectors and most of the industrial companies operating in competitive markets.

Just as in 1981–82 the left had aimed to produce a rupture with the existing system through its programme of reflation and nationalisation, so four years later, this time through privatisation, the right proposed to change the rules of the economic game.[12] Privatisation on a massive scale was viewed by the government as key to preparing France for the single market, to instilling the open, liberal economy, which it considered a prerequisite to success. No fewer than 66 firms,[13] including 27 independent groups, comprising a total of 1,454 companies including subsidiaries,[14] with a total workforce of near 900,000 and an estimated overall value of FF300 billion (one-quarter of the market capitalisation of the Bourse) were to be transferred to private ownership. Edouard Balladur, Minister for the Economy, Finance and Privatisation, described this at the time as 'the most important shift in the boundary between the public and private sectors witnessed so far in the West'.[15] The programme was to be implemented at high speed, with a deadline of March 1991 fixed for its completion.

The political and ideological aspirations invested in the campaign were considerable. A new form of stakeholder capitalism was to replace the old compact between business and the state. Balladur accused the Socialists of having 'mummified' the French economy through nationalisation and a plethora of fruitless controls. He now sought through privatisation to release potentially creative managers and business leaders from the shackles of state control. Market forces were to be given free play to the benefit of consumers who would enjoy greater choice and lower prices. Individual citizens would have a stake in the prosperity of the nation, as share-owning became commonplace rather than the preserve of the wealthy. Employees likewise would share in the success of their companies through schemes to improve productivity and profitability. In short, as the state withdrew, the individual would be handed responsibility and asked to claim his or her economic freedom. None was to be excluded from this great national project. The professed aim of the privatisation programme was thus democratic, not elitist. As Balladur announced after the successful privatisation of Saint-Gobain in December 1986, 'The economic liberty which constitutes the main objective of the government's policy is not the freedom of a chosen few, but concerns all French people.'[16]

At the heart of the proposed social revolution was the creation of a new shareholding class. In the event, privatisation elicited an unexpected public response. By spring 1988 there had been a sixfold increase in the size of the shareholding body from its 1986 level: from 1.2 million individual shareholders in 1986 to more than 7 million two years later, with a further 500,000 employees purchasing stakes in their companies. One in every eight citizens was now a shareholder. There had been a staggering 17 million share applications in all, almost 5 million of which were received in the month of May 1987 alone. From December 1986 to September 1987 France was imbued with a heady air of *fête*. The sales that occurred in quick succession seemed to roll into one vast privatisation jamboree, a merry-go-round of share-buying and selling that seemingly everyone was trying to get on. The overriding impression, as one headline in *L'Humanité* put it, was of 'France on sale'.[17]

It was not, however, entirely plain sailing for the Chirac government. Symbolically, President Mitterrand chose Bastille Day 1986 to refuse to sign the privatisation *ordonnance*; although this delaying tactic slowed the process by just three weeks. The privatisation bill became law on 6 August 1986, with the first sale – that of glassmaker Saint-Gobain – planned for the fortnight beginning 24 November 1986. In the event, the October crash of 1987, coupled with defeat in the 1988 legislative elections, cut short the government's ambition. Nevertheless in a little over a year an extraordinary amount had been achieved. There were 11 flotations, comprising eight large groups (in order of privatisation, Saint-Gobain, Paribas, CGE, CCF, Havas, Société Générale, TF1 and Suez) and three banks (Sogénal, BIMP and BTP). All but the Suez flotation was hugely successful. There were also three off-market sales (MGE, CGCT, IDI). Altogether, the first wave of privatisation amounted to one-third of the government's overall programme, boosting stock market capitalisation by nearly FF100 billion.[18]

For the Chirac government, this represented a prodigious economic and political success, despite accusations from the opposition of *bradage* (selling off the state silver on the cheap) and *copinage* ('cronyism'). However, in terms of opening up the French economy, releasing the corporate sector from the allegedly oppressive tutelage of the state, and empowering small investors and employees, what was achieved was in many ways counter to the professed aims of the government's official discourse. The privatisation programme resulted in a considerable strengthening of the prerogatives of the state over the individual, and a bolstering of the privileges of the establishment elite through the concentration of power in hard cores of stable investors in privatised firms. These were handpicked by Balladur, and often peopled by his personal friends. Ostensibly designed to provide privatised firms with an anchor following their change of status, the more significant function of the *noyaux durs* was to shore up company takeover defences against potential foreign predators. This meant reinforcing the crossed shareholdings that had been the bedrock of French capitalism since the 1960s. Far from giving market forces a free rein, these were ultimately held in check. The government's apparent liberalism – sometimes called 'ultra liberalism', although Balladur rejected the term – did not represent a rupture with the past, and was characterised in many ways by more of the same. As Bauer explains:

> To carry out a programme which was labelled 'liberal' the government was wary of market forces. Nor did it have recourse to an independent commission to which to turn to make a decision after public hearings. All the major decisions that had to be made to implement the policy of privatisation were, on the contrary, left to ministerial discretion. And the minister intervened not only to define the new rules of the game but also to fix the price, choose the shareholders, and decide on the composition of the board. There never was so powerful a Minister of Finance in France: never did the rue de Rivoli matter so much in the business world. The French privatisation programme did not represent any great break with the past. Quite the contrary: it fully illustrated the State's interventionist tradition and even reinforced it.[19]

Acknowledging the paradox, Balladur offered a simple, if unconvincing explanation: 'We needed a greater concentration of power at the time in order to build greater freedom for tomorrow.'[20]

This first wave of privatisation (1986–88) gave an undeniable boost to the Bourse and thereby to equity finance, in a country that had long favoured debt financing over equity. This was important: the high gearing of large French firms had left them exposed when inflation was high, increasing interest payments. Privatisation now sought to attract the interest of the general public in the stock market. Popular capitalism became a reality, in the sense that millions of small shareholders were persuaded to buy shares. It is open to question, however, whether a new risk-taking mentality or a new sense of individual responsibility was instilled in the French populace. The shares were priced to appeal, and all privatisations resulted in huge first-day trading gains for shareholders, with the exception of Suez in October 1987, a victim of the stock-market crash dubbed 'Black Monday'. There was, however, no 'democratisation' of capitalism. On the contrary, privatisation is said to have put in place a 'masked state' by stocking the *noyaux durs* with close political allies of Balladur, reinforcing traditional establishment solidarity. As Jean Peyrelevade, former chairman of Union des Assurances de Paris (UAP) observed, 'Power in the boardroom, as everyone knows, is not for sharing! [...] As all practitioners know, the small shareholder is powerless.'[21]

Nevertheless privatisation was arguably a vital stepping-stone for France along the route towards greater openness in the European and international economy. In releasing privatised firms from public-sector constraints, it left them free to participate in the European wave of mergers and acquisitions fuelled by single-market preparations in the run-up to 1992. It provided much-needed funds for the state, generating about FF85 billion in revenue, used to pay off the national debt, with a proportion going towards the cost of the nationalisations (for which France continued to pay until 1997) and in state aid to public-sector firms (FF27.68 billion).[22] This first wave of privatisation enjoys a relatively positive image, largely because the shares of those companies privatised at the time – sold at bargain prices, unlike those sold off later – have performed on the whole reasonably well.

Privatisation *en masse* was resumed in France with the return of the right to government under the premiership of Balladur in March 1993. However, it would be wrong to think that the process ground completely to a halt during the intervening years. Despite Mitterrand's 1988 electoral pledge that there would be 'neither privatisation nor nationalisation',[23] privatisation continued under the Socialists, albeit in a covert and clandestine manner, presented as enabling the public sector to breathe. The principle of 'ni-ni', as it was called, proved to be extraordinarily flexible in practice. State-owned companies were free to purchase holdings in private companies by decree. Moreover, the way was cleared for 'partial privatisations' by the law of 4 July 1990[24] and the decree of 4 April 1991. The latter opened up public-sector companies to private capital, provided that this remained a minority interest and that a strategic agreement of cooperation had been signed in advance. In the vein of economic realism that characterised the Rocard administration (1988–91), this merely acknowledged in public what had been going on behind the scenes. Soon afterwards, the prerequisite for a strategic agreement of cooperation was abandoned. Between November 1991 and March 1993 four 'partial privatisations' took place, involving the Crédit Local de France, Elf Aquitaine, Total and Rhône-Poulenc.[25]

When the right returned to power in 1993, Prime Minister Balladur set out to complete the job he had left unfinished five years previously. The privatisation law of July 1993 allowed for the sale of 21 state-owned companies, 12 of which had already appeared in the law of August 1986. They came from the banking and insurance sectors, as well as from the industrial sector.[26] They employed a total workforce in excess of 1 million in 1993, and had a combined turnover of FF1,200 billion.

Some critics have argued that this wave of privatisations, notwithstanding its massive scale, was a routine, passionless affair,[27] ideologically spent and budget-driven, motivated above all by the need to reduce the budget deficit in order to qualify for EMU in 1997 or 1999. But this is to miss the point. The lack of controversy surrounding the release of so many firms and jobs into the private sector is a measure not of complacency but of the completeness of the ideological victory that had been won. A new consensus had emerged to the effect that the state should ideally limit its role to macroeconomic management, international relations and the provision of services deemed beyond the scope of the market such as social services, education, policing and defence. The six privatisations carried out by the Balladur administration (1993–95) saw some of the 'heavyweights' of France's industrial and financial sectors returned to private ownership: BNP, Rhône-Poulenc, Elf Aquitaine, UAP, Renault and SEITA. Each of the first four sales attracted some 2–3 million small investors, and all were oversubscribed. Taking into account the partial privatisations of the Crédit Local de France and Total in 1993, the total income generated in two years amounted to FF114 billion.[28] Somewhat controversially, the money was used to finance routine government expenditure,[29] despite the fact that Balladur had once denounced such a policy as 'a waste of the public patrimony'.[30]

Following the 1995 presidential election, the right resumed office with Alain Juppé as Prime Minister (1995–97). The privatisation programme continued, albeit at a slower pace than previously, with fewer flotations and more direct sales to selected buyers. By the time the right lost the legislative elections of 1997, assets exceeding $40 billion in value had been sold.[31] Somewhat ironically, income from privatisation under socialist Prime Minister Lionel Jospin (1997–2002) exceeded the proceeds of the two previous privatisation waves, averaging $10 billion per annum from 1997.[32] This might seem surprising: Jospin's image is that of an unreconstructed socialist, a throwback, quite different from prominent 'third way' politicians like Blair and Schröder. But by the time he came to office any attempt to depart from the new consensus over the proper division of responsibilities between the state and the private sector would have been fruitless and highly divisive. As a concession to lingering sentiment within his own party, the Jospin government avoided using the word privatisation, while selling off stakes in banks, insurance companies and major industrial groups.[33] By 2000 all of France's large banks were in private hands. The partial privatisation in October 1997 of France Télécom (worth an estimated FF130 billion), with a further tranche of shares being sold in November 1998, left 63 per cent of its capital in state hands. The proceeds were partly used to prop up the state pension system, heavily in deficit.

Big is beautiful: the drive for critical mass

The 1985 decision to create a single European market was widely welcomed in French business circles as a means of increasing competitiveness and winning a larger share of world markets. While Japan and the US operated as unified nation-states, Europe remained a plurality. As one director put it, 'Two monolithic blocs, the United States and Japan. And between these two there is a bloc that should be the greatest monolith of all. But instead it is a mosaic of little stones with a bit of cement around them rather than the rock it ought to be.'[34] It became increasingly clear that the days of national champions, often too small for international competition, yet too large to be sustained by domestic markets alone, were over. If European firms were to compete effectively at the international level, Europe's minnows must grow into bigger fish, even at the expense of others being forced out of business.[35]

As 1992 approached, the idea that 'big is best' regained popularity in France. This belief had held sway during the late 1960s and early 1970s, in the era of state-backed mergers, when improving international competitiveness was believed to rest on acquiring critical mass (see Chapter 3). But the concentrations of the 1960s led, in the 1970s, to companies encumbered with debt and inflexible bureaucratic structures. In the mid-1980s, when nationalisation came to be viewed as a costly mistake and large firms were shedding labour on a massive scale, hopes for growth and employment rested much more in small- and medium-sized enterprises, said to be less rigid and more adaptable to changing market conditions.

By 1989, however, size was again in vogue, seen as the key to survival and prosperity in the single market, and as a defence against hostile takeovers. A 1989 survey of 300 large- and medium-sized French industrial and service companies, commissioned by the Ministry of Industry, revealed size (*une taille critique*), as the key strategic objective of 38 per cent of the sample, ahead of profitability.[36] While the concentrations of the Gaullist era had involved mergers between domestic rivals, in the late 1980s expansion no longer needed to be homegrown. With little time remaining before the

1992 deadline, and with the growing need for large French firms to have a European presence, Europe became a leading target for acquisitions. Within Europe, British firms became prime targets, accounting for 18 per cent of acquisitions. This was doubtless influenced by the positive attitude towards takeover that obtains in the UK, where merger is viewed as a legitimate means of replacing poor management by more effective management teams. After Mrs Thatcher came to power in 1979, the British government expressed little interest in intervening in the so-called market for corporate control,[37] in stark contrast to the situation in France and Germany.[38] British firms had few takeover defences, unlike French firms, protected through *autocontrôle* (where a company's shares were safely held by its own subsidiaries, a practice outlawed in 1991), cross shareholdings (where allies hold major stakes in one another), and secret shareholder pacts.

The 1980s ended in a wave of acquisitions. In 1989 a staggering 1,721 successful takeover bids were launched by French companies, 480 on foreign soil, of which 73 per cent were in Europe. Those companies taking part in the survey, conducted by management consultants Bain and Co., anticipated that acquisitions would account for 75 per cent of their growth between 1988 and 1992. Most were expected to involve foreign prey. France's food retailer, BSN, sought to claim first or second place by market share in each segment in which it had a presence. The feeling among large French firms was that unless they were market leaders in Europe, or at least numbers two or three, the game was not worth the candle. Mergers and acquisitions enabled market share to be bought in, albeit at high cost.

By 1989, France was the major cross-border acquirer in Europe, along with the US. This was perhaps surprising, given the country's former insularity and dependence on the state, but there was a large element of playing 'catch-up' here. French M&A activity in Europe increased in volume from $10.7 million in 1985 to $10,888.2 million in 1989. Altogether France spent $26,650.4 million on intra-European transactions over the period.[39] Almost half of France's top companies (43 per cent) launched a successful takeover bid in 1988–89.[40] This included many nationalised firms, trapped in the public sector when Balladur's privatisation programme ended prematurely. To expand, public-sector firms used their subsidiaries, subject to fewer restrictions, as launching-pads for foreign takeover bids, issuing equity substitutes on the Bourse to acquire the necessary financial resources to fund them. Interestingly, it was state-owned companies, together with newly privatised companies, released from public-sector constraints, which emerged as the most aggressive cross-border acquirers. The two largest bids launched in the run-up to 1992 came from one nationalised company (Pechiney for American National Can) and one privatised company (Suez for Société Générale de Belgique), both in pursuit of large businesses abroad.

France's three privately owned water companies exemplify this trend of opportunistic international expansion throughout Europe and beyond.

Lyonnaise des Eaux, Générale des Eaux and SAUR (a subsidiary of Bouygues) embarked in the late 1980s on a wave of acquisitions which saw them purchase numerous foreign water companies – in the US, Canada, Spain, Morocco and the South Pacific. In particular they were attracted by the small English private statutory water companies, in the run-up to the privatisation of the water industry in England and Wales in 1989. The activities of the French water companies were extensively diversified, including energy management, healthcare, leisure and recreational activities, cable television and property development.[41] The rationale was that since local customers came to regard water companies as reliable, here was a chance to use a well-disposed customer base to launch a host of other related and unrelated services. The majority of these services were low-risk, largely unaffected by the vagaries of national economies, and highly cash-generative, helped by the fact that the water companies did not actually own their asset base in France, which they leased from the municipalities. The cost of upgrading facilities, pipes and standards thus lay with the local authorities. The arrival of the three French water companies in the UK coincided with the deregulation of local authority service contracting. The UK-based subsidiaries of Lyonnaise des Eaux (Sita) and Générale des Eaux (Onyx)[42] got themselves on tender lists for waste collection, winning numerous local government contracts. Meanwhile the water companies began to move into the British markets for healthcare, gas and electricity.[43] As the chairman of one British water company remarked at the time, 'This is a bear hug; and it has claws.'[44]

Not all firms were as successful in their strategies for international expansion. Some had 'eyes too big for their bellies', trying to absorb companies that were too large at a time when prices were high. The managers of France's leading firms had been educated and trained in times of high inflation, when the real cost of debt was low, but now France's inflation rate had fallen to just 3 per cent (see Table 6.1). Supposedly rock-solid firms, like Michelin, which bought Uniroyal, then world market leader in

Table 6.1   Inflation in G7 nations, 1987–95 (annual percentage change)

Year	1987	1988	1989	1990	1991	1992	1993	1994	1995
Canada	4.4	4.0	5.1	4.7	5.6	1.5	1.9	0.2	2.2
France	3.3	2.8	3.4	3.4	3.2	2.4	2.1	1.7	1.7
Germ.	0.2	1.2	2.8	2.7	3.6	5.1	4.4	2.7	1.9
Italy	4.7	5.1	6.2	6.5	6.3	5.1	4.5	4.0	5.3
Japan	0.1	0.77	2.2	3.1	3.3	1.7	1.2	0.7	−0.1
UK	4.1	4.8	7.8	9.5	5.9	3.7	1.6	2.5	3.4
USA	3.7	4.0	4.9	5.4	4.2	3.1	2.7	2.6	2.8

Source: World Economic and Social Survey data, *Trends and Policies*, New York, UN, 1997.

Table 6.2 Long-term interest rates in G7 Nations, 1986–95 (annual percentage change)

Year	1986	1987	1988	1989	1990	1991	1992	1993	1994	1995
Can.	9.5	10.0	10.2	9.9	10.9	9.8	8.8	7.8	8.6	8.3
France	**8.6**	**9.4**	**9.1**	**8.8**	**10.0**	**9.1**	**8.6**	**6.9**	**7.4**	**7.6**
Germ.	5.9	5.8	6.1	7.1	8.9	8.6	8.0	6.3	6.7	6.5
Italy	100.5	9.7	10.2	10.7	11.5	13.2	13.3	11.3	10.6	12.2
Japan	4.9	4.2	4.3	5.1	7.4	6.5	4.9	3.7	3.7	2.5
UK	9.9	9.5	9.4	9.6	11.1	9.9	9.1	7.9	8.1	8.3
USA	7.7	8.4	8.9	8.5	8.6	7.9	7.0	5.8	7.1	6.6

Source: World Economic and Social Survey data, 1997, p. 239.

tyres, were not immune. Some financially vulnerable public companies got themselves into difficulties: fearful of being left off the takeover band-wagon, they nevertheless needed to borrow heavily to jump aboard.

The decade ended on a bullish note. The recession that lay in store – the knock-on effect of the slowdown occurring in Britain and the US, and then in Germany, as it grappled with its own mammoth problems of absorption – could hardly have been foreseen. The Bundesbank raised interest rates to attract investment into Germany, helping to pay for unification, and consequentially forcing up interest rates in Europe (and hence the cost of servicing debt). Interest rates in France were more than 6 percentage points above the rate of inflation between 1990 and 1992 (see Table 6.2).

European ambitions

In late 1989 the state-owned computer manufacturer Bull announced its purchase of the American personal computer manufacturer, Zenith Data Systems. One year on, it reported record losses of FF3 billion, the closure of three factories, and 5,000 redundancies (more than 10 per cent of its work-force of 47,332).[45] In March 1991 the company placed an unusual advertise-ment in *Le Monde*. This consisted of a caption typed in small print – 'If European computer firms do not invest and cooperate in these difficult times, here in brief is the future outlook of the European computer industry' – followed by a blank page.[46] That same month, the German computer man-ufacturer Siemens-Nixdorf, whose merger had been organised by the German Cartel Office, placed a trio of ads in the French daily. The theme was of a Pinocchio puppet progressively tied up in its own strings. The ads read respectively: 'Can we reasonably imagine the success of a Europe which failed to master its own intelligence?'; 'Can we honestly believe in the future of a Europe which could not guarantee its own independence?'; and finally, 'Siemens-Nixdorf have united to fight against the absurdity of a Europe without IT.'[47]

These adverts reflected, on the one hand, a fear of subcontractor status, of the branch economy embraced by Britain when its manufacturing base began to erode. In Mitterrand's words, 'We French do not have in our nature the vocation of being subcontractors to others.'[48] The objective of EUREKA (European Research Coordinating Agency), Mitterrand's proposal to group together Europe's high-tech industries for the purposes of facilitating industry-led, market-driven collaborative projects in all sectors of technology, was precisely that subcontractor status should be avoided.

French-style industrial policy was something that France desired to see transferred to the European plane: from 1983 France had sought to convince the Community of the need to create a 'European industrial space'.[49] ESPRIT (European Strategic Programme for Research and Development in Information Technology) aimed to foster collaboration while boosting pre-competitive R&D among Europe's leading firms: Bull, CGE, Thomson (France), as well as GEC, ICL, Plessey (UK), AEG, Siemens, Nixdorf (Germany), Olivetti, Stet (Italy) and Philips (Netherlands). Viscount Davignon, France's EC Commissioner for industrial affairs, played a pivotal role in bringing together these twelve firms in a so-called 'round table' in the search for intra-European networks and cooperation. The proliferation in the late 1980s and early 1990s of Community R&D initiatives in high technology such as RACE (Research and Development in Advanced Communications Technologies in Europe) and SPRINT (Strategic Programme for Innovation and Technology Transfer) is testimony to French success.[50] These projects, however, were both less interventionist and less protectionist than the French would have liked, with non-European partners like IBM being invited to the table.

But the logic of global competition and global markets, and the inherent weakness of European IT, scuppered the strategy of intra-European cooperation, as round-table members actively began to seek partners beyond the EC.[51] The first was ICL, taken over by the Japanese firm Fujitsu in August 1990. In the case of Bull, the battle to avoid the humiliation of subcontractor status, against cutthroat Japanese and American competition, was an unequal one. In November 1991 EC industry ministers, divided on the issue of EC-wide industrial policy, refused to endorse direct subsidies for the struggling electronics sector. With losses of $1 billion for the year 1991, Bull had little option but to open its doors to foreign capital.[52] The company was thrown a lifeline when NEC and IBM purchased stakes of 4.9 per cent and 5.7 per cent respectively.[53] It was agreed that NEC and IBM would henceforth supply Bull with technology, while Zenith's notebook computers would be sold under the IBM label. Bull was also to act as a distributor for NEC mainframes in Europe. This was a serious climb-down for the French. Electronics, described by Edith Cresson as 'the lifeblood of industry', increasingly impacted on other industries, such as cars, aerospace and defence.[54] On the other hand, alliances with leading American and

Japanese electronics firms allowed a holding position to be preserved. The useful life of the one-time national champion was not entirely over; but its dreams were spent.

The above-mentioned adverts also underscored, on the other hand, the growing need for strategic alliances between different international groups. In a complex, uncertain world, characterised by convergent consumer tastes, turbulent technology, and escalating fixed costs, particularly in R&D, it made sense not to go it alone. Partnerships do not require the vast financial outlay exacted by costly acquisitions. Teaming-up facilitates pre-competitive research and product development, which with shortening product life cycles might otherwise prove prohibitively expensive, especially in the more capital-intensive industries (trucks, cars, helicopters, etc.). Technological collaboration, as Sharp and Shearman point out, might also offer something of a 'halfway house'. Firms that had long enjoyed protected domestic markets might gain a breathing space as markets opened up across Europe.[55] Following this logic, Bull could see that a partnership with two of the giants of global capitalism was a safer option than the formation of a European strategic alliance with either Siemens or Olivetti.

An alliance of this kind was formed in April 1990 between Renault and Volvo. Renault was a public flagship. The largest of France's nationalised firms, associated in popular memory with the Liberation, Renault had come to symbolise the marriage of state and industry, as well as French industrial independence.[56] The *régie* had been through difficult times, and in the late 1980s had undergone painful restructuring to shed excess capacity. By 1990, however, the future had begun to look bright again. Thanks to the success of the Renault 19, especially in Germany, the company increased its share of the European car market for the first time in ten years. In April 1990 the Régie Nationale des Usines Renault lost the privileged bankrupt-proof status it had enjoyed since January 1945 to become a *société anonyme* (SA).[57] Three months later it ceded 25 per cent of its voting shares to the Swedish car manufacturer Volvo, with the state retaining 75 per cent.[58] Whatever difficulties the alliance ran into later, at the time it made a new statement to the world.[59] It was a public acknowledgement of the fact that, with the opening up of markets, and the need for the company to open up its capital to other partners, state ownership was no longer sufficient to guarantee survival and prosperity. It also demonstrated the government's willingness to collaborate with private European firms, thus enabling the public sector to gain access to a wider pool of capital.

German comparisons

Increasingly, the main point of reference for French business was Germany, Europe's economic engine and leading exporting nation. Comparison with German rivals did not, however, reflect favourably on French firms. In 1987 the average turnover of the top 250 West German firms was $2.2 billion, whereas the top 250 French firms managed $1.3 billion. French firms had just over a thousand subsidiaries in West Germany, but West German firms had twice that number in France. France's 13,000 patents for 1987 were dwarfed by West Germany's 32,000. This prompted concerns that the French economy was suffering a dearth of investment in R&D, falling behind Germany and Japan. A 1989 report concluded that France was simply too small to sustain comparison with larger industrial nations such as the US, Japan, the Soviet Union and China. 'The ideal', its author, Jean Teillac, argued 'is therefore an economically prosperous France in a Europe playing its full part and assuming its responsibilities on the world stage.'[60]

The unification of Germany on 3 October 1990 was met with some ambivalence in France. Relief that the Cold War was over was mixed with concerns that Germany might lose interest in the European project and the Franco-German partnership, becoming absorbed in internal issues. While some leading managers considered that Europe 'had everything to gain from being strong, from having a strong Germany, a strong Italy, etc.',[61] not all were as confident. Research by the OECD (Organisation for Economic Cooperation and Development) suggested that the growth of the German economy had been at the expense of its partners in the EC, France and Britain in particular. In other words, Germany was not increasing Europe's share of world markets, but merely eroding that of her neighbours.[62] Some of these neighbours, Britain especially, actively blamed Germany for fuelling the recession of the early 1990s because of the interest-rate hike that other European nations were obliged to copy or be starved of investment, thus spreading the costs of German unification throughout Europe.

The years in question were characterised by *rapprochement* with Germany, and by an ever-closer personal bond between President Mitterrand and Chancellor Kohl. For Mitterrand, one of the key lessons of 1982–83 had been that the unity of the Franco-German relationship was an essential prerequisite to extending French influence in the EC and further afield. At the same time, Kohl had made it clear following his election that he was the last Chancellor with whom it would be possible to build Europe: subsequent leaders would be unlikely to share his sense of urgency, nourished by his experience of war.[63] Thereafter the Franco-German axis became the fulcrum of EC politics.[64] Together, Mitterrand and Kohl played a decisive role in the elaboration of the Treaty on European Union (TEU) signed in Maastricht in February 1992. This aimed to respond to geopolitical upheaval in Europe triggered by the collapse of communism, and to endow the Community with a robust social dimension that had been lacking in the single market. The Kohl–Mitterrand tandem likewise played a leading part in the negotiations on Economic and Monetary Union (EMU) that led to the launch of the euro in 1999.

Political cooperation was mirrored in business and economics. French business, encouraged by Bérégovoy, sought actively to emulate the German model of capitalism, based on the close association of banks and industry. This became known as *bancindustrie*. Unfortunately, attempts to establish German-style links between banks and industry led to some notable financial disasters. Lending exploded and poor risks proliferated as banks began to compete with one another for new custom, while still benefiting from the state's ultimate protection and escaping independent professional regulation. The casualties of such a system included Crédit Lyonnais, Crédit Foncier, the Comptoir des Entrepreneurs, GAN and the Banque de Phénix.[65]

Meanwhile, the inflation differential with Germany, a country with a long tradition of price stability following the horror of rampant inflation experienced after the First World War, became almost a national obsession. French pride at achieving a lower inflation rate than Germany in 1991 knew no bounds (see Table 6.1). By 1990, however, the Achilles heel of the French economy was no longer inflation – subjugated by the new policy of the 'franc fort', keeping a strong franc pegged to the German mark within the Exchange Rate Mechanism (ERM) of the European Monetary System (EMS) – but unemployment. Here too France fared considerably worse than Germany, even after unification swelled the German dole queues (see Table 6.3). Half a million new jobs were created in France in the two years from 1988–90, yet there was little erosion of the unemployed population. This was partly due to the continuing rise of France's active population, expected to grow from 24.2 million in 1987 to 24.8 million by the year 2000, while those of Germany and Britain were expected to decline. But the fact that steady growth should have left two-and-a-half million out of work pointed to a more serious structural weakness: the acute shortage of skilled workers in France. Here too France was out of step with Germany, where investment in training is an article of faith. By autumn 1989, 44 per cent of French companies were experiencing recruitment difficulties, a threefold increase since spring 1987. It was suggestive too of the culture of dependency bred

Table 6.3 Unemployment rates in G7 Nations, 1987–95 (percentage of total labour force)

Year	1987	1988	1989	1990	1991	1992	1993	1994	1995
Canada	8.8	7.7	7.5	8.1	10.2	11.3	11.2	10.4	9.5
France	**10.4**	**9.8**	**9.3**	**9.0**	**9.5**	**10.4**	**11.7**	**12.3**	**11.6**
Germ.	6.2	6.2	5.6	4.9	4.2	4.6	7.9	8.4	8.2
Italy	10.9	11.0	10.9	10.3	9.9	10.5	10.3	11.4	11.9
Japan	2.9	2.5	2.3	2.1	2.1	2.2	2.5	2.9	3.1
UK	10.3	8.5	7.1	6.8	8.8	10.1	10.5	9.6	8.8
USA	6.1	5.4	5.2	5.4	6.6	7.3	6.9	6.1	5.6

Source: World Economic and Social Survey data, 1997.

in workers employed in state-owned companies, some of whom were rendered incapable of adapting to the requirements of external labour markets. Renault shed a total of 37,000 jobs in the five years that preceded its alliance with Volvo. A survey of 200 former workers at the Billancourt plant conducted by the Confédération Démocratique du Travail (CFDT) highlighted the extent of this culture of dependency: 'The conclusions are catastrophic. We have found people who, having left behind an existence where they were taken in hand, are completely dependent and sometimes incapable of looking for another job.'[66]

France and Europe: fortress or open house?

As France edged closer to an enterprise culture in the late 1980s and early 1990s, it nevertheless rejected the undiluted free-market ideology embraced by the UK and the US, encapsulated by Thatcherism and Reaganism. At the same time, French emulation of some aspects of the concerted German economy, notably the link between bank and firms, did not lead to the wholesale pursuit of the German model in France. Between these two models, France was engaged in the difficult process of modifying and updating its own national business system. State intervention *tous azimuts* was clearly in the past: this had proved too costly and inefficient. It was increasingly replaced by tactical intervention, or 'arm's length *dirigisme*'.[67] The welfare state, *l'Etat-Providence*, was no longer what it had been in 1981–82. But the role of the state as strategist and defender of the national interest was not being abandoned. Rather, it was being ceded to a Community that France hoped would be strong enough to retain active intervention as a weapon in its economic arsenal. This was a new conceptualisation of an old ambition: that of economic sovereignty, the ability to control one's own destiny.

From this standpoint, the Community of the early 1990s was far from the finished article. It was too often defensive, reactive and on the back foot, seemingly incapable of acting decisively and coherently. It has been suggested that this might be due to its hybrid status, midway between a state and an international organisation. With relatively weak central institutions, and uncertain of its own identity, the Community's capacity for negotiating on behalf of its member states, often unable to agree among themselves, was fundamentally undermined.[68] Competition was one such area where the Community failed to agree. Here, free-marketeers such as Sir Leon Brittan, then head of the Commission's competition directorate (DG IV), for whom competition was 'the guiding force of economic life',[69] were pitched against those who sought greater protectionism and more EC-wide industrial policy, in particular France and Italy. For French Industry Minister Roger Fauroux, Europe was in danger of becoming 'a land open to all the winds'.[70]

This was especially so in the critical sector of cars. France is alone among EU member states in having two volume car manufacturers, both of which relied heavily on the home market despite much reduced domestic market shares. On a domestic level, in 1990 the automobile sector was France's largest single employer (bar the state), accounting for some 320,000 jobs despite the heavy redundancies of the 1980s: 210,000 workers were employed by car manufacturers and a further 110,000 by their suppliers.[71] On a European level, cars accounted for 9 per cent of EC GDP. Yet, when negotiating with the Japanese over the imbalance of trade between Europe and Japan in motor vehicles, little was made of an obvious negotiating advantage. The voluntary limitation agreement of July 1991 brokered by the Commission and the Japanese Ministry for International Trade and Industry (MITI) did little to protect the six European volume manufacturers[72] against what the French perceived as the 'tidal wave' of Japanese cars unfurling over European shores.[73]

The 'agreement' was known as 'elements of consensus', as opposed to anything formal and binding. It concentrated on the following points. First, there was to be a seven-year transition period to 1999, after which the European market would be fully liberalised. Second, all bilateral quotas, such as had prevailed in France, where Japanese imports were restricted to 3 per cent of the market, were to be removed by the end of 1992. Japanese imports were to be 'monitored' until 1999, being kept at around 1.24 million vehicles, while Japanese production in Europe, the so-called 'transplants', could increase sales without restriction. Finally, should market growth be less than the 1–2 per cent annual growth rate expected, the volume 'accorded' to Japanese producers would be 'adjusted' to reflect the new market conditions.

The all-too-glaring weaknesses of an unwritten, 'gentlemen's agreement' have spawned many words. It suffices here to mention briefly its principal lacunae. The agreement made no mention of Japanese cars made in third countries such as the US, Korea or elsewhere, which could continue to be imported freely into Europe. Transplant production was underestimated, according to industry chiefs, who expected it to expand to 2 million units annually by 1999 rather than the 1.2 million predicted by EC officials. That Japanese imports already amounted to 12 per cent of the market in 1991 made nonsense of the 8 per cent objective. No serious attempt was made to ensure the reciprocity that would have benefited European constructors. The Japanese market remained almost hermetically sealed, a true fortress in the eyes of Jacques Calvet, head of Peugeot SA, unlike the 'sandcastle' which, in his perception, Europe seemed intent on building.[74] Sales of European cars, never buoyant, had declined there by 3.9 per cent in the year since 1990.[75]

The European car industry had additional grievances: the seven-year transitionary period, for example, was shorter than they had demanded. The lack of a written contract of any sort left the agreement wide open to interpretation: how then did the Japanese understand it, and would they stick to what they understood? In the event, five of the six European contractors – including Renault – swallowed the pill. Peugeot's Jacques Calvet became a lone Cassandra, resentful of the self-imposed position of weakness from which the EC had negotiated. As one of his senior managers put it, 'We went there as beggars, like the Burghers of Calais, barefoot and with ropes around our necks.'[76] This, in his eyes, was inappropriate for representatives of the world's strongest car market, who ought to have negotiated from a position of strength. Without renegotiation of the contract Calvet predicted industrial defeat: the consequence of a single market that lacked a strong external industrial policy, and which had opened its doors before the house was built. The agreement, however, was not renegotiated.

Top PSA managers were quick to respond when asked in a personal interview how they envisaged the European car market in the twenty-first century: 'There will be some deaths.' Jean-Pierre Lehmann anticipated French industrial defeat as the most likely outcome of the battle: 'In this scenario, either the French automobile industry is relegated to industrial archeology, or – at best – French automotive factories become subcontractors and distributors of Japanese and other foreign multinationals. Renault might become, say, to Toyota what Bull is currently to NEC.'[77] Ironically, in the event Lehmann's prediction was reversed. It was Renault that acquired a Japanese firm, Nissan, in which it purchased a 37 per cent stake in spring 1999, not the other way round. At the time of writing, both Renault and Peugeot continue to survive and prosper. Investment in technology and the exploitation of synergies,[78] as well as alliance building – aggressive and dynamic, not defensive collaboration – are at the heart of their respective strategies (see Chapter 7).

France and world trade: *Realpolitik oblige*?

For French business interests to become fixated on Europe would of course have been dangerous: beyond Europe was the world, an increasingly global economy that could not be ignored. The Uruguay Round of GATT negotiations on international trade (1986–94) was, as *Le Monde* put it, less concerned with matters such as film quotas or the price of wheat than 'a mode of growth, of existence' – literally a mode of being in the world.

Hostility to the Uruguay Round was more acute in France than elsewhere in the EC, especially with respect to agriculture, previously a no-go zone for GATT. This was despite the fact that by 1992 France's share of world exports in manufactured goods was 6.4 per cent, in fourth position behind the US (12.2 per cent), Germany (11.6 per cent) and Japan (9.2 per cent), and ahead of the UK (5.2 per cent).[79] France's share of world exports in services was even more impressive: with 9.4 per cent of the whole in 1991, France was in second position, bettered only by the US (16.7 per cent), and well ahead of Germany (6.7 per cent) and the UK (5.9 per cent).[80] Services accounted for almost two-thirds of world GDP in 1992, equal to $3,000 billion worth of business globally. They represented 20 per cent of world

exports, worth an estimated $900 billion. Their liberalisation was antici-
pated to have far-reaching implications for global trade. French firms in a
range of sectors were well placed to benefit. Overall, the World Bank and
OECD estimated gains from a successful conclusion to the Round to range
from $212 billion to $274 billion annually by the year 2002 (in 1992 dollars). Of this, the EU was expected to win the lion's share, approximately
$80 billion per annum. As a leading producer of luxury goods, France also
stood to benefit from TRIPs (Trade-Related Intellectual Property Rights),
proposals for the protection of intellectual property rights which aimed to
stem the growing traffic in counterfeit goods.[81]

There was a strong feeling in France that some participants to the Round,
particularly the US, had come to the party with a rigged hand. 'Blair House',
the bilateral EC–US agricultural deal of November 1992, became the nexus of
French anger and frustration. EC Agricultural Minister Ray MacSharry
resigned in protest when Jacques Delors intervened directly on behalf of
French farmers. As president of the Commission, Delors was supposed to rise
above national sentiment. French and European farmers were already faced
with major reform of the Common Agricultural Policy (CAP), finalised in
May 1992 and due for implementation in 1993. Now, further reform was in
prospect due to Blair House, which, if implemented, would reduce subsidised
exports by EC member states by 36 per cent in value and 21 per cent in volume over a six-year period.[82] As the main EC exporter of farm produce, producing 22 per cent of EU agricultural output, France would bear the brunt of
the proposed cuts. The US, on the other hand, was expected to increase its
farm exports.[83] In the 1980s the US had lost sizeable market share in farm
produce, much of it to EC, especially French producers – American farm
exports declined dramatically from a peak of $43 billion in 1981 to $26 billion five years later. The French regarded Blair House as a dishonest attempt
on the part of the US to get it back, at French expense, by dint of being
le plus fort, and with the further aim of destroying the CAP in the process.

French hostility to the GATT agricultural talks was exacerbated by CAP
reform. Officially the two were separate. The EC's 1991 reflections paper,
The Development and Future of the CAP, which laid down the principles for
reform, did not mention the GATT, claiming rather that CAP reform was an
internal matter and budget-driven.[84] In reality the two were indivisible.
CAP reform had been prompted by GATT discussions. The Commission
welcomed these, the CAP having long devoured its overall budget to the
detriment of other policies. By 1990 the CAP consumed 56.3 per cent of
the EC budget, equal to ECU (European Currency Unit) 26,431 million.[85]
In the 1970s the CAP had swallowed as much as 75 per cent of the budget;
but there had never been a reduction in CAP expenditure in real terms,
since the overall size of the cake had consistently increased.[86]

In 1993 French farmers were still doing very well from the CAP, earning
in guaranteed receipts ECU8,124 million, about 23.5 per cent of the whole.[87]

As the economic implications of CAP reform crystallised, however, it emerged that, far from reducing EC spending, the cost of support under the new system was likely to rise. Farmers were to be compensated for the loss of revenue resulting from the reduction in levels of price support by direct acreage payments, linked to a set-aside scheme. The burden of the CAP was thus to be shifted away from consumers, who had paid for it in higher prices, more squarely on to the shoulders of taxpayers. The new Delors package envisaged that CAP expenditure would fall beneath 50 per cent of the EU budget for the first time by 1997; but again, the actual amount was set to increase.

Nevertheless, the cocktail of the Maastricht referendum, GATT, Blair House and CAP reform had inflamed the French countryside, its fields spiked with banners urging revolt and prophetic makeshift gallows bearing messages of doom ('Who will feed you tomorrow?'), many of which remain to this day. The separate worlds of *les deux agricultures* were united in an artificial coalition between small and large farmers, demonstrating together over a peasantry threatened, they claimed, with extinction. This was bitterly idiosyncratic as larger farmers – of whom an estimated 50,000 to 200,000 could afford to live without subsidy[88] – were likely to benefit most from the new regime. With the switch to direct payments, the CAP became more transparent. Larger farmers, however, vigorously opposed the principle of modulation, whereby small farmers would be compensated in full and larger farmers only partially beyond a certain size. A degree of embarrassment nevertheless became perceptible among farmers in the wealthy Paris basin, and in the UK, about the size of their payments, with cheques for £1 million seized on by the British press.

At times France's right-wing government, elected in spring 1993 and headed by Balladur, seemed to stir up public opinion, to egg it on, thereby increasing its own negotiating power with the Commission. At others, it seemed to be genuinely out of control, and in need of help.[89] There was much talk at home and abroad that France might torpedo the GATT agricultural deal, either by securing a Council vote against it, or by invoking the 'Luxembourg Compromise', according to which a minority of 23 votes was sufficient to block measures of vital national interest. With hindsight, it might be tempting to view such threats as bluster, designed to win concessions from the Americans (who had always said that they would not renegotiate Blair House); but at the time they were taken very seriously. There was certainly an assumption in the French and British press that the veto would be used. Luc Guyau of the French farmers' union FNSEA (Fédération National des Syndicats des Exploitants Agricoles) wrote convincingly in April 1993 that 'there is bound to be a veto. The case in favour of such a step rests on strong arguments, which go way beyond agriculture.'[90] France's Nobel prize-winning economist, Maurice Allais, fanned the flames by warning that the Uruguay Round would cost France between

3 and 5 million jobs by the year 2000 as a direct result of trade liberalisation.[91] Most others disagreed, estimating that more than 4 million jobs accrued to France as a result of her overseas trade (3,125,000 in industry and 1 million in services), slightly more than those lost to foreign firms due to imports of goods and services (3,332,000 and 700,000 jobs respectively).[92] In the event, President Mitterrand minimised the threat of the veto being used by deciding that the GATT deal should be approved or rejected as a package, thereby making it more difficult to unpick individual items. Balladur embraced this 'all or nothing' approach, often repeating that 'There will be no agreement on anything while there is no agreement on everything' (a phrase he borrowed from Sir Leon Brittan).[93]

By summer 1993, with the deadline (set by President Clinton) of 15 December approaching, there were signs that France's hardline stance over agriculture was beginning to soften. Balladur declared himself 'ready not to be 100 per cent right'.[94] In mid-September, the French requested an EC 'Jumbo Council' (so-called because it involved two separate departments, agriculture and foreign affairs). The meeting emerged as a kind of turning-point: whereas previously the French had been in fighting mode, there was now a sense in which they seemed to acknowledge that in the Blair House deal they had a lot to gain. Foreign Minister Juppé and Agricultural Minister Puech insisted for the first time that they were not interested in reopening Blair House; at the same time, they clearly wanted to see what else they could extract. A commitment was made to the effect that during the coming weeks the Commission would seek 'clarifications, amplifications and additions' to the Blair House farm deal from the US, this form of wording determined by the US's continuing refusal to renegotiate. The modifications that ensued would not have happened without there being something in it for the US.[95] Some of the changes were requested by the US as a quid pro quo; others were welcomed by both sides. Nor would it have happened without change at the top. In 1993 Sir Leon Brittan became EC Commissioner for External Affairs, and Mickey Kantor became US trade representative; both were 54-year-old lawyers of Lithuanian Jewish origin! Sir Leon, moreover, recognised the need to accommodate the French in some way.[96]

The end result was that the constraints on agriculture imposed by GATT were relaxed considerably. The volume of cereals, beef and milk products (cheese in particular, close to French hearts) that the EC would be able to export on a subsidised basis during the implementation period was markedly increased. The 'peace clause', which referred to a period when neither side could take legal action over the farm trading practices of the other, was extended from six to nine years. The market access offer for cereals, rice and certain fruit and vegetables was improved. The French were also successful in their mission to bring about the creation of a 'multilateral trade organisation' – a permanent, supranational body which would limit, if not prevent, US domination of the world trading system.

The Geneva-based WTO (the Americans refused to accept the French choice of name) came into being in 1995. French demands that the audiovisual sector be regarded as a special case – a 'cultural exception' – given the huge trade deficit between the US and the EC in audiovisual products, estimated at $3.37 billion in 1993, were less successful. The audiovisual sector was not removed from the scope of the GATS (General Agreement on Trade in Services), contrary to some reports, but some minor concessions were secured.[97]

What is interesting is that the above concessions were not presented jingoistically in France, although collectively they made a big difference. Perhaps in the eyes of many French farmers they did not go far enough. Perhaps, too, in the final stages of the Round, French perceptions of French interests were undergoing subtle but significant change. The French government was coming round to the view that Blair House was in fact a better deal than the EC might have expected. The IIASA (Institut International pour l'Analyse des Systèmes Appliqués) concluded that the liberalisation of farm trade would mean an increase in EC GDP of between 0.2 and 0.7 per cent.[98]

Despite all the brinkmanship, the attitude that ultimately prevailed was grounded firmly in *Realpolitik*, mindful of France's long-term business interests as a major exporter of goods and services. There was also a perceptible move in favour of efficient agriculture. Agriculture in France has traditionally enjoyed a warm, supportive relationship with government, and mentalities could not be expected to change overnight. The notion of subsidised exports has been around for a very long time. It may well be a very long time before French and Community farmers fully embrace a free trading system in agriculture. But the possibility, formerly taboo, of producing for the world market without export refunds, thus leaving those refunds over for less efficient farmers, had begun to be voiced in France, at least as a theoretical possibility if not an immediate reality.

The Uruguay Round presents an interesting case-study. It demonstrates how concerted action by the French has helped to shape the international institutions and frameworks within which capitalism operates – such as GATT, the WTO, the EU, and within this the CAP, a French initiative which has survived since the 1960s. The cohesive nature of the French politico-administrative system, the particular physiology of government involvement in the economy, has made the French proactive in their determination to set the rules of engagement for enterprise within the European and global economic systems. The *dénouement* to the Round reveals France as having been able to shape the international agenda disproportionately to its size, punching above its weight in the international arena. Technically the French should not have got involved, since article 113 of the Treaty of Rome hands responsibility for external trade negotiations to the Commission. However, other member states may secretly have been thanking the French for having dug in their heels, thus securing a better deal for EC farmers.

An era of scandal

It is an irony of the Mitterrand presidency that Mitterrand, who often expressed his abhorrence of a money-motivated society, should have presided over an era of 'sleaze' with which he himself was not untainted. Hayward observes that the Mitterrand years witnessed 'a dramatic change in official morality'.[99] Much of this scandal had to do with business enterprise. In the late 1980s, scandals involving Carrefour (1986), Société Générale (1988) and Pechiney (1988) turned these companies into household names.[100] In the 1990s, business improprieties forced numerous Cabinet ministers to resign, with several ending up behind bars. By the end of Mitterrand's presidency, a quarter of the bosses of France's top 40 companies were under investigation for fraud or corruption, including those of Saint-Gobain, Bidermann, Bouygues, SNCF, Paribas, EdF, Auchan, GMF and Renault.[101] Others were already in prison, the heads of Schneider (Pineau-Valenciennes) and BTF (Bernard Tapie) being the most infamous.

The Société Générale and Pechiney scandals of 1988–89 illustrate the symbiotic relationship in France between the higher echelons of politics, administration and business, the tight-knit cohesion of the politico-administrative and business establishment. The Société Générale scandal concerned an ill-fated government-backed attempt to break up the 'hard core' of the privatised bank through a dawn raid on the bank's shares orchestrated by Georges Pébereau (former head of CGE and close to Bérégovoy). Friends of the socialist government were able to reap large profits through access to classified information.

Meanwhile, the purchase in November 1988 of the American National Can subsidiary of the US firm Triangle by the nationalised aluminium group, Pechiney, occasioned France's most famous insider trading scandal. Alain Boublil, *directeur de cabinet* of Pierre Bérégovoy, then finance minister, had encouraged Pechiney in the purchase as a means of achieving the critical mass necessary to compete in the international packaging market. That Pechiney was then a public-sector company, not permitted to make acquisitions according to government rules, slowed the takeover while increasing the number of individuals involved in the decision-making process. On the same day that the company's chairman, Jean Gandois, secured the government's green light for the takeover, a businessman closely linked with the Socialist Party, Max Théret, bought 32,000 Triangle shares in his own name. A close friend of Mitterrand, Roger-Patrice Pelat (who introduced him to his wife, Danièle Gouze, and was best man at their wedding), bought a further 20,000 shares through an investment company, having set up a business in Panama through which to launder the profits. Interviewed on television, Mitterrand spoke emotionally of a friendship born in a prisoner-of-war camp, and vehemently of the corrupting influence of money. As Routier observes, 'the wound was too visible for him not to emerge cleansed from the experience, amnestied from the only insider dealing of which he had allowed himself to be guilty – that of friend-ship'.[102] Pelat was never again seen at the Elysée.

That this was all that Mitterrand was culpable of during his long presi-dency has since been called into question by a scandal that has dwarfed all others: that of the oil giant Elf-Aquitaine. It has engulfed Mitterrand's lawyer and *alter ego*, ex-foreign minister Roland Dumas (head of the Constitutional Council, the highest legal authority in the land), as well as his friend Chancellor Kohl and ultimately Mitterrand himself. Mitterrand's son, Jean-Christophe, his father's adviser on Africa (nick-named 'Papa m'a dit'), has also been implicated. Paid by Elf as a consultant from 1992, Jean-Christophe was arrested in December 2000 on suspicion of arms trafficking and money laundering, and admitted receiving £1.3 million in a Swiss bank account. A senior Elf executive, André Tarallo, claimed in summer 2000 that throughout the 1990s the firm had creamed off an annual £40 million from the company into a tax haven located in Liechtenstein. The money was allegedly given to corrupt African heads of state, as well as to political par-ties in France and Germany (Chancellor Kohl's Christlich-Demokratische Union). The CDU is said to have benefited from a £25 million oil refinery kickback,[103] designed to bolster Kohl's chances of re-election in 1994 – viewed by Mitterrand and Kohl as critical to the continuing success of European integration and EMU.[104] Despite his banishment from the party in 1998–99, Kohl always refused to say where the money had come from. At the time of writing, investigations in France are still ongoing. The house of Chirac is similarly under attack, being investigated for alleged party kickbacks during his tenancy as Mayor of Paris. Chirac's oft-repeated line – 'I did not know' – began to wear rather thin when the public discovered the existence of a secret slush fund for the president and his ministers, pay-ing for expensive vacations abroad. One way or another Chirac has been housed and cared for by the state, in luxurious style, for three decades. His re-election in May 2002 was motivated by a common desire to defeat the Far Right rather than any more positive endorsement of Chirac himself.

It is possible to argue that the considerable overlap between politics and business in France creates scope for venality, as the scandal of Elf-Aquitaine highlights, implicating both Mitterrand and Kohl. Large-scale privatisation intensified the need for international standards and codes of practice to be observed. At the same time, comparison with international norms, as European integration and globalisation proceeded apace, put long-established national patterns of doing business under the spotlight for the first time. Openness, transparency and accountability, arguably not intrinsic aspects of the French business culture, were now viewed as desirable at an interna-tional level. The publication of the Cadbury Report in the UK in 1992 on the financial aspects of corporate governance had repercussions in France, leading to the publication in 1995 of the *Rapport Viénot*, which recom-mended certain changes to the board structure of listed companies,

CADBURY	VIÉNOT
(1) Regulatory Regime	
• Self-regulation preferred option. • Centrepiece is Code of Best Practice (CBP). • Compliance with CBP and any variations to be stated in Annual Report and Accounts. • Scope and functioning of CBP to be reviewed by successor committee. • Need for future legislation not ruled out.	• Self-regulation preferred option. • Existing legal framework judged • satisfactory. • Minor modification to existing legislation not ruled out. • Further review to take place after 3 years.
(2) Board Structure, Composition and Procedure	
• Strengthen the unitary board structure rather than replace it. • Minimum of 3 non-executive directors (NEDs) (may include Chairman). • To have formal schedule of matters reserved for collective decision.	• Companies may continue to choose between unitary and dual structure. • Minimum of 2 NEDs (must be shareholders). • Composition of board regularly re-examined to ensure representative of shareholding body. • No change in role but greater formalisation of work required than previously (to allay public concerns). • Directors should represent the general interest, not special interest groups.
(3) Directors' Roles and Responsibilities	
• Chairman and CEO roles clearly separated and responsibilities defined. • NEDs not to participate in share option or pension schemes. • NED appointments require full board approval. • NED appointments for fixed term of 3 years; reappointment requires shareholder approval.	• Advantages seen in continued union of Chairman and CEO roles, but division an option if dual structure adopted. • Individuals to self limit to 5 non-executive directorships and to avoid reciprocal mandates. • NEDs have duty to represent small investors.
(4) Board Committees	
• Audit Committee given central role in monitoring and control (audit objectivity and effectiveness). • Remuneration Committee essential. • Nomination Committee advocated but not insisted upon.	• Audit Committee recommended but no guidelines other than avoidance of reciprocal mandates. • Remuneration Committee recommended and reciprocal mandates to be avoided.

(cont'd)

CADBURY	VIÉNOT
	• Nomination Committee seen as useful but not essential (Remuneration Committee may perform function).
(5) Shareholders and Disclosure of Information	
• Directors' total emoluments (salary, bonuses, stock options, pension contributions) to be disclosed in Annual Reports and Accounts • Directors and auditors to state (with any necessary qualifications) that business is a going concern. • Institutional investors should disclose their policies on the use of their voting rights. • Individual shareholders should have the opportunity to make themselves heard at annual general meetings.	• Disclosure of directors' remuneration not mentioned. • More communication with shareholders encouraged, especially at critical times (such as takeover activity).

Figure 6   Comparative analysis of the Cadbury and Viénot Reports
Compiled by author using data from Cadbury (1992) and Viénot Reports (1995).

summarised in Figure 6.1. In particular, it urged that directors serve on no more than five boards, and that reciprocal mandates be avoided. It stressed the need for independent, non-executive directors (NEDs) to serve on the boards of listed companies. Audit and remuneration committees were advised and nomination committees encouraged. Although the recommendations of the Viénot Report were not binding, nevertheless it represented a significant move towards convergence, as the rules and regulations of corporate governance were harmonised to conform with the new ideology of international capitalism. The *Rapport Marini*, which supported these recommendations, followed in 1996.[105]

Not all scandals have been rooted in corruption, however. One of the most notorious – the bankruptcy of the state-owned bank Crédit Lyonnais in 1993 – was founded in incompetence. It exposed in spectacular fashion the inability of some members of the establishment elite to function as efficient captains of industry in an economy no longer limited by French borders. The osmosis of the elite from administration to business was clearly implicated. The bank's chairman, Jean-Yves Haberer, a technocrat and a former director of the Trésor, found it hard to convert from bureaucrat to businessman. His strategy for the bank's expansion, ill thought-through – including investment in MGM, Groupe Bernard Tapie, and the volatile Parisian property market, which later collapsed – was dreamt up in a sound-proofed office, divorced from the rest of the bank and from reality. No doubt his former colleagues at the Trésor felt uneasy about questioning their ex-director about his commercial ventures. The resulting bill to the taxpayer is estimated at FF190 billion, amounting to the world's largest-ever bail-out. When the bank went up in flames one night in 1994, who knows what incriminating dossiers may have been incinerated in the conflagration.[106]

Conclusion

This chapter has examined the far-reaching privatisation and growing Europeanisation that marked the period 1986–95. In the early 1980s, French business had begun to emerge from the decade of slow growth engendered by the oil price dislocations of the 1970s. However, in many industries, such as cars and IT, confidence remained at low ebb as business leaders struggled to improve competitiveness and prevent further erosion of market shares at home and abroad.[107] The nationalisations of the early Mitterrand era were in essence defensive and reactionary – an unpromising basis for sustained industrial renewal and growth. Yet what followed, once the dogma of old-style socialism had finally been discarded, was highly creditable. French firms confronted and adapted strategically to the pressures of increasing international competition. They showed their resilience in raising national productivity levels to an enviably high level by the best international standards. By 1995 a sharp recovery in the trade figures confirmed the improved competitiveness of the economy, profitability had been restored, and French business was in good shape to address emerging European and global challenges.

Large-scale privatisation served in many respects as a vector for change. It intensified the need for international standards and codes of practice to be observed. Like the numerous financial scandals which came to light in the period, it contributed in this way to the corporate governance changes introduced in France from 1995, in the wake of the Viénot Report, as French rules and regulations were harmonised with international norms.

On the other hand, the privatisation waves of 1986–88 and 1993–95 institutionalised interlocking directorates between banks and firms. These were favoured as a means of preventing foreign takeovers over the 'golden share' option preferred by the British, often held for just a short time before being sold. In this way privatisation in France did not reduce national control. Balladur failed, however, in his avowed objective of introducing economic liberty for all. The charge of cronyism levied against him by left-wing politicians was well merited, as privatisation reinforced business establishment networks through the mechanism of the *noyaux durs*, many of whose members had personal links to the Balladur government.

The main objective for major French companies was to move from being national to international players in Europe, through strategic alliances, mergers and takeovers, joint ventures and licensing deals, many with foreign firms. That this was achieved while retaining national control over privatised firms, enabled the French to 'have their cake and eat it' in the battle to become front-rank European and international firms.[108] With obvious exceptions (such as Bull), the ensuing collaborations revealed French businesses as engaging not in the defensive mergers of the 1960s and 1970s kind, but increasingly in much more aggressive, dynamic and imaginative collaboration. Bull's alliances with NEC and IBM, though, which allowed the company to preserve a holding position in the market, were nevertheless indicative of a new realism driving the relationship between business and government.

The same realism was also evident in the conclusion to the Uruguay Round, in which France's long-term business interests as a major exporter of goods and services were ultimately privileged over the ostensible interests of a powerful national minority. The creation of the WTO in 1995, for which France had campaigned as a counterpoint to American domination, revealed France as able disproportionately to its size to shape the international institutions and frameworks within which capitalism operates. Partly this influence was drawn from the occupancy of coveted top positions in influential organisations. During the early 1990s French nationals presided over the European Commission, the OECD, the IMF, the EBRD (European Bank for Reconstruction and Development), and the secretariat to the Council of Europe. Jacques Delors' long presidency of the European Commission (1985–94) enabled France to exert far-reaching influence over the shape of the institutions determining the form and speed of European integration.[109] French influence in Europe was amplified by the stocking of senior posts with individuals Delors felt he could trust, many of whom were French.[110] Of course, things did not always go France's way. The 1991 EC–Japan car agreement did not suit the French car industry. Realistically, however, in a world in which even French consumers were prepared to purchase Japanese cars, there was little the manufacturers could do about it.[111] Although Peugeot felt let down by the Commission, the agreement brought home to producers the unavoidable fact that sliding back into the protectionism of the past was not an option. Achieving competitiveness depended on confronting competition in the here and now, not seeking to postpone it.

The French business class was nevertheless charged during this time with being exclusively preoccupied with productivity, profitability and competitiveness to the detriment of wider social concerns, with the result that in the industrial sector employment had consistently declined as efficiency gains were achieved (see Table 6.3).[112] The Chirac presidency (1995–) began with a rash of strikes, sparked by welfare cuts and tax increases introduced by premier Alain Juppé (1995–97). The challenge for the incoming socialist administration under Lionel Jospin (1997–2002) was to marry together business success with a more even distribution of its fruits – if indeed so utopian an objective was sustainable in the new, global economy. The years in question were momentous ones for European construction. They embraced the single market programme, the end of the Cold War, German reunification, the two intergovernmental conferences (IGCs) on monetary and political union, the Maastricht Treaty leading to the European Union (TEU), and the preparations for EMU. Much of this was the direct result of French initiatives, amplified by German influence and support – a potent combination. The 1992 Maastricht referendum, though, revealed France not as united over Europe as had been widely assumed, but as deeply divided – even allowing for the fact that the referendum had become bound up with the unpopularity of an ageing president. If the middle ground was broadly supportive of the TEU, the far left and right were opposed.

The departure of Mitterrand and Kohl changed the way in which the EU operated. The EU's enlargement from 12 to 15 members in 1995 (admitting Austria, Finland and Sweden) moved its centre of gravity northwards and eastwards. Mitterrand's successor to the presidency in May 1995, Jacques Chirac, had little rapport with Kohl or Schröder. Elected Chancellor in 1998, Schröder was of a younger generation than Kohl, with no experience of war, and Germany seemed increasingly reluctant to curry favour with the French out of a sense of guilt for crimes carried out under the Nazis. The passing of the Mitterrand–Kohl era thus gave way to a more uncertain future for France in the EU, where the preservation of French interests might no longer be to the fore.

7
French Business and Global Economic Integration

The aim of all public service can only be the general interest.

Michèle Voisset[1]

By spring 2001, it was becoming clear that the US economy, the locomotive of the world economy, was losing momentum, following a long period of expansion spanning most of the Clinton era. French Prime Minister Jospin, nurturing presidential ambitions, urged his country not to be unduly concerned. Despite fear of a global economic slowdown, reflected in weakening share prices, and with oil prices at a ten-year high, France in his view was a pillar of strength within the global economy.[2] Layoffs were bound to occur, such as those announced by the food giant Danone and the retailer Marks and Spencer, which closed its European stores. But they would happen less frequently than previously, Jospin claimed[3] – despite the fact that other large French firms (Bata, Jouef, Moulinex-Brandt, AOM-Air Liberté, Valeo) were also contemplating retrenchment.[4]

This chapter explores the rationale behind Jospin's optimistic assessment of France's economic prospects within the global economy and the consequences of global economic integration for the French national business system and the enduring notion of economic sovereignty. It begins by reviewing the staged build-up to the main economic and political event in France and the European Union (EU) of the late 1990s, the launch of the euro. Though this implied an obvious loss of sovereignty, in fact through EMU France sought to extend its political influence, seeking to tie Germany into the European economy for the good of its trading partners, primarily France, while diminishing German economic hegemony.[5] Our concern here is less with the political aspects of EMU[6] than with its business and economic implications, especially with respect to unemployment, exports and business competitiveness. An important theme, explored through a series of sectoral studies, is the startling internationalisation of French business that took place on the cusp of the new millennium. These reveal a national business system undergoing potentially far-reaching change. It is suggested here, however, that despite the massive penetration of foreign capital in large French companies, the French national business system is in the process of being transformed rather than jettisoned. French business elite networks continue to thrive. Their objective, in response to global pressures, is to maintain or acquire control over European and international enterprises. In this sense, the instinctive reflex towards economic sovereignty continues to prevail despite supranational efforts to manage economic activity across Europe.

The pressures of EMU (1995–99)

The dominant concern of the French government in the mid-1990s was the need to qualify for EMU in 1997 or 1999 (in the event the earlier date was abandoned). This was the top priority on the part of both the Balladur government that preceded Chirac's victory in the 1995 presidential election, and the Juppé administration that succeeded it. It was also the main objective of President Chirac from June 1995, despite his having campaigned on a platform of putting jobs first. Barely five weeks after his election, Chirac reverted to the '*politique unique*' of prioritising the budget deficit to the detriment of employment, promising to keep public spending down in order to meet the Maastricht criteria for EMU.[7] In fact, as Maddison observes, the objective of monetary union was responsible for the persistence in Western Europe of the deflationary policies introduced in response to the oil crises of the 1970s, despite high unemployment and historically low inflation. From an average of 11.2 per cent in 1973–78 and 4.5 per cent in 1983–93, by 1993–98 inflation in Western Europe had fallen to 2.2 per cent, approximately half its rate during the 'golden age' of economic growth.[8]

The Treaty of European Union (TEU), agreed at Maastricht in December 1991 and signed in February 1992, laid down a timetable for EMU in three stages. Stage one began with the completion of the single market in January 1993, by which time all member states were to have joined the Exchange Rate Mechanism (ERM) of the European Monetary System (EMS), designed to function as a 'glide-path' to EMU. The ERM was a system of bilateral exchange rates between member currencies, of which there were two bands: a narrow band, where currencies had a margin of fluctuation of 2.25 per cent, and a broad band, where the margin of variation was 6 per cent. The broader band (which the pound joined when it became a member of the ERM in October 1990) acknowledged the difficulties that weaker European economies might experience in attempting to keep to a tighter 2.25 per cent constraint. From March 1983, the credibility of the system in exchange markets had grown considerably. Membership of the ERM had come to be perceived as a highly effective external discipline for monetary policy, credited with bringing about a downward convergence of inflation rates among member currencies.

Stage two, heralded by the creation of the European Monetary Institute (EMI) in January 1994, was designed to see the progressive reduction of fluctuations in exchange rates between currencies over the following two to five years. By 1999 at the latest, the European Council was to convene to assess on the basis of strict 'convergence criteria' laid down in the Maastricht Treaty whether individual member states had met the conditions for EMU. These criteria were designed to ensure close coordination of economic policies and convergence in economic performance among EU member states. The exchange-rate stability criterion prohibited realignment (which normally meant devaluation, other than for the German mark, regularly revalued *vis-à-vis* other member currencies)[9] in the two years leading up to the permanent fixing of exchange rates. In addition, inflation should not diverge by more than 1.5 per cent, and interest rates not more than 2 per cent above the average of the three best-performing member states. General government financial deficits (which comprised the sum of the central government and local government balances, added to the social security balance) should not exceed 3 per cent of annual GDP, while the ratio of national debt to annual GDP was not to be greater than 60 per cent. The Maastricht criteria owed their stringency to German insistence, prompted by the need to reassure German nationals that the Bundesbank and the Deutschmark, paragons of financial discipline, were not being sacrificed for the lax financial management of an unstable and inflationary European currency.

Finally, stage three was to be marked by the permanent fixing of currencies for those countries meeting the convergence criteria, as well as by the launch of the independent European Central Bank (ECB) in charge of a single currency and a single monetary policy throughout the Eurozone. The distribution of euro coins and banknotes would commence in January 2002. In the intervening period, the euro could be used as a 'virtual', synthetic currency in international financial markets.

In retrospect, the provision that there should be no realignment for two years prior to the irrevocable locking of exchange rates fostered an unnatural rigidity in the system. Realignments that should have taken place were postponed to avoid loss of face, leading to resentment over the Bundesbank's refusal to cut interest rates and thus ease the pressures that had built up in the system. To currency speculators – which included not only individuals such as George Soros, but high-street banks, betting against their own currencies – the provision against realignment served as a red rag to a bull. The combined foreign reserves of EU central banks, which could be tapped to prop up ailing member currencies in danger of falling though their ERM floor, paled into insignificance when compared to global currency transactions. Daily currency transactions in New York, London and Tokyo alone amounted to $623 billion in 1992, almost three times the foreign reserves of the entire G7.

The ERM débâcle of September 1992 saw sterling ousted from the ERM along with the lira and escudo.[10] This, together with the extension of ERM margins of fluctuation to 15 per cent either way[11] following a run on the franc in August 1993, made a nonsense of the ERM as an intended 'glide-path' to EMU.[12] With the exchange rate stability criterion neutered, the importance of the remaining convergence criteria was clearly accentuated. Two emerged as especially important. These concerned the size of budget deficits and the stock of national debt relative to annual GDP.

In 1993, with the French budget deficit approaching 6 per cent of GDP (see Table 7.1), the Balladur government set a government deficit target of 2.5 per cent of GDP by the year 1997. Despite several privatisations,[13] the freezing of FF18 billion of public expenditure, and a growth rate of 2.6 per cent,[14] on the eve of the 1995 presidential election France was still running a budget deficit of FF442 billion equal to 6 per cent of GDP.[15] By 1998, however, the general deficit had fallen to FF229 billion, less than 3 per cent of GDP (see Table 7.2). Meanwhile, the stock of national debt (to which the budget deficit was added at the end of each year) had doubled in the seven

Table 7.1 General government financial balances in G7 Nations, 1986–95 (as percentage of GDP)

Country/ year	1986	1987	1988	1989	1990	1991	1992	1993	1994	1995
Can.	−5.4	−3.8	−2.5	−2.9	−4.1	−6.6	−7.4	−7.3	−5.3	−4.1
France	**−2.7**	**−1.9**	**−1.7**	**−1.2**	**−1.6**	**−2.0**	**−3.8**	**−5.6**	**−5.6**	**4.8**
Germ.	−1.3	−1.9	−2.2	0.1	−2.1	−3.3	−2.8	−3.5	−2.4	−3.5
Italy	−11.7	−11.0	−10.7	−9.9	−11.0	−10.2	−9.5	−9.6	−9.0	−7.1
Japan	−0.9	0.5	1.5	2.5	2.9	2.9	1.4	−1.6	−2.1	3.3
UK	−2.4	−1.4	1.0	0.9	−1.2	−2.5	−6.3	−7.8	−6.8	1.7
USA	−3.5	−2.6	−2.1	−1.7	−2.7	−3.3	−4.4	−3.6	−2.3	3.1

Source: *World Economic and Social Survey 1997: Trends and Policies*, UN, New York, 1997, p. 239.

Table 7.2 French government finances, 1995–2000 (FF billions or percentage of GDP)

Government finances/year	1995	1996	1997	1998	1999	2000
Gen. balance	−434.9	−324.3	−249.2	−228.9	−142.5	−121.7
Gen. balance	−5.6	−4.1	−3.0	−2.7	−1.6	−1.3
Central	−4.7	−3.7	−2.8	−2.9	−2.3	−2.2
Local	−0.2	0.1	0.2	0.3	0.4	0.3
Soc. Sec.	−0.7	−0.4	−0.4	−0.1	0.3	0.6

Sources: EIU, 2000, 2001; INSEE, *Les Comptes de la Nation 1997*, *Les Comptes de la Nation 2000*.

years since 1991, rising from FF2,411 billion in 1991 to FF4,923 billion by 1998 (equal to FF198,000 per employee), a trajectory which augured ill for the future.[16] This level of debt did not infringe the debt convergence criterion *per se*, being expected to attain 58.7 per cent of GDP in 1999 (as against just 20.8 per cent of GDP in 1980). However, in a context of relatively high interest rates and low inflation merely to service it would eat up 15–20 per cent of annual tax receipts.[17]

Clearly, to satisfy the criteria on general government deficits and national debt was a tall order for a country with an unemployment rate in 1995 of 11.6 per cent (as against 8.2 per cent in Germany, and 8.8 per cent in the UK, see Table 6.3). A key indicator of economic health, with major consequences for tax revenue and benefit levels, unemployment was an obvious omission from the Maastricht criteria. This was in tacit recognition of the fact that attempts to reduce government deficits and stocks of national debt, while driving down inflation, were bound at the same time to exacerbate unemployment. At 10.9 per cent in 1995, unemployment in Europe was significantly higher than in the US and Japan, which stood at 5.6 per cent and 3.1 per cent respectively (see Table 6.3). At approximately one percentage point above the EU-15 average, France's chronic unemployment was clearly structural, not cyclical, having been in double figures since 1992 (see Tables 6.3 and 7.3). While France's primary concern was increasingly the need to stimulate growth and hence employment, Germany's main preoccupation was stability. Germany was resistant to the notion that unemployment was a European issue, until it too began to experience its effects, particularly in the former Eastern Länder. Against a background of growing weariness of budgetary austerity in France, Jospin won a major victory at Amsterdam in 1997 when he succeeded in having the words 'and growth' inserted into the Stability Pact, behind which Germany was the driving force – thereby balancing stability with growth and employment.[18]

In May 1998, the European Council formally admitted France, along with ten other EU member states, to the EMU project that commenced in 1999. Budget deficits and debt levels had been eroded to a greater or lesser extent

Table 7.3   Unemployment in France, 1995–2000

Year	1995	1996	1997	1998	1999	2000
Unemployed ('000)*	2,985	3,063	3,102	2,977	2,772	2,338
Rate**	11.6	12.3	12.5	11.8	11.2	9.7
Vacancies ('000)	168	188	209	226	247	263

* Registered unemployed.
** International Labour Organisation definition.

Sources: EIU, 2000, 2001; OECD, *Main Economic Indicators*.

across the EU; although the final decision owed as much, if not more, to political considerations as it did to economic criteria. Despite this successful outcome, the experience of prudent fiscal management that characterised the 1990s threw into sharp relief just how narrow are the straits defining the limits of national government action in the global economy. In particular, the French had become used to, and had even come to tolerate an unemployment rate which, despite its recent reduction, remains high by European and international standards. The EU's Stability and Growth Pact is likely to ensure that unemployment levels in France remain relatively high. It commits France to keep average annual increases in central government spending to just over 0.3 per cent for the period 2001–3, an agreement France may struggle to honour.

That said, the impact of the launch of the euro on France's unemployment rate has been a positive one generally, helped by the relative weakness of the euro *vis-à-vis* the dollar and yen, boosting manufacturing exports. By October 2001, France's unemployment rate had fallen to 8.7 per cent. While this was still above the EU average, significantly it was lower than the German rate, and more than three percentage points beneath its peak in 1997.[19] Nor have the two Aubry laws on working time had a noticeable adverse effect on unemployment, as predicted by Medef (Mouvement des Entreprises de France), who protested that the legislation would act as a disincentive to hiring. In fact, there is some evidence to suggest that the introduction of the 35-hour week may have moderated wage demands.[20] Announced in October 1997, the 35-hour working week came into effect in February 2000 for companies employing 20 workers or more. French employees typically work fewer hours than their counterparts in other industrialised economies. A 56-capital survey by the Swiss bank UBS carried out in summer 2000 placed Paris in fifty-sixth position in terms of the number of hours worked annually. An employee in Paris is estimated to work on average 1,587 hours per annum as against 1,688 hours in Frankfurt, 1,833 hours in London, 1,864 hours in Tokyo and 1,882 hours in New York.[21] Interestingly, Maddison estimated the average annual number of hours worked per employee in France in 1987 at 1,543 hours, even less than the figure reported by UBS thirteen years later. Maddison's data included workers throughout France, however, whereas UBS considered ônly Parisian workers, who might be expected to work longer hours than in the provinces. Notably, however, the improving economic environment of the late 1990s was accompanied by a rise, not a reduction, in the number of unfilled vacancies – an indication that serious skills shortages persist in France (see Table 7.3),[22] and that labour market constraints may continue to impede economic expansion.[23]

The decision to embrace the euro casts France in a less conservative light than is often assumed to be the case. Joining the Eurozone entailed the acceptance of the principle of the subordination of the Banque de France to the ECB, head of the European System of Central Banks (ESCB) – however problematic this might be in practice. France now held only two votes out of 17 on the ECB's Governing Council (18 when Greece joined in 2001). Germany likewise held two votes, in contrast to the situation that had prevailed prior to the launch of the euro, in which the Bundesbank had largely determined French national monetary policy.[24] In the 1990s Germany had imposed punitive interest rates on its EU partners. But in a large Eurozone of 12 members, with a combined population of 300 million, German influence would be considerably diluted. Viewed in this light, EMU appeared as a means of regaining economic sovereignty rather than forgoing it, at least in theory.[25] In practice, though, the Germans were successful in securing Frankfurt as the ECB's location. They also managed to change the name of the single currency from 'écu' to 'euro'. However, the 1998 controversy over who would head the ECB – Wim Duisenberg or Jean-Claude Trichet, former governor of the Banque de France – revealed that the *reflex* of national sovereignty had not deserted France even if it lacked the means to achieve its goals.[26] In the event a non-binding compromise was brokered by the British presidency of the EU, whereby Trichet would take over from Duisenberg four years into the latter's mandate. Comments made subsequently by the incumbent, however, suggested that French pretensions to the ECB chair in 2002 might be premature although in the event the agreement was honoured. Taking up his post in summer 1998, Duisenberg gave a speech in German, in response to which former German Finance Minister Theo Waigel was reported in *Le Monde* as saying: 'The euro speaks German.'[27]

The decision to embrace the euro entailed the abandonment of the franc, symbol *par excellence* of national sovereignty, which ceased to be legal tender in February 2002. The conversion rate of the euro to the French franc had been fixed permanently at FF6.55957 at midnight on 31 December 1998.[28] Despite growing doubt and distrust among the French on the subject of European integration, first highlighted in 1992 by the Maastricht referendum, levels of support for the principle of the euro among the French population, as expressed in national opinion polls, nevertheless remain high, being consistently above 60 per cent.[29]

France and globalisation

In few countries has the phenomenon of globalisation been as widely debated[30] – or as deprecated – as in France.[31] There, globalisation has become synonymous with danger, first and foremost in the form of relocation (*délocalisations*), where multinational companies move production sites to low-wage countries in pursuit of lower costs, and greater flexibility in hiring and firing. This problem was highlighted in France in 1993 when Senator Jean Arthuis warned of the inevitability of firms chasing hourly labour rates of one franc in China as against fifty francs at home.[32] When

Hoover moved production sites from Lyon to the Scottish city of Dundee in 1994 – one of the first cases of Arthuis's prophecy apparently coming true – a predictable public outcry followed. But cheaper labour is not the only reason for relocating abroad. Burdensome legislation in employment or environmental law contributes to 'evasion investment' on the part of large firms, as they seek a less restrictive, less regulated environment in which to do business.[33]

Globalisation has come to signify for many in France – ignoring the more positive messages put forward by Elie Cohen or Michel Rocard – something of an ultraliberal ideology.[34] As such it encourages downsizing, increased capital flows, and a communication revolution. It simplifies and standardises regulations, and breaks down barriers to international trade through the World Trade Organisation (WTO), often perceived in France as an instrument of American imperialism. A survey conducted in June 1997 found that 73 per cent of French people feared the potential impact of globalisation on jobs, pensions, social security and the health service.[35]

For many, globalisation is a threat to national identity, a view championed by sheep farmer José Bové, whose attack on a McDonalds under construction in 1999 earned him international fame, and a prison sentence.[36] The potential threat to national identity was also highlighted by the perceived swallowing up of national assets in the spate of mega-mergers that marked the end of the twentieth century. A number of these mergers and acquisitions (M&As) were strategic deals in oligopolistic markets often characterised by high entry barriers, such as Renault's purchase of a 36.7 per cent stake in Nissan. Several were hostile takeovers launched by French firms on fellow rivals, as exemplified by TotalFina-Elf, or Banque Nationale de Paris (BNP)-Paribas. A number, too, were Franco-German mergers, illustrating the growing industrial and technological cooperation which marks the Franco-German alliance. Notable examples include the merger of Aérospatiale-Matra and Dasa in 1999, leading to the creation of EADS (European Areonautics, Defence and Space Company) in defence and aerospace, and that of Rhône-Poulenc and Hoechst in the pharmaceutical sector, also in 1999, which gave rise to Aventis.[37] Even so, the strength of the German economy often generates irrational fears among the French: in particular that France might become a mere satellite economy to its German neighbours.[38] In 2001, an elite Franco-German working party on global competitiveness sought to bring about potential collective solutions to common challenges, dominated as these often are by national mindsets.[39]

Globalisation implies too the erosion of sovereignty. According to Ulrich Beck, it suggests the transcendence of the nation-state, an '*escape* from the categories of the national state'.[40] Beck argues that while the nation-state delineated the contours of society, the world society created in globalisation's wake undermines the nation-state because 'a multiplicity of social circles, communication networks, market relations and lifestyles, none of them specific to any particular loyalty, now cut across the boundaries of the national state'.[41] Nevertheless, the demise of the nation-state – being too small for the big problems, yet too big for the small problems[42] – may open up new possibilities for networking across national boundaries and conventional loyalties.

Despite the political rhetoric of danger, and threatened sovereignty, however, large French firms have embraced globalisation with a vengeance, displaying a startling internationalisation that has taken others by surprise.[43] Many have shown themselves to be champions of the trend, empire-builders in their respective markets. The closing years of the twentieth century witnessed huge increases in net foreign direct investment (FDI) abroad on the part of large French companies. Total FDI outflows for the year 2000 amounted to FF1.15 trillion, up from FF358.1 billion in 1997, a massive surge of 320 per cent in just three years. With inward investment of FF312.9 billion in 2000, an increase of 30 per cent over 1999 (FF240.9 billion), FDI outflows dwarfed FDI inflows by a factor of four.[44] FDI is a principle vehicle of globalisation, leading as it does to the development of global networks of production and distribution as well as the interpenetration of national value chains, acting as a catalyst for organisational change in the countries involved.[45] Those French firms that are actively pursuing international growth thus become potential agents for change and economic convergence, both in host countries and in France.

The internationalisation of French business

The rapid internationalisation of French business in recent years cannot be explained simply in terms of the orthodox reasoning of mainstream business strategy theories. There is no doubt that members of the French business elite have grown increasingly sophisticated as strategic leaders, embracing in particular the principles of positioning, capability building and value chain configuration across national boundaries. But what is equally true is that business leaders have remained alive to the fact that markets are never completely free; rather, they are socially constructed institutions bound and conditioned by rules and regulations. In particular, French enterprises have colluded with the state whenever possible to manipulate the rules of the game in their favour, with the broad intention of creating opportunities to expand abroad while seeking to exclude foreign competitors from domestic markets. Correspondingly, French firms have been swift to exploit the opportunities created by deregulation elsewhere while resisting liberalisation at home. This tendency reflects the continued impulse of the state towards intervention in pursuit of French national interests, facilitated by the cohesiveness of the ruling elite.

The operation in France of what might be referred to as the *protection–expansion formula* is revealed at the macro level in Tables 7.4 and 7.5.

Table 7.4 FDI inflows and outflows, 1995–2000 ($ millions)

Year	1995	1996	1997	1998	1999	2000
French inflows	23,681	21,996	23,178	31,000	47,000	44,200
French outflows	15,760	30,419	35,591	48,600	120,600	72,500
French inflows as % of outflows	150.3	72.2	65.1	63.7	39.1	25.6
German inflows	12,025	6,572	11,097	24,300	55,900	176,100
German outflows	39,049	50,804	40,733	88,600	109,800	48,600
German inflows as % of outflows	30.8	13.3	27.2	27.4	50.9	362.3
UK inflows	19,969	24,435	33,227	70,600	82,900	130,400
UK outflows	43,562	34,047	61,586	121,800	205,800	249,800
UK inflows as % of outflows	45.8	71.8	54.0	58.0	40.3	52.2
EU inflows	114,387	108,604	128,574	261,100	467,200	617,300
EU outflows	158,990	182,266	233,662	454,300	720,100	772,900
EU inflows as % of outflows	71.9	59.6	55.0	57.5	64.9	79.9

Source: United Nations, *World Investment Report 2000*, UN, New York and Geneva, 2000; United Nations, *World Investment Report 2001*, UN, New York and Geneva, 2001.

Table 7.5 Cross-border M&A sales and purchases, 1995–2000 ($ millions)

Year	1995	1996	1997	1998	1999	2000
French sales	7,533	13,575	17,751	16,885	23,834	35,081
French purchases	8,939	14,755	21,153	30,926	88,656	168,710
French sales as % of purchases	84.3	92.0	83.9	54.6	26.9	20.8
German sales	7,496	11,924	11,856	19,047	39,555	246,990
German purchases	18,509	17,984	13,190	66,728	85,530	58,671
German sales as % of purchases	88.1	66.3	89.9	28.5	46.2	421.0
UK sales	36,392	31,271	39,706	91,081	132,534	180,029
UK purchases	29,641	36,109	58,371	95,099	214,109	382,422
UK sales as % of purchases	122.8	86.6	68.0	95.8	61.9	47.1
EU sales	75,143	81,895	114,591	187,853	357,311	586,521
EU purchases	81,417	96,674	142,108	284,373	517,155	801,746
EU sales as % of purchases	92.3	84.7	80.6	66.1	69.1	73.2

Source: UN, *World Investment Report 2000*; UN, *World Investment Report 2001*.

Table 7.4 charts the flows of foreign direct investment (FDI) into and out of the EU and three of its major economies in recent years. These flows, in an absolute sense, are formidable and sharply rising, reflecting the forward march of international economic integration. Europe, as a highly developed economic region, is a net exporter of FDI, and the UK, as Europe's most open economy, is both the biggest source and recipient of FDI. The large gap between German FDI inflows and outflows is a product of the relative insularity yet immense financial strength of the country's business system. France, on the other hand, has been more welcoming to FDI inflows, but in 1999 and 2000, when outflows forged ahead, a gulf emerged between FDI inflows and outflows, confirming the dualistic character of the national business system.

The same pattern is revealed in Table 7.5, which charts the course of cross-national mergers and acquisitions (M&A) between 1995 and 2000. The relative success of German firms in resisting takeovers by foreigners before 2000 is confirmed, and so too the success of French firms in making large-scale acquisitions abroad while fending off takeovers at home. In 1999, for example, French firms made 16 cross-border acquisitions valued at more than $1 billion (total value of $77.4 billion), while just four French firms worth more than $1 billion (total value of $11.5 billion) were acquired by foreigners. Major acquisitions included TRACTEBEL (Belgium) in electricity, gas and water distribution for $8.2 billion by Suez Lyonnaise des Eaux; United States Filter (US) in machinery for $6.3 billion by Vivendi; Nissan (Japan) in motor vehicles for $5.4 billion by Renault; and Petrofina (Belgium) in oil, gas and petroleum refining for $5.3 billion by Total.[46] The positive, proactive approach to Europeanisation and globalisation displayed by large French firms and supported by the state is evinced in the sectoral case-studies that follow.

French utilities and the *modus operandi* of state-supported strategy

The energy sector provides a good illustration of the kind of state support from which French utilities typically benefit, their pan-European and even global strategies being supported at home by closed and quasi-monopolistic markets, often in direct contravention of EU directives.

French electricity production expanded significantly from 1980, such that production in 1998 was almost twice its 1980 level. At the same time, electricity production benefited from huge cost reductions derived from cheap nuclear energy, confirming the financial wisdom of France's heavy investment in nuclear power in the 1970s and 1980s (if not its environmental wisdom). In the 1980s, France overtook Japan and the former USSR to become the world's second largest producer of electricity generated from nuclear energy, behind only the US.[47] In 1998 almost half (46 per cent) of nuclear-generated electricity in the EU was produced by France's network of 58 nuclear plants, while in the same year Electricité de France (EdF) produced some 76 per cent of its energy from nuclear power stations.[48]

Self-sufficiency in energy is a prodigious achievement for a country with little gas and almost no oil. The pursuit and ultimate achievement of self-sufficiency was the French reaction to the oil crisis which twenty-five years previously sent the country reeling into a decade-long recession. The contrast with the UK, which has benefited since 1975 from North Sea oil, now beginning to run out, but with little to show for it, is stark. With self-sufficiency in energy acquired, EdF and its fellow state monopoly, Gaz de France (GdF), set about capturing international markets through export and acquisition. In doing so, they have benefited from state ownership coupled with closed, *de facto* monopolistic markets at home. This protected position has allowed them to take full advantage of market liberalisation elsewhere in the EU with relative impunity, to the bitter resentment of energy producers in neighbouring EU member states, such as Germany, Spain and the UK.[49]

GdF's expansion strategy seeks to double the company's size in the short space of two or three years. Currently number three in Europe, the company's recent European acquisitions include EMB, a German local distribution company, Degas and Egas, two Hungarian distribution firms, as well as the British shipping company Volunteer Energy, designed to provide access to the British market.[50] For a company that does not produce natural gas, which merely transports and distributes it, and which has a modest turnover (FF60 billion), this is remarkable. Purely a national player five years ago, GdF now distributes gas in Austria, Germany, Hungary, Portugal, Mexico, India and even Britain, which has its own supply of natural gas. The company's two million customers outside France represented 10 per cent of its annual turnover in 2000; the company's objective is for this to rise to 80 per cent.[51]

Meanwhile EdF is now the second largest electricity producer in the world, possessing the greatest export capacity of any EU electricity generator. Embarking on a strategy of international expansion from 1996, acquiring assets (power stations and physical interconnectors) in the EU as well as customers (supply businesses), its primary European export markets include Germany, Italy, Spain, Belgium, Switzerland, Andorra and Britain.[52] Further afield it supplies a growing customer base in Asia, Africa and South America. Altogether it supplied some 15 million customers outside France in 1998.

Five years after the 1996 EU electricity directive on market liberalisation, however, France's electricity market remains the least open in the EU. *Dirigisme* is alive and kicking in France's energy sector, responsibility for policy resting with the Directorate of Energy and Raw Materials, attached to the Ministry of Industry.[53] While other EU member states have broken up their electricity industries, EdF remains integrated and monolithic, handling almost all generation, transmission, distribution and supply, controlling 95.4 per cent of the French retail market in 1998.[54] For all its international expansion, it remains a public-sector monopoly.[55] As such it continues to benefit from the tutelage of the state, including financial support and credit guarantees. The cost of capital advantage derived by EdF from state ownership should not be underestimated. EdF is able to raise money for acquisitions at a rate of interest lower than government bond rates (c. 4 per cent), while its private-sector European competitors, such as British Energy, can do no better than central bank base rates (c. 8 per cent). In short, EdF is using government finance terms to acquire assets abroad, engaging in this way in a strategy of international expansion that is state-funded. EdF's assets include, in the UK, London Electricity and Sweb, as well as generation assets such as Sutton Bridge power station. It has purchased the rights to control the flows of electricity throughout continental Europe, successfully buying up the interconnectors that link France to the UK, France to Spain, and so on.[56] It has also acquired the interconnectors that join continental Europe to external electricity systems such as Eastern Europe and the Nordic countries.

In short, EdF is operating in commercial spheres, but not on commercial terms. It has no shareholders to satisfy, nor any stock price sensitivity. Its expansion abroad is supported by protection at home, coupled with unrivalled access to low-cost capital. It is a formidable combination and a unique source of competitive advantage. As the company becomes increasingly internationalised, however, questions of its ownership may loom large. But with parliamentary and presidential elections scheduled for 2002, the privatisation of EdF or GdF is not even in the offing. State subsidy is permissible under EU rules where it meets a social objective, or alternatively to enable a state-owned company to restructure or privatise as preparation for entering the market economy, neither of which applies in this case. Justification for non-competitive behaviour comes instead from a variety of sources and amounts to little more than a smokescreen. In this case, union entitlement to a percentage of EdF/GdF income (for pension funds) is the reason commonly cited for the alleged difficulties concerning privatisation, restructuring or market access in France.[57]

At the Stockholm summit of March 2001, Jospin, in electioneering mode, presented his government as a staunch defender of public services, vowing that the national market for utilities would remain closed.[58] With a coalition government that includes Communist Party members firmly wedded to the principle of public monopolies as the basis for energy production and distribution, Jospin had little reason to support the Commission's proposals for full market liberalisation by 2005.[59] In this his government is backed by powerful public-sector unions, keen to avoid competition in energy and rail services.[60] For the French in general, public service is endowed with special meaning. This cultural specificity is used opportunistically by the French government as a convenient shield to market opening. Once again, the Commission's proposals for market liberalisation were effectively torpedoed by French objections, combined with German reluctance to provoke another Franco-German conflict – a potent combination for inertia.[61] There is no doubt that the French have used their considerable influence in Brussels effectively to counter obvious complaints from fellow member states that have opened their markets already. Regular bilateral Franco-German summits and ministerial meetings, dubbed 'Sauerkraut diplomacy', enable France and Germany to reach prior agreement on contentious issues in advance of EU summits. Despite presenting itself as one of the more pro-European member states, France is now bottom of the table, behind Greece, in terms of implementing EU single-market legislation.[62] Ignoring the obvious contradictions of the pan-European aspirations of its public utilities with its desire for market protection, the French government treads an increasingly lonely – but highly profitable – path in Europe. French attachment to protectionism within these sectors stands in flagrant contradiction to its economic aspirations for European construction. As Alain Vernholes observes, 'It is incoherent to rejoice that a firm such as EdF should control a large part of electricity distribution in London while refusing – or deferring – reciprocity on national territory on the pretext of protecting the general interest which depends on a public monopoly.'[63]

That said, the French energy market has gone some way along the path to greater openness. In December 1998 the Jospin government approved the draft bill transposing the EU electricity directive into French law. In February 1999 it was passed to the National Assembly for consideration, and in February 2000 the directive finally appeared on French statute books,[64] one year behind the EU's official deadline.[65] It seems, however, that the new law may infringe the EU directive on electricity liberalisation, containing as it does two amendments designed to protect the home market. First, it stipulates that any company importing electricity into France must have a proportion of its electricity generation in France. Second, it insists that any company operating in France must adhere to French public-sector salary and benefit rules.[66]

Many critics regard further liberalisation of the French electricity market as inevitable.[67] EdF's current chairman, François Roussely, for instance, preaches the virtues of an open electricity market across Europe.[68] Talk, however, is cheap, especially when government views on the subject are well known. That the EU electricity directive was implemented minimally and with substantial delay has given French utility companies a significant in-built advantage over their European counterparts, enhancing the company's existing dual legacy of nuclear power stations and domestic dominance.

Likewise, the minimal interpretation and belated implementation of the EU gas directive, which sought to liberalise the European gas market and ensure competition between and across member states, has enabled France to remain one of the most closed markets of the EU. The directive came into force in August 1998, with the requirement that it should be on member states' statute books by August 2000. Through initial stalling, followed by minimal opening,[69] GdF is likely to continue to dominate the French gas market, with no more than 22 per cent of those customers who are eligible expected to change suppliers by 2005.[70] In contrast, competition in the British market was introduced in 1996, with mainland Britain effectively fully open to supply competition from 1998.[71] Similarly, foreign inroads into France's electricity market may well inflict little damage on EdF's monopolistic fortress, in that nuclear-generated electricity is so cost-effective that foreign rivals are unlikely to be able to compete.[72] In 2001 only a tiny fraction of France's electricity market (1.3 per cent) was in foreign hands.[73] Large domestic conglomerates such as Suez-Lyonnaise des Eaux and Vivendi may well present more formidable competition, while new entrants, such as GdF, may be enticed into the market.[74] That said, EdF is set to retain ownership of the national transmission grid, to be managed by an autonomous operator. Its distribution monopoly is likely to remain relatively unbreached.

In summary, the French are seriously (and successfully) playing the market opening game long. Unless and until EdF and GdF are restructured and the ownership of transmission, generation and supply separated, they will always effectively be able to shield themselves behind barriers to entry into their home market.[75] Meanwhile EdF's international strategy remains fundamentally unaltered: to expand internationally in new and developing markets, where demand for electricity is rising sharply at more than three times the European rate, while strengthening its leadership position in Europe.[76] EdF clearly perceives itself as destined now to play a major role not only on the European stage (where it expects to control 20 per cent of the market by 2010), but also on a global stage.[77]

This protection–expansion formula is repeated in other industries, particularly those that continue to benefit in some measure from the tutelage of the state, such as transport and telecommunications. France's state-of-the art transport infrastructure – including relatively decongested motorways, a growing high-speed train network, and an efficient suburban rail system complemented by a modern urban metro in Paris – has served France well, boosting tourism in particular, such that Paris is now the most visited capital city in the world. France's efficient transport infrastructure was a key consideration in the choice of Paris as the location for Disney's first park in Europe. Established in 1992, Disneyland Paris is now the most visited tourist attraction in France, with 12 million visitors annually. The contrast with public transport in Britain could not be more glaring, with a growing British international reputation for faulty railway tracks and gridlocked motorways. The end-of-century achievements of French railways have been exceptional, with the extension of the TGV (*train à grande vitesse*) network northwards to Lille, Brussels and London, and southwards to the Mediterranean. Opened in May 2001, the TGV Méditerrané brings the south coast within three hours of Paris. Taking more than a decade to plan and six years to build, it illustrates what the French state is capable of achieving through its centralised structure, a belief in progress and a willingness to back this with taxpayers' money. Since 1981, the TGV has rejuvenated regions and transformed travel customs.[78] The Thalys service, which uses TGV technology, now operates to Amsterdam and Cologne, and will soon include Dortmund and Düsseldorf among its international destinations. Restructured in 1997, the SNCF (Société nationale des chemins de fer) transferred the management of its track to the newly created Réseau ferré de France (RFF). Significantly, Transport Minister Jean-Claude Gayssot rejected EU attempts to dent the monopoly which SNCF enjoys by refusing to consider EU proposals to open up the French railway network to foreign freight operators. He did so despite the fact that two French operators, SNCF and Vivendi-Connex, had exploited already the opening up of Deutsche Bahn's lines by launching ultra-modern trains in Germany, while Vivendi-Connex operates a franchise in southern England. In a stark case of 'what's mine is mine, what's yours is negotiable', this exemplifies the furthering of French interests in Europe while deferring reciprocity.[79]

The telecommunications industry is viewed as critical to national competitive advantage in the new global economy.[80] Following a number of foreign acquisitions in 1999 and 2000, France Télécom became the leading telecom operator in Europe and the second largest in the world.[81] Thanks to its purchase of Orange, the UK's second largest mobile phone operator, the company is now also the second largest mobile phone operator in Europe. In 2000 France Télécom had 28 million subscribers worldwide. With more than 26 international subsidiaries it employed a total of 24,000 workers.[82] France Télécom has benefited from the rise in Internet use in France, which rose dramatically in 2000, with France displaying one of the fastest rates of increase in the EU. Prior to the acquisition of Orange, sales for the first six months of 2000 were buoyant, with earnings up 19.8 per cent.[83] But the flotation of Orange in spring 2001 flopped, achieving a share price much lower than anticipated. Should the acquisition fail in the long run, potential losses could amount to double those incurred by Crédit Lyonnais.[84]

That the state continues to hold a sizeable majority stake in France Télécom (62 per cent) following its partial privatisation in 1997, gives its foreign rivals pause for thought. Company strategy is still heavily influenced by government policy, currently the so-called strategy 'of the public service':[85] to serve all customers throughout the national territory as soon as possible.[86] However, the company has saddled itself with debt of E61 billion ($53 billion), much of it short-term at high interest rates, as the price of international empire building.[87] This debt is set to increase in 2001 with the purchase of an operating licence for third-generation (3G) mobile phones using UMTS (Universal Mobile Telecommunications Standard) technology, four of which are for sale in France at a cost of FF32.5 billion each.[88] The French government has already earmarked licence receipts for the Fond de réserve des retraités, to bolster the national pay-as-you-go pension system – in the same way as the British government enthusiastically auctioned 3G licences to supplement revenues. Bidding companies have been burdened consequently with massive debt resulting in higher prices for consumers. The levels of debt assumed by telecommunication firms in pursuit of acquisitions and 3G licences led to a dramatic fall in telecommunication stocks in December 2000. By May 2001 shares in France Télécom had fallen to E63.70, amounting to a loss of 70 per cent since March 2000, when the company share price peaked.[89] As a public-sector firm, however, there is always the chance that France Télécom may be subject to different rules. In particular, there is the suspicion that debt may be written by the state, a tactic outlawed by the European Commission, but still employed in France. (This was amply demonstrated by the rehabilitation and partial privatisation of Crédit Lyonnais in July 1999 at an estimated cost of FF190 billion or $29.7 billion to the French taxpayer following its bankruptcy in the mid-1990s).[90] The objective is to halve the company's debt by 2003.[91]

International expansion in manufacturing

The economic rationale for a European single currency – regardless of any political motivation on the part of France or Germany – focused on two key benefits: more trade and lower costs for business. In the event, the first was amply delivered, though perhaps less due to any integral advantage deriving from membership of the euro than to its weakness *vis-à-vis* the US dollar and the Japanese yen. French export competitiveness in manufacturing has benefited singularly since 1999 from the weak euro relative to the dollar, supported until 2001 by a strong US economy. The appreciation of the dollar relative to the euro was arguably beyond any conceivable productivity gains the US economy may have made relative to the Eurozone.[92] However, the weak euro increased some business costs by accentuating the effect of rising international commodity prices, in particular oil.

Following its untroubled launch as a virtual currency in 1999 at a rate of $1.17, the euro depreciated sharply in value, falling beneath the psychological barrier of $1 one year later and reaching a low of $0.84 in October 2000.[93] French manufacturing exports outside the Eurozone were correspondingly cheaper than prior to the advent of the euro – as much as 28 per cent cheaper in autumn 2000. By June 2001, exports were still approximately 26 per cent cheaper than in January 1999, the euro having fallen to a six-month low against the dollar, now worth $0.86, as the markets reflected growing pessimism concerning growth prospects for Europe. The surge in French exports in 2000 was particularly marked outside the Eurozone, especially in non-OECD countries, but demand rose across the majority of France's export markets. Export earnings for the year totalled FF2,123.5 billion, as against FF1,857.3 billion in 1999, an increase of 12.5 per cent in twelve months.[94] The impact of the undervalued euro on British exports to Europe, on the other hand, has been severe, all the more so given the closeness of the economic ties linking Britain with Euroland, whatever the popular rhetoric of being semi-detached from the continent.

However, with European growth expected to outstrip growth in the US, some recovery in the value of the euro in 2002–3 is likely.[95]

Growth industries in France are increasingly those with a high R&D input, in railway engineering and telecommunications, aerospace, construction, pharmaceuticals, cars and food processing. Large increases in exports were registered in 2000 for investment goods, which includes Airbus airplanes and cars. Airbus Industries is a four-country consortium, but its large passenger aircraft are manufactured in Toulouse. Sales of Airbus large passenger aircraft were buoyant in 2000, with orders beginning to flow in for its giant, double-decker A3XX plane or 'Superjumbo', which fortuitously Boeing decided not to build. In fact, the extra earnings from export sales of Airbus passenger planes in 2000 were sufficient in themselves to compensate for the increase in the international price of oil.

Military equipment too is a traditional French export strength, with a cluster of leading companies in this sector: Dassault, GIAT, Thales (formerly Thomson-CSF) and EADS. Following the end of the Cold War defence equipment sales fell in the 1990s as a proportion of total French product exports: from 3 per cent in 1990 to 1.6 per cent in 1997–98.[96] With international arms markets flooded with cheap discarded weapons from Eastern and Central Europe, France has sought to find new export markets, not all of these entirely legitimate. In spring 2001 Britain and the US challenged French contracts to Iraq worth almost £1 billion, under the so-called 'oil for food' programme. British shadow foreign secretary, Francis Maude, accused the French of actively flouting UN and security council controls 'in a massive export programme designed to enhance their economic power'.[97] The changing security climate following the terrorist attacks on the World Trade Centre in September 2001 may signal more lucrative times ahead for French defence sales.

Likewise, in the automobile sector, Peugeot-Citroën and Renault have gone on the attack, investing heavily in technology. Together they represented 22 per cent of cars sold in Western Europe in 1998.[98] Car exports were buoyant in 2000, against the global trend, boosted by the weak euro. Domestic car sales were likewise strong in 2000–2001, boosted by the need to spend undeclared cash holdings in advance of the introduction of the euro in 2002.[99] In an industry burdened by over-capacity,[100] where price competition is intense, teaming up with other players through mergers and acquisitions and strategic alliances makes increasing sense. Would-be predators, though, may view mergers as an answer to their own decline, as exemplified by Renault's purchase of a 36.7 per cent stake in Nissan following the erosion of its market share from 8.03 per cent in 1998 to 7.65 per cent in 1999.[101] The merger with Nissan was a gamble, designed (if it paid off) to take Renault to a new plane as a global company. But though the motivation for the merger may have been defensive, company behaviour since the merger has been intensely competitive, with both Renault and

Nissan engaging in cost-cutting and cost-sharing exercises,[102] and expanding vigorously into new markets and businesses. Dubbed 'le cost killer',[103] Nissan's chairman Carlos Ghosn has ended the privileged, quasi-paternalist relations Nissan enjoyed with its suppliers, forcing the latter to cut their prices by up to 30 per cent or forgo their supplier status.[104] By 2001, Nissan was once again back in the black, while Renault was expanding into the luxury car business.[105]

Ignoring the current merger fashion, Renault's rival Peugeot has concentrated instead on technology joint ventures and partial alliances.[106] These include joint ventures with Renault (on large engines), Fiat and Ford. Performing well in recent years, perhaps against the odds, Peugeot has increased its market share in Europe to 12 per cent, in second place behind Volkswagen (VW), by focusing on product innovation, especially in low-cost diesel models. From an operating margin of 4.4 per cent, its net profit margin of 1.9 per cent in 1999, though narrow, was higher than any other European car manufacturer. Likewise, its return of capital employed rose from 2.6 per cent in 1997 to 14.2 per cent in 1999.[107]

The dual challenge for Renault and Peugeot in the twenty-first century is to expand their market share outside Europe while seeking to grow in size.[108] Both have gone on the offensive in Latin America, opening greenfield-site factories in Brazil and Argentina, an experiment viewed as a test case for further expansion into Asia and Eastern Europe. Designed to give them a foothold in the new 'common market' of Mercosur (Brazil, Argentina, Uruguay and Paraguay), this offensive will bring them into direct competition with global manufacturers Fiat, Ford, General Motors (GM) and VW, all of which are active in the region. It will also force them to keep costs down by creating efficient global supply chains, the starting prices for new cars in developing markets being situated at ever-lower levels.[109]

Financial services

In a similar vein, consolidation and expansion have characterised French financial services in recent years. In banking, mergers and acquisitions have been boosted by the euro, the liberalisation of financial services in Europe, and the IT revolution which is emblematic of the new economy. The French banking sector performed poorly in the 1990s, burdened by low efficiency and over-capacity, lagging far behind its European counterparts.[110] Despite the privatisation of the major retail banks from 1987 to 1999, the legacy of state ownership is a heavy one, resulting in an excess of branches, over-manning and impediments to restructuring due to employment protection. The mutual bank sector has detracted further from industry performance.[111] Mutual banks are able to acquire French commercial banks while enjoying protection from takeovers themselves. In 1997 Crédit Mutuel purchased a 67 per cent stake in Crédit Industriel et Commercial (CIC), a state-owned regional banking network, at a cost of FF20 billion.

This offer was lower than that made by ABN Amro, but contained significant job guarantees. The focus of mutual banks has been on market share rather than shareholder value. Offering services at reduced prices while paying high-yielding interest rates on savings, understandably they have provoked claims of unfair competition from commercial banks, which in these circumstances cannot reasonably compete.[112]

A sea-change in French banking was nevertheless signalled in 1999 by the hostile takeover of Paribas by BNP, through which BNP-Paribas became France's largest bank, scuppering the would-be friendly merger of Paribas with BNP's rival Société Générale in the process. What is noteworthy here is that this hostile takeover – which BNP attributed to the introduction of the euro and the consequent need to reposition as a European bank – was not a European affair but a purely French one. Banks that had previously co-existed in cosy complacency (even to the extent of colluding to agree financial results)[113] were now rivals engaged in a fierce competition for survival and supremacy.[114] The Franco-French nature of the consolidation was not coincidental. The French banking sector remains tightly guarded. Foreign banks are detracted from investing in France due to the well-known dislike of hostile takeovers on the part of successive French governments, as well as to the formidable power of existing state-owned banks.

France's leading insurance companies were likewise involved in aggressive empire building in Europe, facilitated by the privatisation in 1994 and 1996 respectively of Union des Assurances de Paris (UAP) and Assurances Générales de France (AGF). A pan-European insurance market had been slow to develop, despite EU directives on market liberalisation. This was partly because life insurance depends on national tax regimes, which have yet to be harmonised, and partly because non-life insurance calculations are determined by risk, which varies according to local circumstances. A sea-change nevertheless occurred in the late 1990s, such that all of Europe's leading five insurers (AXA, Allianz, Generali, CGU and Zurich Financial Services) grew through mergers and acquisitions. In 1997 UAP teamed up with AXA, the leading private French insurer, to form the world's largest insurer by assets under management and the second largest by turnover. Dwarfing all domestic competition (including AGF and the loss-making state-owned insurer Groupe des Assurances Nationales, GAN), the AXA-UAP merger created the largest accident and property insurance group in Europe. Its empire embraced Sun Life, Provincial and Guardian Royal Exchange, as well as Axa Colonia. The merger gave rise to a group with significant shareholdings in Paribas and BNP in particular (now BNP-Paribas), in a sector of the economy that is highly cash-generative.[115] As far as the privatised AGF is concerned, however, the boot was on the other foot, disappearing almost without trace in 1998 when swallowed up by the German insurance group Allianz, to French dismay. In November 1999, the former state-owned Caisse Nationale de Prévoyance (CNP) joined forces with

Prudential of the UK and Signul Iduna of Germany to sell co-branded products through local distribution channels.[116]

Over the past two decades, since the 1979 Loi Monory and the 1983 share savings plans helped to revitalise an otherwise moribund stock exchange, the development of the Paris bourse has been spectacular (see Chapter 5).[117] Waves of privatisations occurring under liberalising right-wing governments, as well as under the socialists, accompanied by groundbreaking legislation brought about a staged, but fundamental transformation of the Parisian and regional exchanges. In 1999 the Paris bourse overtook Frankfurt to become the second largest stock exchange after London. In 2000 it merged with the Dutch and Belgian stock exchanges to form Euronext. With a market capitalisation of E2,419.7 billion in December 2000, Euronext is currently second in Europe to the London Stock Exchange (LSE) (E2,744.7 billion in December 2000),[118] whose projected merger with Deutsche Börse to form iX (International Exchanges) foundered on the incompatibility of the electronic trading platforms of the two exchanges. Euronext, on the other hand, benefits from its rationalised structure, operating a unified trading platform, clearing system and settlement platform. At the time of writing, Euronext is engaged in discussions with seven other international exchanges outside Europe – New York, Tokyo, Australia, Hong Kong, Toronto, Mexico and Sao Paolo – regarding the possibility of forming a global equity market. The proposed global partnership would allow individual brands and lists of stocks to be retained, while enabling equities trading to 'follow the sun'.[119] The rationale driving consolidation is to achieve the financial strength and scale economies needed to play a leading role in the development of European and global trading markets, creating benefits for customers and value for shareholders. Driving this, in turn, is the desire to be the premier European and international exchange network and provider of exchange-related services. At the moment it appears to be Euronext, not the LSE, which is closest to achieving this objective.

Food retailing: market consolidation and pan-European expansion

The European food industry has been viewed traditionally as more fragmented and regionally oriented than most sectors – especially in France, characterised by rich regional variation in dairy produce, wine, fruit and vegetables. In the merger wave that marked the run-up to the single market, few of Europe's food companies had the inclination or confidence to take over foreign rivals from other parts of the continent. A pan-European market could exist in many things, but not perhaps in food, dominated by regional produce, custom and taste.

Recently, however, the food industry has shown marked signs of consolidation. This has occurred in three phases: national consolidation, leading to minor cross-border consolidation, and finally major alliances on the European stage. The merger of French food retailers Carrefour and Promodès in August 1999 to create the biggest supermarket retailer in Europe illustrates the first phase, while the second is typified by the takeover of retailers in developing world markets of southern Europe. Seven major mergers occurred in European food retailing in 1995, 17 in 1996, 18 in 1997 and more than 20 in 1998.[120] Food retailing naturally complements France's status as the world's second largest exporter of agricultural produce (after the US), which in turn owes much to the benefits French farmers derive from the Common Agricultural Policy (CAP).[121] As many as five out of the top ten European food retailers in 1998 were French (see Table 7.6), with a combined share of 18.5 per cent of the European market, including Central Europe. The merger of Carrefour and Promodès in 1999 took the new company to the top of the table, with a total market share of 7.6 per cent.

It is French retailers that have taken the lead in the process of consolidation, acquiring market share in southern Europe in particular, such that they now control much of the Spanish food market.[122] Carrefour-Promodès operates in more than 20 countries. Auchan has been active in Italy, where in 1998 it became the second largest player (following its purchase of Rinascente and Colmark), with Carrefour-Promodès occupying the number three position. Large French food retailers, like their European counterparts, have been on the hunt for minor acquisitions in Central Europe, their ability to acquire local firms enhanced by the cash-generative nature of their business in fast-moving consumer goods.[123]

The final stage of consolidation, that of major alliances, is exemplified by US retailer Wal-Mart's takeover of Asda in 1999, its founder ousting Bill Gates as the world's richest man two years later. It is expected that the coming years will witness further strategic alliances between top European

Table 7.6 Estimated market share of top 10 European retailers,* 1998 (as percentage)

Rank	Firm	Country	European market share
1	Metro	Denmark	5.0
2	Tesco	UK	4.4
3	*Intermarché*	*France*	4.1
4	*Promodès*	*France*	3.9
5	*Carrefour*	*France*	3.7
6	Rewe	Denmark	3.7
7	*Auchan*	*France*	3.6
8	Aldi	Denmark	3.3
9	*Leclerc*	*France*	3.2
10	J. Sainsbury	UK	3.1

* Includes Central Europe.

Source: Adapted from *Empire Building: the Future of European Food Retailing*, Reuters Business Insight Report, 1999.

food retailers, with French companies well placed to take advantage. Further consolidation makes sense because critical mass means more purchasing power for large-scale operators – increasingly necessary given the fiercely competitive market conditions that prevail – translating in turn, through economies of scale and scope, into lower prices for consumers.

Like Carrefour-Promodès, the dairy company Danone – one of a number of top French firms announcing large redundancies at home in 2001, blamed on globalisation – emerges as one of the most internationalised firms of the CAC-40, operating in more than 22 countries. Danone's long list of subsidiaries, from all parts of Europe (including Eastern Europe) and indeed the world, testifies to a prodigious strategy of international expansion. It is a strategy that acknowledges the role of regional preferences, and does not seek to homogenise these but rather to incorporate them under one umbrella.[124] Danone is world market leader in fresh dairy produce, competing with the likes of Nestlé, Fromagerie Bel and Suiza Foods. The group has three separate dairy businesses: Danone, Beldina and Galbani. However, the Danone range of branded products accounts for 71 per cent of global sales and 73 per cent of dairy profits. At the time of writing, the French domestic market has been displaying sluggish growth. As Danone's largest market, slow growth in France gives cause for concern, encouraging restructuring at home as well as entry into new markets further afield, perhaps in Asia. New product development is critical to the group, and considerable investment in R&D and in product innovation has helped Danone to remain dominant in the global dairy market.[125] With slow growth at home, product innovation is likely to remain central to the group's continued international expansion.[126]

The French national business system revisited

The above case-studies shed light on a national business system potentially undergoing far-reaching change. They demonstrate that despite the political rhetoric, much of which is anti-globalisation, leading French firms have been to the fore in dynamically engaging in strategies of international expansion and alliance-building. In this they clearly recognise the need to reap economies of scale and scope, which is the logic underpinning the growth of large-scale enterprises and mega-mergers. Their approach to Europeanisation and globalisation is proactive, a far cry from the chronic under-performance, defensive collaboration and so-called 'Malthusianism' of the past. To what extent, however, are these empire-builders breaking the mould of the French business model, strongly network-based, traditionally *dirigiste* and governed by long-term inter-personal and inter-corporate relationships between different corporate constituencies?

As the above examples illustrate, expansion abroad is regularly accompanied by protectionism at home. This is often achieved by denying or deferring key EU legislation that aims to ensure reciprocity, on the pretext that the general interest depends on public monopolies. The minimalist approach to market opening on the part of successive French governments is supported by a strong popular mandate, which has the backing of political parties and unions alike. This allows French firms to establish themselves in the marketplace while postponing competition at home, thus achieving a preemptive in-built and potentially lasting advantage over foreign rivals. This obvious double standard rests on a vision of Europe run by powerful nation-states, in which the accumulation of negotiating power is a legitimate course of action, actively employed. As a founding member state, France's influence in the EU over the years has been greater than that of any other member state. Though enlargement may reduce its influence, it is nevertheless the case that old members wield more influence than new arrivals.[127] This double standard also rests, as Raymond observes, on a long-standing protectionist reflex of national sovereignty, of 'economic patriotism', suggesting that some aspects of what is apparently new in French business are in fact recast elements of continuity.

The large-scale privatisation of state-owned companies from 1986 onwards served as stimulus to far-reaching cultural change in France. The transfer of public assets to private hands was one of the most spectacular developments of the late twentieth century, not only in Europe but also elsewhere in the world.[128] Described by Crozier as a country of bureaucrats, France now has more shareholders than civil servants. There is no doubt that privatisation bolstered existing establishment solidarity through the introduction of the *noyaux durs*, hard cores of stable investors designed to shore up company defences against foreign predators. In this way it concentrated power in the hands of a relatively small domestic business elite.[129] A large number of directorships were held by a small group of people: a mere 75 individuals filled the 300 board-seats of the CAC-40 in 1995.[130]

In the mid-1990s, however, some of these hard cores began to disintegrate, especially in non-financial firms, unable to withstand the new financial pressures associated with globalisation, which promoted to centre stage issues of shareholder value. It was not clear how shareholder value was to be released through unprofitable non-core shareholdings that offered few, if any, synergies. Stakes in industrial French firms, for example, offered low annual returns of no more than 2 per cent.[131] The pressure to sell stakes in domestic firms that did not make financial or strategic sense was all the more acute when board members were not only French but increasingly also European and international. Many observers were understandably sceptical about privatisation at the outset, Edouard Balladur seemingly implementing a state-directed model of privatisation that was wary of market forces, exemplifying and strengthening the state's interventionist tradition.[132] In retrospect, though, privatisation in France may have served a more useful function, facilitating the internationalisation of French business that currently obtains, and in which the hard cores may have provided a useful temporary 'halfway house'. Privatisation served as a catalyst in terms of getting France's former state-owned public sector to think about and assume risk, and to do deals.[133] In creating employee-shareholders, mainly the salaried employees of large firms, who grew in number from 500,000 in 1988 to 1.5 million in 2001, it could be argued that privatisation encouraged this risk-taking mentality to spread more widely than the boards of the CAC-40.[134]

Who owns French business?

There is now compelling evidence to suggest that the cross-shareholdings that have been at the heart of French capitalism since the 1960s have begun to disintegrate.[135] This is largely the result of the massive penetration of foreign capital in French companies, which took place from the late 1990s, and which continues to rise. Arguably the high gearing (debt-to-equity ratios) of French firms, coupled with the long-standing lack of interest in equity among the general public, made them vulnerable to foreign raids. In this sense, large French firms must have appeared relatively soft targets to foreign investors hungry for equity and control. At the same time, corporate governance initiatives introduced by Marc Viénot and Senator Philippe Marini sought to limit to five the number of directorships an individual business leader could assume. These initiatives targeted reciprocal mandates (where directors of two or more companies serve on each other's boards) which, like cross-shareholdings, reinforced the mutual interests of the French business elite.[136]

France is now, according to some commentators, an economy in transition, moving from a financially networked economy to a financial market economy.[137] As François Morin writes:

> The French economy is beginning to operate in the same way as the American and British economies and is distancing itself from the German and Japanese models of capitalism which had, to some extent, previously motivated its shareholding system. The extent to which US and British norms have penetrated the system is impressive and total.[138]

In 1997, the proportion of share capital held by foreign investors stood at 5 per cent in the US, 9 per cent in the UK and 11 per cent in Japan. In France it stood at an astonishing 35 per cent. By November 2000 foreign ownership of the equity of the top 40 companies had reached an average of more than 40 per cent, a record among the world's leading industrial nations (see Table 7.7). The most international firm by ownership of France's CAC-40 was TotalFinaElf, with 65 per cent of its equity in the hands of foreigners. In second place was Dexia, with 55.7 per cent of its share capital owned by foreign investors.[139] In third place came Suez-Lyonnaise des Eaux,

Table 7.7 Share capital held by foreign investors in CAC-40 companies, 2000 (as percentage)

Company	Share capital in foreign hands, 2000	Share capital in foreign hands, 1999	Part-owned by US/UK investors, 2000	Part-owned by US/UK investors, 1999
TotalFinaElf	65.0	77.0	20.0	33.0
Dexia	55.7	49.7	9.1	21.9
Suez-Lyonnaise	55.0	54.2	17.6	15.3
Vivendi	53.4	51.5	25.0	27.0
Alstom	53.0	Not present in CAC-40	21.0	Not present in CAC-40
Lafarge	51.0	42.0	29.0	32.5
Société Générale	50.8	48.1	–	29.0
Alcatel	50.0	49.0	40.0	30.0
Lagardère	49.0	47.0	35.0	36.7
Axa	46.0	44.0	25.0	28.0
Groupe Danone	42.0	40.0	24.0	35.0
Accor	40.8	48.0	16.9	30.0
Saint-Gobain	40.5	44.0	24.4	27.0
Valeo	40.0	45.0	23.0	33.0
Cap Gemini	36.0	33.0	19.0	25.0
Equant	32.9	34.0	26.3	22.0
Schneider Electric	32.0	31.0	20.0	18.0
Carrefour	30.0	30.0	20.0	20.0
Peugeot PSA	30.0	34.2	20.0	25.3
TF1	28.6	Not present in CAC-40	–	Not present in CAC-40
Canal+	28.3	30.0	17.0	22.0
Air liquide	26.0	25.0	12.5	10.4
Sanofi-Synthélabo	23.9	22.0	14.7	13.0
AGF*	23.0	25.0	6.7	16.5
Bouygues	22.0	Not present in CAC-40	17.0	Not present in CAC-40
Pinault-Printemps-Redoute	21.3	21.7	8.5	13.5
Sodexho Alliance	19.1	24.0	10.0	14.0
Renault	19.0	30.0	14.0	12.7
L'Oréal	17.0	17.0	–	4.1
France Télécom	12.8	9.1	–	1.6
Crédit Lyonnais	10.5	Not present in CAC-40	0.0	Not present in CAC-40
Casino	9.0	10.0	4.5	7.0
EADS	8.5	Not present in CAC-40	4.5	Not present in CAC-40
BNP Paribas	–	45.0	23	20.4
Aventis**	–	59.6	–	14.4
LVMH**	–	18.0	–	8.0
Michelin**	–	45.0	–	14.7

Table 7.7   (Continued)

Company	Share capital in foreign hands, 2000	Share capital in foreign hands, 1999	Part-owned by US/UK investors, 2000	Part-owned by US/UK investors, 1999
STMicroelectronic	–	35.0	–	25
Thalès**	–	14.6	–	11.1
Thomson Multimédia	–	Not present in CAC-40	–	Not present in CAC-40

* Does not include majority share of Allianz.
** Aventis, LVMH, Michelin and Thalès did not respond.

Source: *L'Expansion* survey, November 2000; see De Tricornot, A., 'Qui possède les entreprises européennes?', *L'Expansion*, 21 December 2000–3 January 2001, p. 77.

55 per cent of whose share capital was in foreign hands following its takeover of Générale de Belgique.[140]

The presence of US institutional investors in the share capital of French firms has reached extraordinary and unprecedented levels. This in itself is a huge vote of confidence in French business and the French economy. In the late 1990s these investors sought to invest their capital internationally, targeting firms in continental Europe, buying up released equity as governments and non-financial firms reduced their involvement in non-core business sectors, thereby inducing a trend shift in shareholding classes.[141] By 1998, the Californian public-sector employees' pension fund, Calpers, had significant holdings in all of France's top 40 companies. Other North American mutual funds, such as Templeton and Fidelity, chose to target specific companies: Fidelity began buying shares in Total and Alcatel in December 1996 and March 1997 respectively, while Templeton targeted Elf-Aquitaine and BNP from 1997. Foreign mutual funds are thus in a powerful position to influence and monitor management methods and decisions, and to make their voices heard, encouraging a new shareholder activism.[142] This is in stark contrast to the traditionally passive French shareholder, who in the past enjoyed few rights, receiving financial statements, company reports or auditors' reports only when these were specifically requested. Some top 40 companies, however, remain resistant to the global push towards transparency and accountability; these include Aventis, LVMH, Michelin and Thalès (see Table 7.7). Institutional equity ownership is likely to increase further given the relative absence of French pension funds and the recognised need to promote these to complement France's struggling pay-as-you-go national pension scheme.[143] However, French proposals to develop privately funded pensions have yet to be implemented.

Insider control, interlocking shareholdings within a group, has not been abandoned, continuing to account for a small but significant proportion of shares in some companies. In 1998 insider control represented 6.4 per cent of shares at Elf-Aquitaine, 5.2 per cent at Société Générale, 5.5 per cent at AXA, and 10 per cent at Paribas (a sizeable share, but not enough to prevent the hostile takeover of the investment bank by BNP in 1999). Cross-shareholdings retain an important presence. Among the best-known cross-shareholdings in 1999 were those between Saint-Gobain and Vivendi; Suez-Lyonnaise des Eaux and Saint-Gobain; BNP and AXA; Havas and Canal Plus; Alcatel and Vivendi; Alcatel and Société Générale. AXA in particular retains the means to allow it to exercise a pivotal strategic role as 'the key actor and central fulcrum of the French financial network', a role occupied by its predecessor, UAP, in the early 1990s.[144] Concentrating financial holdings on a massive scale, AXA enjoys extensive power to coordinate and regulate economic activities in France – even if the group's management team, led by Claude Bébéar, a prominent member of the French business elite, has so far eschewed the possibility of so doing.[145] However, despite the obvious importance of these interlocking shareholdings from a political and strategic viewpoint, they are clearly dominated by the far larger percentages of shares now in the hands of foreign investors (see Table 7.7).

Similarly, familial groups and family control persist among France's leading companies despite the far-reaching internationalisation of French business. Even some very large companies remain family-dominated, such as Michelin, the former world leader in tyres,[146] and the somewhat unorthodox retailer Leclerc, three of the family being board members. Peugeot-Citroën SA, one of only six European volume car manufacturers remaining, has several family members on its board. The company's reluctance to contemplate a merger or major alliance is clearly motivated by its desire to hold on to power: the Peugeot family retains 38.5 per cent of voting shares. It is estimated that almost half of France's top 100 businesses are family-dominated. At the time of the Popular Front, 'les 200 familles' were said to have a stranglehold on the French economy. Recently, however, the founders of family firms like François de Wendel, Paul Ricard and Pierre Taittinger were venerated in the pages of *L'Expansion* for their ambition and foresight. The de Wendel family recently sponsored a chair in family capitalism at INSEAD.[147] The stocking of boards with family members ensures continuity in management, enabling families such as Peugeot to keep control of their 'birthright' in the event of an attempted takeover. The persistence of family capitalism also enables the old ways of doing things to endure, at least to a certain extent. The Peugeot family is not the only family in the car industry to operate in this way. The German luxury car manufacturer BMW similarly runs a very tight ship as a family-controlled firm, with 46 per cent of voting shares held by the Quandt family, ruthlessly pulling out of Rover in 1999 lest its patrimony be damaged by an ailing brand. The powerful Italian Agnelli dynasty likewise holds 46 per cent of shares in Fiat. In all, founding families control approximately one-quarter of the global car industry.[148]

That said, family capitalism in large French firms might be expected to decline further as financially constrained families turn to the capital markets for external finance. Yet some are determined to hold on to the reins of power. Among these is the Bouygues family, which retains control through the medium of cross-shareholdings. While the family owns just 23.6 per cent of the Bouygues share capital, it controls 57.3 per cent when the holdings of the hard core of stable shareholders (company personnel, Crédit Lyonnais, UAP and Nippon Life) are taken into account.[149] Arguably, the era of cross-shareholdings, including family-dominated enterprises, is far from over.

The enduring nature of business networks

It would be unwise to toll the knell for French-style capitalism too soon. Success in the global economic era requires effective networking and sophisticated political skills. Cultural understanding is likewise needed for firms to operate effectively across a multitude of frontiers. International firms increasingly must face up to challenges of contextual complexity. The proven diplomatic and networking skills of French business elites arguably provide a potent competitive advantage, one little understood or appreciated by many US multinationals wherein protestations of corporate social responsibility and good citizenship serve as a doubtful substitute for in-depth understanding of local communities.

The business networks, the ties of kinship and friendship that underlie the exercise of power in French business go far beyond cross shareholdings and reciprocal mandates, of which these are merely one form. They are supported by a commonality of membership of organisation, such as schools, *grandes écoles*, *grands corps*, *cabinets ministériels* and state institutions. The French business elite is 'multipositional', to borrow from Pierre Bourdieu, operating simultaneously in different 'fields' of business, and exploiting different kinds of capital, social and cultural as well as economic.[150] The bonds of friendship forged at *grandes écoles* and *grands corps* are often cemented, as Bourdieu observes, through marriage, where graduates marry the sisters and daughters of their colleagues, giving rise to a tightly-knit oligarchy. That the offspring of political administrative and business elites go on in their turn to be educated by members of the intellectual elite, and are initiated through their education into a network of power and influence, ensures the survival of such elites and the preservation of the status quo. Bourdieu highlights an important dialectical relationship between the formal and informal, the official and unofficial, as informal familial relations feed and support the strictly economic networks of the circulation of capital. In this way, 'a network of family relations can be the locus of an unofficial circulation of capital that enables the networks of official circulation to function and in turn blocks any effects of the latter that would be contrary to family interests'.[151] And while 'social capital' of this type is difficult to reduce to economic capital, nevertheless each individual member of the group has a share by proxy in the capital possessed by all others, whether family or *grand corps*, etc. The maximisation of this capital depends in particular, according to Bourdieu, on the *degree of integration of the group*. Elite networks that are mutually supportive, which feed off one another in a variety of 'fields' are by definition highly integrated and robustly cohesive, fully in tune with the institutions and structures they serve. They function too at the EU's central locus of power, the Commission. The networks that form there mirror those of the 'tightly-knit world of the Parisian political-administrative-commercial elite',[152] reflecting the dominant groups involved in its establishment and development,[153] many of whom were French statesmen and technocrats. The pivotal Franco-German relationship is essentially a relationship of political and technocratic elites, 'an informal, often invisible compact, driven by networks of officials sharing common understandings and engaged in inter-elite bargaining and policy learning'.[154] As it has grown in importance over the years, so the cohesion of elite networks in France and Germany has strengthened correspondingly. This type of behaviour, though, has not gone entirely unchallenged in Brussels. Commissioner Edith Cresson was accused of nepotism for bringing almost her whole team with her from Paris, following the practice adopted by the majority of her French ministerial predecessors. This ultimately contributed to the resignation of the Commission *en masse* in 1999. Reproducing the strongly clientilistic social patterns of 'latin', southern European member states was not an offence in Cresson's eyes. When questioned by a journalist she allegedly retorted, 'Should we only work with people we have never seen before?'[155]

The symbolic value of the networks that underpin and sustain the exercise of power in France is highlighted by the extraordinary case of Jean-Yves Haberer, former PDG (Président Directeur Général) of Crédit Lyonnais. When Haberer's misconceived strategy of expansion brought the bank to its knees in 1993, he was not dismissed. Instead he was parachuted into a new position as chairman of Crédit National. On being removed from this post six months later, Haberer was given an office and an extra pension. Revealingly, where he was 'punished' was in the expunction of his biographical entry from *Who's Who*, a sanction akin to banishment to a member of the French establishment.[156] This reveals the symbolic power of membership of elite networks, which transcends material gain, as well as the symbolic violence of exclusion from the group.

Ezra Suleiman suggests that these networks, all the stronger for having other fields of meaning than mere business, are sufficiently robust and integrated to withstand the ravages of globalisation.[157] Whitley supports this view. Regardless of the degree of international influence to which the host economy is subjected, he argues that where national business systems are cohesive and supported by integrated institutions in a close-knit system of economic coordination and control, so the domestic economy will be less susceptible to change due to internationalisation:

> The likelihood that inward foreign investment and control of economic activities and the internationalization of financial flows, will significantly change business system characteristics is similarly structured by the strength and cohesion of host economy institutions and their closeness to particular characteristics of the economic coordination and control system.[158]

Whitley concludes that there is no reason to presume that increasing international competition, such as France has witnessed in recent years, will in itself bring about far-reaching business system change, let alone that it will do so in one, Anglo-American direction.[159] Despite the substantial transfers of ownership that have taken place, coupled with the unprecedented increase in the presence of US institutional investors in the share capital of top French firms (see Table 7.7), national institutional arrangements and business systems are tenacious. The limited importance of supranational pan-European agencies and institutions, despite the existence and development of the Community over fifty years, testifies to their tenacity.[160] Supranational institutions of the EU, which *de jure* may have authority and competency, *de facto* often kowtow to national governments.[161] It is still the national arena that matters most.[162] This is amply demonstrated by the Commission's reluctance to take on the French government over its failure to liberalise fully its energy markets. The lasting imprint of national (especially French) institutions and structures on the make-up and management of the EU is exemplified most spectacularly by the CAP. A French invention designed to solve the problems of financing French farming, the CAP has survived almost entirely as it was conceived originally by de Gaulle in the 1960s. It is illustrated too by EMU, a project driven by the French since the Giscard years as a solution to the problems of asymmetrical interdependence with Germany, now brought to fruition.

One of the key signs of difference between national business systems is extent of the market for corporate control. While a subdued market for corporate control normally characterises network-based systems, the market-based system is marked by contestation. We have noted the heightened merger activity of French firms, especially during the 'equity decade' of the 1990s. A recent study of changes in the market for corporate control in a number of leading industrialised countries (France, Germany, Britain and the US) compared takeover activity in the period 1984–89 to that which took place between 1991 and 1996. Interestingly, this revealed France as the country with the largest increase in total takeover activity. More importantly, while other countries registered a decline in hostile takeover activity as a percentage of GDP over the two periods, France alone recorded an

Table 7.8   Changes in the market for corporate control between 1984–89 and 1991–96 in France, Germany, the UK and the US (as percentage of GDP)

	Total takeover activity		Hostile takeover activity	
Period	1984–89	1991–96	1984–89	1991–96
Germany	0.20	0.81	0.08	0.01
France	**0.83**	**2.45**	**0.35**	**1.03**
UK	5.55	7.93	1.93	0.36
US	2.18	4.13	0.37	0.05

Source: Amdata; Carati, G. and Tourani Rad, A., 'Convergence of corporate governance systems', *Managerial Finance*, vol. 26, no. 10, 2000, p. 77.

increase (see Table 7.8). The stock market capitalisation of the Paris bourse increased by a staggering 50 per cent in 1999 alone, a further indication of convergence towards a market-based business system.[163]

While the evidence seemingly points to an important paradigm shift in the French business model, protectionism nevertheless persists in various guises, often going hand in hand with adventurous internationalisation strategies. Jean-Marie Messier, one of the most progressive of French business leaders, promised in 2000 while seeking to promote his company's proposed merger with Seagram that Vivendi would be a model of good governance. Once agreement on the merger had been reached, however, Messier restricted shareholders' voting rights to ensure that Vivendi Universal (and its management team) remained insulated from unwanted takeover. According to Messier's new system, shareholders with 2 per cent of company shares or more should forgo their voting rights if the turnout at the annual general meeting (AGM) was significantly less than 100 per cent. Far from listening to the voices of major investors, this measure effectively removed their voting rights, since turnout at annual meetings is normally low.[164]

Protectionism persists as a cost of capital advantage in the purchase of foreign acquisitions by state-owned firms, as we have seen with EdF. It is apparent in the minimal interpretation and delayed implementation of EU directives on market liberalisation in utilities. It remains in the form of measures designed to safeguard employment (job guarantees and penalties for laying off workers in France), which in turn discourage foreign entrants in banking. The implementation of the protection–expansion formula rests on a long-standing national consensus on protectionism, supported by the expert defence of the national interest in Brussels, which in turn stems from the enduring influence of a founding member state. These are elements of continuity within French business culture, albeit recast. The central position of AXA in the domestic economy and the persistence of family capitalism suggest that cross-shareholdings are not entirely a thing of the past. While the French are content to purchase foreign firms, as the BNP-Paribas affair clearly demonstrates, they prefer French structures within their own borders. It is likely too that when markets are eventually deregulated, invisible barriers to competition may come into play. Thus, a company such as British Energy, in trying to avail itself of the limited opening of the French electricity market, finds itself consistently barred by the instinctive French preference to the domestic incumbent, making market entry impossible in fact even if it is possible in theory.[165] Or a British airline may find itself repeatedly delayed at Charles de Gaulle airport, headquarters of Air France, its slots occupied on arrival, its passengers unable to disembark.[166] In this way, the instinctive reflex of national economic sovereignty prevails over parallel supranational attempts to manage, regulate and govern economic activity across Europe.

Conclusion

There is much good news behind Jospin's claim, seemingly far-fetched, that France is now a motor force within the world economy. Despite the uncertainty induced by the terrorist attacks on the US, France remains the fastest growing economy of the Eurozone. Real GDP growth was expected to be 1.9 per cent in 2001 before falling to 1.3 per cent in 2002, while Germany and the US were expected to experience negative growth.[167] Economic growth has been led by business investment spending on capital and equipment. French exports have been boosted by an undervalued euro, and there has been a huge increase in net FDI abroad. Businesses are operating at near full-capacity levels (88 per cent in 2001), and order books are relatively full.[168] Unemployment has fallen to 8.7 per cent, beneath the German rate. This represents one million fewer unemployed than in 1997. Even the long-term unemployed have benefited. There were 300,000 fewer in 2001 than in 1997. Employment growth, moreover, has tended to be in quality jobs. Growth industries are increasingly those with a high R&D input, and many of the jobs created in 2000 were in managerial posts. Consumer confidence remains fairly buoyant, while inflation, at 1.9 per cent, is lower than the Eurozone average.[169] Only high taxes, now at a record level (45.7 per cent of GDP in 1999), the continuing failure of governments to grasp the pensions nettle, and the succession of scandals and high-level prosecutions detract from this rosy picture. France's political class is fully implicated in the financial scandals that have come to light. There is now an emerging crisis of legitimacy in French democratic institutions, triggered by a loss of confidence in the political elite which has found expression in the rise of the Far Right.

This chapter has examined, through a series of sectoral case-studies, the extraordinary internationalisation of French business, which accelerated dramatically in the closing years of the twentieth century. These point to a national business system potentially undergoing radical change. Leading

French firms are engaging dynamically in strategies of international expansion and alliance building. By 2010 we may expect to see more liberal markets in France (although invisible barriers to competition are likely to persist), as well as more listed companies, listing being viewed by large French companies as a mark of their success.

However, despite an obvious and on-going progression towards a market-based economy, French business elites are not seeking to embrace in its entirety the market-based Anglo-American system. On the contrary, many of the features traditionally associated with the French system continue to play a key role. These include *dirigisme*, which is down but not out, coupled with continuing protectionism, especially in markets associated with public service. Similarly, long-term inter-personal and inter-corporate relationships between different corporate constituencies still dominate business life. Effective networking continues to serve the country well, and is more suited to the ways of continental Europe and many other countries, not least Japan. Elite networking drives the Franco-German relationship, which spawns a large number of economic and industrial projects. It is also at the nucleus of EU politicking and diplomacy. Cross-shareholdings survive, particularly in family-dominated companies, which continue to thrive. Where internation-alisation entails a loss of majority control, hard cores of shareholders still have a role to play, although they may come from further afield than in the past (as exemplified by Nippon Life, a member of the hard core of Bouygues). Moreover, they increasingly include company personnel.

It is argued here that in spite of an obvious loss of economic sovereignty through European construction and integration, the French have continued to protect and advance national business interests through expert manage-ment of the institutional landscape. As the above case-studies demonstrate, French business elites are successfully manipulating and playing global capitalism to their advantage, pre-emptively and proactively engaging in the strategic logic of globalisation. The objective is to maintain or acquire hegemonic control of leading domestic and European enterprises. Far more likely than the complete undoing of the French network-based business model is the adaptation of international market-based structures to suit the national system. In a society still wedded to its history, which remains more stakeholder- than shareholder-oriented, *franco-français* shareholdings are being ceded for a stake in a wider European and international game.

Conclusion

> The union of Europe cannot be based on goodwill alone: rules are needed.... Men pass away; others will take their place. We cannot bequeath them our personal experience. But we can leave them institutions. The life of institutions is longer than that of men; if they are well built, they can accumulate and hand on the wisdom of succeeding generations.
>
> Jean Monnet[1]

The foremost theme of this book is that of economic management and the modernisation of French business since 1945. Economic management has been used as shorthand for the collection of policies and practices used by the state in pursuit of economic growth and structural change. At the end of the Second World War, still reeling from the traumatic effects of Occupation and Liberation, France experienced a deep-seated national crisis that opened the way for radical economic change. Jean Monnet and his fellow luminaries, backed by General Charles de Gaulle, supplied the vision needed to unite the nation and galvanise its resources in pursuit of a brighter future. The modernisation of the French economy became a national crusade spearheaded by the state, not by the business community, widely regarded as having failed the nation in the past. So it was that the Planning Commission, supported by other ministries and agencies, emerged for a time as the principal institutional repository of authority in matters of business, economics and finance. Under its guidance, the French economy was boosted by capital investment on an unprecedented scale, with selected key industries targeted as the main beneficiaries. Meanwhile, technical, organisational and managerial know-how flowed across the North Atlantic from the US to France on a prodigious scale, ensuring that large-scale investments were matched by equally large increases in output and productivity.

No one should doubt the enduring influence of the commitment made after the war to the modernisation of French business structures, methods and processes. In few countries outside the US has the pursuit of economies of scale and scope been taken so far as in France, which is all the more remarkable in view of the low level of concentration in most industries before the war. It finds expression today not only on the domestic front, but in the ambitious pursuit by French companies of cross-border mergers and acquisitions. Likewise, firms have embraced the need for mass production and automation such that nowadays France stands second only to Belgium in Europe in terms of GDP per person employed ($50,680 1990 international dollars in 1998 compared to $52,642 for Belgium and $55,618 for the US). And when looked at in terms of GDP per hour worked, France came second only to the US in 1998 with an index score of 98 per cent the US level, compared to 77 per cent for Germany and 79 per cent for the UK.[2] French firms moreover have embraced more completely the need to invest systematically in the development of core capabilities than many of their counterparts. This is not surprising in view of the extent and quality of business education in France, reflecting a widespread interest in management thought and methods, which again can be traced back directly to US influence on Monnet and others among the influential modernising French elite.

These observations nonetheless should not mask the fact of numerous changes in economic management during the postwar era. These have been documented and explained in previous chapters. The broad picture is one of government progressively ceding influence and authority, redefining its role as an influential actor, supreme negotiator in pursuit of the French national interest, within a complex of transnational institutions. However, what stands out above all is the diminution over time in the freedom of governments and officials to determine the course of national economic policy at the macro level. Hence the disparity between the ideal of economic sovereignty, on which de Gaulle set his sights in the aftermath of war and Occupation, and economic management, as European construction and globalisation, moving on apace, served to circumscribe and constrain French aspirations for independence and status in the world. The establishment of the European Community in 1958, which France joined as a founder member, and which coincided with the birth of the new Fifth Republic, marked the beginning of a new openness. Thereafter French economic management in an increasingly internationalised economy was bound at times to conflict with the desire for national independence and sovereignty. The replacement of the 'nouveau franc' – itself intended in 1960 as a symbol of economic stability, revival and autonomy – by the euro in 2002 epitomises the ostensible abandonment of national sovereignty in order to share in the wider benefits that may accrue to a larger European currency area.

In order better to understand the dynamics of economic management and business modernisation, this book has explored a second, related theme: the ongoing reconstitution of the French national business system. With globalisation looming large at the start of the new millennium, particularly in France where the phenomenon has sparked wide-ranging debate, the present tendency is to view the world in terms of rapid change, to which businesses must swiftly adapt or perish. Internationalisation is perceived to act as a powerful motor for the convergence of national business systems. The massive penetration of foreign capital in large French companies that occurred very rapidly in the closing years of the twentieth century, and which is still ongoing, exemplifies this trend. The increasing involvement of foreign, especially US actors in large French firms encourages comparison with international norms. It is likely to focus corporate minds in France on issues such as transparency and openness, auditing and accountability, board effectiveness, structures and procedures, potentially effecting change in company rules and regulations (i.e. in the area at the top of the pyramid, see Figure 1, in the Introduction).

The recommendations of the Viénot and Marini reports on matters of corporate governance, particularly board composition, have already brought about some change in this direction (see Figure 6.1). In 1997, a KPMG survey of the evolution of governance practices of French listed companies found evidence of such change.[3] A majority of CAC-40 companies (32) was found to have introduced at least one committee, normally the remuneration committee, with 29 having an audit committee, but only 17 a nomination committee. The survey identified, however, confusion as to the meaning of 'independent'. Major shareholders (*actionnaires de référence*) were often regarded as independent if they were not part of the executive management team. Such an interpretation of independent or non-executive directors clearly leaves the way open for cross-shareholdings and reciprocal mandates to continue. Many companies had the strong sentiment that Viénot's recommendations applied to others, not to themselves, for reasons of their weaker stock market capitalisation or the continuing dominance of the board by family members. However, one positive effect of the governance debate identified by the survey has been to make French listed companies more sensitive to the needs of minority shareholders, previously ignored, and to improve the quality of information communicated to them. Arguably the historical lack of openness on the part of large French companies, which did not tend to make information available to the public, contributed to the latter's detachment from economic and business affairs and general lack of interest in shareholding. This, coupled with high debt-to-equity ratios, made them vulnerable to foreign actors on the hunt for international equity and for control.

The argument revisited

Notwithstanding the profundity of recent developments, the argument presented here is that there are strong elements of continuity over the postwar period, while necessarily also important changes. It is argued that French capitalism forms a distinctive set of social relations, founded on relationships between constituent agencies and on a particular concordat between state and business, by which it is conditioned and structured. However, in terms of the fundamental characteristics of the French business model, there is a paradox, in that features once seen as stultifying, bureaucratic and inflexible have in the new era of Euro-capitalism emerged as vital sources of strength. Four features of the French business system stand out in this regard.

Stable entities

First of all, the French system, by virtue of its integrated nature, leads to organisational stability, which is essentially a belief that you are going to be there tomorrow, and hence can look to the longer term. This is manifest in the longevity of French firms. In an era when mergers, start-ups and failures occur often at a vertiginous pace, all the more so in the so-called 'new economy', where many 'dot.com' companies have been snuffed out as swiftly as they came into being, the life-span of large French companies is noteworthy. Numerous leading companies survived the upheavals of nationalisation in 1982 (even if some of their chairmen did not) at a time when many of their British counterparts were allowed to go under. Many survived privatisation in the late 1980s and 1990s – the so-called 'popularisation' of capital which Balladur aimed to bring about did not lead to democratisation – as well as several merger waves. Crédit Lyonnais survived bankruptcy, admittedly at enormous cost to the taxpayer (FF190 billion), and is now part of Crédit Agricole. The materials mega-company Saint-Gobain, now operating in 42 countries, has been in existence since 1665; this is no small achievement.[4]

Executive appointments and board directorships are also often of a lasting nature. Jean-Louis Beffa, Saint-Gobain's Président Directeur Général (PDG), has been in post since 1986, seeing through the ups and downs of privatisation and even charges of business irregularities. This is a long-standing feature of business in France. As Ehrmann noted in the 1950s, the postwar boards of French corporations consisted almost entirely of the same men as before the war, and almost always of the same social groups. In the 1960s, Postan observed that the control of banks and industrial enterprises was shared by largely the same groups of men.[5] While, from an Anglo-Saxon governance perspective, this might imply a certain immunity to the mechanisms of corporate governance, cushioning poor management from the harsh realities of business life (cf. Jean-Yves Haberer), on the positive side continuity of leadership at the top promotes organisational stability. Reputedly ailing British companies, on the other hand, such as British Airways in 1999, or Marks and Spencer in 2001, tend to see change at the top as a potential answer to financial difficulties. Often this merely exacerbates the company's turbulence, as company strategies are symbolically abandoned and others adopted in their stead.

Commercial contracts too are typically of longer duration in France than in the UK. Water giants Vivendi (formerly Compagnie Générale des Eaux) or Suez-Lyonnaise des Eaux, for example, typically acquire *concessions* to supply a particular city or region with water over 30 years. Since the late 1980s, they have been winning 30-year contracts not just in France but also abroad.[6] Arguably, when the contract eventually expires, three decades of good service will ensure that the incumbent enjoys a powerful in-built advantage over potential bidders. French water companies have used their good reputations as stable, reliable entities to launch a host of other related and unrelated services, at home and abroad.

The key point about organisational stability is that it creates a capacity to plan in the belief that the organisation is going to be there tomorrow. In marked contrast to the myopic focus on quarterly returns which prevails in the City of London, allegedly in the service of shareholder value, French managers can afford to take a much longer-term and broader perspective of value-creating strategies than their UK counterparts.[7] Planning has been a distinctive characteristic of the French economy in the postwar period, especially during the 'thirty glorious years', although it has since fallen largely into disuse despite the survival of the Commissariat Général du Plan in diluted, essentially tokenistic form. Transferred to business strategy, the French capacity to plan coupled with the luxury of being able to assume a longer-term view of business enterprise continues to pay dividends.

Ability to assume a long-term strategic view

The second key feature flows directly from this. Organisational stability promotes a long-term, strategic perspective. French political and business leaders have grown in strategic sophistication over recent years, since the 1980s in particular, in their approach to Euro-capitalism within the context of the global economy. This has manifested itself in two main ways. The first is a concerted attempt to shape the international institutions within which capitalism operates. These include first and foremost the European Union (EU), French influence being apparent in the survival of the Common Agricultural Policy (CAP) as well as the coming to fruition of Economic and Monetary Union (EMU). It is manifest too in GATT (General Agreement in Tariffs and Trade) negotiations, most notably in the agricultural domain, where French obstinacy delivered a better deal for European farmers, and in its successor institution, the World Trade Organisation (WTO), whose creation France demanded and won in 1995. By the early 1990s, France presided over numerous linchpin institutions, European and international. Included in the list were the European Commission (led for a decade by Jacques Delors), the European Bank for Reconstruction and Development (managed in its early years by Jacques Attali, adviser to President Mitterrand), the International Monetary Fund, the Organisation for Economic Cooperation and Development, and the Council of Europe.

Less well known is the fact that it was France that initiated the annual meetings of the group of seven industrial nations (G7), now the G8 following the inclusion of Russia. The stocking of key European and world institutions with members of its politico-administrative elite has enabled France to exercise greater influence over European and international affairs than might be warranted by its size or status. More recently, Jean-Claude Trichet has secured the governorship of the European Central Bank.

As a key founding member of the Community, France was particularly active when the initial rules of the game were being shaped. Often critical negotiations involved relatively few actors. The Maastricht negotiations in the early 1990s, for example, involved Mitterrand, Bérégovoy (as Finance Minister), Guigou (Minister of European Affairs) and Dumas (Foreign Minister), as well as several key figures in administration, notably Trichet as governor of the Banque de France, and high-ranking cabinet members.[8] The elite networks and relationships that dominate French politics, business and administration extend to the EU's centre of gravity, the Commission. In short, France has had, and continues to have significant input into the establishment of the institutions responsible for running the EU. As Jean Monnet expressed it in 1952, men may come and go, but the institutions they legate are potentially far more powerful, being able to shape policy and events over long spans of time.

France has a good track-record of achieving its objectives at the European level. One current French crusade is for an EU constitution. A former president, Giscard d'Estaing, is to chair the group that examines its feasibility. Another concerns the harmonisation of business taxes throughout the EU, on the grounds that high business taxes in France relative to other EU member states encourage French firms to register, and hence pay taxes, in EU countries where lower business rates obtain, such as the UK. At the time of writing, a European Commission paper on corporate tax barriers to the completion of the single market is keenly awaited. This will be a hard-fought battle, attracting fierce opposition from Britain and Denmark, and the outcome is by no means guaranteed; but on past performance, the possibility of an outcome that is favourable to the French should not be discounted.

The cohesive nature of French capitalism has made French business leaders proactive in their determination to shape the rules of engagement for private enterprise within the framework of the European and international economic systems. The French are pursuing the logic of Euro-capitalism within the global economy. In this they recognise the need to reap economies of scale and scope, which is fundamental to the logic of large-scale enterprise and mega-mergers. The closing years of the twentieth century saw the creation of French-based mega-companies in insurance (AXA-UAP-Royal Sunlife Alliance), banking (BNP-Paribas), cars (Renault-Nissan), food retailing (Carrefour-Promodès), utilities and entertainment (Vivendi Universal), dairy produce (Danone), and so on, the products of deliberate strategies of international expansion. Franco-German mergers have featured prominently, underlining the growing industrial cooperation that marks the Franco-German alliance: 1999 saw the creation of EADS (European Aeronautics, Defence and Space Company) and Aventis in defence and pharmaceuticals respectively. Less glamorously, in 1998 the French insurer AGF was subsumed as part of Allianz, to French dismay.

The pivotal Franco-German relationship is driven by political and technocratic elites. The recent rush of Franco-German mergers demonstrates that business elites are now exploiting the partnership for mutual advantage. It is argued here, following the analysis of Suleiman, that French business networks are sufficiently robust and integrated to withstand the ravages of globalisation.[9] As Whitley observes, where national business systems are coherent and supported by fully integrated institutions in a tightly knit system of coordination and control, so the host economy may be less susceptible to the myriad influences of internationalisation.[10] The view presented here is that the French model of elite networking, which has served France well in the postwar period, and which is well suited to the ways of continental Europe, will continue to be used effectively by French business and political leaders on a European and international level. The internationalisation of the French economy is startling and ongoing. An average of 40 per cent of the share capital of CAC-40 (Cotation assistée en continu) firms is now in foreign hands. That said, the year 2000 witnessed record foreign direct investment (FDI) outflows of FF1.15 trillion, notably dwarfing inflows by a ratio of four to one (FF358.1 billion). It is argued here, provisionally at least, that *franco-français* shareholdings are being ceded for a stake in a wider European and international game. In this way, the French business elite is seeking to maintain control of leading domestic and European enterprises, pre-emptively and proactively engaging with the structural logic of globalisation.[11] This argument is in sympathy with Whitley's view that ownership, control and governance in the emerging international business order will be strongly influenced by those of the leading economies, rather than an institutionally disembodied, idealised market.[12]

Managing the competitive landscape

The third key characteristic of French capitalism is the readiness of the state to manage the competitive landscape in favour of French firms. A long-standing defining feature of the French business system, despite far-reaching privatisation in the late 1980s and 1990s, is the traditionally strong, interventionist role of the state, although both sides of the political divide are now, in the twenty-first century, challenging this. From prominent socialists such as Martine Aubry and Jacques Delors to right-wing thinkers Alain Minc and Alain Madelin, the contemporary 'pensée unique' in France is that the role of the state is excessive and should be reduced.[13]

Nevertheless, an obvious double standard prevails in that numerous companies in pivotal markets continue to benefit from state ownership coupled with closed *de facto* monopolistic markets at home. The protected position enjoyed by firms in utilities and transport, such as Eléctricité de France (EdF), Gaz de France (GdF), Société National des Chemins de Fer (SNCF) and Réseau Ferré de France (RFF), has allowed them to take full advantage of market liberalisation elsewhere in the EU while denying or deferring reciprocity on French soil. Despite their overt and doubtless heartfelt enthusiasm for the single market, French interpretation of EU directives on market liberalisation has been purposely minimal, with implementation subject to lengthy delays. Several years after the EU directives on the liberalisation of energy markets, for example, France's electricity industry remains the least open in the EU. While other EU member states have privatised their energy industries, EdF and to a lesser extent GdF remain integrated and monolithic, the unions' entitlement to a share of EdF/GdF income (for pension funds) being the main reason given for the reputed difficulties with privatisation. As public-sector monopolies, they continue to benefit from the tutelage of the state, enjoying financial support and credit guarantees. The significant cost of capital advantage derived from state ownership has enabled state-owned utilities to embark on prodigious international expansion strategies, to the chagrin of privatised utilities in Britain and Spain. The state's deep pockets provide them with the capacity to act. EdF and GdF are able to raise money for acquisitions at a rate of interest lower than government bond rates, while privatised European competitors can do no better than central bank base rates. In short, state-owned French utilities are operating in commercial markets but not on a fully commercial basis, with no shareholders to satisfy, nor any stock price sensitivity to distract or concern them. Expansion abroad is supported by protection at home, this protection–expansion formula proving a tough one with which to compete. In the meantime, the French are determined to play the market opening game long. The intention is that when energy markets are eventually liberalised in France, French incumbents will enjoy a considerable inherent advantage over new market entrants. While they remain monoliths, moreover, without an ownership separation of transmission, generation and supply, effectively barriers to competition will persist.[14]

This state-funded strategy has proved highly effective for manipulating the rules of the game. EdF, for example, has purchased the rights to control the flows of electricity throughout continental Europe, from France to the UK, France to Spain, from the West European grid to Central Europe, and to Scandinavia. This allows the French quite literally to manage the competitive landscape, as well as to generate the financial surpluses required to fund large-scale international expansion. Some of the businesses in which the French have a strong European and international presence are, indeed, highly cash-generative. (This applies not only to utilities, such as energy, water and waste, but also to French insurance companies, headed by AXA, now the largest accident and property insurance group in Europe.) State ownership, however, is not entirely costless to the utilities concerned. The government has earmarked some of the surpluses generated by EdF and GdF to boost falling tax receipts in 2002.

Sustained investment in internal capabilities

The fourth key feature is the sustained investment in developing internal capabilities, in particular research and development (R&D) and information systems. Heavy investment in R&D is an enduring feature of the French business system. While the job of engineer lacks prestige in the UK, the profession of *ingénieur* in France commands significant respect, reflecting an education spent at one of the country's leading *grandes écoles* often accompanied by membership of a prestigious *grand corps*. Whereas 'screwdriver' assembly plants burgeoned in Britain in the 1980s and 1990s, the French in sharp contrast recognised the importance of attracting and retaining the 'grey matter' of company research centres.

The GDP growth displayed by France at the dawn of the twenty-first century is primarily investment-led, sparked by business spending on capital and equipment. Growth industries in France are increasingly those with a high R&D input, such as railway engineering, telecommunications, aerospace, cars, construction and pharmaceuticals. This success is also export-driven, sales of manufactured goods with a high R&D content benefiting from the appreciation of the dollar *vis-à-vis* the euro following the latter's launch in 1999. In the critical automotive sector, one of the most internationalised and technologically mature of sectors, high spending on R&D, together with improved efficiency, has ensured the survival of Renault and Peugeot thus far. Renault has recently increased its European market share, with sales of French cars accounting for approximately one-fifth of total sales in Western Europe.[15] Similarly, the high R&D investment in the four-country consortium Airbus has paid off handsomely, with sales of its large passenger aircraft booming. At the Paris air show of June 2001, orders for its new military aircraft flowed in; in the past, many of these would have gone to Boeing. The downturn in air-travel that followed the terrorist attacks on the US did not, paradoxically, lead to the cancellation of Airbus orders, some of which were placed after 11 September 2001. Even industries not normally associated with investment in R&D, such as the food industry, find themselves needing to invest in research and innovation in order to keep ahead of the game. Investment in product innovation, for example, has enabled Danone, world market leader in fresh dairy produce, to remain dominant in the global dairy market; it is likely to remain central to the group's continued international expansion.

This continued boom in business investment spending is related in turn to the historically high capacity utilisation in factories: at over 88 per cent in 2001, this is higher than during the economic upswing of the late 1980s. This has an obvious knock-on effect for employment. With growth industries increasingly those with a significant R&D input, employment growth has tended to be in quality jobs, with many of the jobs created in 2000 in the management category. Interestingly, some observers attribute the high levels of production currently experienced in France to the introduction of the 35-hour week. Despite increasing hourly wage rates, it seems that far from detracting from national competitive advantage, as anticipated by the employers' association Medef (Mouvement des Entreprises de France), the working-time laws may have boosted productivity while seemingly moderating wage demands.

An ideological revolution?

The argument that runs throughout this book is that the French business system is marked by strong elements of continuity over the postwar period, albeit recast, and that features once viewed as rigid and stultifying have emerged in the era of Euro-capitalism as sources of strength and dynamism. If this is the case, then what led the French to pursue the logic of the new, revived capitalism? What prompted the big change?

The contention here is that this change in attitude occurred at the level of an ideological struggle, in which ultimately the forces of modernisation and change won out over the old guard of French nationalism. 'The terrain of ideas', writes Alain Vernholes, 'is the only battle worth fighting.'[16] As the economist Jacques Plassard explained in 1985, businessmen do not have a 'revolutionary' agenda in any political sense. But the 'flourishing of human beings' to which they aspire is nevertheless a powerful, compelling message in its own right, and hence in this sense ideological:

> If entrepreneurs are heard in politics, it is because they are the bearers of certain truths. The camp of entrepreneurs does not defend interests and certainly not individual interests... [Entrepreneurs] are interested in an aspiration toward progress, toward the flourishing of human beings.... Developed countries are those in which merchants and producers, liberal professions and artisans play the main role. Countries in which wealth is captured and sterilized by a leading class whose power rests on political domination (party or army) remain underdeveloped.[17]

The last battle of this ideological revolution occurred in 1983, when left and right were finally reconciled as to the importance of business enterprise, healing the two-hundred-year-old schism of a conflict-ridden society. The socialists, in their naïvety, had endeavoured on coming to power

(1981–83) to resist the operation of market forces and had grossly overestimated their freedom to dictate policy. They learned the hard way that it was near impossible to go it alone in the era of international economic integration: the policy switch was soon thrown from radical to orthodox. What the complete about-turn in economic policy in the early 1980s – from nationalisation to austerity and ultimately conversion to the market – revealed above all was the extent to which governments and firms alike can be punished by the markets for denying their constraints. Retribution was visible in the snowballing of the budget deficit and national debt, the worsening trade balance and unemployment statistics, and in three ignominious currency devaluations.

The year 1983 also signalled the birth of a new consensus on Europe, the product of a new understanding on the part of France's political leaders and populace that the country's economy was inextricably linked with those of its partners in the Community. This consensus enabled successive French governments to pursue clear, coherent European policies at critical stages in the process of European integration, without being constantly obliged to canvass public opinion or hedge their bets, a luxury that British governments have scarcely known.[18] It is obvious that unambiguous strategies are likely to be more effective ones. The decision to remain in the European Monetary System in 1983 was critical, at the heart of which was a new awareness that Europe might prove to be the means for the realisation of national goals which national action could clearly no longer deliver.[19] The sacrifice of a measure of national sovereignty was arguably a price worth paying in the pursuit of welfare, prosperity, and an enhanced role on the world stage.

Pragmatism lay at the heart of the new consensus in favour of business enterprise and European integration. The consensus evident after 1983, however, was the outcome of developments that dated back to the watershed years between 1945 and 1950 when the need for economic modernisation was accepted and embraced as a primary objective of national policy.[20] Progressive liberalisation, the release of the entrepreneurial spirit, was implicit in the building of the new Europe, in which France played such a leading role. Yet this was for long tempered by state involvement by multifarious means in the affairs of business, revealing the depth of the old urge in France towards planning, predictability and stability. All this was called into question after 1974–75 when the problems induced by the first oil crisis made it far more difficult to plan and predict. Beginning in 1976, the execution of the Barre plan promoted a greater economic realism, taken up again by the socialists after their brief attempt to resurrect radical alternative principles of economic management. The 1983 U-turn on economic policy, the decision to remain in the EMS and the emergence of a new mentality more conducive to business enterprise followed in swift succession. Privatisation from 1986 onwards was a critical stepping-stone along the route to the internationalisation of French business that currently obtains.

The intention here is not to underestimate the importance of the war and the Liberation as a watershed. Some of the changes discussed here do not make sense unless a long-term perspective is adopted, unless we go back to the drive to modernise the economy which crystallised in 1945, itself the product of France's humiliating capitulation in 1940 in a matter of a few weeks. Nor should we misjudge the importance of the oil shocks of the 1970s. The reaction to that crisis determined the pursuit and ultimate achievement of self-sufficiency in energy, a huge achievement for a country with few natural energy sources.

It is argued here that the key point of transformation in this ideological struggle is nevertheless the turning-point, *l'année-charnière*, of 1983, leading to a new, reborn cohesiveness and greater confidence of the French elite – paradoxically, given its proximity to the nationalisations of 1982. The economic strategy of Raymond Barre (1976–81) was a small step along the way; but it was not in itself sufficient. The coming to power of the left, and the pursuit and renunciation of its reformist agenda were necessary preconditions for the emergence of greater economic realism. Arguably, what made France's new business orientation so potent was the fact that it was forged under a socialist administration – an improbable midwife to this conversion, but perhaps all the more effective in consequence.

The new attitude that prevails is very much associated with the French *grandes écoles* and business schools, which have been instrumental in changing attitudes, especially among the managerial class. Of the two leading *grandes écoles*, the Ecole Nationale d'Administration (ENA) and Polytechnique, which together educated two-thirds of the current chairmen of the CAC-40, the former we should remember was a postwar invention.[21] There is now also a growing band of leading PDGs who attended other, less elitist stables such as HEC (Hautes Etudes Commerciales) or ESSEC (Ecole Supérieure des sciences économiques et commerciales), or business schools which teach American management principles, such as INSEAD, or even the Harvard Business School. The growing number of provincial business schools, as well as leading universities such as Paris-Dauphine which seek to emulate these, have played a key role in broadening France's managerial base, especially at middle-management level and among medium-sized firms – the ruling business elite jealously guarding its privileges at the top. The current prestige of a top-level business education, in marked contrast to the former disparagement of business enterprise, reflects the new ideology, which essentially concerns the projection of French interests through European institutions, and which seeks to manipulate and play global capitalism to its advantage, in a 'savvy, street-wise' way. It is distinctively French and European because values such as stability, long-term planning, and a measured, considered approach to all they do have not been abandoned. On the contrary, all of this remains. The perception of business enterprise as a constellation of long-term inter-personal and inter-corporate relationships is still a valid one, suited to the ways of continental Europe, to the workings of the EU, and to the pivotal Franco-German axis. However, it is arguably much more powerful in practice now that the central role of long-term relationships (including those with the state) to business enterprise is infused by market forces, economic realism and the 'killer instinct' to succeed.

Summation

The French economy has performed extremely well over the postwar period by international comparative indicators. The world's fourth economy, behind only the US, Japan and Germany, France enjoys a strong growth record, coupled with a progressive structural change. Currently the fastest growing economy of the Eurozone, her real GDP growth was expected to be 1.9 per cent in 2001 and 1.3 per cent in 2002, avoiding the negative growth expected to befall Germany and the US.[22] That the economy is broadly based, being especially strong in terms of the balance between sectors – agriculture, industry, services and commerce – adds to its robustness.

It is argued here that the French economy has performed so well in recent years because of the particular form of capitalism that obtains there. This explanation of French economic success is also institutional, determined by the particular physiology, or physiognomy of the French economy. This is characterised by stable institutions as well as by long-term relationships between different corporate constituencies – inter-personal, inter-corporate, between government and business, and business and politics – all pulling since 1983 in the same direction, at times caricatured as 'la pensée unique'. Individual cross-shareholdings may come and go, ravaged by the winds of globalisation; but the strength and cohesiveness of French and increasingly European business elites, and the robustness of their economic networks arguably transcend these.

Finally, it is argued that as a result of the particular characteristics of French capitalism, French business leaders have been able to extend very quickly on to a European stage, carrying forward their ideology and institutions. An institutional explanation of French success is also informed by the make-up of the EU, heavily influenced by the input of French founding fathers and subsequent active participation in the process of European integration. The influence of Schuman and Monnet in the conception, gestation and infancy of the Community is matched by that of de Gaulle (cf. the CAP) and above all Mitterrand (cf. the single market, the Maastricht Treaty, the 'social chapter' and EMU) in its later development. The institutional innovations introduced by French nationals over the years, including Giscard d'Estaing and Jacques Delors, have paved the way for French business success in Europe and beyond, a scenario now playing itself out on a bigger European and international stage.

That said, the constellation of power and interests in the EU is currently changing. It has not been easy for France to come to terms with a larger Germany, run by a younger generation of politicians, less willing to subordinate German interests to French interests, and eager to engage in new relationships with new partners. With the EU now on the verge of a significant enlargement to the east, the privileged status France has come to enjoy as co-leader of the EU with Germany is no longer guaranteed, with implications for French influence in Europe. Indeed, the Nice summit of December 2000 may have signalled the end of French dominance of the EU. Not only did it highlight Franco-German differences, but also in agreeing the extension of qualified majority voting, the allocation of only one commissioner per country from 2005, and the reweighting of votes,[23] it privileged small countries over larger ones to a greater extent than before. Since it is intended that a rotational system for the allocation of commissioners will apply when the EU reaches 26 members, this means that at some stage in the future France may be without a commissioner, since member states are to be treated equally.

Enlargement provides Germany with a huge adjacent market, but offers the French nothing. The CAP remains a significant budgetary obstacle in its way: either existing beneficiaries, primarily France, will lose out, or the burden will fall on net contributors. Agenda 2000 recognised that CAP reform was long overdue. Without radical reform, the next enlargement involving East European countries with sizeable agrarian populations will make its financing unbearable. The accession of all current candidate countries would double the EU's agricultural labour force and increase its agricultural area by 50 per cent. The EU cannot afford to encompass candidate countries in an unreformed CAP. The consequence would be a rise in CAP-related expenditure of E11 billion per annum, two-thirds of which would be in the form of direct payments to farmers. Should candidate countries be excluded from the CAP, however, this would be at odds with the EU's principles of solidarity and cohesion.[24] One possible scenario to ensure the smooth accession of candidate countries might be to 'buy off' the French by allowing France to retain some of the considerable benefits it currently enjoys from the CAP – a scenario in which French interests are notably protected.[25]

'Globalisation', writes Graham Searjeant, financial editor of *The Times*, should start at home.' As Searjeant observes, France recognises – perhaps because of its underlying belief in the legitimacy of national self-expression – that globalisation works in national interests if as many domestic companies as possible can be helped into the driving-seat.[26] In the twenty-first century, economic sovereignty may no longer be a realistic ideal, if indeed it ever was. But skilful economic management in the defence and promotion of national business interests, which rests on the continuing reflex of national sovereignty, provides an effective and arguably superior substitute.

Notes

Introduction

1. Landes, D.S., *The Unbound Prometheus*, Cambridge, Cambridge University Press, 1969; Mentré, P., *Gulliver enchaîné*, Paris, Editions la Table Ronde, 1982.
2. Landes, D.S., 'French Entrepreneurship and Industrial Growth in the Nineteenth Century', *Journal of Economic History*, No. 9, 1949, pp. 45–61; Landes, D.S., 'French Business and the Businessmen in Social and Cultural Perspective', in Earle, E.M., ed., *Modern France: Problems of the Third and Fourth Republics*, New York, Russell & Russell, 1951, pp. 334–53; Crozier, M., *La Société bloquée*, Paris, Seuil, 1970; Crozier, M., *Le Phénomène bureaucratique*, Paris, Seuil, 1963.
3. Ehrmann, H.W., *Organized Business in France*, Princeton, Princeton University Press, 1957, p. 111.
4. Fourastié, J., *Les Trente glorieuses ou la révolution invisible de 1946 à 1970*, Paris, Fayard, 1979.
5. This is one of the main arguments put forward by Marie-Laure Djelic in her book *Exporting the American Model: the Postwar Transformation of European Business*, Oxford, Oxford University Press, 1998.
6. Williams, K., 'From Shareholder Value to Present-day Capitalism', *Economy and Society*, Vol. 29, No. 1, 2000, pp. 1–12; Froud, J., Haslam, C., Johnal, S. and Williams, K., 'Shareholder Value and Financialization: Consultancy Promises, Management Moves', *Economy and Society*, Vol. 29, No. 1, 2000, pp. 80–110.
7. Tainio, R., 'Effects of Foreign Portfolio Investors on Finnish Companies and their Management', paper presented to 17th EGOS (European Group for Organizational Studies) Colloquium, July 2001, Lyon.
8. DiMaggio, P. and Powell, W.W., 'The Iron Cage Revisited: Institutional Isomorphism and Collective Rationality in Organisational Fields', in Powell, W.W. and DiMaggio, P., eds, *The New Institutionalism in Organisational Analysis*, Chicago, University of Chicago Press, 1991, pp. 63–82.
9. Hofstede, G., *Culture's Consequences*, London, Sage, 1980.
10. This framework draws on the author's work with Charles Harvey, Bristol Business School, University of the West of England, as part of a project entitled 'Business Elites and Corporate Governance in France and the UK', funded by Reed Charity.
11. Association Française des Entreprises Privées/Conseil National du Patronat Français, *Le Conseil d'Administration des Sociétés Cotées*, CNPF, Paris, 1995, known as the 'Rapport Viénot' after its author Marc Viénot. A follow-up to this report was published in 1999. See too Marini, P., *La Modernisation du droit des sociétés*, Paris, La Documentation française, 1996 (the 'Rapport Marini'); Maclean, M., 'Towards a European Model? A Comparative Evaluation of Recent Corporate Governance Initiatives in France and the UK', *Journal of European Area Studies*, Vol. 7, No. 2, 1999, pp. 227–45.
12. I owe this observation to Marie-Laure Djelic, ESSEC, July 2001, Lyon.
13. Djelic, M-L., *Exporting the American Model*.
14. Bourdieu, P., *Outline of a Theory of Practice*, Cambridge, Cambridge University Press, 1977, p. 214, cited in Swartz, D., *Culture and Power: the Sociology of Pierre Bourdieu*, Chicago, University of Chicago Press, 1997, p. 70.

15. 'EU looks into tax regimes', *The Times*, 7 July 2001, p. 29.
16. The ECB is alleged to suffer from an accountability problem. See Elgie, R., 'Democratic Accountability and Central Bank Independence: Historical and Contemporary, National and European Perspectives', *West European Politics*, Vol. 21, No. 3, July 1998, pp. 53–76; Elgie, R., 'Central Bank Independence: a Reply to Various Critics', *West European Politics*, Vol. 24, No. 1, January 2001, pp. 217–21.
17. Crozier, M., *La Société bloquée*.
18. 'Cause to rail at Brussels diktat', *The Times*, 23 June 2001.
19. Berstein, S., *The Republic of de Gaulle 1958–1969*, translated by P. Morris, Cambridge, Cambridge University Press/Editions de la Maison des Sciences de l'Homme, 1993, p. 102.
20. Hall, P.A., *Governing the Economy: the Politics of State Intervention in Britain and France*, Cambridge, Polity Press, 1986.
21. Porter, M.E., *Competitive Strategy: Techniques for Analyzing Industries and Competitors*, New York, Macmillan, 1980; Porter, M.E., *Competitive Advantage: Creating and Sustaining Superior Performance*, New York, Macmillan, 1985.
22. Balladur, E., *Je crois en l'homme plus qu'en l'Etat*, Paris, Flammarion, 1987, p. 84. Unless otherwise stated, all translations are by the author.
23. Maclean, M. and Trouille, J.-M., eds, *France, Germany and Britain: Partners in a Changing World*, Palgrave – now Palgrave Macmillan, Basingstoke, 2001.
24. Vernholes, A., 'La France n'accepte pas de payer le prix de ses ambitions', *Modern and Contemporary France*, Vol. 9, No. 3, August 2001, pp. 289–300.
25. Readers are referred to the recent study by Steve Jeffreys, *European Working Lives: Continuities and Change in Management and Industrial Relations in France, Scandinavia and the UK*, Aldershot, Edward Elgar, 2001. Susan Milner provides a useful overview of French industrial relations during the Mitterrand era in 'Industrial Relations in France: Towards a New Social Pact?', in Maclean, M., ed., *The Mitterrand Years: Legacy and Evaluation*, Macmillan Press – now Palgrave Macmillan, Basingstoke, 1998, pp. 169–84. See also her article, 'Globalisation and Employment in France: Between Flexibility and Protection?', *Modern and Contemporary France*, Vol. 9, No. 3, August 2001, pp. 327–37.
26. Kindleberger, C.P., *Economic Growth in France and Britain 1851–1950*, Cambridge MA, Harvard University Press, 1964, p. 108.

1 Enduring Influences: French Business and the State

1. Jean-Jacques Rousseau, *Du Contrat social*, Paris, Garnier-Flammarion, 1966, p. 63.
2. Parodi, M., *L'Economie et la société française de 1945 à 1970*, Paris, Armand Colin, 1971, p. 62.
3. Fourastié, J., *Les Trente glorieuses ou la révolution invisible de 1946 à 1970*, Paris, Fayard, 1979; Maddison, A., *The World Economy: a Millennial Perspective*, Paris, OECD, 2001, p. 125.
4. Figures cited in Maddison, A., *The World Economy: a Millennial Perspective*, p. 261. For 2000 estimates see Economist Intelligence Unit, *Country Profile 2001: France*, London, EIU, 2001, p. 25. For 1997 figures, see *L'Expansion*, 8–22 July 1999, p. 26.
5. Elie Cohen, annual conference of the Association for the Study of Modern and Contemporary France, Royal Holloway, September 1996.
6. Albert, M., *Capitalisme contre capitalisme*, Paris, Seuil, 1991.
7. Albert, M., *Capitalisme contre capitalisme*, p. 87.

8. Harvey, C., Maclean, M. and Hayward, A., 'From Knowledge Dependence to Knowledge Creation: Industrial Growth and the Technological Advance of the Japanese Electronics Industry', *Journal of Industrial History*, Vol. 4, No. 2, 2001, pp. 1–22; Harvey, C., Hayward, A. and Maclean, M., 'Good luck or fine judgement?', *Asia Pacific Business Review*, Vol. 10, No. 1, 2002.

9. On the distinction between internationalisation and globalisation, see Lane, C., *Industry and Society in Europe: Stability and Change in Britain, Germany and France*, Aldershot, Edward Elgar, 1995, pp. 82–3.

10. Giddens, A., *Runaway World: How Globalisation is Shaping Our Lives*, London, Profile, 1999, p. 3. See also Regini, M., 'Between Deregulation and Social Pacts: the Responses of European Economies to Globalization', *Politics and Society*, Vol. 28, No. 1, March 2000, pp. 5–33, and the special issue of *Modern and Contemporary France* on 'France and Globalisation', Vol. 9, No. 3, August 2001.

11. Schmidt, V., 'Globalization, Europeanization, and the Loss of National Autonomy and Control', and Krugman, P., 'Growing World Trade: Causes and Consequences', *Brookings Papers on Economic Activities*, 1995, pp. 327–62.

12. Figures cited in Sage. A., 'Gallic culture embraces shock of new as Left Bank loses panache', *The Times*, 27 September 1999, p. 12, and Bremner, C., 'French unite against US trade domination', *The Times*, 24 September 1999, p. 21. See also Gordon, P. and Meunier, S., 'Globalization and French Cultural Identity', *French Politics, Culture and Society*, Vol. 19, No. 1, spring 2001, pp. 22–41.

13. Rousseau, J.-J., *Du Contrat social*, p. 146. For an illuminating interpretation of this work, see Crocker, L.G., *Rousseau's Social Contract: an Interpretive Essay*, Cleveland, Ohio, the Press of Case Western Reserve University, 1968.

14. Plassard, J., 'Editorial', *Les Quatre vérités*, No. 129, November 1985, cited and translated by Berger, S., 'Liberalism reborn: the New Liberal Synthesis in France', in Howorth, J. and Ross, G., eds, *Contemporary France: a Review of Interdisciplinary Studies*, 1, London, Pinter, 1987, p. 98; Landes, D.S., 'French Entrepreneurship and Industrial Growth in the Nineteenth Century', *Journal of Economic History*, No. 9, 1949, p. 61.

15. See Stanley Hoffmann on sovereignty, 'Thoughts on Sovereignty and French Politics', in Flynn, G., ed., *Remaking the Hexagon: the New France in the New Europe*, Boulder, Westview Press, 1995, pp. 251–8.

16. See the definition given by Kuisel, R.F., *Capitalism and the State in Modern France: Renovation and Economic Management in the Twentieth Century*, Cambridge, Cambridge University Press, 1981, p. ix: '"Economic Management" means conscious direction from above. In this case the state became the manager; it came to rely on a wide range of controls and incentives as well as on the collaboration of private interests with public authorities. Management thus complemented and substituted for market forces without supplanting them.'

17. Cohen, E., 'France: National Champions in Search of a Mission', in Hayward. J., ed., *Industrial Enterprise and European Integration: from National to International Champions in Western Europe*, Oxford, Oxford University Press, 1995, pp. 30–1.

18. Kuisel, R.F., *Capitalism and the State in Modern France*, p. 202.

19. Malraux, A., *Les Chênes qu'on abat*, Paris, Gallimard, 1971, p. 29.

20. Cited in Hall, P.A., *Governing the Economy: the Politics of State Intervention in Britain and France*, Cambridge, Polity Press, 1986, p. 204.

21. Hayward, J., '*Moins d'Etat* or *Mieux d'Etat*: the French Response to the Neo-Liberal Challenge', in Maclean, M., ed., *The Mitterrand Years: Legacy and Evaluation*, Basingstoke, Macmillan Press – now Palgrave Macmillan, 1998, pp. 23–35.

22. I owe this information to Armand Bizaguet of the French Section of the Centre Européen des Entreprises à Participation Publique. See CEEP, *L'Importance et l'évolution des entreprises à participation publique et des entreprises d'intérêt économique général dans l'économie française depuis 1996*, Paris, CEEP, 2000.

23. Hoffmann, S., 'France and Europe: the Dichotomy of Autonomy and Cooperation', in Howorth, J. and Ross, G., eds, *Contemporary France*, 1, p. 49.

24. Hall, P.A., *Governing the Economy*, p. 196.

25. Dunham, A.L., 'A New Perspective on the Industrial Revolution in France', *Michigan Alumnus Quarterly Review*, Vol. 57, No. 14, pp. 148–59. See also the seminal work by Jean-François Gravier, *Paris et le désert français*, 2nd edition, Paris, Flammarion, 1958.

26. Feinstein, C.H. *et al.*, *The European Economy between the Wars*, Oxford, Oxford University Press, 1997, p. 36.

27. Ehrmann, H.W., *Organized Business in France*, Princeton, Princeton University Press, 1957, p. 111.

28. Kindleberger, C.P., *Economic Growth in France and Britain 1851–1950*, Cambridge MA, Harvard University Press, 1964, p. 160.

29. Fridensen, P., 'France: the Relatively Slow Development of Big Business in the Twentieth Century', in Chandler, A.D. *et al.*, eds, *Big Business and the Wealth of Nations*, Cambridge, Cambridge University Press, 1997, p. 207. Fridensen cites as worthy exceptions the work of James M. Laux, Claude Fohlen, François Caron and Maurice Lévy-Leboyer. See also Moutet, A., *Les Logiques de l'entreprise: la rationalisation dans l'industrie française de l'entre-deux-guerres*, Paris, Editions de l'Ecole des Hautes Etudes en Sciences Sociales, 1997.

30. Vinen, R., *Bourgeois Politics in France 1945–1951*, Cambridge, Cambridge University Press, 1995, p. 19.

31. The work of the historian Jean Bouvier is worthy of note in this regard. Bouvier collaborated appropriately with a civil servant. See Bloch-Lainé, F. and Bouvier, J., *La France restaurée: dialogue sur le choix d'une modernisation*, Paris, 1986.

32. See, for example, Parodi, M., *L'Economie et la société française de 1945 à 1970*, Paris, Armand Colin, 1971, updated as a collective work under Parodi's direction in three volumes, *L'Economie et la société françaises au second XXe siècle*, Paris, Armand Colin, 1998.

33. Landes, D.S., 'French Entrepreneurship and Industrial Growth in the Nineteenth Century', p. 45.

34. Landes, D.S., 'French Business and Businessmen in Social and Cultural Perspective', in Earle, E.M., ed., *Modern France: Problems of the Third and Fourth Republics*, New York, Russell & Russell, 1951, p. 336. See also 'Social Attitudes, Entrepreneurship and Economic Development', *Explorations in Entrepreneurial History*, Vol. 6, No. 4, May 1954, pp. 245–72.

35. Landes, 'French Entrepreneurship and Industrial Growth in the Nineteenth Century', p. 50.

36. Landes, 'French Entrepreneurship and Industrial Growth in the Nineteenth Century', p. 49.

37. See Dautry, *Notice sur la vie et les travaux de M. Eugène Schneider*, Paris, 1948, p. 6, cited in English translation in Ehrmann, *Organized Business in France*, p. 328.

38. Kindleberger, C., *Economic Growth in France and Britain*, pp. 88–112.

39. Kindleberger, C., *Economic Growth in France and Britain*, p. 114; p. 134.

40. Febvre, L., in Introduction to Morazé, C., *La France bourgeoise, XVIIIe–Xxe siècles*, Paris, Armand Colin, 1946, p. ix, cited in Landes, 'French Entrepreneurship and Industrial Growth in the Nineteenth Century', p. 61.

41. Kindleberger, C., *Economic Growth in France and Britain*, p. 111.
42. Cited in Smith, W.R., '"We can make the Ariane but we can't make washing machines"': the State and Industrial Performance in Post-war France', in Howorth, J. and Ross, G., eds, *Contemporary France*, Vol. 3, p. 181.
43. Fourastié illustrates this point with reference to the Hall of Mirrors at Versailles. Each mirror of 4 square metres cost 2,750 *livres* to produce in 1702, and took 30,000–35,000 man hours to make, whereas due to the technical progress achieved during the intervening centuries, the cost in 1950 would have been FF10,000, amounting to 160 wage hours. See Fourastié, J., 'Productivity and Economics', *Political Science Quarterly*, Vol. 66, No. 2, 1951, p. 222.
44. Kindleberger, C., *Economic Growth in France and Britain*, p. 181.
45. Vinen, R., *Bourgeois Politics in France*, pp. 265–6.
46. Berger, A., 'Sortir du malthusianisme économique', *Esprit*, January 1954, pp. 20–32, p. 24; Ehrmann, *Organized Business in France*, p. 322.
47. Berger, A., 'Sortir du malthusianisme économique', p. 24.
48. Fouillée, A., *Esquisse psychologique des peuples européens*, Paris, Alcan, 1903, p. 507, cited in Kindleberger, C., *Economic Growth in France and Britain*, p. 39.
49. Uncertainty avoidance was one of four dimensions measured in Hofstede's study. The others were 'power distance', tolerance of inequalities of power, in which France likewise achieved a high score; 'masculinity', the extent to which behaviour tends to be aggressive or materialistic, which may be interpreted as 'masculine'; and 'individualism', the degree to which individuals regard themselves as autonomous or influenced by community solidarity. Hofstede, G., *Culture's Consequences*, London, Sage, 1980.
50. Lewis, M., Fitzgerald, R. and Harvey, C., *The Growth of Nations: Culture, Competitiveness and the Problem of Globalization*, Bristol, Bristol Academic Press, 1996, p. 45.
51. Hall, P.A., *Governing the Economy*.
52. Verba, S., 'Comparative Political Culture', in Pye, L. and Verba, S., eds, *Political Culture and Political Development*, Princeton, Princeton University Press, 1965, p. 513, cited in Hall, P.A., *Governing the Economy*, p. 8.
53. Hall, P.A., *Governing the Economy*, p. 283.
54. Hayward, J., 'Institutional Inertia and Political Impetus in France and Britain', *European Journal of Political Research*, No. 4, pp. 341–59, cited in Hall, P.A., *Governing the Economy*, p. 8.
55. Zysman, J., *Governments, Markets and Growth: Financial Systems and the Politics of Industrial Change*, Ithaca, Cornell University Press, 1983. See too Zysman, J., *Political Strategies for Industrial Order: State, Market and Industry in France*, Berkeley, University of California Press, 1977.
56. Kuisel, R.F., *Capitalism and the State in Modern France*, p. 275.
57. Hayward, J., *The State and the Market Economy*, Brighton, Wheatsheaf, 1986, p. ix.
58. Berger, S., 'Liberalism Reborn: the New Liberal Synthesis in France'. That said, Loriaux argues that financial liberalisation under the left actually paved the way for greater government control over monetary policy. See Loriaux, M., *France after Hegemony: International Change and Financial Reform*, Ithaca, Cornell University Press, 1991.
59. Schmidt, V.A., *From State to Market? The Transformation of French Business and Government*, Cambridge, Cambridge University Press, 1996.
60. Hayward, J., '*Moins d'Etat* or *Mieux d'Etat*: the French Response to the Neo-Liberal Challenge', p. 33.

61. Suleiman, E.N., *Les Ressorts cachés de la réussite française*, Paris, Seuil, 1995, pp. 23, 213, 258.
62. Williams, K., 'From Shareholder Value to Present-day Capitalism', *Economy and Society*, Vol. 29, No. 1, 2000, pp. 1–12; Froud, J., Haslam, C., Johnal, S. and Williams, K., 'Shareholder Value and Financialization: Consultancy Promises, Management Moves', *Economy and Society*, Vol. 29, No. 1, 2000, pp. 80–110.
63. Charkham, J., *Keeping Good Company: a Study of Corporate Governance in Five Countries*, Oxford, Clarendon Press, 1994, p. 154.
64. Morin, F., 'A Transformation in the French Model of Shareholding and Management', *Economy and Society*, Vol. 29, No. 1, February 2000, pp. 31–53. See also Letreguilly, H., 'France', *International Financial Law Review*, Supplement on Corporate Governance, April 1998, pp. 18–22; Windolf, P., 'The Governance Structures of Large French Corporations: a Comparative Perspective, *Columbia Law Review Sloan Project*, 1998, pp. 705–35; Maclean, M., 'Towards a European Model? A Comparative Evaluation of Recent Corporate Governance Initiatives in France and the UK', *Journal of European Area Studies*, Vol. 7, No. 2, 1999, pp. 227–45
65. Cassis, Y., *Big Business: the European Experience in the Twentieth Century*, Oxford, Oxford University Press, 1997, p. 236.
66. Lannoo, K., 'A European Perspective on Corporate Governance', *Journal of Common Market Studies*, Vol. 37, No. 2, June 1999, pp. 269–94.
67. The directive on European works councils (94/95/EC) gave new impetus to the question of worker involvement. The 1995 White Paper on European Social Policy led to the setting up of a Group of Experts to consider European systems of worker participation, headed by former commissioner Viscount Davignon. The final report of the working party noted in particular 'the diversity of national models [...] which it is difficult to harmonise'. Tailored solutions were therefore recommended, as opposed to any uniformly imposed model. See European Commission, *European Systems of Worker Involvement Final Report*, Luxembourg, Office for Official Publications of the European Communities, 1997, p. 11. The issue of worker representation remains unresolved, however, and at the time of writing is under discussion in the European Council.
68. Cassis, Y., *Big Business*, p. 1.
69. DiMaggio, P. and Powell, W.W., 'The Iron Cage Revisited: Institutional Isomorphism and Collective Rationality in Organisational Fields', in Powell, W.W. and DiMaggio, P., eds, *The New Institutionalism in Organisational Analysis*, Chicago, University of Chicago Press, 1991, pp. 63–82.
70. This is emphasised by Lane, *Industry and Society in Europe: Stability and Change in Britain, Germany and France*, pp. 82–3. See also Evans, *Embedded Autonomy: States and Industrial Transformation*, Princeton, Princeton University Press, 1995.
71. This point is noted by Jones, G., 'Great Britain: Big Business, Management, and Competitiveness in Twentieth-Century Britain', in Chandler, A.D. *et al.*, eds, *Big Business and the Wealth of Nations*, p. 111.
72. Buck, T. and Tull, M., 'Anglo-American Contributions to Japanese and German Corporate Governance after World War II', *Business History*, Vol. 42, No. 2, 2000, pp. 119–40.
73. Cited in Djelic, M.-L., *Exporting the American Model: the Postwar Transformation of European Business*, Oxford, Oxford University Press, 1998, p. 281.

2 Liberation, Modernisation and the Fourth Republic

1. De Gaulle, C., *Salvation, 1944–1946*, translated by R. Howard, London, Weidenfeld and Nicolson, 1960, p. 100.
2. The Allied landings in Normandy in June 1944, involving US, British and Canadian forces, were on a larger scale than those in the Midi, which tend to be neglected in comparison. The Riviera landings commenced 15 August 1944 and lasted four to five days. A massive Allied force landed on a 100-mile front stretching from Nice to Marseilles.
3. Ehrmann, H.W., *Organized Business in France*, Princeton, Princeton University Press, 1957, p. 79.
4. Ehrmann, H.W., *Organized Business in France*, p. 95.
5. Vinen, R., *Bourgeois Politics in France 1945–1951*, Cambridge, Cambridge University Press, 1995, p. 267.
6. Weber, H., *Le Parti des patrons: le CNPF (1946–1986)*, Paris, Seuil, 1986, p. 68.
7. Pickles, D.M., *France Between the Republics*, London, 1946. Synchronic to the events concerned, it provides a perceptive analysis of the legacy of the Vichy regime.
8. See in particular *Le Salut, 1944–1946*, Plon, Paris, 1959.
9. Pickles, D., *France Between the Republics*, p. 125.
10. De Gaulle, C., *Salvation, 1944–1946*, p. 8.
11. Pickles, D., *France Between the Republics*, p. 123.
12. Pickles, D., *France Between the Republics*, p. 123.
13. Pickles, D., *France Between the Republics*, p. 125.
14. Pickles, D., *France Between the Republics*, p. 124.
15. Pickles, D., *France Between the Republics*, p. 125.
16. De Gaulle, C., *Salvation, 1944–1946*, p. 229.
17. Pickles, D., *France Between the Republics*, p. 125.
18. Clout, H., *The Geography of Post-war France, a Social and Economic Approach*, Pergamon, 1972, cited in Hough, J.R., *The French Economy*, Croom Helm, London, 1982, p. 110.
19. Pickles, D., *France Between the Republics*, p. 127.
20. De Gaulle, C., *Salvation, 1944–1946*, p. 231. See also 'The Human Casualties of War', *20th Century Day by Day*, London, Dorling Kindersley, 1999, p. 633.
21. Where October 1938 equalled 100, prices had risen to between 300 and 1,000 by autumn 1944, according to de Gaulle, C., *Salvation, 1944–1946*, p. 40.
22. A social insurance scheme predated the Second World War, complementary to private insurance. Introduced in 1930, the scheme covered reimbursement of sickness expenses, accidents at work and maternity benefits, and set up a fund for worker disability and retirement. Prior to this, in the 1890s, free medical care had been available for the poor and needy, as well as an insurance fund to cover injuries at work. The social protection of children was introduced in 1904, of the elderly in 1905, and of expectant mothers in 1913. See Catrice-Lorey, A., *Dynamique interne de la sécurité sociale*, Paris, 1980.
23. Cassis, Y., 'Financial Elites in Three European Centres: London, Paris, Berlin', in Jones, G., ed., *Banks and Money: International and Comparative Finance in History*, London, Cass, 1991, pp. 53–71.
24. Vinen, R., *Bourgeois Politics in France 1945–1951*.
25. Barsoux, J.-L. and Lawrence, P., *Management in France*, London, Cassell, 1990, pp. 118–19; Ehrmann, H., *Organized Business in France*, p. 210.

26. Bloch-Lainé, F., *Profession: fonctionnaire*, Paris, Seuil, 1976. It was not until the late 1980s that the image of French businessmen became more positive. See Servan-Schreiber, J.-L., *Le Métier de patron*, Paris, Fayard, 1990.

27. Forty years later, François Ceyrac, a former president of the CNPF (Conseil National du Patronat Français, renamed MEDEF, Mouvement des Entreprises de France, in 1998), offered a potential reply to the General's rhetorical question: 'I would have replied [...] "No, General, we were not in London. We are business leaders and, as such, are responsible for the industries and wage earners of this country. We were in our factories, with our workers, trying to prevent the military débâcle from turning into economic ruin and the direct stranglehold of the occupier on our resources. Numerous business leaders [...] slowed down production for the German war machine. Our *résistance professionnelle* was less visible than armed resistance, but it was no less efficient or dangerous." ' Cited in Weber, H., *Le Parti des patrons: le CNPF 1946–1986*, Paris, Seuil, 1986, p. 68.

28. Ehrmann, H., *Organized Business in France*, p. 94.

29. Guéhenno, January 1945, cited in Pickles, D., *France Between the Republics*, p. 139. Eric Duhamel observes that, 'Being French [between 1940 and 1944] was to find a place on the spectrum accommodating all shades between ideological collaboraton with the Nazis and Resistance born of rejection of the Armistice. [...] Resistance fighters included those who were *maréchaliste* and those who were not, those who were Pétainist, non-Gaullist and even those who moved from being *maréchaliste* to Giraudism and then Gaullism.' Duhamel, E., 'François Mitterrand between Vichy and the Resistance', in Maclean, M., ed., *The Mitterrand Years: Legacy and Evaluation*, Basingstoke, Macmillan Press – now Palgrave Macmillan, 1998, p. 227.

30. Jeanneney, J.N., *François de Wendel en République: l'argent et le pouvoir*, Paris, 1975.

31. Kolboom, I., *La Revanche des patrons: le patronat français face au front populaire*, Paris, 1986, cited in Vinen, R., *The Politics of French Business 1936–1945*, Cambridge, Cambridge University Press, 1991, p. 98.

32. Aron, R., *Histoire de l'épuration, 1. Le Monde des affaires, 1944–1953*, Paris, Fayard, 1974; Weber, H., *Le Parti des patrons: le CNPF (1946–1986)*, p. 68.

33. Aron, R., *Histoire de l'épuration, 1. Le Monde des affaires, 1944–1953*, p. 234.

34. See in this regard Turkle, S.R., 'Symbol and Festival in the French Student Uprising (May–June 1968)', in Falk Moore, S. and Myerhoff, B., eds, *Symbol and Politics in Communal Ideology*, Ithaca, Cornell University Press, 1975. I am grateful to Dr Margaret Taylor for drawing my attention to this.

35. Ehrmann, H., *Organized Business in France*, p. 104.

36. Vinen, R., *Bourgeois Politics in France 1945–1951*, p. 1.

37. Ehrmann, H., *Organized Business in France*, p. 109.

38. De Gaulle, C., *Salvation, 1944–1946*, p. 109. If spontaneous, 'popular' tribunals are included in the reckoning, as many as 10,000 may have been executed. See Goubert, P., *The Course of French History*, translated by M. Utlee, London, Routledge, 1991, p. 300.

39. De Gaulle, C., *Salvation, 1944–1946*, p. 96.

40. Kuisel, R.F., *Capitalism and the State in Modern France*, p. 202.

41. Cited in Bizaguet, A., *Le Secteur public et les privatisations*, Paris, PUF, 1988, p. 22.

42. Kuisel, R.F., *Capitalism and the State in Modern France*, p. 202.

43. Kuisel, R.F., *Capitalism and the State in Modern France*, p. 203.

44. De Gaulle, C., *Salvation, 1944–1946*, p. 98.

240   *Notes*

45. Choinel, A. and Rouyer, G., *Le Système bancaire français*, 5th ed., Paris, PUF, 1996, p. 8. The same act classified French banks as three types: deposit banks, *banques d'affaires*, and *banques de crédit à long et moyen terme*, medium or long-term credit banks. Restrictions were imposed on what each type could or could not do.
46. De Gaulle, C., *Salvation, 1944–1946*, p. 98.
47. 1998 study by Korn Ferry International. See Basini, B., 'Patronat: les parrains ne sont plus ce qu'ils étaient', *Le Nouvel Economiste*, 11 December 1998, p. 49.
48. Malraux, A., *Les Chênes qu'on abat*, Paris, Gallimard, 1971, p. 29. This interview with de Gaulle was conducted in December 1969. It is especially penetrating, partly because Malraux was a long-standing friend and ally of the general's, and partly because, released from the burdens of office, and in the twilight of his life, de Gaulle was able to look back on his achievements with lucidity and objectivity.
49. Henri Weber recounts a meeting in 1961 between Pierre Massé, Commissaire Général du Plan, and de Gaulle, the latter in the process of preparing a speech. On reading de Gaulle's words, 'the State must direct the economy', Massé is reported to have suggested replacing 'direct' (*diriger*) with 'orient' (*orienter*), to which de Gaulle allegedly retorted: 'It's [direct] or nothing', and then proposed, after reflection, to use the verb 'conduct' (*conduire*). Cited in Weber, H., *Le Parti des patrons: le CNPF 1946–1986*, p. 125.
50. De Gaulle, C., *Salvation, 1944–1946*, p. 100.
51. De Gaulle, C., *Mémoirs d'Espoir*, Vol. 1, *Le Renouveau*, Paris, Plon, 1980, cited in Fysh, P., 'Gaullism and Liberalism', in Flood, C. and Bell, L., eds, *Political ideologies in Contemporary France*, London, Pinter, 1997.
52. De Gaulle, C., *The Call to Honour 1940–1942*, translated by J. Griffin, Collins, London, 1955, p. 9.
53. De Gaulle, C., *The Call to Honour 1940–1942*, p. 14.
54. De Gaulle, C., *The Call to Honour 1940–1942*, p. 9.
55. De Gaulle, C., *Salvation, 1944–1946*, p. 25.
56. Kuisel, R.F., *Capitalism and the State in Modern France*, pp. 279–80.
57. Cited in Ehrmann, H., *Organized Business in France*, p. 284.
58. See Barsoux, J.-L. and Lawrence, P., *Management in France*, p. 144, or Kindleberger, C.P., *Economic Growth in France and Britain 1851–1950*, p. 110.
59. Goubert, P., *The Course of French History*, p. 300.
60. Berstein, S., *The Republic of de Gaulle 1958–1969*, translated by P. Morris, Cambridge, Cambridge University Press/Editions de la Maison des Sciences de l'Homme, 1993, p. 102.
61. Berstein, S., *The Republic of de Gaulle 1958–1969*, p. 102.
62. France withdrew from Indochina in 1954, and Tunisia and Morocco were liberated in 1956. The situation was more complicated in Algeria, where conflict dragged on until April 1962, when under de Gaulle's presidency Algeria was accorded independence.
63. Berstein, S., *The Republic of de Gaulle 1958–1969*, p. 107.
64. Berstein, S., *The Republic of de Gaulle 1958–1969*, pp. 101–3.
65. The minimum wage was named the SMIG in 1950.
66. Eck, J.-F., *Histoire de l'économie française depuis 1945*, 2nd edition, Paris, Armand Colin, 1988, p. 21.
67. Goubert, P., *The Course of French History*, p. 300.
68. Cohen, E., 'France: National Champions in Search of a Mission', in Hayward, J., ed., *Industrial Enterprise and European Integration: from National to International Champions in Western Europe*, Oxford, Oxford University Press, 1995, pp. 26–7.

69. Clough, S.B. *et al.*, eds, *Economic History of Europe: Twentieth Century*, New York and London, Harper, 1968, p. 328.
70. Clough, S.B. *et al.*, eds, *Economic History of Europe: Twentieth Century*, p. 329.
71. Committee of European Economic Cooperation, *General Report*, vol. 1, London, HMSO, 1947, pp. 3–8.
72. Lieberman, S., *The Growth of European Mixed Economies 1945–1970*, New York, Wiley, 1977, p. 7.
73. Lynch, F., *France and the International Economy from Vichy to the Treaty of Rome*, London, Routledge, 1997, p. 55.
74. Lynch, F., *France and the International Economy*, p. 109.
75. Lynch, F., *France and the International Economy*, p. 68.
76. Lynch, F., *France and the International Economy*, p. 79.
77. Under the Marshall Plan, the US government provided finance for increased imports on the condition that bilateral trade agreements were abolished. The Organisation for European Economic Cooperation was then established, with rules and targets for the gradual freeing of international trade from quotas and similar discriminatory impediments. See Postan, M.M., *An Economic History of Western Europe 1945–1964*, London, Methuen, 1967, p. 98.
78. Monnet, J., *Mémoires*, Paris, Fayard, 1976, pp. 275–6.
79. Quotations extracted from *Rapport général sur le Premier Plan de Modernisation et d'équipement*, Paris, Commissariat général du Plan de modernisation et d'équipement, 1947, pp. 9–34, translated by and cited in Clough, S.B. *et al.*, *Economic History of Europe*, pp. 345–54.
80. Monnet, J., *Mémoires*, p. 278.
81. Henri Guillaume, cited in *Cinquante ans de planification à la française*, Paris, Commissariat Général du Plan, 1998, p. 7.
82. Letter to the author from Rémi Lallement, adviser, Commissariat Général du Plan, December 1999.
83. Hall, P.A., *Governing the Economy*, p. 141.
84. Monnet, J., *Mémoires*, cited in *Cinquante ans de planification à la française*, p. 6.
85. Quotations extracted from *Rapport général sur le Premier Plan de Modernisation et d'équipement*, cited in Clough, S.B. *et al.*, *Economic History of Europe*, pp. 345–54.
86. Lynch, F., *France and the International Economy*, p. 99.
87. Hough, J.R., *The French Economy*, p. 111.
88. Hall, P.A., *Governing the Economy*, p. 143.
89. Lieberman, S., *The Growth of European Mixed Economies 1945–1970*, p. 13.
90. Lieberman, S., *The Growth of European Mixed Economies 1945–1970*, p. 186.
91. Maddison, A., *The World Economy: a Millennial Perspective*, Paris, OECD, 2001, p. 276.
92. Postan, M.M., *An Economic History of Western Europe 1945–1964*, p. 91.
93. Djelic, M.-L., *Exporting the American Model: the Postwar Transformation of European Business*, Oxford, Oxford University Press, 1998, p. 137.
94. Djelic, M.-L., *Exporting the American Model*, p. 141.
95. Lynch, F., *France and the International Economy*, p. 98.
96. Caron, F., *An Economic History of Modern France*, translated by B. Bray, London, Methuen, 1979, p. 223.
97. Djelic, M.-L., *Exporting the American Model*, pp. 94–103.
98. Djelic, M.-L., *Exporting the American Model*, p. 206.
99. De Gaulle, C., *Salvation, 1944–1946*, p. 98.

3   The 'Golden Age' of the Gaullist Era

1. De Gaulle, C., *War Memoirs: Salvation, 1944–1946*, translated by R. Howard, London, Weidenfeld and Nicolson, 1960, p. 120.
2. Lévy-Leboyer, M., 'La grande entreprise française: un modèle français?', in Lévy-Leboyer, M., and Casanova, J.-C., *Entre l'Etat et le marché: l'économie française des années 1880 à nos jours*, Paris, 1991.
3. Hough, J.R., *The French Economy*, London, Croom Helm, 1982.
4. Vinen, R., *France, 1934–1970*, Basingstoke, Macmillan Press – now Palgrave Macmillan, 1996, p. 111.
5. Fourastié, J., *Les Trente glorieuses ou la révolution invisible*, Paris, Fayard, 1979, p. 261.
6. Cassis, Y., *Big Business: the European Experience in the Twentieth Century*, Oxford, Oxford University Press, 1997, p. 236.
7. Berstein, S., *The Republic of de Gaulle 1958–1969*, translated by P. Morris, Cambridge, CUP/Editions de la Maison des sciences de l'homme, 1993, p. 211.
8. Fourastié, J., *Les Trente glorieuses ou la révolution invisible*, p. 285.
9. Fourastié, J., *Les Trente glorieuses ou la révolution invisible*, p. 285.
10. Crozier, M., ed., 'L'Administration face aux problèmes du changement', special issue of *Sociologie du Travail*, 1966; and *La Société bloquée*, Paris, Seuil, 1970.
11. Servan-Schreiber, J.-J., *Le Défi américain*, Paris, Denoël, 1967.
12. Vinen, R., *France, 1934–1970*, p. 111.
13. See Vinen, R., *Bourgeois Politics in France*, Cambridge, Cambridge University Press, 1995, pp. 220–1.
14. Cited in Berstein, S., *The Republic of de Gaulle 1958–1969*, p. 106.
15. Berger, S., 'Liberalism Reborn: the New Liberal Synthesis in France', in Howorth, J. and Ross, G., eds, *Contemporary France: a Review of Interdisciplinary Studies*, Vol. 1, London, Pinter, 1987, pp. 84–110.
16. Here, Kuisel borrows from Jean Bouvier. Kuisel, R.F., 'The France We Have Lost: Social, Economic and Cultural Discontinuities', in Flynn, G., ed., *Remaking the Hexagon: the New France in the New Europe*, Oxford, Westview Press, 1995, p. 39.
17. Rueff, J., *Combats pour l'ordre financier*, Paris, Plon, 1972.
18. Eck, J.-F., *Histoire de l'économie française depuis 1945*, 2nd edition, Paris, Armand Colin, 1990, p. 169.
19. Cohen, E., 'France: National Champions in Search of a Mission', in Hayward, J., ed., *Industrial Enterprise and European Integration: from National to International Champions in Western Europe*, Oxford, Oxford University Press, 1995, pp. 26–7.
20. De Gaulle was encouraged in this view by his economic adviser Jacques Rueff, who exhorts in his memoirs, 'Exact financial order or accept slavery!' Rueff, J., *Combats pour l'ordre financier*, p. 16.
21. For a résumé of this press conference, see Berstein, S., *The Republic of de Gaulle 1958–1969*, p. 166.
22. For detailed accounts of individual plans, see Hall, P.A., *Governing the Economy: the Politics of State Intervention in Britain and France*, Cambridge, Polity Press, 1986, chapter 7; Hough, J.R., *The French Economy*, pp. 111–17; or Baleste, M., *L'Economie française*, 11th edition, Paris, Masson, 1991, pp. 22–4.
23. Hough, J.R., *The French Economy*, p. 110.
24. Hough, J.R., *The French Economy*, p. 112.
25. The numbers of those completing the *baccalauréat* swelled from 32,362 in 1950 to 139,541 in 1970. Berstein, S., *The Republic of de Gaulle 1958–1969*, p. 127.

26. Hall, P.A., *Governing the Economy*, p. 143.
27. Hall, P.A., *Governing the Economy*, p. 143.
28. The population swelled from 47 million to 50 million from 1962 to 1969, although from 1964 onwards the fertility rate again began to decline.
29. Berstein examines the case for the 'embourgeoisement' of the working classes. According to opinion polls of the day, many believed that this was happening. Mallet argues that, on the contrary, the working class was expanding through the absorption of minor civil servants, employees and artisans, giving rise to a new working class elite of industrial wage-earners whose demands were no longer quantitative (e.g. higher wages, shorter working hours) but qualitative (e.g. status in the firm). Mallet, S., *La Nouvelle Class ouvrière*, Paris, Seuil, 1963, cited in Berstein, S., *The Republic of de Gaulle 1958–1969*, p. 137.
30. Cited in *Cinquante ans de planification à la française*, p. 17.
31. Radio broadcast, 8 May 1961.
32. Cited in Baleste, M., *L'Economie française*, p. 23.
33. On 19 December 1965, de Gaulle polled 54.5 per cent of the vote, compared to 45.5 per cent for Mitterrand. The latter emerged from defeat as a credible leader of the left-wing opposition to de Gaulle.
34. Hough, J.R., *The French Economy*, p. 116.
35. Cited in Baleste, M., *L'Economie française*, p. 23.
36. Carré, J.-J. *et al.*, *French Economic Growth*, translated by J.P. Hatfield, London, Oxford University Press, 1976, p. 274. Here, Carré *et al.* borrow from the ideas of A. Cotta, presented in 'La Croissance de l'économie française', *Analyse et prévision*, Vol. 11, No. 1.2, July–August 1966.
37. Hough, J.R., *The French Economy*, p. 126.
38. Hall, P.A., *Governing the Economy*, p. 163.
39. Eck, J.-F., *Histoire de l'économie française depuis 1945*, p. 32.
40. Cited in Hough, J.R., *The French Economy*, p. 123.
41. Fourastié, J., *Les Trente glorieuses ou la révolution invisible*, p. 284.
42. This threefold strategy was made explicit in the *Livre Blanc sur la Défense Nationale* published in 1972, and popularised in the notion of three concentric circles devised by General Poirier, explained in *Des Stratégies nucléaires*, Paris, Hachette, 1977. Howorth, J., 'France and the Defence of Europe: Redefining Continental Security', in Maclean, M. and Howorth, J., eds, *Europeans on Europe: Transnational Visions of a New Continent*, Basingstoke, Macmillan Press – now Palgrave Macmillan, 1992, p. 77.
43. Berstein, S., *The Republic of de Gaulle 1958–1969*, p. 168.
44. Berstein, S., *The Republic of de Gaulle 1958–1969*, p. 164.
45. Berstein, S., *The Republic of de Gaulle 1958–1969*, p. 165.
46. De Gaulle's announcement in January 1963 is quoted in Berstein, S., *The Republic of de Gaulle 1958–1969*, p. 173: 'It may be that one day England will manage the transformation that would enable it to become a member of the European Community, without restriction and without hesitation and in preference to anything else.... It may also be the case that England is not yet ready for such a change and this is certainly what appears to emerge from the oh so lengthy conversations in Brussels.'
47. Mayall, quoted in Tsoukalis, L., *The New European Economy Revisited*, Oxford, Oxford University Press, 1997, p. 22.
48. Tsoukalis, L., *The New European Economy Revisited*.

49. Berger, S., 'Lame Ducks and National Champions: Industrial Policy in the Fifth Republic', in Andrews, W.G. and Hoffmann, S., eds, *The Fifth Republic at Twenty*, Albany, State University of New York Press, 1981, p. 295.
50. On this theme see Balassa, B., 'The French Economy under the Fifth Republic, 1958–1978', in Andrews, W.G. and Hoffmann, S., eds, *The Fifth Republic at Twenty*, pp. 204–25.
51. Balassa, B. 'The French Economy under the Fifth Republic, 1958–1978', p. 207.
52. Berger, S., 'Lame Ducks and National Champions: Industrial Policy in the Fifth Republic', p. 295.
53. BRP founding charter.
54. Smith, J.G., *The Origins and Early Development of the Heavy Chemical Industry in France*, Oxford, Clarendon Press, 1979.
55. Berstein, S., *The Republic of de Gaulle 1958–1969*, p. 109.
56. As Postan notes, 'The influence of private banks in industrial and commercial enterprises was not [...] rooted in their ownership of large pockets of shares (*paquets de contrôle*) but in personal links of cross-ownership and of multiple directorates. The links created close associations between certain banks and industrial enterprises, the control of which was shared by largely the same groups of men.' See Postan, M.M., *An Economic History of Western Europe 1945–1954*, London, Methuen, 1967, p. 368.
57. Carré, J-J. *et al.*, *French Economic Growth*, p. 167.
58. See Schmidt, V., *From State to Market: the Transformation of French Business and Government*, Cambridge, Cambridge University Press, 1996, pp. 79–80.
59. Schmidt, V., *From State to Market*, p. 206.
60. Berger, S., 'Lame Ducks and National Champions: Industrial Policy in the Fifth Republic'.
61. Carré, J-J. *et al.*, *French Economic Growth*, pp. 173–5.
62. De Monton, J. and Harvard Business School, 'Carrefour, S.A.', Harvard Business School case study no. 273–099, 1974.
63. French pioneers in distribution, Marcel Fournier or Jacques and Denis Defforey, attended the seminars given in Dayton, Ohio in the early 1960s by Bernard Trujillo, the American producer of NCR cash registers, who preached 'no parking, no business'. See Parodi, M. *et al.*, *L'Economie et la société françaises au second XXe siècle*, Vol. 2, *Les Mutations sectorielles*, Paris, Armand Colin, 1998, p. 229.
64. Baleste, M., *L'Economie française*, pp. 249–52.
65. *L'Entreprise*, 15 September 1972, p. 75, cited in de Monton, J. and Harvard Business School, 'Carrefour, S.A.', p. 3.
66. De Monton, J. and Harvard Business School, 'Carrefour, S.A.', p. 2.
67. Cited in Baleste, M., *L'Economie française*, p. 250.
68. De Monton, J. and Harvard Business School, 'Carrefour, S.A.', p. 3.
69. Amann, P.H., *The Corncribs of Buzet: Modernizing Agriculture in the French Southwest*, Princeton, Princeton University Press, 1990, p. 267.
70. Amann, P.H., *The Corncribs of Buzet*, p. 229.
71. On the relative decline of French agriculture, see Parodi, M., *L'Economie et la société française de 1945 à 1970*, Paris, Armand Colin, 1971, pp. 99–121.
72. Atlas, C. and Linotte, D., *Le Remembrement rural*, Paris, Librairies techniques, 1980.
73. Carré, J-J. *et al.*, *French Economic Growth*, p. 173.
74. Amann, P.H., *The Corncribs of Buzet*, p. 231.
75. Carré, J-J. *et al.*, *French Economic Growth*, p. 173.
76. Figures cited in Caron, F., *An Economic History of Modern France*, p. 222.

77. Hough, J.R., *The French Economy*, p. 66.
78. Caron, F., *An Economic History of Modern France*, p. 223.
79. Berger, S., 'Lame Ducks and National Champions: Industrial Policy in the Fifth Republic', p. 296.
80. Carré, J-J. *et al.*, *French Economic Growth*, pp. 165–6. Percentages for Germany, the US and Belgium refer to 1961, 1963 and 1963 respectively.
81. Cassis, Y., *Big Business*, p. 231. See too Trouille, J.-M. and Uterwedde, H., 'Franco-German Relations and Globalisation', *Modern and Contemporary France*, Vol. 9, No. 3, August 2001, pp. 339–53, which contains a useful chart documenting Franco-German mergers in the period 1989–2000.
82. Carré, J-J. *et al.*, *French Economic Growth*, p. 169.
83. Carré, J-J. *et al.*, *French Economic Growth*, p. 176.
84. Vinen, R., *France, 1934–1970*, p. 126.
85. De Gaulle, C., *Salvation, 1944–1946*, p. 174.
86. De Gaulle stressed this point to President Truman: 'My Government and I must therefore take the necessary measures to prevent the German threat from ever reappearing. Our intention, of course, is not to drive the German people to despair. On the contrary, we want the people to live, to flourish, and even to draw closer to us. But we must have guarantees.' De Gaulle, C., *Salvation, 1944–1946*, p. 208.
87. De Gaulle, C., *Salvation, 1944–1946*, p. 204.
88. Berstein, S., *The Republic of de Gaulle 1958–1969*, p. 177.
89. Zettelmeier, W., 'Franco-German University Co-operation: the Position Today and Prospects within a European Higher Educational System', in Maclean, M. and Trouille, J.-M., eds, *France, Germany and Britain: Partners in a Changing World*, Basingstoke, Palgrave – now Palgrave Macmillan, 2001, pp. 151–66.
90. Berstein, S., *The Republic of de Gaulle 1958–1969*, p. 176.
91. On the development of the Franco-German partnership since 1945, see Maclean, M. and Trouille, J.-M., 'Introduction: France, Germany and Britain: Partners in a Changing World', in Maclean, M. and Trouille, J.-M., eds, *France, Germany and Britain*, pp. 1–17.
92. Webber, D., ed., *The Franco-German Relationship in the European Union*, London, Routledge, 1999.
93. The Elysée Treaty provided for quarterly meetings between finance ministers, while ministers of defence, youth exchanges and education met every two months.
94. Trouille, J.-M., 'Re-defining the Franco-German Relationship: Divergences and Perspectives', paper presented at the annual conference of the Association for the Study of Modern and Contemporary France, Cardiff, September 1999.
95. This conversation reputedly took place in 1984. Attali, J., *Verbatim I 1981–1986*, Paris, Fayard, 1993, p. 642, cited in Webber, D., ed., *The Franco-German Relationship in the European Union*, p. 12.
96. On French and German involvement in EMU negotiations, see Howarth, D.J., *The French Road to European Monetary Union*, Palgrave – now Palgrave Macmillan, Basingstoke, 2001, and Dyson, K. and Featherstone, K., *The Road to Maastricht: Negotiating Economic and Monetary Union*, Oxford, Oxford University Press, 1999.
97. Dyson, K. and Featherstone, K., 'EMU and Presidential Leadership under François Mitterrand', in Maclean, M., ed., *The Mitterrand Years: Legacy and Evaluation*, Macmillan Press – now Palgrave Macmillan, Basingstoke, 1998, pp. 89–111.

98. Wallace, H., 'Bilateral, Trilateral and Multilateral Negotiations in the European Community', in Martin, R. and Bray, C., eds, *Britain, France and Germany: Partners and Rivals in Western Europe*, Aldershot, Gower, 1986, p. 162. Webber, D., ed., *The Franco-German Relationship in the European Union*, p. 12.
99. Hough, J.R., *The French Economy*, p. 197.
100. Berstein, S., *The Republic of de Gaulle 1958–1969*, p. 171.
101. Pivot, C., 'Costs and Benefits of the Common Agricultural Policy for France', in Dreyfus, F.-G. *et al.*, eds, *France and EC Membership Evaluated*, London, Pinter, 1993, p. 59.
102. Vinen, R., *France, 1934–1970*, p. 112.
103. The East European candidate nations have large agrarian populations. Those of the Czech Republic and Hungary represented 7 and 8 per cent respectively of the total population in 1996. The Bulgarian and Romanian agrarian populations were estimated at 14 and 40 per cent respectively.
104. Pivot, C., 'Costs and Benefits of the Common Agricultural Policy for France', p. 60.
105. Cole, A., *Franco-German Relations: Political Dynamics of the European Union*, Harlow, Pearson, 2001, p. 140.
106. Hough, J.R., *The French Economy*, p. 69.
107. Consumers in the European Community Group, *Eurospeak Explained*, London, CECG, 1990.
108. The agricultural support system resulted in higher prices for consumers since when Community market prices fell 5–7 per cent below world prices, this triggered support buying as well as levies on imports from outside the EEC to guarantee parity with Community prices. Hough, J.R., *The French Economy*, p. 69.
109. Tsoukalis, L., *The New European Economy: the Politics and Economics of Integration*, 2nd edition, Oxford, Oxford University Press, 1993, p. 33.
110. Crozier, M., cited in Barsoux, J.-L. and Lawrence, P., *Management in France*, London, Cassell, 1990, p. 83.
111. Berstein, S., *The Republic of de Gaulle 1958–1969*, p. 190.
112. Berstein, S., *The Republic of de Gaulle 1958–1969*, p. 216.
113. Berstein makes this point, *The Republic of de Gaulle 1958–1969*, p. 183.
114. Malraux, A., *Les Chênes qu'on abat*, Paris, Gallimard, 1971, p. 28.
115. Lauber, V., 'The Gaullist Model of Economic Modernization', in Andrews, W.G. and Hoffmann, S., eds, *The Fifth Republic at Twenty*, p. 229.
116. Malraux, A., *Les Chênes qu'on abat*, p. 30.
117. See 'Dessine-moi un salarié capitaliste', *L'Expansion*, 20 January–3 February 2000, pp. 32–3; '1 million de golden salariés dans les groupes français', *L'Expansion*, 20 January–3 February 2000, pp. 34–5.
118. Lyon Business School, Lyon, July 1985.
119. Goubert, P., *The Course of French History*, translated by Utlee, M., London, Routledge and Franklin Watts, 1991, p. 312.

4 The Giscard Years: from Prosperity to Deepening Crisis

1. Giscard d'Estaing, V., *L'Etat de la France*, Paris, Fayard, 1981, p. 3.
2. The nine changes included reduced income inequality, equal opportunities and equal rights, better working conditions, better transport and hospitals. Frears, J.R., *France in the Giscard Presidency*, London, George Allen & Unwin, 1981, pp. 14–15.

3. Cohen, S.S., 'Twenty Years of the Gaullist Economy', in Hoffmann, S. and Andrews, W.G., eds, *The Fifth Republic at Twenty*, Albany, State University of New York Press, 1981, p. 242.

4. British oil imports were cut by 15 per cent in October 1973. Oil began to flow from the Argyll field in the North Sea on 18 June 1975.

5. PS, *Propositions pour l'actualisation du Programme commun de gouvernement de la gauche*, Paris, Flammarion, 1978, p. 63.

6. The eighth plan, published in 1979, explained the omission of quantitative targets by stating: 'This technique has been rendered obsolete by the fluctuations of a new era and the growing uncertainties that result from them.' Commissariat Général du Plan: cited in Hall, P., *Governing the Economy: the Politics of State Intervention in Britain and France*, Cambridge, Polity Press, 1986, p. 186.

7. Peyrefitte, A., *Le Mal français*, Paris, Plon, 1976. Other key works of the period which signalled the dangers of sliding into uncompetitiveness, particularly in manufacturing industry, include Stoffaes, C., *La Grande Menace industrielle*, Paris, Calmann-Lévy, 1978, and Cotta, A., *La France et l'impératif mondial*, Paris, PUF, 1978.

8. Peyrefitte, A., *Le Mal français*, p. viii. This view is shared by Sir Antony Wrigley, who attributes the growth of the English economy in the seventeenth and eighteenth centuries to the existence of cheap thermal energy in the form of coal. Wrigley, E.A., 'The Divergence of England: the Growth of the English Economy in the Seventeenth and Eighteenth Centuries', *Transactions of the Royal Historical Society*, Cambridge, Cambridge University Press, 2000, pp. 117–41.

9. This is confirmed by the extraordinary performance of the energy sector between 1952 and 1972, when it outperformed all other sectors, being the only one to show an accelerated increase in productivity in both capital and labour. See Caron, F., *An Economic History of Modern France*, translated by B. Bray, Columbia, Columbia University Press, 1979, p. 229.

10. Caron, F., *An Economic History of Modern France*, p. 227.

11. Caron, F., *An Economic History of Modern France*, p. 228.

12. The elements of the so-called 'French system' included graphite, metallic natural uranium and gas cooling.

13. Cited in Derogy, J. and Pontaut, J.-M., *Investigation, passion: enquête sur 30 ans d'affaires*, Paris, Fayard, 1993, p. 415. See Derogy and Pontaut for an amusing account of the sniffer plane scandal, pp. 409–26.

14. Derogy, J. and Pontaut, J.-M., *Investigation, passion: enquête sur 30 ans d'affaires*, p. 417.

15. Derogy, J. and Pontaut, J.-M., *Investigation, passion: enquête sur 30 ans d'affaires*, p. 426.

16. Smith, W.R., '"We can make the Ariane, but we can't make washing machines": the state and industrial performance in post-war France', in Howorth, J. and Ross, G., eds, *Contemporary France: a Review of Interdisciplinary Studies*, Vol. 3, London, Pinter, 1989, p. 190.

17. See 'Nombre record de faillites', *L'Année économique et sociale: 1975, 'la crise'*, *Le Monde Dossiers et Documents Supplément*, January 1976, p. 9.

18. Cited in 'L'année noire', *L'Année économique et sociale: 1975, 'la crise'*, p. 14.

19. Hall, P.A., *Governing the Economy*, p. 184.

20. Fonteneau, A. and Muet, P.-A., *La Gauche face à la crise*, Paris, Presses de la Fondation nationale des sciences politiques, 1985, p. 90.

21. Weber, H., *Le Parti des patrons (1946–1986)*, Paris, L'Epreuve des Faits/Seuil, 1986, p. 228.

22. See 'Les plus touchés en France', *L'Année économique et sociale: 1975, 'la crise'*, p. 14.
23. Thevenot, L., 'Les catégories sociales en 1975', *Economie et statistique*, 91, July–August 1977, p. 47, cited in Cohen, S.S., 'Twenty Years of the Gaullist Economy', in Hoffmann, S. and Andrews, W.G., eds, *The Fifth Republic at Twenty*, note 25, p. 250.
24. Balassa estimates that the quadrupling of oil prices in the first oil crisis amounted to a 'tax' of 3 per cent on domestic incomes and expenditure in France, involving an equivalent income transfer to the oil states. Balassa, B., 'The French Economy under the Fifth Republic, 1958–1978', in Hoffmann, S. and Andrews, W.G., eds, *The Fifth Republic at Twenty*, p. 212. Amouyel calculates the first oil crisis to have cost approximately 4 per cent of GDP. Amouyel, P., 'L'Avenir énergetique de la France', *Project*, 1979, pp. 844–55, cited in Hall, P.A., *Governing the Economy*, p. 184.
25. 'La plus forte récession industrielle depuis quarante ans', *L'Année économique et sociale: 1975, 'la crise'*, p. 7.
26. 'La plus forte récession industrielle depuis quarante ans', *L'Année économique et sociale: 1975, 'la crise'*, p. 7.
27. 'Automobile: la chute des "géants américains"', *L'Année économique et sociale: 1975, 'la crise'*, p. 10.
28. Fonteneau, A. and Muet, P.-A., *La Gauche face à la crise*, p. 62. Fonteneau and Muet draw on the theory of Eckstein, O., *The Great Recession*, North-Holland, 1979.
29. See 'Epargne: une abondance paradoxale', *L'Année économique et sociale: 1975, 'la crise'*, p. 13.
30. Smith, W.R., '"We can make the Ariane, but we can't make washing machines"': the state and industrial performance in post-war France', p. 190.
31. Hall, P.A., *Governing the Economy*, p. 183.
32. Hall, P.A., *Governing the Economy*, p. 184.
33. Tsoukalis, L., *The New European Economy Revisited*, Oxford, Oxford University Press, 1997.
34. Boyer, R., 'The Current Economic Crisis: its Dynamics and its Implications for France', in Ross, G., Hoffmann, S., and Malzacher, S., eds, *The Mitterrand Experiment*, New York, Oxford University Press, 1987, pp. 34–5.
35. The sixth plan introduced an early warning system of *clignotants* designed to alert decision-makers should a vital economic indicator veer off course.
36. This point is made by Diana Green in 'The Seventh Plan – the Demise of French Planning', *West European Politics*, February 1978.
37. The eighth plan, designed to cover the period 1981–85, was rejected by the incoming socialist administration, under whom planning was reduced essentially to an information-gathering exercise.
38. Fonteneau, A. and Muet, P.-A., *La Gauche face à la crise*, p. 50.
39. Szarka, J., *Business in France: an Introduction to the Economic and Social Context*, London, Pitman, 1992, p. 173.
40. Weber, H., *Le Parti des patrons (1946–1986)*, p. 330.
41. Economic Intelligence Unit (EIU), *Country Report: France*, October 2000, p. 8.
42. For a full breakdown of the plans, see Fonteneau, A. and Muet, P.-A., *La Gauche face à la crise*, p. 132.
43. This practice of combining a number of government posts had been widely used during the Third and Fourth Republics. General de Gaulle himself had assumed the joint responsibilities of president of the Council and head of national defence in 1958, but the practice had since fallen into disuse. Laurens, A., 'Le changement dans la stabilité', *Le Monde*, 29–30 August 1976, p. 2.

44. See 'M. Barre n'obtient du RPR qu'une confiance réservée au lieu d'un soutien sans équivoque', *Le Monde*, 30 April 1977, p. 6.
45. Economist Intelligence Unit, *Country Profile: France*, EIU, London, 2001, p. 9.
46. Chirac's protégé, Alain Juppé, took over as RPR head in 1994, followed by Philippe Séguin in 1997 and Michèle Alliot-Marie in 1999. In the municipal elections of March 2001, the right lost the Paris *mairie* to the socialists.
47. Cited in Mathieu, G., 'Le chevalier de l'austérité', *Le Monde*, 27 August 1976, p. 1.
48. Mathieu, G., 'Le chevalier de l'austérité', p. 1.
49. Hall, P.A., *Governing the Economy*, p. 188.
50. Income tax was increased by 4 per cent for annual incomes between FF4,500 and FF20,000. For those earning more than FF20,000, income tax was raised by 8 per cent. If a five-year government bond paying 6.5 per cent interest per year was purchased, taxpayers in the lower bracket could forgo the rise while those in the higher bracket need only pay half.
51. Vernholes, A., 'Le Plan Barre soumis au conseil des ministres', *Le Monde*, 24 September 1976, p. 1.
52. At 20 per cent, France already had the highest basic VAT rate in the European Community, compared to a normal rate of 11 per cent in West Germany, 18 per cent in Belgium, 18 per cent in the Netherlands, 10 per cent in Luxembourg, 12 per cent in Italy and 8 per cent in Britain.
53. Dumont, J.-H., and Labarde, P., 'Les syndicats demandent à M. Barre une réduction des inégalités sociales et le patronat une relance de l'investissement', *Le Monde*, 7 September 1976, p. 1.
54. See 'Vers une action commune, CGT, CFDT, FEN', *Le Monde*, 23 September 1976, p. 3; Mathieu, G. and Fabra, P., 'Un entretien avec M. Raymond Barre', *Le Monde*, 5 October 1976, p. 1.
55. Barrillon, R., 'Le malaise politique, économique et social', *Le Monde*, 29 April 1977, p. 1; 'Grèves: malgré les menaces', *Le Nouvel Observateur*, 31 January 1977, p. 20.
56. Laurent Fabius, also a professor of economics at the Ecole Normale Supérieure, sums up his objections to the plan in 'Ce qui manque au plan Barre', *Le Nouvel Observateur*, 31 January 1977, p. 19.
57. Dumont, J.-P., 'Le refus des cadres', *Le Monde*, 28 September 1976, p. 1.
58. 'La CGC et la CFTC manifestent leur inquiétude', *Le Monde*, 23 November 1976, p. 40.
59. Dumont, J.-P., and Labarde, P., 'M. Barre reçoit les partenaires sociaux', *Le Monde*, 7 September 1976, pp. 1–2.
60. See 'M. Barre confirme qu'il ne relancera pas l'activité', *Le Monde*, 8 January 1977, p. 26.
61. Cited in 'Grèves: malgré les menaces', *Le Nouvel Observateur*, 31 January 1977, p. 20.
62. Frears, J.R., *France in the Giscard Presidency*, p. 21.
63. Hall, P.A., *Governing the Economy*, p. 188.
64. Barre, R., *The Times*, 10 November 1978, cited in Hall, P.A., *Governing the Economy*, p. 188.
65. Giscard clarifies his views on economic liberalism in his book *Démocratie française*, Paris, Fayard, 1976. See also Giscard d'Estaing, V., 'Humaniser la croissance', *Preuves*, 10, 1972, pp. 7–12.
66. Hall, P.A., *Governing the Economy*, pp. 188–9.
67. Frears, J.R., *France in the Giscard Presidency*, p. 131.
68. Balassa, B., 'The French Economy under the Fifth Republic, 1958–1978', p. 218.
69. Frears, J.R., *France in the Giscard Presidency*, p. 132.
70. Frears, J.R., *France in the Giscard Presidency*, p. 133.

71. Cited in Berger, S., 'Lame Ducks and National Champions; Industrial Policy in the Fifth Republic', in Hoffmann, S. and Andrews, W.G., eds, *The Fifth Republic at Twenty*, p. 294.
72. As one top executive at Saint-Gobain put it, 'The fault was that we nationalised', personal interview with the author, Courbevoie, July 1990.
73. Maclean, M., 'L'actualité dans le monde des affaires', in Denby, D. and Hayward, S., eds, *ACTIF*, AMLC, Birmingham, 1986, p. 35.
74. Berger, S., 'Lame Ducks and National Champions', p. 302.
75. *Le Monde*, 23 March 1979, cited in Frears, J.R., *France in the Giscard Presidency*, p. 132.
76. Stoléru, L., *L'Impératif industriel*, Paris, Seuil, 1969, p. 267.
77. On Japanese participation, see Harvey, C., Maclean, M. and Hayward, A., 'From Knowledge Dependence to Knowledge Creation: Industrial Growth and the Technological Advance of the Japanese Electronics Industry', *Journal of Industrial History*, Vol. 4, No. 2, 2001, pp. 1–22.
78. Hough, J.R., *The French Economy*, London, Croom Helm, 1982, p. 75.
79. Balassa, B., 'The French Economy under the Fifth Republic, 1958–1978', p. 220.
80. Fonteneau, A. and Muet, P.-A., *La Gauche face à la crise*, p. 91.
81. Fonteneau, A. and Muet, P.-A., *La Gauche face à la crise*, pp. 93–4.
82. Frears, J.R., *France in the Giscard Presidency*, p. 115.
83. Cited in Frears, J.R., *France in the Giscard Presidency*, p. 17.
84. Bassi, M., *Valéry Giscard D'Estaing*, Paris, Grasset, 1968, p. 122, quoted in Frears, J.R., *France in the Giscard Presidency*, p. 28.
85. I owe this observation to Guy Benoist, Professor in Marketing, Lyon Business School, July 1985.
86. Quoted in Frears, J.R., *France in the Giscard Presidency*, p. 14.
87. Televised broadcast to the nation, 30 June 1977, quoted in Frears, J.R., *France in the Giscard Presidency*, p. 28.
88. In return, Giscard asked for a salary similar to that earned by the Commission President (E17,000 per month, or £10,500). However, he was awarded only expenses. 'D'Estaing snub', *The Times*, 25 January 2002, p. 17.
89. For a moving account of the last execution in France, see Derogy, J. and Pontaut, J.-M., *Investigation, passion: enquête sur 30 ans d'affaires*, pp. 175–85.
90. This point is stressed by Alain Vernholes, 'La France n'accepte pas de payer le prix de ses ambitions', *Modern and Contemporary France*, Vol. 9, No. 3, August 2001, pp. 289–300.
91. Shakespeare, W., *Macbeth*, 1, vii, 25.

5   The Socialist Experiment: Coming to Terms with Economic Realities

1. Minc, A., 'L'Entreprise: horizon indépassable', *L'Expansion*, October–November 1985, p. 351.
2. Televised debate with Giscard d'Estaing, 5 May 1981.
3. Machin, H. and Wright, V., 'Economic Policy under the Mitterrand Presidency, 1981–1984: an introduction', in Machin, H. and Wright, V., eds, *Economic Policy and Policy-Making under the Mitterrand Presidency 1981–84*, London, Pinter, 1985, p. 2.
4. Cited in Machin, H. and Wright, V., eds, *Economic Policy and Policy-Making under the Mitterrand Presidency 1981–84*, p. 1.

5. *Projet socialiste pour la France des années 1980*, Paris, Club socialiste du livre, 1980, cited in Fonteneau, A. and Muet, P-A., *La Gauche face à la crise*, Paris, Presses de la Fondation Nationale des Sciences Politiques, 1985, p. 87.
6. *Projet socialiste pour la France des années 1980*.
7. Machin, H. and Wright, V., eds, *Economic Policy and Policy-Making under the Mitterrand Presidency 1981–84*, p. 2.
8. Hough, J.R., *The French Economy*, London, Croom Helm, 1982.
9. Hayward, J., *The State and the Market Economy: Industrial Patriotism and Economic Intervention in France*, Brighton, Wheatsheaf, 1986, p. 234.
10. Cameron, D.R., 'Exchange Rate Politics in France, 1981–1983: the Regime-Defining Choices of the Mitterrand Presidency', in Flynn, G., ed., *Remaking the Hexagon: the New France in the New Europe*, Oxford, Westview Press, 1996, pp. 117–57.
11. Gattaz, Y. and Simonnot, P., *Mitterrand et les patrons 1981–1986*, Paris, Fayard, 1999, p. 16.
12. Gattaz, Y. and Simonnot, P., *Mitterrand et les patrons 1981–1986*, p. 10.
13. Weber, H., *Le Parti des patrons: le CNPF (1946–1986)*, Paris, L'Epreuve des Faits/Seuil, 1986, pp. 322–43.
14. Gattaz, Y. and Simonnot, P., *Mitterrand et les patrons 1981–1986*, p. 16.
15. Fonteneau, A. and Muet, P-A., *La Gauche face à la crise*, p. 19.
16. Muet, P-A., 'Economic Management and the International Environment', in Machin, H. and Wright, V., eds, *Economic Policy and Policy-Making under the Mitterrand Presidency 1981–84*, p. 72.
17. Cameron, D.R., 'Exchange Rate Politics in France, 1981–1983: the Regime-Defining Choices of the Mitterrand Presidency', p. 128.
18. *Le Témoignage Chrétien*, 11 July 1983, cited in Hall, P.A., *Governing the Economy: the Politics of State Intervention in Britain and France*, Cambridge, Polity Press, 1986, p. 195.
19. This did not apply to Mitterrand himself, who had served as a minister in the Fourth Republic eleven times in as many years, under governments of both right and left. His portfolios included that of minister of overseas territories (1950–51), minister of the interior (1954–55) and minister of justice (1956–57).
20. In addition to the 40-hour week, the Matignon Agreements of 1936 consecrated collective bargaining, paid holiday and trade union rights.
21. The death penalty was also abolished. Robert Badinter, a close friend of Mitterrand's, had been present at the last execution in France in 1972, having acted as defence lawyer for Roger Bontems, condemned for a murder at which he was present but in which he did not participate. Badinter fought tirelessly thereafter for the abolition of the death penalty. Derogy, J. and Pontaut, J-M., *Investigation, passion: enquête sur 30 ans d'affaires*, Paris, Fayard, 1993, pp. 175–85.
22. Gattaz, Y. and Simonnot, P., *Mitterrand et les patrons 1981–1986*, p. 63.
23. Gattaz, Y. and Simonnot, P., *Mitterrand et les patrons 1981–1986*, p. 75.
24. Weber, H., *Le Parti des patrons: le CNPF (1946–1986)*, pp. 330–1. The Mauroy government disputed these calculations, estimating the combined cost to business at FF15–18 billion, with additional costs bringing the total to FF20–23 billion.
25. During the Giscard years the overall tax and social security burden had risen from an estimated 35 per cent to 42.5 per cent of GDP. Weber, H., *Le Parti des patrons: le CNPF (1946–1986)*, p. 330.
26. Cited in Weber, H., *Le Parti des patrons: le CNPF (1946–1986)*, p. 330.
27. Data from INSEE, cited in Blotnicki, L. and Heckly, C., 'France', in Messere, K., ed., *The Tax System in Industrialized Countries*, Oxford, Oxford University Press, 1998, p. 94.

28. Muet, P-A., 'Economic Management and the International Environment', p. 74.
29. There had been three previous waves of nationalisations: immediately after the First World War; in 1936, at the time of the Popular Front, which saw the nationalisation of the Banque de France, the SNCF (Société Nationale des Chemins de Fer); and in the aftermath of the Liberation (in particular the four main deposit banks, and the Régie Renault).
30. Speech by Pierre Mauroy on the nationalisation programme, reported in *Le Monde*, 1 July 1981.
31. The money was to be paid through the Caisse Nationale de l'Industrie and the Caisse Nationale des Banques, established for the purposes of administering compensation. Stoffaes, C., 'The Nationalizations: an Initial Assessment', in Machin, H. and Wright, V., eds, *Economic Policy and Policy-Making under the Mitterrand Presidency 1981–84*, p. 145.
32. Stoffaes, C., 'The Nationalizations: an Initial Assessment', p. 145.
33. Bizaguet, A., *Le Secteur public et les privatisations*, Paris, PUF, 1988, p. 23.
34. Hall, P.A., 'The Evolution of Economic Policy under Mitterrand', in Ross, G., Hoffmann, S. and Malzacher, S., eds, *The Mitterrand Experiment*, New York, Oxford University Press, 1987, p. 59.
35. Extracts from nationalisation laws, cited in Bizaguet, A., *Le Secteur public et les privatisations*, p. 23.
36. Milner, S., 'Industrial Relations in France: Towards a New Social Pact?', in Maclean, M., ed., *The Mitterrand Years: Legacy and Evaluation*, Basingstoke, Macmillan Press – now Palgrave Macmillan, 1998, p. 170.
37. Cohen, E., 'A *Dirigiste* End to *Dirigisme*?', in Maclean, M., ed., *The Mitterrand Years: Legacy and Evaluation*, p. 38.
38. Milner, S., 'Industrial Relations in France: Towards a New Social Pact?', p. 174.
39. Figures from Lyon Business School.
40. Milner, S., 'Industrial Relations in France: Towards a New Social Pact?', p. 169.
41. Porter, M.E., *Competitive Strategy: Techniques for Analyzing Industries and Competitors*, London, Macmillan, 1980; Porter, M.E., *Competitive Advantage: Creating and Sustaining Superior Performance*, London, Macmillan, 1985.
42. Morvan, Y., 'Industrial Policy', in Machin, H. and Wright, V., eds, *Economic Policy and Policy-Making under the Mitterrand Presidency 1981–84*, p. 123.
43. Green, D., 'Comment', in Machin, H. and Wright, V., eds, *Economic Policy and Policy-Making under the Mitterrand Presidency 1981–84*, p. 143.
44. Jublin, J., 'Les nationalisées ont perdu 16 milliards de F en 1983', *Le Monde*, 12 March 1984.
45. Le Boucher, E., 'En 1982, les entreprises nationalisées n'ont pas joué leur rôle d'entrainement', *Le Monde*, 10 September 1983.
46. Auberger, P., *Rapport*, No. 580, Annexe 15, Vol. 2, Paris, Assemblée Nationale, 1993, p. 145.
47. Figures cited in *Rapport sur les opérations réalisées par la caisse d'amortissement de la dette publique*, annexed to *Projet de loi de finances*, Paris, Assemblée Nationale, 1988, p. 9.
48. Muet, P-A., 'Economic Management and the International Environment', in Machin, H. and Wright, V., eds, *Economic Policy and Policy-Making under the Mitterrand Presidency 1981–84*, p. 73.
49. See Hall, P.A., *Governing the Economy*, p. 195.
50. I owe this observation to Gordon Shenton, Lyon Business School.
51. 'Le temps du pouvoir', 15 November 1991, televised documentary on Mitterrand's first ten years in power.

52. McCormick, for example, defines the period of *rigueur* as March 1982 to March 1983, and austerity as March 1983 to July 1984. McCormick, J., 'Apprenticeship for Governing: an Assessment of French Socialism in Power', in Machin, H. and Wright, V., eds, *Economic Policy and Policy-Making under the Mitterrand Presidency 1981–84*, pp. 52–6.

53. Gattaz, Y. and Simonnot, P., *Mitterrand et les patrons 1981–1986*, p. 21.

54. This point is argued by Elie Cohen, 'A *Dirigiste* End to *Dirigisme*?', p. 36.

55. This proved a point of contention at the 1996 annual ASMCF (Association for the Study of Modern and Contemporary France) conference held at Royal Holloway, University of London. Serge Berstein insisted that there had been a debate.

56. McCormick, J., 'Apprenticeship for governing: an assessment of French Socialism in Power', in Machin, H. and Wright, V., eds, *Economic Policy and Policy-Making under the Mitterrand Presidency 1981–84*, p. 55.

57. Hayward, J., *The State and the Market Economy: Industrial Patriotism and Economic Intervention in France*, p. 234.

58. Cameron, D.R., 'Exchange Rate Politics in France, 1981–1983: the Regime-Defining Choices of the Mitterrand Presidency', in Daley, A., ed., *The Mitterrand Era: Policy Alternatives and Political Mobilization in France*, Basingstoke, Macmillan Press – now Palgrave Macmilan, 1996, p. 61.

59. On 4 October 1981 the franc was devalued by 3 per cent, while the mark appreciated by 5.5 per cent. On 12 June 1982 the franc lost 5.75 per cent while the mark gained 4.25 per cent in value. And on 21 March 1981 the franc lost 2.5 per cent of its value as against an appreciation of 5.5 per cent by the mark.

60. President Mitterrand, televised address to the nation, March 1983, cited in McCormick, J., 'Apprenticeship for Governing: an Assessment of French Socialism in power', in Machin, H. and Wright, V., eds, *Economic Policy and Policy-Making under the Mitterrand Presidency 1981–84*, p. 55.

61. Vernholes, A., 'La France n'accepte pas de payer le prix de ses ambitions', *Modern and Contemporary France*, Vol. 9, No. 3, 2001, p. 298.

62. Hayward, J., *The State and the Market Economy: Industrial Patriotism and Economic Intervention in France*, p. 235.

63. Economist Intelligence Unit, *France*, EIU, January 2001, p. 25; Economist Intelligence Unit, *France*, EIU, July 2001, p. 25.

64. Dyson, K. and Featherstone, K., 'EMU and Presidential Leadership under François Mitterrand', in Maclean, M., ed., *The Mitterrand Years: Legacy and Evaluation*, pp. 89–111; Cameron, D.R., 'Exchange Rate Politics in France, 1981–1983: the Regime-Defining Choices of the Mitterrand Presidency', in Daley, A., ed., *The Mitterrand Era*, pp. 56–82; Cameron, D.R., 'From Barre to Balladur: Economic Policy in the Era of the EMS', in Flynn, G., ed., *Remaking the Hexagon*, pp. 117–57.

65. Personal interview with the author, 6 August 1990, Le Défense, Paris.

66. For an overview of the development of the Bourse under the socialists, see 'La Bourse', *Le Monde Dossiers et Documents*, No. 131, March 1986, pp. 1–4. See also Gallois, D., *La Bourse*, Paris, Marabout, 1995. The reconstruction of the Bourse had begun in 1978 with the 'SICAV 5,000', known as the SICAV Monory, when Finance Minister René Monory had allocated a FF5,000 tax discount in return for the purchase of shares.

67. Dethomas, B., 'La déréglementation en cours', *Le Monde*, 8 October 1985, p. 23.

68. For a useful account of the development of the Paris Bourse under the socialists and afterwards see Flockton, C., 'The Frankfurt Börse, the Paris Bourse and the City: Competition and Co-operation within a Unifying EU Financial Market', in

Maclean, M. and Trouille, J.-M., eds, *France, Germany and Britain: Partners in a Changing World*, Basingstoke, Palgrave – now Palgrave Macmillan, 2001, pp. 37–49.

69. Pébereau, M., 'Les promesses de la privatisation', *Problèmes Economiques*, No. 2018, 1 April 1987, p. 4.

70. The planning process was marginalised from the mid-1980s, as the ideology of less state ('moins d'Etat') gathered momentum. Since 1995, planning has seen a modest revival. Commissions have been established with briefs relating to the problems of twenty-first-century France, its role in the EU, its partnership with Germany, and the future of social security provision.

71. Jaffré, J., 'Le retournement de l'opinion', *Le Monde (Supplément)*, 1 January 1984, p. III, cited in Berger, S., 'The Socialists and the *patronat*', in Machin, H. and Wright, V., eds, *Economic Policy and Policy-Making under the Mitterrand Presidency 1981–84*, p. 228.

72. Cited in Colombini, J.-M., 'A la fois "plus d'Etat" et "moins d'Etat"', *Le Monde*, 15 December 1982.

73. Hayward, J., '*Moins d'Etat* or *Mieux d'Etat*: the French Response to the Neo-Liberal Challenge', in Maclean, M., ed., *The Mitterrand Years: Legacy and Evaluation*, pp. 23–35.

74. Speech to National Assembly, July 1984.

75. Mitterrand, F., televised address to the nation, 15 January 1984. It is possible that these words may have been influenced by Gattaz, then head of the CNPF, who in the course of 14 interviews with the president during the period repeatedly stressed 'the irreplaceable role [of the firm] in the creation of wealth and jobs'. Gattaz, Y. and Simonnot, P., *Mitterrand et les patrons 1981–1986*, p. 20, p. 44, p. 78.

76. Gattaz, Y. and Simonnot, P., *Mitterrand et les patrons 1981–1986*, p. 26.

77. Gattaz, Y. and Simonnot, P., *Mitterrand et les patrons 1981–1986*, p. 27.

78. Berger, S., 'The Socialists and the *patronat*', in Machin, H. and Wright, V., eds, *Economic Policy and Policy-Making under the Mitterrand Presidency 1981–84*, p. 236.

79. Crozier, M., *La Société bloquée*, Paris, Seuil, 1970, or *Le Phénomène bureaucratique*, Paris, Seuil, 1964; see also Crozier, M. and Friedberg, E., *L'Acteur et le système*, Paris, Seuil, 1977.

80. Cited in Servan-Schreiber, J.-L., *Le Métier de patron*, Paris, Fayard, 1990, p. 35.

81. Barsoux, J.-L., and Lawrence, P., *Management in France*, London, Cassell, 1990, p. 76.

82. Bulletin officiel des annonces civiles et commerciales, cited in *Le Monde*, 3 May 1985, p. 32.

83. Mazey, S., 'Power outside Paris', in Hall, P.A. *et al.*, *Developments in French Politics*, Macmillan Press – now Palgrave Macmillan, Basingstoke, 1990, pp. 152–67.

84. Szarka, J., 'French Business in the Mitterrand Years: the Continuity of Change', in Maclean, M., ed., *The Mitterrand Years: Legacy and Evaluation*, pp. 156–7.

85. Basini, 'Patronat: les parrains ne sont plus ce qu'ils étaient', *Le Nouvel Economiste*, 11 December 1998, p. 49.

86. The traditional *grandes écoles* have also become more international in focus. Mr Jacques Maisonrouge, former President of IBM's World Trade Corporation, provided an interesting illustration of this point. When he graduated from the Ecole Centrale de Paris, only two out of 300 fellow graduands ventured abroad for further training. Forty years later, 85 chose to spend a year abroad from a graduating class of 370. Personal interview with the author, 21 November 1990, Paris.

87. Reinhard, P., *Bernard Tapie ou la politique au culot*, Paris, France-Empire, 1992, p. 206. See also Maclean, M., 'Dirty Dealing: Business and Scandal in Contemporary France', *Modern and Contemporary France*, NS1, 2, pp. 161–70.

88. Cresson's opening speech at the Carrefour National des Créateurs d'Entreprise, 23–25 May 1985, Marseille, cited in Fabra, P., 'La fiction de l'Etat actionnaire', *Le Monde*, 1 October 1985, p. 34.
89. 'Sept questions clés pour un retour au privé', *Libération*, 21 October 1985, p. 3.
90. Gloaguen, J., 'La vérité des chiffres', *Le Nouvel Economiste*, No. 527, 7 February 1986, pp. 54–8.
91. Dethomas, B., 'La privatisation en marche', *Le Monde*, 1 October 1985, p. 34.
92. Le Boucher, E., 'Nationalisations: la fin du dogme', *Le Monde*, 21 April 1985.
93. Dethomas, B., 'La déréglementation en cours', *Le Monde*, 8 October 1985, p. 23.
94. De Closets, F., *Toujours plus!*, Paris, Editions Grasset & Fasquelle, 1982.
95. Mentré, P., *Gulliver enchaîné*, Paris, Editions La Table Ronde, 1982.
96. Cited in 'Le retour de l'industrie', *French Politics and Society*, Vol. 10, No. 2, Spring 1992, p. 30.
97. Stanley Hoffmann argues this point in 'France and Europe: the Dichotomy of Autonomy and Cooperation', in Howorth, J. and Ross, G., eds, *Contemporary France: a Review of Interdisciplinary Studies*, Vol. 1, pp. 46–54.
98. Minc, A., 'L'Entreprise: horizon indépassable', p. 351.
99. Cited in Servan-Schreiber, J.-L., *Le Métier de patron*, Paris, Fayard, 1990.

6 Competitive Liberalism and European Ambitions

1. Delors, J. and Clisthène, *La France par l'Europe*, Paris, Editions Grasset et Fasquelle, 1988, pp. 13–14.
2. Servan-Schreiber, J.-J., *Le Défi américain*, Paris, Denoël, 1967.
3. These became known as the 'four freedoms', article 8a, Single European Act.
4. Albert, M. and Ball, R.J., *Towards European Economic Recovery in the 1980s*, Report to the European Parliament, 1983.
5. Commission of the EC, *Completing the Internal Market: White Paper from the Commission to the European Council*, Luxembourg, Office for Official Publications of the European Communities, June 1985.
6. Cited in Maclean, M., 'The Unfinished Chrysalis: Market Forces and Protectionist Reflexes in France', in Maclean, M. and Howorth, J., eds, *Europeans on Europe: Transnational Visions of a New Continent*, Basingstoke, Macmillan Press – now Palgrave Macmillan, 1992, p. 21.
7. Mr Alain Raoux, director of international affairs, Elf-Aquitaine, personal interview with the author, 6 August 1990, Courbevoie, Paris.
8. Barsoux, J.-L., and Lawrence, P., *Management in France*, London, Cassell, 1990, p. 219.
9. Consensus Research survey commissioned by management consultants Ernst and Whinney. See 'British not prepared', *The Times*, 2 March 1988, p. 2.
10. Mr Michel Pauwels, former director of Esso France, personal interview with the author, 7 August 1990, Versailles.
11. Berger, S., 'Liberalism reborn', in Howorth, J. and Ross, G., eds, *Contemporary France: a Review of Interdisciplinary Studies*, Vol. 1, London, Pinter, 1987, pp. 84–108.
12. Maclean, M., 'Privatisation in France 1993–94: New Departures, or a Case of *plus ça change?*', *West European Politics*, Vol. 18, No. 2, April 1995, pp. 273–90.
13. The list of companies to be privatised given in the annex to article 4 of law no. 86-793 of 2 July 1986 comprised 65 firms. The figure of 66 includes television channel TF1.
14. Diner, A. and Tricou, J., 'Les procédures de la privatisation', *Problèmes Economiques*, 31 December 1986, p. 7.

15. Balladur, E., *Je crois en l'homme plus qu'en l'Etat*, Paris, Flammarion, 1987, p. 84.
16. Cited in 'Balladur: la première privatisation réussie', *Le Figaro*, 15 December 1986, p. 8.
17. 'La France en solde', *L'Humanité*, 23 January 1987, p.12.
18. Bauer, M., 'The Politics of State-Directed Privatisation: the Case of France', *West European Politics*, Vol. 11, No. 4, October 1988, pp. 49–60.
19. Bauer, M., 'The Politics of State-Directed Privatisation: the Case of France', p. 57. Balladur drew a different conclusion: the concentration of power in the hands of one minister saved so much time and discussion! Balladur, E., *Je crois en l'homme plus qu'en l'Etat*, p. 96.
20. Balladur, E., *Je crois en l'homme plus qu'en l'Etat*, p. 170.
21. Peyrelevade, J., *Pour un capitalisme intelligent*, Paris, Editions Grasset & Fasquelle, 1993, pp. 52–5.
22. The money was channelled through the Caisse d'Amortissement de la Dette Public (CADEP), created by Poincaré in 1926, and revived by Balladur in July 1986. See article 32 of law no. 86-824 of 11 July 1986.
23. Mitterrand, F., *Lettre aux Français*, 22 March 1988.
24. The law of April 1990 opened up the former Régie Renault, now with limited company status, to private and foreign capital in order to facilitate its (abortive) merger with Volvo.
25. Centre Européen des entreprises à participation publique (section française), *Les Evolutions doctrinales et structurelles du secteur public français (1989–1993)*, Paris, CEEP, 1994.
26. Earmarked for privatisation were Aérospatiale, Air France, Banque Hervet, BNP, Caisse Centrale de Réassurance, Caisse Nationale de Prévoyance, Bull, Compagnie Générale Maritime, Crédit Lyonnais, Pechiney, Renault, Rhône-Poulenc, Assurances Générales de France, Groupe des Assurances Nationales, UAP, Société nationale d'exploitation industrielle des tabacs et allumettes, Société nationale d'étude et de construction de moteurs d'aviation, Elf Aquitaine, Thomson and Usinor Sacilor.
27. Wright, V., 'Privatisations sans passion', *Le Monde Dossiers et Documents*, June 1994, p. 1.
28. 'Privatisations: 114 milliards engrangés par l'Etat', *La Tribune Desfossés*, 11 May 1995.
29. Jacques Lauze, personal interview with the author, Commission des Finances, Assemblée Nationale, 3 June 1994, 20 June 1995.
30. Balladur, E., *Je crois en l'homme plus qu'en l'Etat*, p. 88.
31. Maclean, M., 'Privatisation, *dirigisme* and the Global Economy: an End to French Exceptionalism?', *Modern and Contemporary France*, Vol. 5, No. 2, pp. 215–28.
32. Brown, K., 'Sell-offs transform economic landscape', *The Financial Times*, Supplement, 'Europe Reinvented', 2, 19 January 2001, p. 6.
33. These included Bull (1997), Thomson-CSF (1998), GAN (1998), CNP-Assurances (1998), Crédit Industriel et Commercial (1998), Société Marseillaise de Crédit (1998), Aérospatiale (1999), Air France (1999) and Crédit Lyonnais (1999).
34. Mr Georges Cagnard, director of international affairs, Renault, personal interview with the author, 21 November 1990, Boulogne-Billancourt.
35. A point stressed by Sharp, M. and Shearman, C., *European Technological Collaboration*, London, Routledge and Kegan Paul, 1987, p. 104.
36. Bain and Co., *La Stratégie des entreprises industrielles face à la demande mondiale*, 1989. For a summary of the survey's findings, see 'Les grandes entreprises sont

trop petites', *La Tribune de l'Expansion*, 5 July 1989, p. 7, or Graham, G., 'Time to take the war to the enemy', *The Financial Times*, 9 November 1989.

37. The purchase by Fujitsu of an 80 per cent stake in ICL, the leading British computer manufacturer, in August 1990, one month before EC merger legislation was introduced which would have outlawed the takeover, is a case in point.

38. In the 1999 takeover of the German telecommunications and engineering group Mannesmann by the British mobile phone company Vodafone, for example, Chancellor Schröder intervened to try to stop the merger. Prime Minister Blair responded by saying that in the single market and the global economy, political attempts to block it were wrong. See *The Telegraph*, 22 November 1999, p. 1.

39. Smith, R.C. and Walter, I., 'Reconfiguration of Global Financial Markets in the 1990s', in Buckley, P.J., ed., *New Directions in International Business: Research Priorities for the 1990s*, Aldershot, Edward Elgar, 1992, p. 59.

40. Banque de France, *La Croissance externe des entreprises françaises à l'étranger*, August 1989; or 'Extérieures, toutes...', *Le Monde*, 4 October 1989, pp. 29, 44.

41. Maclean, M., *French Enterprise and the Challenge of the British Water Industry*, Aldershot, Avebury, 1991, p. 64.

42. A joint venture with Cory Waste Management.

43. In 1990 Générale des Eaux announced its purchase of AMI Healthcare, Britain's leading chain of private clinics, through its subsidiary Générale de Santé, at a cost of £245 million. The company's subsidiary Associated Gas Services (AGS) entered the British gas market, followed by its sister, Associated Heat Services, lured by electricity privatisation in the UK.

44. Personal interview with the author, June 1989, Bristol.

45. Vaysse, F., 'Bull lance un plan de restructuration pour retrouver l'équilibre en 1992', *Le Monde*, 10 November 1990.

46. *Le Monde*, 29 March 1991, p. 7.

47. *Le Monde*, 12 March 1991.

48. Address to the Centre des Jeunes Dirigeants d'Entreprise, Palais des Congrès, 18 June 1987.

49. Pearce, J., and Sutton, J., *Protection and Industrial Policy in Europe*, London, Routledge and Kegan Paul, 1986.

50. Department of Trade and Industry, *A Guide to European Community Research & Development Programmes*, DTI, March 1993.

51. Tsoukalis, L., *The New European Economy: the Politics and Economics of Integration*, Oxford, Oxford University Press, 1993, pp. 49–50.

52. Hill, A., 'Ministers draw line at subsidies for electronics', *The Financial Times*, 19 November 1991, p. 2.

53. Dawkins, W., 'French pick IBM alliance with Bull', *The Financial Times*, 29 January 1992, p. 1; Cane, A., 'French computer industry thrown a lifeline', *The Financial Times*, 29 January 1992, p. 24.

54. Cited in 'Industrie – le coup d'Etat', *L'Expansion*, 6–19 February 1992, p. 84.

55. See Sharp, M. and Shearman, C., *European Technological Collaboration*.

56. See *Renault de 1898 à nos jours*, Boulogne-Billancourt, Histoire et Patrimoine, 1990.

57. This had been made possible by the law of 3 January 1983.

58. Law no. 90-560, see *Journal Officiel*, 6 July 1990.

59. A photo published in Swedish newspapers at the time of the alliance, showing PDG Gérard Longuet holding hands with Volvo heads Louis Schweitzer and Pehr Gyllenhammar, caused a furore in Sweden. It suggested that part of the national patrimony – Volvo accounted for 8 per cent of Swedish GDP – was

being ceded to French control. Swedish shareholders voted against the merger, scuppering the deal. See Fortin, D., 'Renault–Volvo: la fêlure', *L'Expansion*, 25 November–8 December 1993, p. 36.

60. See Conseil Economique et Social, *L'Economie française souffre-t-elle d'une insuffisance de recherche?*, Paris, Journal Officiel, 1989.
61. Mr Alain Raoux, personal interview with the author, 6 August 1990, Paris.
62. 'Le boom économique en RFA devrait se poursuivre et profiter aussi à ses partneraires', *Le Monde*, 7 July 1990, p. 21.
63. Dyson, K. and Featherstone, K., 'EMU and Presidential Leadership under François Mitterrand', in Maclean, M., ed., *The Mitterrand Years: Legacy and Evaluation*, Basingstoke, Macmillan Press – now Palgrave Macmillan, 1998, p. 90.
64. Cole, A., *Franco-German Relations: Political Dynamics of the European Union*, Harlow, Pearson, 2001.
65. Cohen, E., 'A *Dirigiste* End to *Dirigisme?*', in Maclean, M., ed., *The Mitterrand Years: Legacy and Evaluation*, p. 43.
66. 'Renault esquisse un nouveau modèle social', *Le Monde*, 12 April 1990.
67. Cerny, P.G., 'From *Dirigisme* to Deregulation? The case of financial markets', in Godt, P., ed., *Policy-Making in France*, London, 1989, p. 158.
68. Allen, D., 'The United States, the European Community and the GATT', *Journal of Area Studies*, No. 2, 1992; Tsoukalis, L., *The New European Economy*, p. 297.
69. Cited in 'A Delicate Case of Jurisdictions', *The Financial Times*, 20 September 1990.
70. Cited in 'Business in Europe', *The Economist*, June 1991.
71. 'Plan: l'Etat devra payer pour sauver l'automobile', *La Tribune de l'Expansion*, 2 March 1992.
72. These were: Volkswagen AG and SEAT, the Fiat group, PSA, Renault, Ford Europe and General Motors Europe.
73. Jack Lang, cited in 'Le gouvernement justifie l'accord CEE–Japon', *Le Figaro*, 1 August 1991.
74. 'L'Europe, forteresse de sable', *Le Monde*, 6 January 1990, p. 2.
75. Béjat, E., 'Spécial Accord CEE–Japon', *Avec Renault*, No. 88, 4 October 1991, p. 28 (Renault in-house magazine).
76. Personal interview with the author, PSA, 18 December 1991, Paris.
77. Lehmann, J.-P., 'France, Japan, Europe and Industrial Competition: the Automotive Case', *International Affairs*, Vol. 68, No. 1, 1992, p. 50; Mason, M., 'Elements of Consensus: Europe's Response to the Japanese Automotive Challenge', *Journal of Common Market Studies*, Vol. 32, No. 4, December 1994, pp. 433–53.
78. I owe this information to Professor Paul Stewart, Bristol Business School, University of the West of England.
79. GATT.
80. GATT.
81. One of the main culprits was Italy, responsible for 7 per cent of world trade in counterfeit luxury goods.
82. This implied an estimated reduction in EC exports of 6.6 million tonnes of cereal, 2.4 million tonnes of milk and milk products, and 183,000 tonnes of beef by 1999. Henry de Frahan, B., 'Les enjeux de la libéralisation mondiale de l'agriculture', *Politique Etrangère*, Vol. 58, No. 2, 1993, p. 271.
83. US exports in wheat and beef were expected to rise by 5–10 per cent, eggs and poultry by 10 per cent and tobacco by 15 per cent.
84. Commission of the European Communities, *The Development and Future of the CAP*, COM(91)100, Brussels, CEC, 1991.

85. Tsoukalis, L., *The New European Economy*, p. 271. This does not include money spent on agricultural subsidies.

86. I owe this information to Jackie Cahill, Ministry of Agriculture, Fisheries and Food (MAFF).

87. Guarantee receipts received by EU member states for 1993, in millions of ECU, were as follows: Belgium 1,292; Denmark 1,328; Germany 4,930; Spain 4,173; Ireland 1,637; Italy 4,754; Luxembourg 3; Netherlands 2,327; Portugal 478; UK 2,736. Source: MAFF.

88. 'Il existe aussi des paysans heureux...', *L'Expansion*, 23 September–6 October 1993, p. 110.

89. Personal interview with the author, Commission of the European Communities, 11 July 1994, Brussels.

90. Guyau, L., 'Seeds of crisis in a flawed deal', *The Financial Times*, 13 April 1993, p. 15.

91. 'Gatt: les vrais enjeux du 15 décembre', *L'Expansion*, 25 November–8 December 1993, p. 67.

92. Vimont, C., *Le Commerce extérieur français créateur ou destructeur d'emplois?*, Paris, Economica/institut de l'entreprise, 1993.

93. Balladur's initial discourse had seemed to promise a veto. See 'Gatt: le non d'Edouard Balladur', *Le Figaro*, 11 June 1993, p. 1.

94. Cited in 'Agriculture: inventaire avant révolution', *L'Expansion*, 1–12 July 1993, p. 63.

95. Mary Minch, personal interview with the author, 11 July 1994, Brussels.

96. Katrina Williams, UK Permanent Representation, personal interview with the author, 11 July 1994, Brussels.

97. GATT, 'The Final Act of the Uruguay Round – Press Summary as of 14 December', *The World Economy*, Vol. 17, No. 3, May 1994, p. 393.

98. Henry de Frahan, B., 'Les enjeux de la libéralisation mondiale de l'agriculture', p. 313.

99. Hayward, J., '*Moins d'Etat* or *Mieux d'Etat*: the French Response to the Neo-Liberal Challenge', in Maclean, M., ed., *The Mitterrand Years: Legacy and Evaluation*, p. 28.

100. Bornstein, S., 'The Politics of Scandal', in Hall, P.A. *et al.*, *Developments in French Politics*, 2nd edition, London, Macmillan Press – now Palgrave Macmillan, 1994, pp. 269–81; Maclean, M., "Dirty Dealing: Business and Scandal in Contemporary France', *Modern and Contemporary France*, NS1, No. 2, April 1993, pp. 161–70.

101. 'France', *Corporate Governance: an International Review*, Vol. 5, No. 1, January 1997, p. 46.

102. Routier, A., *La République des loups*, Paris, Calmann-Lévy, 1989, p. 234.

103. Lichfield, J., 'French VIPs at risk if "Mr Chips" talks', *The Independent on Sunday*, 11 February 2001, p. 19.

104. Bremner, C., 'The French Revolution', *The Times 2*, 16 January 2001, pp. 2–3.

105. *Report of the Committee on the Financial aspects of Corporate Governance*, London, 1992 ('the Cadbury Report'); Association Française des Entreprise Privées (AFEP)/CNPF, *Le Conseil d'Administration des Sociétés Cotées*, Paris, CNPF, 1995 ('the Viénot Report'); Marini, P., *La Modernisation du droit des sociétés*, Paris, La Documentation Française, 1996 ('the Marini Report').

106. Leser, E., *Crazy Lyonnais: les infortunes d'une banque publique*, Paris, Calmann-Lévy, 1995; Pourardier, G. and Perucca, F., *Crédit Lyonnais: le casse du siècle*, Paris, Transparence, 1995.

107. 'Entre 1979 et 1986, la France a perdu des parts de marché industriel', *Horizon 1993, Economie et statistique*, No. 217–18, January–February 1989, pp. 37–49.
108. Cohen, E., 'France: National Champions in Search of a Mission', in Hayward, J., ed., *Industrial Enterprise and European Integration: from National to International Champions in Western Europe*, Oxford, Oxford University Press, 1995, pp. 23–47.
109. Economic Intelligence Unit, *Country Profile 2001: France*, EIU, London, 2001, pp. 13–14.
110. Ross, G., *Jacques Delors and European Integration*, Cambridge, Polity Press, 1995, p. 158; Stevens, A. with Stevens, H., *Brussels Bureaucrats? The Administration of the European Union*, Palgrave – now Palgrave Macmillan, Basingstoke, 2001, p. 238.
111. A 1990 ESOP survey on French attitudes to Japan discovered that 55 per cent of interviewees feared Japanese economic muscle. Yet 54 per cent were not averse to purchasing a Japanese car. 'On peut craindre les Japonais et avoir envie de leurs voitures', *Le Monde*, 30 March 1990, p. 35.
112. In 1994, Chirac accused employers of a 'headlong rush to productivity'. Chirac, J., *Une Nouvelle France: réflexions 1*, Paris, Nil Editions, 1994, p. 24.

7 French Business and Global Economic Integration

1. Voisset, M., 'Les Services publics en France', *Europe concurrence et service public*, Centre Européen des entreprises à participation publique, Paris, April 1995, p. 59.
2. Jospin was not alone in making this claim: other EU political leaders had angered the US financial and political administration by declaring Europe ready to become the engine of global economic growth. Duncan, G., 'G7 ready for conflict – in the meetings', *The Times*, 26 April 2001, p. 27.
3. Televised address to the nation, April 2001.
4. Syfuss-Arnaud, S., 'Licencier sans trop de casse', *L'Expansion*, 30 August–13 September 2001, pp. 14–15; 'Lionel's share', *The Economist*, 21–7 April 2001, pp. 47–8.
5. Cole, A., *Franco-German Relations: Political Dynamics of the European Union*, Harlow, Pearson, 2001, p. 103.
6. See Dyson, K. and Featherstone, K., *The Road to Maastricht: Negotiating Economic and Monetary Union*, Oxford, Oxford University Press, 1999; Howarth, D.J., *The French Road to European Monetary Union*, Palgrave – now Palgrave Macmillan, Basingstoke, 2001; special issue of *Cahiers Français*, no. 297, July–August 2000.
7. A report on the future of France to the year 2000 insisted that job creation on a scale sufficient to bring down unemployment was incompatible with parallel attempts to reduce public deficits. Barbier, B., 'Une projection à moyen terme (1994–2000): tendances macroéconomiques et perspectives pour les finances publiques', *Les Rapports du Sénat*, no. 293, 1995, p. 14.
8. Maddison, A., *The World Economy: a Millennial Perspective*, Paris, OECD, 2001, p. 132.
9. Between September 1979 and May 1993, 17 realignments occurred relative to the German mark. Eijfinger, S.C.W. and De Haan, J., *European Monetary and Fiscal Policy*, Oxford, Oxford University Press, 2000, p. 13.
10. Maclean, M., 'Le "Mercredi noir" et le dilemme britannique du système monétaire européen: coopération européenne ou splendide isolement?', *Relations Internationales et Stratégiques*, no. 11, autumn 1993, pp. 151–64.
11. This did not apply to the German mark or the Dutch guilder.

12. Its successor, ERM II, was an anodyne mechanism. Membership remains compulsory for any currency wishing to join the Eurozone, but is voluntary for other currencies, such as the pound, which has an opt-out clause. Eijfinger, S.C.W. and De Haan, J., *European Monetary and Fiscal Policy*, pp. 71–3.

13. According to TEU convergence criteria, member states were not permitted to use the proceeds from the sale of state-owned assets to reduce their budget deficits in order to facilitate comparison between federal states, such as Germany, and non-federal states. The proceeds could be used to reduce the national debt.

14. 'Les comptes de la nation', *Les Notes bleues de Bercy*, no. 64, 1–15 June 1995, p. 4.

15. The 1994 budget deficit was compounded by a debt write-off of FF22 billion owed by developing African nations and former French colonies.

16. INSEE, *Tableaux de l'économie française 1999–2000*, Paris, INSEE, 1999, p. 116; CNPF, *Cartes sur table 1995*, Paris, CNPF, p. 56.

17. INSEE, *Tableaux de l'économie française 1999–2000*, p. 116; CNPF, 'Il n'y a pas de marge de manoeuvre budgétaire', *Cartes sur table 1994*, Paris, CNPF, p. 27.

18. Jospin stressed at Amsterdam that a budget deficit of 'drei komma nil nil' was not his overriding objective. When France achieved the required budget deficit of 3 per cent, there was some irritation at the Finance Ministry that the estimate of 3.1 per cent had been overshot. Reland attributes this to the importance of EMU's political aspects for France, as opposed to its economic aspects, which were secondary. Reland, J., 'The Euro Contest: a Franco-German Affair', in Haseler, S. and Reland, J., eds, *Britain and Euroland: a Collection of Essays*, Federal Trust, 2000, p. 129.

19. EIU, *Country Report: France*, July 2001, p. 24; EIU, *Country Report: France*, October 2001, p. 26.

20. EIU, *Country Report: France*, January 2001, p. 26.

21. UBS survey, 2000, see Lesniak, I., 'Ça bosse dur...sauf à Paris', *L'Expansion*, 1–14 March 2001, p. 81.

22. Maddison, A., *Explaining the Economic Performance of Nations*, Aldershot, Edward Elgar, 1995, p. 43.

23. EIU, *Country Profile 2001: France*, p. 29.

24. Dyson, K. and Featherstone, K., 'EMU and Presidential Leadership under François Mitterrand', in Maclean, M., ed., *The Mitterrand Years: Legacy and Evaluation*, Macmillan Press – now Palgrave Macmillan, Basingstoke, 1998, p. 89.

25. Cole, A., *Franco-German Relations*, p. 93.

26. This point was made by Gino Raymond, 'The End of Sovereignty?', paper presented to the Conference of the South Wales and West of England Regional Centre for Contemporary French Studies, University of Bristol, May 2001.

27. Delhomais, P.-A., *Le Monde*, 22 September 1998, cited in Reland, J., 'The Euro Contest: a Franco-German Affair', p. 117.

28. Conversion rates between the euro and participating currencies were fixed as follows: one euro would equal 40.3399 Belgian francs; 1.95583 German marks; 166.386 Spanish pesetas; 0.787564 Irish pound; 1936.27 Italian lira; 40.3399 Luxembourg francs; 2.20371 Dutch guilders; 13.7603 Austrian schillings; 200.482 Portuguese escudo; and 5.94573 Finnish markka.

29. Chris Flood, 'Eurosceptics – Rearguard of the Republic?', paper presented to the Conference of the South Wales and West of England Regional Centre for Contemporary French Studies, University of Bristol, May 2001.

30. Giddens, A., *Runaway World: How Globalisation is Reshaping our Lives*, London, Profile, 1999; Hirst, P.K. and Thompson, G., *Globalization in Question: the International Economy and Possibilities of Governance*, Cambridge, Polity Press, 1996.

31. Balladur, E., 'Y a-t-il un avenir pour nos entreprises?', *Le Monde*, 13 November 1997; Pasqua, C., 'La mondialisation n'est pas inéluctable', *Le Monde*, 8 December 1999; Rocard, M., 'Le développement, oui, mais comment', *La Vie*, 10 February 2000. See the special issue of *Modern and Contemporary France* on this topic, co-edited by Mairi Maclean and Susan Milner, Vol. 9, No. 3, 2001.

32. Arthuis, J., *L'Incidence économique et fiscale des délocalisations hors du territoire national des activités industrielles et de services*, Commission des Finances au Sénat, no. 337, 4 June 1993.

33. Lallement, R., ' Foreign Direct Investment and the Diversity of Socio-Economic Systems in Europe: France, Germany and Britain Compared', in Maclean, M. and Trouille, J.-M., eds, *France, Germany and Britain: Partners in a Changing World*, Basingstoke, Palgrave – now Palgrave Macmillan, 2001, p. 88.

34. Cohen, E., 'On met n'importe quoi sur le dos de la mondialisation', *La Croix*, 4 January 1997; Rocard, M., 'Le développement, oui, mais comment', *La Vie*, 10 February 2000.

35. Lavialle survey for Credoc; see 'Les Français redoutent la mondialisation', *La Tribune*, 2 July 1997.

36. Le Billon, V. and Bouvais, W., 'Mondialisation: cette France qui dit non', *L'Expansion*, 7–20 October 1999, pp. 64–8.

37. Trouille, J.-M., and Uterwedde, H., 'Franco-German Relations, Europe and Globalisation', *Modern and Contemporary France*, Vol. 9, No. 3, August 2001, pp. 339–53.

38. Trouille, J.-M., 'The Franco-German Economic and Industrial Partnership', in Maclean, M. and Trouille, J.-M., eds, *France, Germany and Britain: Partners in a Changing World*, p. 80.

39. Commissariat Général du Plan, Deutsch-Französisches Institut, *Compétitivité globale: une perspective franco-allemande*, Paris, La Documentation Française, 2001.

40. Beck, U., *What is Globalization?*, translated by P. Camiller, Cambridge, Polity Press, 2000, p. 1.

41. Beck, U., *What is Globalization?*, p. 4.

42. Bell, D., 'The World and the Unites States in 2013', *Daedelus*, Vol. 116, No. 3, 1987, pp. 1–31.

43. Ministère de l'Economie, des Finances et de l'Industrie, *Industrie française et mondialisation*, Paris, SESSI, 1998.

44. EIU, *Country Report: France*, April 2001, p. 30.

45. Lallement, R., ' Foreign Direct Investment and the Diversity of Socio-Economic Systems in Europe: France, Germany and Britain Compared', in Maclean, M. and Trouille, J.-M., eds, *France, Germany and Britain: Partners in a Changing World*, p. 85.

46. UN, *World Investment Report 2000: Cross-border Mergers and Acquisitions and Development*, New York and Geneva, UN, 2000, pp. 234–8.

47. EIU, *Country Profile 2000: France*, EIU, London, 2000, p. 21.

48. EIU, *Country Profile 2000: France*, EIU, London, 2000, p. 21.

49. David Love, Head of Regulation, British Energy, personal interview with the author, 11 May 2001.

50. Meziane, Z., *The European Gas Markets*, Reuters Business Insight Report, June 2000.

51. Mattei, J., 'Gaz de France, prêt pour l'explosion?', 21 December 2000–4 January 2001, pp. 69–71.

52. EdF has been so competitive that French imports have come to be seen as a permanent feature of Britain's baseload supply. Cooke, S., 'Iniquities of the French connection', *Management Today*, March 1993, p. 38.

53. Nardoni, L., *The European Electricity Markets*, Reuters Business Insight Report, June 2000.
54. Nardoni, L., *The European Electricity Markets*.
55. Tizier, P.-E., and Mauchamp, N., *EdF-GdF: une entreprise publique en mutation*, Paris, La Découverte, 2000.
56. Access to the British market is provided through the interconnector that lies on the seabed, equivalent to having a large power-station in Sussex.
57. I owe this information to David Love, British Energy.
58. Gino Raymond, 'The End of Sovereignty?'.
59. The proposed market liberalisation was designed to occur in three stages. From January 2003 all business customers were to have a free choice of electricity supplier; from January 2004 all business customers were to have a free choice of gas supplier; and from January 2005 free choice was to be extended to all remaining gas and electricity users.
60. 'Liberalise? Regulate? Both', *The Economist*, 10 March 2001, pp. 50–5.
61. EIU, *Country Report: France*, April 2001, pp. 18–19.
62. Lister, D., 'EU attacks Britain on directives backlog', *The Times*, 29 May 2001, p. 19.
63. Vernholes, A., 'La France n'accepte pas de payer le prix de ses ambitions', *Modern and Contemporary France*, Vol. 9, No. 3, August 2001, p. 291.
64. The new law means that the market over 40 GWh, about 800 customers, is open to competition, at least in theory, accounting for 30 per cent of electricity use. By 2003, customers over 20 GWh will be able to choose their supplier and from 2006 all customers over 9 GWh may choose. In practice, the incumbent supplier will have significant advantages over newcomers, since EdF will remain as grid operator. Evans, A., *Energy: Customer Retention and Acquisition*, Reuters Business Insight Report, 2000, p. 13.
65. The parallel directive for gas has yet to be implemented in France.
66. Evans, A., *Energy: Customer Retention and Acquisition*, p. 14.
67. David Love, British Energy, personal interview with the author, 11 May 2001.
68. 'Electricité de France: a giant awakes', *The Economist*, 4 November 2000, p. 71.
69. Minimal opening of 20 per cent in 2000, 28 per cent in 2003, and 33 per cent in 2008 is expected. Meziane, Z., *The European Gas Markets*, Reuters Business Insight Report, June 2000.
70. Evans, A., *Energy: Customer Retention and Acquisition*, p. 15.
71. Meziane, Z., *The European Gas Markets*.
72. Nardoni, L., *The European Electricity Markets*.
73. Foreign competitors include the German operators Rheinisch-Westfälisches Elektrizitätswerk (RWE) and Hamburgische Electricitätswerke (HEW), as well as the Belgian Electrabel. Mattai, J., 'Ils ont osé s'attaquer à la forteresse EDF', *L'Expansion*, 1–15 February 2001, pp. 66–8.
74. Some of the emerging competition may come from EdF's own subsidiaries, such as the Société nationale d'électricité et de thermique (SNET), jointly owned with Charbonnages de France.
75. David Love, British Energy, personal interview with the author, 4 June 2001.
76. 'Electricité de France: a giant awakes', p. 71.
77. 'Electricité de France: a giant awakes', p. 71.
78. Bremner, C., 'London to the Med in six hours on new TGV', *The Times*, 24 May 2001, p. 11.
79. Vernholes, A., 'La France n'accepte pas de payer le prix de ses ambitions'; EIU, *Country Profile 2000: France*, pp. 19–20.

80. Thatcher, M., *The Politics of Telecommunications: National Institutions, Convergence and Change in Britain and France*, Oxford, Oxford University Press, 2000.

81. These include the British mobile phone operator Orange (at a cost of $40 billion), the British internet service provider Freeserve ($2.5 billion), the data service provider Equant ($4 billion), and a 28.5 per cent stake in the German phone company MobilCom ($3.5 billion).

82. Deschamps, P.-M, and Dumont, L., 'L'armée de France Télécom à la conquête de la tribu Orange', *L'Expansion*, 7–20 December 2000, pp. 98–101.

83. 'France Télécom's $53 billion debt burden', *Business Week*, 8 January 2001, p. 22.

84. Deschamps, P.-M, and Dumont, L., 'L'armée de France Télécom à la conquête de la tribu Orange', p. 98.

85. See Haut Conseil du Secteur Public, *Les Services publics en réseaux face au progrès technique et à la mondialisation*, 1998.

86. Barberi, J.-L., 'En France, quatre champions qui ont beaucoup à perdre', *L'Expansion*, 18–31 January 2001, p. 39.

87. See 'Europe's Telco's: Sliding toward Junk?', *Business Week*, 26 March 2001, p. 65.

88. EIU, *Country Report: France*, July 2000, p. 19.

89. EIU, *Country Report: France*, April 2001, p. 27.

90. Jack, A., 'Plus ça change…(Successful Privatization of Credit Lyonnais Reflects Many Problems in French Banking Sector)', *The Banker*, Vol. 149, No. 882, August 1999, p. 21.

91. In June 2001 France Télécom announced its intention to sell its 9.9 per cent stake in Sprint, the US long-distance telecoms group, as well as holdings in STMicroelectronics and the French cable company Noos, as part of a debt-reduction strategy. See Mathieson, C. 'France Telecom to raise up to £1.1 bn by selling Sprint stake', *The Times*, 1 June 2001, p. 26.

92. EIU, *Country Report: France*, October 2001, p. 12.

93. For an overview of the performance of the euro, see Trichet, J.-C., 'The Euro after Two Years', *Journal of Common Market Studies*, Vol. 39, No. 1, March 2001, pp. 1–13.

94. INSEE, EIU, *Country Report: France*, April 2001, p. 28.

95. This view is expressed by Buiter, W.H., 'Ugly Things Can Happen', *The World Today*, Vol. 57, No. 5, May 2001, p. 12.

96. EIU, *Country Profile 2001: France*, EIU, London, 2001, p. 37.

97. 'French "weapons grade" exports to Iraq blocked', *The Sunday Times*, 22 April 2001, p. 26.

98. EIU, *Country Profile 2000: France*, EIU, London, 2000, p. 36.

99. EIU, *Country Report: France*, October 2001, p. 24.

100. European manufacturers are able to produce 18 million cars annually, but only 15 million new cars are sold in Europe each year.

101. Society of Motor Manufacturers and Traders, cited in C. Brabbs, 'Will Renault's focus on its marque build sales?', *Marketing*, 22 March 2001, p. 17.

102. Brabbs, C., 'Renault and Nissan in joint initiatives', *Marketing*, 18 May 2000, p. 4.

103. 'Who says it's iffy now?', *Business Week*, 23 October 2000, p. 64.

104. Kohiyama, M., 'Renault, bulldozer dans l'empire des équipementiers', *L'Expansion*, 1–15 February 2001, pp. 62–5.

105. 'Now Renault is driving upmarket', *Business Week*, 19 March 2001, p. 22.

106. Burt, T., 'The End of the Road', *Financial Times Supplement*, Part 4, 'Europe's New Capitalism', February 2001, p. 13.

107. 'PSA Peugeot Citroen – Sturdy Independent', *The Economist*, 11 March 2000, p. 70.

108. In 2000, Peugeot depended on the European market for 86 per cent of its sales.

109. Gallard, P., 'Renault et Peugeot, conquistadors du Mercosur', *L'Expansion*, 7–20 December 2000, pp. 104–8.
110. Candida, D., *The Future of European Retail Banking*, Reuters Business Insight, 2000, p. 17.
111. Candida, D., *The Future of European Retail Banking*, p. 17.
112. Drury, S., *Diversification in European Insurance and Financial Services*, Reuters Business Insight, 1999, p. 112.
113. Leser, E., *Crazy Lyonnais: les infortunes d'une banque publique*, Paris, Calmann-Lévy, 1995, p. 224; Maclean, M., 'Corporate Governance in France and the UK: Long-term Perspectives on Contemporary Institutional Arrangements', *Business History*, Vol. 41, No. 1, January 1999, p. 103.
114. Suez opted out of banking entirely: in 1996 it sold the Banque Indosuez to Crédit Agricole, turning to water and energy distribution through its alliance in 1997 with Lyonnaise des Eaux. EIU, *Country Profile 2001: France*, EIU, London, 2001, pp. 33–4.
115. Drury, S., *Diversification in European Insurance and Financial Services*, p. 110.
116. Parry, D., *The Future of European Insurance*, Reuters Business Insight, 2000, pp. 16–18.
117. Flockton, C., 'The Frankfurt Börse, the Paris Bourse and the City: Competition and Cooperation within a Unifying EU Financial Market', in Maclean, M. and Trouille, J.-M., eds, *France, Germany and Britain: Partners in a Changing World*, pp. 42–3.
118. Boland, V., 'Merger Fever grips Europe's Exchanges', *Financial Times Supplement*, Part 2, 'Europe Reinvented', February 2001, pp. 8–9.
119. Richard Grasso, New York Stock Exchange chairman, cited in *The Financial Times*, 7 June 2000.
120. Dodgson, N., *Empire Building: the Future of European Food Retailing*, Reuters Business Insight Report, September 1999.
121. France's net contribution to the EU budget in 1999 was E0.8 billion, as against E10.9 billion contributed by Germany: a hefty 60 per cent of the EU budget, and thirteen times the French contribution. Gougeon, J.-P., 'Les raisons d'une crispation', *Libération*, 10 March 1999.
122. Carrefour, Promodès and Auchan own the largest Spanish firms, Pryca, Continente, and Alcampo respectively.
123. Dodgson, N., *Empire Building: the Future of European Food Retailing*.
124. Maclean, M., Harvey, C. and Press, J., 'Elites, Ownership and the Internationalisation of French Business', *Modern and Contemporary France*, Vol. 9, No. 3, August 2001, pp. 313–25.
125. Actimel, launched in 1996, has been particularly successful, enjoying global sales in 2000 of $170 million in a total of 14 countries.
126. Nunny, S., *Growth Strategies in Dairy*, Reuters Business Insight, January 2001.
127. Of EU member states, France, Austria and the UK were least in favour of enlargement. Eurobarometer survey no. 54, November–December 2000.
128. Brown, K., 'Sell-offs transform economic landscape', *Financial Times Supplement*, Part 2, 'Europe Reinvented', February 2001, p. 6.
129. Maclean, M., 'Privatisation, *Dirigisme* and the Global Economy: an End to French Exceptionalism?', *Modern and Contemporary France*, Vol. 5, No. 2, 1997, pp. 215–28.
130. International Capital Market Group, *International Corporate Governance: Who Holds the Reins?*, London, ICMG, 1995, p. 42.
131. Jean-Pierre Helbert, CNPF, personal interview with the author, Paris, January 1995.

132. Bauer, M., 'The Politics of State-Directed Privatisation: the Case of France', *West European Politics*, Vol. 11, No. 4, October 1988, p. 57.
133. Timmins, N., 'Europe adopts UK approach to spreading the risk', *Financial Times Supplement*, Part 2, 'Europe Reinvented', February 2001, p. 7.
134. Dedieu, F. and Hénisse, P., 'Les salariés actionnaires voient s'envoler leurs rêves de fortune', *L'Expansion*, 4–17 January 2001, p. 90.
135. Basini, B., 'Patronat: les parrains ne sont plus ce qu'ils étaient', *Le Nouvel Economiste*, 11 December 1998, p. 49.
136. Association Française des Entreprises Privées/Conseil National du Patronat Français, *Le Conseil d'Administration des Sociétés Cotées*, Paris, 1995 (the 'Rapport Viénot'). A follow-up was published in 1999. See too Marini, P., *La Modernisation du droit des sociétés*, Paris, 1996 (the 'Rapport Marini').
137. Maclean, M., Harvey, C., and Press, J., 'Elites, Ownership and the Internationalisation of French Business'.
138. Morin, F., 'A Transformation in the French Model of Shareholding and Management', *Economy and Society*, Vol. 29, No. 1, February 2000, pp. 36–53, p. 37.
139. Dexia was formed by the merger of Crédit Communal de Belgique and Crédit Local de France.
140. De Tricornot, A., 'Qui possède les entreprises européennes?', *L'Expansion*, 21 December 2000–3 January 2001, p. 76.
141. Carati, G. and Tourani Rad, A., 'Convergence of Corporate Governance Systems', *Managerial Finance*, Vol. 26, No. 10, pp. 66–83.
142. Morin, F., *Le Modèle français de détention et de gestion du capital*, Paris, Editions de Bercy, 1998.
143. The elderly dependency ratio (the population aged 65 and above as a percentage of those aged 15–64) is expected to rise in France from 20.8 per cent in 1990 to 39.1 per cent by 2030. Davis, E.P., *Can Pension Systems Cope? Population Ageing and Retirement Income Provision in the European Union*, London, Royal Institute of International Affairs, 1997, pp. 6, 43.
144. Morin, F., 'A Transformation in the French Model of Shareholding and Management', p. 41.
145. Maclean, M., 'Corporate Governance and Business Cultures in France, Germany and Britain', in Maclean, M. and Trouille, J.-M., eds, *France, Germany and Britain: Partners in a Changing World*, pp. 53–69.
146. While François and Edouard Michelin run the company as executive managers, Daniel and Pierre Michelin are members of the supervisory board.
147. Jacquin, J.-B., 'OPA sur les grandes familles', *L'Expansion*, 7–21 June 2001, pp. 56–9.
148. Barberi, J.-L., 'Automobile: les enfants aux commandes', *L'Expansion*, 7–21 June 2001, p. 76.
149. Meignan, G., 'Famille "je rachète" les Bouygues', *L'Expansion*, 7–21 June 2001, p. 66.
150. Bourdieu, P., *The State Nobility*, translated by R. Nice, Cambridge, Polity Press, 1996.
151. Bourdieu, P., *The State Nobility*, p. 292.
152. Cited in Stevens, A. with Stevens, H., *Brussels Bureaucrats? The Administration of the European Union*, Basingstoke, Palgrave – now Palgrave Macmillan, 2001, p. 237.
153. Whitley, R., *Divergent Capitalisms: the Social Structuring and Change of Business Systems*, Oxford, Oxford University Press, 1999, p. 133.
154. Cole, A., *Franco-German Relations*, p. 150.
155. *The Economist*, 6 March 1999, quoted in Stevens, A. with Stevens, H., *Brussels Bureaucrats? The Administration of the European Union*, p. 70.

156. Jack, A., 'Plus ça change ... (successful privatization of Credit Lyonnais reflects many problems in French banking sector)', p. 21.
157. As Suleiman notes: 'At best, you are dealing with a capitalism of connivance in transition. Our "ivy leagues" and "old boy networks" are a joke compared to the *grandes écoles*, the French networks and their godfathers, whether they are grandads like Ambroise Roux, in their prime like Claude Bébéar, or an apprentice like Jean-Marie Messier'. Cited in Basini, B., 'Patronat: les parrains ne sont plus ce qu'ils étaient', *Le Nouvel Economiste*, 11 December 1998, p. 49.
158. Cited in Whitley, R., *Divergent Capitalisms*, p. 127.
159. Whitley, R., *Divergent Capitalisms*, p. 120.
160. Dimitrakopoulos examines the reactions by the French National Assembly to the process of European integration, and finds these to be path-dependent and wholly consistent with long-established national patterns. Dimitrakopoulos, D., 'Incrementalism and Path Dependence', *Journal of Common Market Studies*, Vol. 39, No. 3, September 2000, pp. 405–22.
161. Thomas Lawton, 'Regulating Business, Constricting Strategy: the Emerging Role of the WTO in International Commerce', paper presented at the University of the West of England, 23 May 2001.
162. Gueldry argues that the process of European integration is a permanent negotiation between 'Community interests which assert themselves rather lamely, and pugnacious national interests'. Gueldry, M., 'Le présidence française au Conseil de l'Union européenne', *French Politics, Culture and Society*, Vol. 19, No. 2, summer 2001, pp. 1–20, p. 19.
163. Targett, S., 'Europe places its bets on the equity culture', *Financial Times Supplement*, Part 2, 'Europe Reinvented', February 2001, p. 12.
164. 'French corporate governance – ambivalent', *The Economist*, 7 October 2000, p. 73.
165. David Love, British Energy, 4 June 2001.
166. I owe this information to Dr Thomas Lawton, Imperial College, University of London.
167. EIU, *Country Report: France*, October 2001, p. 11; Shah, S., 'OECD praises Britain's performance but America slips into recession', 27 November 2001, p. 17.
168. 'Looking fitter than its neighbors', *Business Week*, 19 February 2001, p. 30.
169. EIU, *Country Report: France*, April 2001, pp. 24–5.

Conclusion

1. Jean Monnet, address to the Parliamentary Assembly of the European Coal and Steel Community, June 1952, cited in Webber, D., 'Conclusion', in Webber, D., ed., *The Franco-German Relationship in the European Union*, London, Routledge, 1999, p. 178.
2. Maddison, A., *The World Economy: a Millennial Perspective*, Paris, OECD, 2001, pp. 349, 353.
3. KPMG, *Gouvernement d'entreprise: évolution de la pratique deux ans après le rapport Viénot*, Paris, KPMG, 1997. The survey embraced the CAC-40 as well as the SBF (Sociétés des Bourses Françaises) 120 and SBF 250.
4. 'Compagnie de Saint-Gobain', *Industry Week*, 7 June 1999, p. 38.
5. Postan, M.M., *An Economic History of Western Europe 1945–1954*, London, Methuen, 1967, p. 368.

6. 'Casablanca water deal for Suez-Lyonnaise des Eaux', *Middle East Economic Digest*, 28 April 2000, Vol. 44, Issue 17, p. 22.
7. Dockey, E. *et al.*, 'Corporate Governance, Managerial Strategies and Shareholder Wealth Maximisation: a Study of Large European Companies', *Managerial Finance*, Vol. 26, No. 9, 2000, pp. 21–35.
8. Menon, A., 'France', in Kassim, H. *et al.*, eds, *The National Co-ordination of EU Policy: the Domestic Level*, Oxford, Oxford University Press, 2000, p. 93.
9. Basini, B., 'Patronat: les parrains ne sont plus ce qu'ils étaient', *Le Nouvel Economiste*, 11 December 1998, p. 49.
10. Whitley, R., *Divergent Capitalisms: the Social Structuring and Change of Business Systems*, Oxford, Oxford University Press, 1999, p. 133.
11. Maclean, M., Harvey, C. and Press, J., 'Elites, Ownership and the Internationalisation of French Business', *Modern and Contemporary France*, Vol. 9, No. 3, August 2001, pp. 313–25.
12. Whitley, R., *Divergent Capitalisms*, p. 135.
13. See Minc, A., *www.capitalisme.fr*, Paris, Grasset, 2000.
14. David Love, Head of Regulation, British Energy, personal interview with the author, 4 June 2001.
15. EIU, *Country Profile 2000: France*, London, EIU, 2000, p. 36.
16. Vernholes, A., 'La France n'accepte pas de payer le prix de ses ambitions', *Modern and Contemporary France*, Vol. 9, No. 3, August 2001, p. 295.
17. Plassard, J.P., 'Editorial, *Les Quatre Vérités*, no. 128, November 1985, translated by S. Berger, cited in Berger, S., 'Liberalism reborn', in Howorth, J. and Ross, G., eds, *Contemporary France: a Review of Interdisciplinary Studies*, I, London, Pinter, 1987, p. 98.
18. Menon, A., 'France', in Kassim, H., Peters, B.G. and Wright, V., eds, *The National Co-ordination of EU Policy*, p. 96.
19. Hoffmann, S., 'France and Europe: the Dichotomy of Autonomy and Cooperation', in Howorth, J. and Ross, G., eds, *Contemporary France: a Review of Interdisciplinary Studies*, Vol. 1, pp. 49–50.
20. Djelic, M.-L., *Exporting the American Model: the Postwar Transformation of European Business*, Oxford, Oxford University Press, 1998.
21. 1998 study by Korn Ferry International, see Basini, B., 'Patronat: les parrains ne sont plus ce qu'ils étaient', *Le Nouvel Economiste*, 11 December 1998, p. 49.
22. EIU, *Country Report: France*, April 2001, p. 11.
23. France, with a population of 59.2 million, has been allocated 29 votes, along with Germany, the UK and Italy. The smallest existing member state, Luxembourg, with a population of 400,000, has four votes. The weighting of candidate countries ranges from 27 votes (Poland) to three votes (Malta). It is intended that these weightings will be revised in 2005.
24. Enlargement negotiations were suspended temporarily in April 2000 due to problems with the agricultural 'chapter' of the *acquis communautaire*. Candidates were keen to increase their agricultural output following membership, with obvious consequences for existing member states. The EU refused, prompting a breakdown in negotiations. *European Voice*, 13–19 April 2000, p. 1.
25. I owe this observation to Caroline Jackson MEP, Bristol, March 2001.
26. Searjeant, G., 'Globalisation should start at home', *The Times*, 18 January 2001, p. 31.

Bibliography

Adams, W.J., 'France and Global Competition', in Flynn, G., ed., *Remaking the Hexagon: the New France in the New Europe*, Boulder, Colorado, Westview Press, 1995, pp. 87–116.

Adams, W.J., *Restructuring the French Economy: Government and the Rise of Market Competition since World War II*, Washington, DC, the Brookings Institution, 1989.

Albert, M., *Capitalisme contre capitalisme*, Paris, Seuil, 1991.

Albert, M. and Ball, R.J., *Towards European Economic Recovery in the 1980s*, Report to the European Parliament, 1983.

Allen, D., 'The United States, the European Community and the GATT', *Journal of Area Studies*, No. 2, 1992.

Amann, P.H., *The Corncribs of Buzet: Modernizing Agriculture in the French Southwest*, Princeton, Princeton University Press, 1990.

Amouyel, P., 'L'Avenir énergetique de la France', *Project*, 1979, pp. 844–55.

Aron, R., *Histoire de l'épuration, 1: le Monde des affaires, 1944–1953*, Paris, Fayard, 1974.

Arthuis, J., *L'Incidence économique et fiscale des délocalisations hors du territoire national des activités industrielles et de services*, Commission des Finances au Sénat, No. 337, 4 June 1993.

Association Française des Entreprises Privées/Conseil National du Patronat Français, *Le Conseil d'Administration des Sociétés Cotées*, Paris, CNPF, 1995 (the 'Rapport Viénot').

Atlas, C. and Linotte, D., *Le Remembrement rural*, Paris, Librairies techniques, 1980.

Attali, J., *Verbatim I 1981–1986*, Paris, Fayard, 1993.

Auberger, P., *Rapport*, No. 580, Annexe 15, Vol. 2, Paris, Assemblée Nationale, 1993.

Bain and Co., *La Stratégie des entreprises industrielles face à la demande mondiale*, 1989.

Balassa, B., 'The French Economy under the Fifth Republic, 1958–1978', in Andrews, W.G. and Hoffmann, S., eds, *The Fifth Republic at Twenty*, Albany, State University of New York Press, 1981, pp. 204–25.

Baleste, M., *L'Économie française*, 11th edition, Paris, Masson, 1991.

Balladur, E., *Je crois en l'homme plus qu'en l'Etat*, Paris, Flammarion, 1987.

Balladur, E., 'Y a-t-il un avenir pour nos entreprises?', *Le Monde*, 13 November 1997.

Banque de France, *La Croissance externe des entreprises françaises à l'étranger*, August 1989.

Barberi, J.-L., 'En France, quatre champions qui ont beaucoup à perdre', *L'Expansion*, 18–31 January 2001, pp. 38–41.

Barberi, J.-L., 'Automobile: les enfants aux commandes', *L'Expansion*, 7–21 June 2001, pp. 74–6.

Barbier, B., 'Une projection à moyen terme (1994–2000): tendances macroéconomiques et perspectives pour les finances publiques', *Les Rapports du Sénat*, No. 293, 1995, p. 14.

Barrillon, R., 'Le malaise politique, économique et social', *Le Monde*, 29 April 1977, p. 1.

Barsoux, J.-L and Lawrence, P., *Management in France*, London, Cassell, 1990.

Basini, B., 'Patronat: les parrains ne sont plus ce qu'ils étaient', *Le Nouvel Economiste*, 11 December 1998, p. 49.

Bassi, M., *Valéry Giscard d'Estaing*, Paris, Grasset, 1968.

Bauer, M., 'The Politics of State-Directed Privatisation: the Case of France', *West European Politics*, Vol. 11, No. 4, October 1988, pp. 49–60.

Beck, U., *What is Globalization?*, translated by P. Camiller, Cambridge, Polity Press, 2000.

Béjat, E., 'Spécial Accord CEE–Japon', *Avec Renault*, No. 88, 4 October 1991, p. 28.

Bell, D., 'The World and the United States in 2013', *Daedalus*, Vol. 116, No. 3, 1987, pp. 1–31.

Berger, A., 'Sortir du malthusianisme économique', *Esprit*, January 1954, pp. 20–32.

Berger, S., 'Lame Ducks and National Champions: Industrial Policy in the Fifth Republic', in Andrews, W.G. and Hoffmann, S., eds, *The Fifth Republic at Twenty*, Albany, State University of New York Press, 1981, pp. 292–310.

Berger, S., 'Liberalism Reborn: the New Liberal Synthesis in France', in Howorth, J. and Ross, G., eds, *Contemporary France: a Review of Interdisciplinary Studies*, Vol. 1, London, Pinter, 1987, pp. 84–108.

Berger, S., 'The Socialists and the *patronat*', in Machin, H. and Wright, V., eds, *Economic Policy and Policy-Making under the Mitterrand Presidency 1981–84*, London, Pinter, 1985, pp. 225–44.

Berstein, S., *The Republic of de Gaulle 1958–1969*, translated by P. Morris, Cambridge, Cambridge University Press/Paris, Éditions de la Maison des Sciences de l'Homme, 1993.

Bizaguet, A., *Le Secteur public et les privatisations*, Paris, PUF, 1988.

Bloch-Lainé, F., *Profession: fonctionnaire*, Paris, Seuil, 1976.

Bloch-Lainé, F. and Bouvier, J., *La France restaurée: dialogue sur le choix d'une modernisation*, Paris, 1986.

Blotnicki, L. and Heckly, C., 'France', in Messere, K., ed., *The Tax System in Industrialized Countries*, Oxford, Oxford University Press, 1998, pp. 93–127.

Boland, V., 'Merger Fever Grips Europe's Exchanges', *Financial Times Supplement*, Part 2, 'Europe Reinvented', February 2001, pp. 8–9.

Bornstein, S., 'The Politics of Scandal', in Hall, P.A. *et al.*, eds, *Developments in French Politics*, 2nd edition, London, 1994, pp. 269–81.

Bourdieu, P., *Distinction: a Social Critique of the Judgement of Taste*, translated by R. Nice, London, Routledge, 1984.

Bourdieu, P., *The State Nobility*, translated by L.C. Clough, Cambridge, Polity Press, 1996.

Bourdois, J.-H., 'Trente ans d'essor industriel (1945–1974)', *Les Cahiers Français*, 211, May–June 1983, pp. 4–12.

Boyer, R. and Mistral, J., *Accumulation, Inflation, Crises*, Paris, PUF, 1978.

Boyer, R., 'The Current Economic Crisis: its Dynamics and its Implications for France', in Ross, G., Hoffmann, S., and Malzacher, S., eds, *The Mitterrand Experiment*, New York, Oxford University Press, 1987, pp. 33–53.

Brabbs, C., 'Renault and Nissan in joint initiatives', *Marketing*, 18 May 2000, p. 4.

Brabbs, C., 'Will Renault's focus on its marque build sales?', *Marketing*, 22 March 2001, p. 17.

Bremner, C., 'French unite against US trade domination', *The Times*, 24 September 1999, p. 21.

Bremner, C., 'The French Revolution', *The Times 2*, 16 January 2001, pp. 2–3.

Bremner, C., 'London to the Med in six hours on new TGV', *The Times*, 24 May 2001, p. 11.

Brown, K., 'Sell-offs transform economic landscape', *The Financial Times*, Supplement, Part 2, 'Europe Reinvented', 19 January 2001, p. 6.

Buck, T. and Tull, M., 'Anglo-American Contributions to Japanese and German Corporate Governance after World War II', *Business History*, Vol. 42, No. 2, 2000, pp. 119–40.

Buiter, W.H., 'Ugly Things Can Happen', *The World Today*, Vol. 57, No. 5, May 2001.

Burt, T., 'The End of the Road', *Financial Times Supplement*, Part 4, 'Europe's New Capitalism', February 2001, p. 13.

Cameron, D.R., 'Exchange Rate Politics in France, 1981–1983: the Regime-Defining Choices of the Mitterrand Presidency', in Daley, A., ed., *The Mitterrand Era: Policy Alternatives and Political Mobilization in France*, Basingstoke, Macmillan Press – now Palgrave Macmillan, 1996, pp. 56–82.

Cameron, D.R., 'From Barre to Balladur: Economic Policy in the Era of the EMS', in Flynn, G., ed., *Remaking the Hexagon: the New France in the New Europe*, Oxford, Westview Press, 1996, pp. 117–57.

Candida, D., *The Future of European Retail Banking*, Reuters Business Insight, 2000.

Cane, A., 'French computer industry thrown a lifeline', *The Financial Times*, 29 January 1992, p. 24.

Carati, G. and Tourani Rad, A., 'Convergence of Corporate Governance Systems', *Managerial Finance*, Vol. 26, No. 10, 2000, pp. 66–83.

Caron, F., *An Economic History of Modern France*, translated by B. Bray, London, Methuen, 1979.

Carré, J.-J., Dubois, P., and Malinvaud, E., *French Economic Growth*, translated by J.P. Hatfield, Stanford, Stanford University Press, 1976.

Cassis, Y., *Big Business: the European Experience in the Twentieth Century*, Oxford, Oxford University Press, 1997.

Cassis, Y., 'Financial Elites in Three European Centres: London, Paris, Berlin', in Jones, G., ed., *Banks and Money: International and Comparative Finance in History*, London, Cass, 1991, pp. 53–71.

Centre Européen des Entreprises à Participation Publique, *Les Entreprises à participation publique dans l'Union Européenne: Annales du CEEP 1994*, Brussels, CEEP, 1994.

Centre Européen des entreprises à participation publique (section française), *Les Evolutions doctrinales et structurelles du secteur public français (1989–1993)*, Paris, CEEP, 1994.

Cerny, P.G., 'From *Dirigisme* to Deregulation? The Case of Financial Markets', in Godt, P., ed., *Policy-Making in France*, London, 1989.

Charkham, J., *Keeping Good Company: a Study of Corporate Governance in Five Countries*, Oxford, Clarendon Press, 1994.

Chirac, J., *Une Nouvelle France: réflexions 1*, Paris, Nil Editions, 1994.

Chirac, J., *La France pour tous*, Paris, Nil Editions, 1994.

Choinel, A. and Rouyer, G., *Le Système bancaire français*, 5th ed., Paris, PUF, 1996.

Clough, S.B. *et al.*, eds, *Economic History of Europe: Twentieth Century*, New York and London, Harper, 1968.

Cohen, E., 'A *Dirigiste* End to *Dirigisme*?', in Maclean, M., ed., *The Mitterrand Years: Legacy and Evaluation*, Basingstoke, Macmillan Press – now Palgrave Macmillan, 1998, pp. 36–45.

Cohen, E., 'France: National Champions in Search of a Mission', in Hayward, J., ed., *Industrial Enterprise and European Integration: from National to International Champions in Western Europe*, Oxford, Oxford University Press, 1995, pp. 23–46.

Cohen, E., *La Tentation hexagonale: la souveraineté à l'épreuve de la mondialisation*, Paris, Fayard, 1996.

Cohen, E., 'On met n'importe quoi sur le dos de la mondialisation', *La Croix*, 4 January 1997.

Cohen, S.S., 'Twenty Years of the Gaullist Economy', in Andrews, W.G. and Hoffmann, S., eds, *The Fifth Republic at Twenty*, Albany, State University of New York Press, 1981, pp. 240–50.

Cole, A., *Franco-German Relations: Political Dynamics of the European Union*, Harlow, Pearson, 2001.

Colombini, J.-M., 'A la fois "plus d'Etat" et "moins d'Etat"', *Le Monde*, 15 December 1982.

Commissariat Général du Plan, *Cinquante ans de planification à la française*, Paris, Commissariat Général du Plan, 1998.

Commissariat Général du Plan, Deutsch-Französisches Institut, *Compétitivité globale: une perspective franco-allemande*, Paris, La Documentation Française, 2001.

Commission of the European Communities, *Completing the Internal Market: White Paper from the Commission to the European Council*, Luxembourg, Office for Official Publications of the European Communities, June 1985.

Commission of the European Communities, *The Development and Future of the CAP*, COM(91)100, Brussels, CEC, 1991.

Committee of European Economic Cooperation, *General Report*, Vol. 1, London, HMSO, 1947.

'Les Comptes de la nation', *Les Notes bleues de Bercy*, No. 64, 1–15 June 1995, p. 4.

Conseil Economique et Social, *L'Economie française souffre-t-elle d'une insuffisance de recherche?*, Paris, Journal Officiel, 1989.

Conseil National du Patronat Français, *Cartes sur table 1994*, Paris, CNPF, 1994.

Conseil National du Patronat Français, *Cartes sur table 1995*, Paris, CNPF, 1995.

Consumers in the European Community Group, *Eurospeak Explained*, London, CECG, 1990.

Cooke, S., 'Iniquities of the French Connection', *Management Today*, March 1993.

Cotta, A., 'La Croissance de l'économie française', *Analyse et prévision*, Vol. 11, No. 1.2, July–August 1966.

Cotta, A., *La France et l'impératif mondial*, Paris, PUF, 1978.

Crocker, L.G., *Rousseau's Social Contract: an Interpretive Essay*, Cleveland, Ohio, the Press of Case Western Reserve University, 1968.

Crozier, M., ed., 'L'Administration face aux problèmes du changement', special issue of *Sociologie du Travail*, 1966.

Crozier, M., 'Les Intellectuels et la stagnation française', *Esprit*, December 1953, pp. 771–82.

Crozier, M., *Le Phénomène bureaucratique*, Paris, Seuil, 1963.

Crozier, M., *La Société bloquée*, Paris, Seuil, 1970.

Crozier, M., *The Stalled Society*, New York, Viking, 1973.

Crozier, M. and Friedberg, E., *L'Acteur et le système*, Paris, Seuil, 1977.

Davis, E.P., *Can Pension Systems Cope? Population Ageing and Retirement Income Provision in the European Union*, London, RIIA, 1997.

Dawkins, W., 'French pick IBM alliance with Bull', *The Financial Times*, 29 January 1992, p. 1.

De Closets, F., *Toujours plus!*, Paris, Editions Grasset & Fasquelle, 1982.

Dedieu, F. and Hénisse, P., 'Les salariés actionnaires voient s'envoler leurs rêves de fortune', *L'Expansion*, 4–17 January 2001, p. 90.

De Gaulle, C., *The Call to Honour 1940–1942*, translated by J. Griffin, Collins, London, 1955.

De Gaulle, *Mémoirs d'Espoir*, Vol. 1, *Le Renouveau*, Paris, Plon, 1980.

De Gaulle, C., *Mémoirs de guerre: Le Salut, 1944–1946*, Plon, Paris, 1959.

De Gaulle, C., *War Memoirs: Salvation, 1944–1946*, translated by R. Howard, London, Weidenfeld and Nicolson, 1960.

Delors, J. and Clisthène, *La France par l'Europe*, Paris, Editions Grasset & Fasquelle, 1988.

De Monton, J. and Harvard Business School, 'Carrefour, S.A.', Harvard Business School case study No. 273–099, 1974.

Department of Trade and Industry, *A Guide to European Community Research & Development Programmes*, DTI, March 1993.

Derogy, J. and Pontaut, J.-M., *Investigation, passion: enquête sur 30 ans d'affaires*, Paris, Fayard, 1993.

Deschamps, P.-M, and Dumont, L., 'L'armée de France Télécom à la conquête de la tribu Orange', *L'Expansion*, 7–20 December 2000, pp. 98–101.

Dethomas, B., 'La déréglementation en cours', *Le Monde*, 8 October 1985, p. 23.

Dethomas, B., 'La privatisation en marche', *Le Monde*, 1 October 1985, p. 34.

De Tricornot, A., 'Qui possède les entreprises européennes?', *L'Expansion*, 21 December 2000–4 January 2001, pp. 76–9.

DiMaggio, P. and Powell, W.W., 'The Iron Cage Revisited: Institutional Isomorphism and Collective Rationality in Organisational Fields', in Powell, W.W. and DiMaggio, P., eds, *The New Institutionalism in Organisational Analysis*, Chicago, University of Chicago Press, 1991, pp. 63–82.

Dimitrakopoulos, D., 'Incrementalism and Path Dependence', *Journal of Common Market Studies*, Vol. 39, No. 3, September 2000, pp. 405–22.

Diner, A. and Tricou, J., 'Les procédures de la privatisation', *Problèmes Economiques*, 31 December 1986.

Djelic, M.-L., *Exporting the American Model: the Postwar Transformation of European Business*, Oxford, Oxford University Press, 1998.

Dockey, E. *et al.*, 'Corporate Governance, Managerial Strategies and Shareholder Wealth Maximisation: a Study of Large European Companies', *Managerial Finance*, Vol. 26, No. 9, 2000, pp. 21–35.

Dodgson, N., *Empire Building: the Future of European Food Retailing*, Reuters Business Insight Report, September 1999.

Dombey, D., 'EU ditches proposed takeover directive', *The Financial Times*, 5 July 2001, p. 1.

Drury, S., *Diversification in European Insurance and Financial Services*, Reuters Business Insight, 1999.

Duhamel, E., 'François Mitterrand between Vichy and the Resistance', in Maclean, M., ed., *The Mitterrand Years: Legacy and Evaluation*, Basingstoke, Macmillan Press – now Palgrave Macmillan, 1998, pp. 217–32.

Dumont, J.-P., 'Le refus des cadres', *Le Monde*, 28 September 1976, p. 1.

Dumont, J.-P. and Labarde, P., 'M. Barre reçoit les partenaires sociaux', *Le Monde*, 7 September 1976, pp. 1–2.

Dumont, J.-P. and Labarde, P., 'Les syndicats demandent à M. Barre une réduction des inégalités sociales et le patronat une relance de l'investissement', *Le Monde*, 7 September 1976, p. 1.

Duncan, G., 'G7 ready for conflict – in the meetings', *The Times*, 26 April 2001, p. 27.

Dunham, A.L., 'A New Perspective on the Industrial Revolution in France', *Michigan Alumnus Quarterly Review*, Vol. 57, No. 14, February 1951, pp. 148–59.

Dyson, K. and Featherstone, K., 'EMU and Presidential Leadership under François Mitterrand', in Maclean, M., ed., *The Mitterrand Years: Legacy and Evaluation*, Basingstoke, Macmillan Press – now Palgrave Macmillan, 1998, pp. 89–111.

Dyson, K. and Featherstone, K., *The Road to Maastricht: Negotiating Economic and Monetary Union*, Oxford, Oxford University Press, 1999.

Earle, E.M., ed., *Modern France: Problems of the Third and Fourth Republics*, New York, Russell & Russell, 1964.

Eck, J-F., *Histoire de l'économie française depuis 1945*, 2nd edition, Paris, Armand Colin, 1990.

Economist Intelligence Unit, *Country Profile 2000: France*, London, EIU, 2000.

Economist Intelligence Unit, *Country Profile 2001: France*, London, EIU, 2001.

Economist Intelligence Unit, *Country Report: France*, London, EIU, May 2000.

Economist Intelligence Unit, *Country Report: France*, London, EIU, July 2000.

Economist Intelligence Unit, *Country Report: France*, London, EIU, October 2000.

Economist Intelligence Unit, *Country Report: France*, London, EIU, January 2001.

Economist Intelligence Unit, *Country Report: France*, London, EIU, April 2001.

Economist Intelligence Unit, *Country Report: France*, London, EIU, July 2001.

Ehrmann, H.W., *Organized Business in France*, Princeton, Princeton University Press, 1957.

Eijfinger, S.C.W. and De Haan, J., *European Monetary and Fiscal Policy*, Oxford, Oxford University Press, 2000.

'Electricité de France: a giant awakes', *The Economist*, 4 November 2000, p. 71.

Elgie, R., 'Democratic Accountability and Central Bank Independence: Historical and Contemporary, National and European Perspectives', *West European Politics*, Vol. 21, No. 3, July 1998, pp. 53–76.

Elgie, R., 'Central Bank Independence: a Reply to Various Critics', *West European Politics*, Vol. 24, No. 1, January 2001, pp. 217–21.

European Commission, *European Systems of Worker Involvement Final Report*, Luxembourg, Office for Official Publications of the European Communities, 1997.

European Voice, 13–19 April 2000, p. 1.

Evans, A., *Energy: Customer Retention and Acquisition*, Reuters Business Insight Report, 2000.

Fabius, L., 'Ce qui manque au plan Barre', *Le Nouvel Observateur*, 31 January 1977, p. 19.

Fabra, P., 'La fiction de l'Etat actionnaire', *Le Monde*, 1 October 1985, p. 34.

Fauroux, R., 'Le retour de l'industrie', *French Politics and Society*, Vol. 10, No. 2, Spring 1992.

Feinstein, C.H. *et al.*, *The European Economy Between the Wars*, Oxford, Oxford University Press, 1997.

Flockton, C., 'The Frankfurt Börse, the Paris Bourse and the City: Competition and Cooperation within a Unifying EU Financial Market', in Maclean, M. and Trouille, J.-M., eds, *France, Germany and Britain: Partners in a Changing World*, Basingstoke, Palgrave – now Palgrave Macmillan, 2001, pp. 37–49.

Flood, C., 'Eurosceptics – Rearguard of the Republic?', paper presented to the Conference of the South Wales and West of England Regional Centre for Contemporary French Studies, University of Bristol, May 2001.

Fonteneau, A. and Muet, P.-A., *La Gauche face à la crise*, Paris, Presses de la Fondation Nationale des Sciences Politiques, 1985.

Fortin, D., 'Renault-Volvo: la fêlure', *L'Expansion*, 25 November–8 December 1993, p. 36.

Fouillée, A., *Esquisse psychologique des peuples européens*, Paris, Alcan, 1903.

Fourastié, J., 'Productivity and Economics', *Political Science Quarterly*, Vol. LXVI, No. 2, 1951, pp. 216–25.

Fourastié, J., *Les Trente Glorieuses ou la révolution invisible de 1946 à 1970*, Paris, Fayard, 1979.

'France', *Corporate Governance: an International Review*, Vol. 5, No. 1, January 1997, p. 46.

Frears, J.R., *France in the Giscard Presidency*, London, George Allen & Unwin, 1981.

Fridensen, P., 'France: the Relatively Slow Development of Big Business in the Twentieth Century', in Chandler, A. D. *et al.*, eds, *Big Business and the Wealth of Nations*, Cambridge, Cambridge University Press, 1997, pp. 207–45.

Friend, J.F., *The Long Presidency: France in the Mitterrand Years, 1981–1995*, Boulder, Colorado, Westview Press, 1998.

Froud, J. *et al.*, 'Shareholder Value and Financialization: Consultancy Promises, Management Moves', *Economy and Society*, Vol. 29, No. 1, 2000, pp. 80–110.

Fysh, P., 'Gaullism and Liberalism' in Flood, C. and Bell, L., eds, *Political Ideologies in Contemporary France*, London, Pinter, 1997.

Gallard, P., 'Renault et Peugeot, conquistadors du Mercosur', *L'Expansion*, 7–20 December 2000, pp. 104–8.

Gallois, D., *La Bourse*, Paris, Marabout, 1995.

GATT, 'The Final Act of the Uruguay Round – Press Summary as of 14 December', *The World Economy*, Vol. 17, No. 3, May 1994, p. 393.

Gattaz, Y. and Simonnot, P., *Mitterrand et les patrons 1981–1986*, Paris, Fayard, 1999.

Giddens, A., *Runaway World: How Globalisation is Shaping Our Lives*, London, Profile, 1999.

Giscard d'Estaing, V., *Démocratie française*, Paris, Fayard, 1976.

Giscard d'Estaing, V., *L'Etat de la France*, Paris, Fayard, 1981.

Giscard d'Estaing, V., 'Humaniser la croissance', *Preuves*, 10, 1972, pp. 7–12.

Gloaguen, J., 'La vérité des chiffres', *Le Nouvel Economiste*, No. 527, 7 February 1986, pp. 54–8.

Gordon, P. and Meunier, S., 'Globalization and French Cultural Identity', *French Politics, Culture and Society*, Vol. 19, No. 1, spring 2001, pp. 22–41.

Goubert, P., *The Course of French History*, translated by M. Utlee, London, Routledge and Franklin Watts, 1991.

Gougeon, J.-P., 'Les raisons d'une crispation', *Libération*, 10 March 1999.

Graham, G., 'Time to take the war to the enemy', *The Financial Times*, 9 November 1989.

Gravier, J.-F., *Paris et le désert français*, 2nd edition, Paris, Flammarion, 1958.

Green, D., 'Comment', in Machin, H. and Wright, V., eds, *Economic Policy and Policy-Making under the Mitterrand Presidency 1981–84*, London, Pinter, 1985, pp. 139–43.

Green, D., 'The Seventh Plan – the Demise of French Planning', *West European Politics*, Vol. 1, February 1978.

Gueldry, M., 'La présidence française au Conseil de l'Union européenne', *French Politics, Culture and Society*, Vol. 19, No. 2, summer 2001, pp. 1–20.

Guyau, L., 'Seeds of crisis in a flawed deal', *The Financial Times*, 13 April 1993, p. 15.

Guyomarch, A. *et al.*, *France in the European Union*, Basingstoke, Palgrave – now Palgrave Macmillan, 1998.

Hall, P.A., 'The Evolution of Economic Policy under Mitterrand', in Ross, G., Hoffmann, S. and Malzacher, S., eds, *The Mitterrand Experiment*, New York, Oxford University Press, 1987, pp. 54–72.

Hall, P.A., *Governing the Economy: the Politics of State Intervention in Britain and France*, Cambridge, Polity Press, 1986.

Hanley, D.L., Kerr, A.P. and Waites, N.H., *Contemporary France: Politics and Society since 1945*, London, Routledge & Kegan Paul, 1979.

Harvey, C., Maclean, M. and Hayward, A., 'From Knowledge Dependence to Knowledge Creation: Industrial Growth and the Technological Advance of the Japanese Electronics Industry', *Journal of Industrial History*, Vol. 4, No. 2, 2001, pp. 1–22.

Harvey, C., Hayward, A. and Maclean, M., 'Good luck or fine judgement?', *Asia Pacific Business Review*, Vol. 8, No. 1, 2002.

Hattemer-Lefèvre, S. with Arnoux, P., 'Les sociétés qui traitent le mieux leurs actionnaires', *Le Nouvel Economiste*, 3 July 1998, pp. 67–71.

Haut Conseil du Secteur Public, *Les Services publics en réseaux face au progrès technique et à la mondialisation*, Paris, 1998.

Hayward, J., 'Institutional Inertia and Political Impetus in France and Britain', *European Journal of Political Research*, No. 4, 341–59.

Hayward, J., *'Moins d'Etat* or *Mieux d'Etat*: the French Response to the Neo-Liberal Challenge', in Maclean, M., ed., *The Mitterrand Years: Legacy and Evaluation*, Basingstoke, Macmillan Press – now Palgrave Macmillan, 1998, pp. 23–35.

Hayward, J., *The State and the Market Economy: Industrial Patriotism and Economic Intervention in France*, Brighton, Wheatsheaf, 1986.

Henry de Frahan, B., 'Les enjeux de la libéralisation mondiale de l'agriculture', *Politique Etrangère*, Vol. 58, No. 2, 1993, pp. 309–24.

Hill, A., 'Ministers draw line at subsidies for electronics', *The Financial Times*, 19 November 1991, p. 2.

Hirst, P.K. and Thompson, G., *Globalization in Question: the International Economy and the Possibilities of Governance*, Cambridge, Polity Press, 1996.

Hoffmann, S. *et al.*, *France: Change and Tradition*, London, Victor Gollancz, 1963.

Hoffmann, S., 'France and Europe: the Dichotomy of Autonomy and Cooperation', in Howorth, J. and Ross, G., eds, *Contemporary France: a Review of Interdisciplinary Studies*, Vol., 1, London, Pinter, 1987, pp. 46–54.

Hoffmann, S., 'Thoughts on Sovereignty and French Politics', in Flynn, G., ed., *Remaking the Hexagon: the New France in the New Europe*, Boulder, Colorado, Westview Press, 1995, pp. 251–8.

Hofstede, G., *Culture's Consequences*, London, Sage, 1980.

Hough, J.R., *The French Economy*, London, Croom Helm, 1982.

Howarth, D.J., *The French Road to European Monetary Union*, Basingstoke, Palgrave – now Palgrave Macmillan, 2001.

Howorth, J., 'France and the Defence of Europe: Redefining Continental Security', in Maclean, M. and Howorth, J., eds, *Europeans on Europe: Transnational Visions of a New Continent*, Basingstoke, Macmillan Press – now Palgrave Macmillan, 1992, pp. 77–97.

Institut National de la Statistique et des Etudes Economiques, *Tableaux de l'économie française 1999–2000*, Paris, INSEE, 2000.

International Capital Market Group, *International Corporate Governance: Who Holds the Reins?*, London, ICMG, 1995.

Jack, A., 'Plus ça change … (successful privatization of Crédit Lyonnais reflects many problems in French banking sector)', *The Banker*, Vol. 149, No. 882, August 1999.

Jackson, J., 'General de Gaulle and his Enemies: Anti-Gaullism in France since 1940', *Transactions of the Royal Historical Society*, IX, Cambridge, Cambridge University Press, 1999, pp. 43–65.

Jacquin, J.-B., 'OPA sur les grandes familles', *L'Expansion*, 7–21 June 2001, pp. 56–9.

Jaffré, J., 'Le retournement de l'opinion', *Le Monde (Supplément)*, 1 January 1984, p. III.

Jeanneney, J-N., 'The Legacy of Traumatic Experiences in French Politics Today', in Flynn, G., ed., *Remaking the Hexagon: the New France in the New Europe*, Boulder, Colorado, Westview Press, 1995, pp. 17–29.

Jeffrey, S., *European Working Lives: Continuities and Change in Management and Industrial Relations in France, Scandinavia and the UK*, Aldershot, Edward Elgar, 2001.

Jones, G., 'Great Britain: Big Business, Management, and Competitiveness in Twentieth-Century Britain', in Chandler, A.D. *et al.*, eds, *Big Business and the Wealth of Nations*, Cambridge, Cambridge University Press, 1997, pp. 102–38.

Jublin, J., 'Les nationalisées ont perdu 16 milliards de F en 1983', *Le Monde*, 12 March 1984.

Kindleberger, C.P., *Economic Growth in Britain and France 1851–1950*, Cambridge MA, Harvard University Press, 1964.

Kipping, M., 'A Slow and Difficult Process: the Americanization of the French Steel-Producing and Using Industries after the Second World War', in Zeitlin, J. and Herrigel, G., eds, *Americanization and its Limits: Reworking US Technology and Management in Post-War Europe and Japan*, Oxford, Oxford University Press, 2000, pp. 209–35.

Kohiyama, M., 'Renault, bulldozer dans l'empire des équipementiers', *L'Expansion*, 1–15 February 2001, pp. 62–5.

KPMG, *Gouvernement d'entreprise: évolution de la pratique deux ans après le rapport Viénot*, Paris, KPMG, 1997.

Krugman, P., 'Growing World Trade: Causes and Consequences', *Brookings Papers on Economic Activities*, 1995, pp. 327–62.

Kuisel, R.F., *Capitalism and the State in Modern France: Renovation and Economic Management in the Twentieth Century*, Cambridge, Cambridge University Press, 1981.

Kuisel, R.F., 'The France We Have Lost: Social, Economic and Cultural Discontinuities', in Flynn, G., ed., *Remaking the Hexagon: the New France in the New Europe*, Boulder, Colorado, Westview Press, 1995, pp. 31–48.

Kuisel, R.F., 'French Post-war Economic Growth: a Historical Perspective on the *Trente Glorieuses*', in Ross, G. *et al.*, eds, *The Mitterrand Experiment*, New York, Oxford University Press, 1987, pp. 18–32.

Kuznets, S., 'Quantitative Aspects of the Economic Growth of Nations, I. Levels and Variability of Rates of Growth', *Economic Development and Cultural Change*, Vol. 5, No. 1, October 1956, pp. 1–94.

Kuznets, S., 'Quantitative Aspects of the Economic Growth of Nations, II. Industrial Distribution of National Product and Labor Force', *Economic Development and Cultural Change*, Vol. 5, No. 4, Supplement, July 1957, pp. 1–111.

Lallement, R., 'Foreign Direct Investment and the Diversity of Socio-Economic Systems in Europe: France, Germany and Britain Compared', in Maclean, M. and Trouille, J.-M., eds, *France, Germany and Britain: Partners in a Changing World*, Basingstoke, Palgrave – now Palgrave Macmillan, 2001, pp. 85–99.

Landes, D.S., 'French Business and Businessmen in Social and Cultural Perspective', in Earle, E.M., ed., *Modern France: Problems of the Third and Fourth Republics*, New York, Russell & Russell, 1951, pp. 334–53.

Landes, D.S., 'French Entrepreneurship and Industrial Growth in the Nineteenth Century', *Journal of Economic History*, No. 9, 1949, pp. 45–61.

Landes, D.S., 'Social Attitudes, Entrepreneurship and Economic Development', *Explorations in Entrepreneurial History*, Vol. 6, No. 4, May 1954, pp. 245–72.

Landes, D.S., *The Unbound Prometheus*, Cambridge, Cambridge University Press, 1969.

Lane, C., *Industry and Society in Europe: Stability and Change in Britain, Germany and France*, Aldershot, Edward Elgar, 1995.

Lannoo, K., 'A European Perspective on Corporate Governance', *Journal of Common Market Studies*, Vol. 37, No. 2, June 1999, pp. 269–94.

Lauber, V., 'The Gaullist Model of Economic Modernization', in Albany, W.G. and Hoffmann, S., eds, *The Fifth Republic at Twenty*, Albany, State University of New York Press, 1981, pp. 227–39.

Laurens, A., 'Le changement dans la stabilité', *Le Monde*, 29–30 August 1976, p. 2.

Le Billon, V. and Bouvais, W., 'Mondialisation: cette France qui dit non', *L'Expansion*, 7–20 October 1999, pp. 64–8.

Le Boucher, E., 'En 1982, les entreprises nationalisées n'ont pas joué leur rôle d'entrainement', *Le Monde*, 10 September 1983.

Le Boucher, E., 'Nationalisations: la fin du dogme', *Le Monde*, 21 April 1985.

Lehmann, J.-P., 'France, Japan, Europe and Industrial Competition: the Automotive Case', *International Affairs*, Vol. 68, No. 1, 1992.

Leser, E., *Crazy Lyonnais: les infortunes d'une banque publique*, Paris, Calmann-Lévy, 1995.

Lesniak, I., 'Ça bosse dur ... sauf à Paris', *L'Expansion*, 1–14 March 2001, p. 81.

L'Etat de la France 1998–1999, Paris, Editions la Découverte & Syros, Paris, 1998.

L'Etat de la France 1999–2000, Paris, Editions la Découverte & Syros, Paris, 1999.

Letreguilly, H., 'France', *International Financial Law Review*, Supplement on Corporate Governance, April 1998, pp. 18–22.

Lévy-Leboyer, M., 'La grande entreprise française: un modèle français?', in Lévy-Leboyer, M. and Casanova, J.-C., eds, *Entre l'Etat et le marché: l'économie française des années 1880 à nos jours*, Paris, 1991.

Lewis, M., Fitzgerald, R. and Harvey, C., *The Growth of Nations: Culture, Competitiveness and the Problem of Globalization*, Bristol, Bristol Academic Press, 1996.

Lieberman, S., *The Growth of European Mixed Economies 1945–1970*, New York, Wiley, 1977.

Lichfield, J., 'French VIPs at risk if 'Mr Chips' talks', *The Independent on Sunday*, 11 February 2001, p. 19.

Lister, D., 'EU attacks Britain on directives backlog', *The Times*, 29 May 2001, p. 19.

Loriaux, M., *France after Hegemony: International Change and Financial Reform*, Ithaca, N.Y., Cornell University Press, 1991.

Lynch, F., *France and the International Economy from Vichy to the Treaty of Rome*, London, Routledge, 1997.

Machin, H. and Wright, V., 'Economic Policy under the Mitterrand Presidency, 1981–1984: an introduction', in Machin, H. and Wright, V., eds, *Economic Policy and Policy-Making under the Mitterrand Presidency 1981–84*, London, Pinter, 1985, pp. 1–43.

Maclean, M., 'L'actualité dans le monde des affaires', in Denby, D. and Hayward, S., eds, *ACTIF*, AMLC, Birmingham, 1986, pp. 28–37.

Maclean, M., *French Enterprise and the Challenge of the British Water Industry*, Aldershot, Avebury, 1991.

Maclean, M., 'The Unfinished Chrysalis: Market Forces and Protectionist Reflexes in France', in Maclean, M. and Howorth, J., eds, *Europeans on Europe: Transnational Visions of a New Continent*, Basingstoke, Macmillan Press – now Palgrave Macmillan, 1992, pp. 21–39.

Maclean, M., 'Dirty Dealing: Business and Scandal in Contemporary France', *Modern and Contemporary France*, Vol. NS1, No. 2, May 1993, pp. 161–70.

Maclean, M., 'Le "Mercredi noir" et le dilemme britannique du système monétaire européen: coopération européenne ou splendide isolement?', *Relations Internationales et Stratégiques*, No. 11, autumn 1993, pp. 151–64.

Maclean, M., 'Privatisation in France 1993–94: New Departures, or a Case of *plus ça change*?', *West European Politics*, Vol. 18, No. 2, April 1995, pp. 273–90.

Maclean, M., 'Privatisation, *Dirigisme* and the Global Economy: an End to French Exceptionalism?', *Modern and Contemporary France*, Vol. 5, No. 2, 1997, pp. 215–28.

Maclean, M., ed., *The Mitterrand Years: Legacy and Evaluation*, Basingstoke, Macmillan Press – now Palgrave Macmillan, 1998.

Maclean, M., 'Corporate Governance in France and the UK: Long-term Perspectives on Contemporary Institutional Arrangements', *Business History*, Vol. 41, No. 1, January 1999, pp. 88–116.

Maclean, M., 'Towards a European Model? A Comparative Evaluation of Recent Corporate Governance Initiatives in France and the UK', *Journal of European Area Studies*, Vol. 7, No. 2, autumn 1999, pp. 227–45.

Maclean, M. and Trouille, J.-M., 'Introduction: France, Germany and Britain: Partners in a Changing World', in Maclean, M. and Trouille, J.-M., eds, *France, Germany and Britain: Partners in a Changing World*, pp. 1–17.

Maclean, M., Harvey, C. and Press, J., 'Elites, Ownership and the Internationalisation of French Business', *Modern and Contemporary France*, Vol. 9, No. 3, August 2001, pp. 313–25.

Maddison, A., *Explaining the Economic Performance of Nations*, Aldershot, Edward Elgar, 1995.

Maddison, A., *The World Economy: a Millennial Perspective*, Paris, OECD, 2001.

Mallet, S., *La Nouvelle Class ouvrière*, Paris, Seuil, 1963.

Malraux, A., *Les Chênes qu'on abat*, Paris, Gallimard, 1971.

Marini, P., *La Modernisation du droit des sociétés*, Paris, la Documentation française, 1996 (the 'Rapport Marini').

Marras, M.R. and Paxton, R.O., *Vichy et les juifs*, Paris, Calmann-Lévy, 1981.

Mason, M., 'Elements of Consensus: Europe's Response to the Japanese Automotive Challenge', *Journal of Common Market Studies*, Vol. 32, No. 4, December 1994, pp. 433–53.

Mathieson, C., 'France Telecom to raise up to £1.1bn by selling Sprint stake', *The Times*, 1 June 2001, p. 26.

Mathieu, G., 'Le chevalier de l'austérité', *Le Monde*, 27 August 1976, p. 1.

Mathieu, G. and Fabra, P., 'Un entretien avec M. Raymond Barre', *Le Monde*, 5 October 1976, p. 1.

Mattei, J., 'Gaz de France, prêt pour l'explosion?', *L'Expansion*, 21 December 2000–4 January 2001, pp. 69–71.

Mazey, S., 'Power outside Paris', in Hall, P.A. *et al.*, eds, *Developments in French Politics*, Basingstoke, Macmillan Press – now Palgrave Macmillan, 1990, pp. 152–67.

McCormick, J., 'Apprenticeship for governing: an assessment of French Socialism in Power', in Machin, H. and Wright, V., eds, *Economic Policy and Policy-Making under the Mitterrand Presidency 1981–84*, London, Pinter, 1985, pp. 44–63.

Meignan, G., 'Famille "je rachète" les Bouygues', *L'Expansion*, 7–21 June 2001, p. 66.

Mendès-France, P., *Choisir: conversations avec Jean Botheral*, Paris, Stock, 1974.

Mendès-France, P., *Œuvres complètes II: une politique de l'économie 1943–1954*, Paris, Gallimard, 1985.

Menon, A., 'France', in Kassim, H. *et al.*, eds, *The National Co-ordination of EU Policy: the Domestic Level*, Oxford, Oxford University Press, 2000.

Mentré, P., *Gulliver enchaîné*, Paris, Editions la Table Ronde, 1982.

Meziane, Z., *The European Gas Markets*, Reuters Business Insight Report, June 2000.

Milner, S., 'Globalisation and Employment in France: Between Flexibility and Protection?', *Modern and Contemporary France*, Vol. 9, No. 3, August 2001, pp. 327–37.

Milner, S., 'Industrial Relations in France: Towards a New Social Pact?', in Maclean, M., ed., *The Mitterrand Years: Legacy and Evaluation*, Basingstoke, Macmillan Press – now Palgrave Macmillan, 1998, pp. 169–84.

Minc, A., 'L'Entreprise: horizon indépassable', *L'Expansion*, October–November 1985, p. 351.

Minc, A., *www.capitalisme.fr*, Paris, Grasset & Fasquelle, 2000.

Ministère de l'Economie, des Finances et de l'Industrie, *Industrie française et mondialisation*, Paris, SESSI, 1998.

Mitterrand, F., *Lettre aux Français*, 22 March 1988.

Mitterrand, F., *Mémoires interrompus*, Paris, Odile Jacob, 1996.

Mitterrand, F., *De l'Allemagne, de la France*, Paris, Odile Jacob, 1996.

Monnaie et politique monétaire en Europe, Cahiers français, No. 297, July–August 2000.

Monnet, J., *Mémoires*, Paris, Fayard, 1976.

Morin, F., *Le Modèle français de détention et de gestion du capital*, Paris, Editions de Bercy, 1998.

Morin, F., 'A Transformation in the French Model of Shareholding and Management', *Economy and Society*, Vol. 29, No. 1, February 2000, pp. 31–53.

Morvan, Y., 'Industrial Policy', in Machin, H. and Wright, V., eds, *Economic Policy and Policy-Making under the Mitterrand Presidency 1981–84*, London, Pinter, 1985, pp. 117–39.

Moutet, A., *Les Logiques de l'entreprise: la rationalisation dans l'industrie française de l'entre-deux-guerres*, Paris, Editions de l'Ecole des Hautes Etudes en Sciences Sociales, 1997.

Muet, P-A., 'Economic Management and the International Environment', in Machin, H. and Wright, V., eds, *Economic Policy and Policy-Making under the Mitterrand Presidency 1981–84*, London, Pinter, 1985, pp. 70–96.

Nardoni, L., *The European Electricity Markets*, Reuters Business Insight Report, June 2000.

North, D.C. and Miller, R.L., *The Economics of Public Issues*, New York, Harper & Row, 1971.

Nunny, S., *Growth Strategies in Dairy*, Reuters Business Insight, January 2001.

Parodi, M., *L'Économie et la société française de 1945 à 1970*, Paris, Armand Colin, 1971.

Parodi, M. et al., *L'Économie et la société française au second XXe siècle*, Vol. 2, Paris, Armand Colin, 1998.

Parry, D., *The Future of European Insurance*, Reuters Business Insight, 2000.

Parti Socialiste, *Propositions pour l'actualisation du Programme commun de gouvernement de la gauche*, Paris, Flammarion, 1978.

Pasqua, C., 'La mondialisation n'est pas inéluctable', *Le Monde*, 8 December 1999.

Pearce, J. and Sutton, J., *Protection and Industrial Policy in Europe*, London, Routledge and Kegan Paul, 1986.

Pébereau, M., 'Les promesses de la privatisation', *Problèmes Economiques*, No. 2018, 1 April 1987, p. 4.

Peyrefitte, A., *Le Mal français*, Paris, Plon, 1976.

Peyrelevade, J., *Pour un capitalisme intelligent*, Paris, Editions Grasset & Fasquelle, 1993.

Pickles, D., *France Between the Republics*, London, 1946.

Pivot, C., 'Costs and Benefits of the Common Agricultural Policy for France', in Dreyfus, F.-G. et al., eds, *France and EC Membership Evaluated*, Pinter, London, 1993, pp. 59–67.

Plassard, J., 'Editorial', *Les Quatre vérités*, No. 129, November 1985.

Porter, M.E., *Competitive Advantage: Creating and Sustaining Superior Performance*, New York, Macmillan Press – now Palgrave Macmillan, 1985.

Porter, M.E., *Competitive Strategy: Techniques for Analyzing Industries and Competitors*, New York, Macmillan Press – now Palgrave Macmillan, 1980.

Postan, M.M., *An Economic History of Western Europe 1945–1964*, London, Methuen, 1967.

Pourardier, G. and Perucca, F., *Crédit Lyonnais: le casse du siècle*, Paris, Transparence, 1995.

Projet socialiste pour la France des années 1980, Paris, Club socialiste du livre, 1980.

Rapport sur les opérations réalisées par la caisse d'amortissement de la dette publique, Projet de loi de finances, Paris, Assemblée Nationale, 1988.

Raymond, G., 'The End of Sovereignty?', paper presented to the Conference of the South Wales and West of England Regional Centre for Contemporary French Studies, University of Bristol, May 2001.

Redlich, F., 'German Economic Planning for War and Peace', *The Review of Politics*, Vol. 6, 1944, pp. 315–35.

Regini, M., 'Between Deregulation and Social Pacts: the Responses of European Economies to Globalization', *Politics and Society*, Vol. 28, No. 1, March 2000, pp. 5–33.

Reinhard, P., *Bernard Tapie ou la politique au culot*, Paris, France-Empire, 1992.

Reland, J., 'The Euro Contest: a Franco-German Affair', in Haseler, S. and Reland, J., eds, *Britain and Euroland: a Collection of Essays*, Federal Trust, 2000, pp. 117–38.

Renault de 1898 à nos jours, Boulogne-Billancourt, Histoire et Patrimoine, 1990.

Report of the Committee on the Financial Aspects of Corporate Governance, London, Gee, 1992 ('the Cadbury Report').

Reynaud, J.-D., *Les Syndicats, les patrons et l'Etat*, Paris, Les Editions Ouvrières, 1978.

Rocard, M., 'Le développement, oui, mais comment', *La Vie*, 10 February 2000.

Ross, G., *Jacques Delors and European Integration*, Cambridge, Polity Press, 1995.

Rousseau, J.-J., *Du Contrat social*, Paris, Garnier-Flammarion, 1966.

Routier, A., *La République des loups*, Paris, Calmann-Lévy, 1989.

Rueff, J., *Combats pour l'ordre financier*, Paris, Plon, 1972.

Sage, A., 'Gallic culture embraces shock of new as Left Bank loses panache', *The Times*, 27 September 1999, p. 12.

Schmidt, V., *From State to Market? The Transformation of French Business and Government*, Cambridge, Cambridge University Press, 1996.

Searjeant, G., 'Globalisation should start at home', *The Times*, 18 January 2001, p. 31.

Servan-Schreiber, J.-J., *Le Défi américain*, Paris, Denoël, 1967.

Servan-Schreiber, J.-L., *Le Métier de patron*, Paris, Fayard, 1990.

Sharp, M. and Shearman, C., *European Technological Collaboration*, London, Routledge and Kegan Paul, 1987.

Smith, J.G., *The Origins and Early Development of the Heavy Chemical Industry in France*, Oxford, Clarendon Press, 1979.

Smith, R.C. and Walter, I., 'Reconfiguration of Global Financial Markets in the 1990s', in Buckley, P.J., ed., *New Directions in International Business: Research Priorities for the 1990s*, Aldershot, Edward Elgar, 1992.

Smith, W.R., ' "We can make the Ariane but we can't make washing machines": the State and Industrial Performance in Post-war France', in Howorth, J. and Ross, G., eds, *Contemporary France: a Review of Interdisciplinary Studies*, Vol. 3, London, Pinter, 1989, pp. 175–202.

Stevens, A. with Stevens, H., *Brussels Bureaucrats? The Administration of the European Union*, Basingstoke, Palgrave – now Palgrave Macmillan, 2001.

Stoffaes, C., *La Grande Menace industrielle*, Paris, Calmann-Lévy, 1978.

Stoffaes, C., 'The Nationalizations: an Initial Assessment', in Machin, H. and Wright, V., eds, *Economic Policy and Policy-Making under the Mitterrand Presidency 1981–84*, London, Pinter, 1985, pp. 144–69.

Stoléru, L., *L'Impératif industriel*, Paris, Seuil, 1969.

Suleiman, E.N., *Elites in French Society: the Politics of Survival*, Princeton, Princeton University Press, 1978.

Suleiman, E.N., *Les Ressorts cachés de la réussite française*, Paris, Seuil, 1995.

Suleiman, E.N., 'Change and Stability in French Elites', in Flynn, G., ed., *Remaking the Hexagon: the New France in the New Europe*, Boulder, Colorado, Westview Press, 1995, pp. 161–79.

Swartz, D., *Culture and Power: the Sociology of Pierre Bourdieu*, Chicago, University of Chicago Press, 1997.

Syfuss-Arnaud, S., 'Licencier sans trop de casse', *L'Expansion*, 30 August– 13 September 2001, pp. 14–15.

Szarka, J., *Business in France: an Introduction to the Economic and Social Context*, London, Pitman, 1992.

Szarka, J., 'French Business in the Mitterrand Years: the Continuity of Change', in Maclean, M., ed., *The Mitterrand Years: Legacy and Evaluation*, pp. 156–7.

Tainio, R., 'Effects of Foreign Portfolio Investors on Finnish Companies and their Management', paper presented to 17th EGOS (European Group for Organizational Studies) Colloquium, 5–7 July, Lyon, France.

Targett, S., 'Europe places its bets on the equity culture', *Financial Times Supplement*, Part 2, 'Europe Reinvented', February 2001, p. 12.

Thatcher, M., *The Politics of Telecommunications: National Institutions, Convergence and Change in Britain and France*, Oxford, Oxford University Press, 2000.

Thevenot, L., 'Les catégories sociales en 1975', *Economie et statistique*, 91, July–August 1977.

Timmins, N., 'Europe adopts UK approach to spreading the risk', *Financial Times Supplement*, Part 2, 'Europe Reinvented', February 2001, p. 7.

Tizier, P.-E. and Mauchamp, N., *EdF-GdF: une entreprise publique en mutation*, Paris, La Découverte, 2000.

Trichet, J.-C., 'The Euro after Two Years', *Journal of Common Market Studies*, Vol. 39, No. 1, March 2001, pp. 1–13.

Trouille, J.-M., 'Re-defining the Franco-German Relationship: Divergences and Perspectives', paper presented at the annual conference of the Association for the Study of Modern and Contemporary France, Cardiff, September 1999.

Trouille, J.-M., 'The Franco-German Economic and Industrial Partnership', in Maclean, M. and Trouille, J.-M., eds, *France, Germany and Britain: Partners in a Changing World*, Basingstoke, Palgrave – now Palgrave Macmillan, 2001, pp. 70–84.

Trouille, J.-M. and Uterwedde, H., 'Franco-German Relations and Globalisation', *Modern and Contemporary France*, Vol. 9, No. 3, August 2001, pp. 339–53.

Tsoukalis, L., *The New European Economy: the Politics and Economics of Integration*, 2nd edition, Oxford, Oxford University Press, 1993.

Tsoukalis, L., *The New European Economy Revisited*, Oxford, Oxford University Press, 1997.

Turkle, S.R., 'Symbol and Festival in the French Student Uprising (May–June 1968)', in Falk Moore, S. and Myerhoff, B., eds, *Symbol and Politics in Communal Ideology*, Ithaca and London, Cornell University Press, 1975.

Vaysse, F., 'Bull lance un plan de restructuration pour retrouver l'équilibre en 1992', *Le Monde*, 10 November 1990.

Verba, S., 'Comparative Political Culture', in Pye, L. and Verba, S., eds, *Political Culture and Political Development*, Princeton, Princeton University Press, 1965.

Vernholes, A., 'Le Plan Barre soumis au conseil des ministres', *Le Monde*, 24 September 1976, p. 1.

Vernholes, A., 'La France n'accepte pas de payer le prix de ses ambitions', *Modern and Contemporary France*, Vol. 9, No. 3, August 2001, pp. 289–300.

Vimont, C., *Le Commerce extérieur français créateur ou destructeur d'emplois?*, Paris, Economica/institut de l'entreprise, 1993.

Vinen, R., *The Politics of French Business 1936–1945*, Cambridge, Cambridge University Press, 1991.

Vinen, R., *Bourgeois Politics in France 1945–1951*, Cambridge, Cambridge University Press, 1995.

Vinen, R., *France, 1934–1970*, Basingstoke, Macmillan Press – now Palgrave Macmillan, 1996.

Voisset M., 'Les services publics en France', *Europe concurrence et service public*, Paris, Centre Européen des entreprises à participation publique, April 1995.

United Nations, *World Investment Report 2000: Cross-border Mergers and Acquisitions and Development*, New York and Geneva, UN, 2000.

Wallace, H., 'Bilateral, trilateral and multilateral negotiations in the European Community', in Martin, R. and Bray, C., eds, *Britain, France and Germany: Partners and Rivals in Western Europe*, Aldershot, Gower, 1986.

Webber, D., ed., *The Franco-German Relationship in the European Union*, London, Routledge, 1999.

Weber, H., *Le Parti des patrons: le CNPF (1946–1986)*, Paris, L'Epreuve des Faits/Seuil, 1986.

Whitley, R., *Divergent Capitalisms: the Social Structuring and Change of Business Systems*, Oxford, Oxford University Press, 1999.

Williams, K., 'From Shareholder Value to Present-day Capitalism', *Economy and Society*, Vol. 29, No. 1, 2000, pp. 1–12.

Wilson, S., *Ideology and Experience*, London, Associated University Presses, 1982.

Windolf, P., 'The Governance Structures of Large French Corporations: a Comparative Perspective, *Columbia Law Review Sloan Project*, 1998, pp. 705–35.

Wright, V., *The Government and Politics of France*, 3rd edition, London, Routledge, 1989.

Wright, V., 'Privatisations sans passion', *Le Monde Dossiers et Documents*, June 1994, p. 1.

Wrigley, E.A., 'The Divergence of England: the Growth of the English Economy in the Seventeenth and Eighteenth Centuries', *Transactions of the Royal Historical Society*, Cambridge, Cambridge University Press, 2000, pp. 117–41.

Zettelmeier, W., 'Franco-German University Co-operation: the Position Today and Prospects within a European Higher Educational System', in Maclean, M. and Trouille, J.-M., eds, *France, Germany and Britain: Partners in a Changing World*, Basingstoke, Palgrave – now Palgrave Macmillan, 2001, pp. 151–66.

Zysman, J., *Governments, Markets and Growth: Financial Systems and the Politics of Industrial Change*, Ithaca, Cornell University Press, 1983.

Zysman, J., 'The Interventionist Temptation: Financial Structure and Political Purpose', in Andrews, W.G. and Hoffmann, S., eds, *The Fifth Republic at Twenty*, Albany, State University of New York Press, 1981, pp. 252–69.

Zysman, J., *Political Strategies for Industrial Order: State, Market and Industry in France*, Berkeley, University of California Press, 1977.

Index